THE LITURGICAL YEAR

THE
LITURGICAL YEAR

Volume One

ADVENT, CHRISTMAS, EPIPHANY

by

Adrian Nocent, O.S.B.

Translated by

Matthew J. O'Connell

THE LITURGICAL PRESS

COLLEGEVILLE   MINNESOTA

Cover design by Clement Schmidt.

Available in four volumes, THE LITURGICAL YEAR is the authorized English version of *Célébrer Jésus-Christ, L'année Liturgique*, published by Jean-Pierre Delarge, 10, rue Mayet, 75006 Paris, France.

Texts from the Revised Standard Version — Catholic Edition of the Holy Bible contained in this book are used by permission, copyright © 1965 and 1966 by the Division of Christian Education of the National Council of Churches of Christ in the United States of America. All rights reserved.

English translation of excerpts from the Roman Missal, The Roman Calendar, Rite of Marriage, Rite of Baptism for Children, Rite of Blessing of Oils, Rite of Consecrating the Chrism, Rites for Holy Week, original texts of Alternative Opening Prayers, Invitatories and Penitential Rites, the Liturgy of the Hours, Lectionary for Mass, copyright © 1969, 1970, 1972, 1973, 1974, 1975. International Committee on English in the Liturgy, Inc. All rights reserved.

Nihil obstat: William G. Heidt, O.S.B., S.T.D., *Censor deputatus.*
Imprimatur: ✝ George H. Speltz, D.D., Bishop of St. Cloud, October 12, 1977.

Copyright © 1977, The Order of St. Benedict, Inc., Collegeville, Minnesota.

All rights reserved under United States copyright law, and the International and Pan-American Conventions, including the right to reproduce this booklet, or parts thereof, in any form, by mimeograph, or other mechanical or electronic devices.

Printed in the United States of America. ISBN 0-8146-0962-7

PREFACE

I began this work only after a good deal of hesitation. A simple revision of some older book in the light of the new lectionary seemed hardly worthwhile. On the other hand, I could not but ask whether there was any point to publishing, in our day, several volumes on the liturgical year. The very name "liturgical year" seemed terribly dated, with its overtones of facile spirituality and love of the old texts and rituals dear to earlier generations. Would I be doing anything more than disturbing the dust on antiques now lodged in a museum that is often closed and is in any case inaccessible to the crowds of today's faithful?

After inquiries of my own among the young, the faithful of all ages, and priests and religious, and after careful inquiry on the part of the publisher, it became clear that the treasures contained in the new lectionary will be a source of confusion rather than a help unless they are presented in a simple straightforward way. To many, the connection between the various readings and other elements of a celebration is not always clear, nor is the broad overall theme of a liturgical season. More importantly, many do not see these celebrations as being in any way relevant to their life in the modern world. There seemed to be room, then, for a simple presentation of the liturgical year as envisaged in the reform which Vatican Council II initiated; in such a presentation I would try to meet the needs expressed to me in various pastoral circles.

My purpose explains the threefold division of each volume. First come biblico-liturgical reflections on the particular phase of the liturgical year. Has this celebration, connected as it is with the history of salvation, anything to do with us today? Next I take up the structure and themes of

the season. How are the readings and celebrations of the
season organized? How are we to read the Scripture texts
that the liturgy inserts into a specific context? Finally there
are suggestions from the past. In order to widen our field of
vision and to supply material for celebrations of the word,
may we not draw upon the local churches of the past and
share their experience of the liturgical seasons as these
gradually took shape in the life of these churches?

These volumes make no claim to be complete. Their aim
is simply to offer lines of thought and subjects for reflection
to the faithful and their pastors, to those in charge of various
groups, and above all, to those who wish to experience the
Church's liturgy more fully. At no point have I felt I was
being unfaithful to scientific standards or to a method that
should never be set aside, even in pastoral work. My work
is intended to be readable, but as the notes will suggest at
times, it is also based on strict scholarly principles without
which any work, even if it be pastoral or "spiritual," will
lack objectivity and solidity.

I have not thought it advisable to supply a bibliography.
The reformed liturgical year has not yet been studied as a
whole. There do exist collections providing essays on each
Sunday or feast; but these are well known and will be of
help to any who wish to undergird their celebrations with a
more profound liturgical and spiritual theology. There are
also a good many articles on the new lectionary and its
composition, good points, and limitations, but citation of
these would be out of place in a work that does not aim to
give the reader a complete inventory of studies done on the
new liturgy or to guide him in future study of his own. This
work, like every other, must be faithful to its own purpose
and corresponding structure.

My desire is to serve as many as I can of those faithful
who wish to experience the greatest treasure and most vital
stimulus the Church has to offer them: the presence of the
Lord in her word and her Eucharist.

Adrian Nocent, O.S.B.

CONTENTS

vii

THE EPIPHANY MYSTERY

SUNDAYS IN ORDINARY TIME

CYCLE A

CYCLE B

CYCLE C

THE LITURGICAL YEAR

ADVENT, CHRISTMAS, EPIPHANY

INTRODUCTION
to
THE LITURGICAL YEAR

Does the "Church year" have a meaning?

"Church year" and "liturgical year" are very ancient phrases and may be suspect today. Suspect, among other things, of expressing ideas that are outdated and unrealistic, having nothing to do with the expectations of our present-day world. Suspect, too, as representing the escapism of those who are frightened by the dogmatic and moral upheaval going on in contemporary religious life, and are looking for security. These people take comfortable refuge in a "contemplation" supposedly based on solid theology but in fact on neo-romantic yearnings; they turn their back on the volcano and gaze toward a distant, peaceful, soothing horizon. Their prayer is a retreat, a way of building up psychological security, a dam against the mounting flood of the sexual revolution, a source of tranquillity for tense neurotics. Such at least are the attitudes attributed to an inoffensive group living out what they call the "liturgical year."

And yet Vatican Council II, with open enthusiasm, set about revitalizing the celebration of the liturgy and making it a genuine response to the needs of contemporary man. The Council regarded the liturgy as the summit and source of the Church's activity, and the source of sanctification as well.[1]

For the vast majority of people this represented a discovery. In their eyes, the liturgy had previously been the preserve of sacristans and rubricists; to a few others, the liturgy had had a higher status, as being a field of research on which the sciences of paleography, history, and archeology were brought to bear. After the Council a bishop was heard to say that he had been converted to the liturgy — once they had made the sacraments part of it! And, in fact, some theologians (not always just the ones unknown to the general public) go on teaching the theology of the sacraments without the least reference to the liturgy; in their view, the liturgy has no authority as a theological source.

The situation in the past was not unfairly described by saying that, to some, the liturgy was a kind of religious luxury reserved for distinguished persons who seemed beyond the reach of ordinary life's many problems.

Now, almost miraculously, the Church took the liturgy in hand at the Second Vatican Council. It did not touch on disputes over technical matters and details, but did affirm the ontological (as distinct from the merely moralistic) value of the liturgical celebration as being the summit of the Church's activity. The Church did so because it saw in that celebration the saving mysteries of Christ made present here and now, and rendered visible through signs. "Summit of the Church's activity, and source of sanctification!" What a brilliant light radiated from these words! They became the starting point for a renewed spiritual life that would be centered upon reality and protected against all abstractionism. Such at least was the objective proposed for the reform of the liturgy. Many believed in the reform and its aims, especially such individuals as bore the responsibility for Catholic communities.

Was it all a delusion? Have we been the victims of a collective hallucination? For, as we now realize, it was not quite such a simple matter as it seemed. The immense enthusiasm seems to have faltered somewhat, and there are those who think that the reform has petered out.

At the very moment when the rich values of tradition were being rediscovered and seemed capable of inspiring the masses, new problems arose to absorb the attention of our contemporaries. In consequence, the renewal seemed hardly to have begun when it risked being overwhelmed by a psychological and philosophical tidal wave. Desacralization, secularization, secularism, the claims of psychoanalysis, a new anthropology, problems of languages, the demand for total commitment on the part of the Church, the call for a politically oriented worship — all these stormed the temple whose façade had been remodeled only shortly before.

The paradox of a secularized liturgy

Contemporary Christians do not think they have lost their faith when a toothache drives them to the dentist rather than to St. Apollonia. Workingmen are much less likely to pray to the patron saint of their trade than to set up a union when they want to improve their working conditions. The hot-tempered man who feels himself in danger of committing a criminal act knows that it is time to get his thyroid gland examined. Experience shows that when a person obsessed with sex prays and meditates, he often only strengthens the hold of the obsession; such activities are more likely to intensify rather than alleviate the problem. In a land beset by persistent drought, people turn, not to Rogation processions, but to the building of an artificial lake that will serve when the rain fails.

We must not be blind to this phenomenon. People today will not accept a liturgy that is offered as a sacred moment apart, detached from life and everyday affairs, as if the created order and the world of technology were evil and heavenly blessing had to be pronounced on everything — the world, times, places — before it could be used. They may understand and know from experience the world's limitations, but they will not therefore be resigned to celebrating a liturgy that is cut off from the world and represents a flight from the world, a kind of transcending of the world so as later to bring back to it a sanctification that will render it fit to share in the praise of God. People are convinced that the world itself provides the material for the building of something new and great, that the liturgy is not "the sacred" and the world "the profane," and that worship is not meant to be an action and a moment "apart from the world" so as to sanctify the world.

In short, hardly has the renewal of the liturgy begun in the West when we see the irresistible growth of a secularization that is seemingly incompatible with one type of worship.

A *Report of the Theological Commission on Worship* (Geneva, 1963) states that the term "worship" has lost its meaning for contemporary man and rouses no interest any more. But in that same year the report on the sessions of the Fourth World Conference on Faith and Order (Montreal) claims that Christian worship is profoundly compatible with the life of man today.[2] However, the Conference also shows itself aware that a new attitude is abroad in the world:

> The Churches carry on their worship today in a world that is proud of its technological success, but at the same time is deeply troubled. In ways old and new our world shows itself opposed or indifferent to Christian worship and apathetic to the Good News of Jesus Christ. Sometimes simply ignorant of man's transcendent destiny, sometimes full of seeming contempt for it, the modern world seems willing to accept absurdity, once daily worries have been overcome or, on the other hand, material security is wholly lacking.[3]

But the Conference is realistic; it states:

> In these circumstances we must very carefully examine the worship of the Churches. The Churches must ask themselves whether or not the liturgical language, images, and symbols they use are intelligible to our contemporaries, and whether or not preachers are able to explain the Christian heritage in language that is meaningful to modern men.[4]

This is undoubtedly what Vatican Council II attempted to do. But is such a task feasible on the whole? Is it enough to concede the adaptations that science and politico-social ideas seem to call for? The danger of such a procedure is that we may reach an illusory answer by papering over a house that is full of holes; it can only be a stage in a longer process, a temporary solution dictated by necessity. The real need is to work from inside and start taking into account the real circumstances in which men find themselves. In the last analysis, what is needed is greater confidence in the capacity of the Church to find embodiment in human values, a full acceptance of all earthly things that are good, and an effort to become a guiding force in men's daily lives.

In short, we are confronted here with one application of the law of incarnation that Christ willed should reign. In this sense the Church becomes a missionary, and the vocation that is inseparable from her being requires of her a "secularization" that will take various forms in various times and places. In thus "secularizing" herself, the Church will be in continuity with the prophets, who were so careful to avoid absorption in worship and, above all, any connection with the kind of cultic institution that would dispense men from genuine faith and love.

But there is danger of great confusion here, since the road of secularization is not easy and simple. Observers have criticized the snobbism typical of much closet secularization, where the latter is seen simply in intellectual terms (and not always with all desirable clarity). They have sometimes attacked it on good grounds:

> The abusive, unthinking, commercialized use of "secularization" and related words is disagreeable and wearying. Thinking men do not thus deal with realities profoundly rooted in man's being nor attack, in such a blanket, confused, and partisan fashion, a set of values intimately connected with God.[5]

And yet there is a real problem behind it all. For how can we settle for a liturgy that has no connection with men's temporal activities? The problem is by no means new, of course; the liturgical reform has certainly been aware of it. But what remedy is to be applied in this scandalous situation? Are we to consider temporal activity something untouchable and adjust the liturgy to it? Are we to insert the liturgical signs among the signs proper to temporal life, with its program that is geared to earth and time?

Such an approach is harsh and simplistic. No matter — the mentality it presents is in fact widespread. It is not always officially expressed, but it corresponds to an instinct of our contemporaries. At the very moment when the liturgy and its incomparable values were being rediscovered, man and his world were also being exalted.

Consequently, it is difficult for our contemporaries to think of Christianity simply as something given, and imposed on them by God. Rather, man and the world think they have the right to question God and to receive an answer. In other words, the new-found consciousness of human and worldly values does not dispose people to accept readily the values of a ready-made liturgy, a sort of "take out" affair that needs only to be adjusted a bit (what all parties would agree to call "adaptation"). Such a liturgy would be incapable of confronting or challenging man, and consequently it would lose its whole justification. For man thinks he has the right to challenge God in turn. This is why he instinctively rejects the whole idea of a "sacred time," texts imposed by authority, and a prefabricated ritual, no matter how traditional. As some people would put it, don't we men of today have our own "scriptures," written by our daily lives? Shouldn't we be reading, during the liturgy of "the world," the records jotted down in our diaries? Should they, have they the right to, oblige us to certain prayer formularies and specific themes for celebration? And so on, until the challenge becomes a claim to exercise an unlimited creativity.

Given these conditions, how can we possibly ignore these various reactions (some of them quite justified) and offer the reader a commentary on the texts of the liturgical year universally used by the Roman Catholic Church?

Spiritual worship

As we pointed out above, the term "worship" is no longer acceptable to many, or at best they have little use for it. They have little use for it because they have a false idea of it. In fact, many Christians really have a pagan idea of worship, and many theological books only keep them locked up in their misconceptions. To think of worship as an act in which the spirit is raised to God in order to honor him and to acknowledge our dependence on him is to have but a partial vision of it and a very rudimentary and textbookish theology.

Vatican Council II, profiting by the studies that preceded it, has given us access to a much richer and more vibrant reality. The Council sees Catholic worship as a dialogue of God with man. In this dialogue God takes the initiative; he solicits and expects man's response in the form of praise and prayer, but also in the form of questions. Here we have the biblical attitude as represented in chapter 19 of the Book of Exodus, where the *Qahal*, or "called community," is described. God gathers his people in order to speak to them through Moses. The people listen and then answer; their response takes the form of praise and petition, and culminates in the offering of sacrifice.

We must bear in mind the dynamic character of this divine intervention that initiates dialogue. For God, the word is a form of action; in his word he gives himself as a savior, and his very word is already a saving gift. Our response, therefore, cannot be simply an empty rite; it too must be the offering of life. That is what St. Paul is telling the Romans when he exhorts them to offer their bodies as a living sacrifice that is holy and acceptable to God (Rom. 12:1-2). This is spiritual worship. Spiritual worship embraces life in its entirety: all that is interior to man, his orientation to others and to the community, his openness to the world's needs and the world's progress.

We might be tempted to think that Paul is here establishing a clear break between conceptions proper to the New Testament and conceptions proper to the Old, the latter being much more "cult-bound." But this view is certainly extreme; in fact, it is even inaccurate. The Book of Joshua already suggests a service of Yahweh that is not simply cultic but embraces the whole of life through the fulfillment of the law (Josh. 24:21-24).[6] Later on, the prophets even challenged the value of the cultic institutions. "To obey is better than sacrifice, and to hearken than the fat of rams" (1 Sam. 15:22). And recall the well-known words of Hosea: "For I desire steadfast love and not sacrifice, the knowledge of God, rather than burnt offerings" (6:6). Christ would make these themes his own in an emphatic way in Matthew 9:13 and 12:7. In the Old Testament there was an increasing spiritualization of worship, but after the Exile came a new wave of institutionalization, as feasts, days, Sabbaths, seasons, and holy places took on increasing importance; thus, for example, the Sabbath, a day of rest (Exod. 20:8), became a day of worship (Book of Jubilees 2, 30–31).

The New Testament has a resolutely spiritualist vision of worship, as we have already pointed out. Worship means the offering of the person (1 Cor. 16:15; Rom. 16:5; Heb. 9:14-28; 1 Peter 2:5; Apoc. 14:4). But it also means that the Christian's entire life is placed at the service of evangelization, faith, and brotherly love. In 2 Corinthians 9:11-12, St. Paul writes: "You will be enriched in every way for great generosity, which through us will produce thanksgiving to God; for the rendering of this service not only supplies the wants of the saints but also overflows in many thanksgivings to God." The Letter to the Philippians (4:18) contains the same theology: the charitable offering of the Philippians is a sacrifice that God finds pleasing and acceptable. In a sterner way the Letter of St. James confirms this spiritualization of worship with its aspect of gift: "Religion that is pure and undefiled before God and the Father is this: to visit orphans and widows in their affliction, and to keep oneself unstained from the world" (1:27).

We noted above, and shall not delay on it here, that the handing on of the faith and the preaching of the gospel are also a worship and a liturgy. The whole apostolic life of Paul is a sharing in the sacrificial offering of Christ (Col. 1:24; 2 Cor. 4). Paul thinks of himself as the liturgical minister of Jesus Christ among the pagans, as priest of God's gospel; and the goal of his work is to help the pagans become a pleasing sacrifice that is consecrated by the Holy Spirit (Rom. 15:15-16). The Letter to the Hebrews thinks of Jesus' redemptive action in cultic terms; herein lies the originality of the Letter (see especially Hebrews 5-10).

Worship, then, as seen by the Scriptures, is spiritual and leads toward a future. Christ is its high priest (Heb. 2:17; 7:1-14, 23-28); he transcends the whole created order, thus showing the limitations of all cultic paraphernalia and filling the world with his light and power.

Now, these are the realities that lay hold of our everyday life through the mediation of the signs, words, and gestures that make up the liturgy.

There is now no separation of sacred and profane, although the world has not yet achieved the full dimensions of the kingdom. It is because the world has not yet done so that the Church and its sacraments are indispensable as means of laying hold of the world and building the king-dom.[7]

To think of the liturgy in the way we have been indicat-ing is to orient oneself toward the future. The Christian must use the world as building material for a new world. If we take the world as it is, without fearing it, we open it to God's action and our own action; we offer it the possibility of being reshaped in accordance with God's original plan for it. But the world is not simply something to be rebuilt, and it is not rebuilt simply because the Church pours out upon it the transforming gifts of heaven. Rather, it takes an active part in its own rebuilding. The Catholic, therefore, does not condemn the world as such, though he does con demn its present sinful limitations. Thereby he commits himself to the creation of that future in which the material world itself will be redeemed.

Worship gathers up all these aspects. Worship is God's descent, but it is also man's ascent in which he uses the created world to reach its, and his, God, and offers his daily life and loving service of others; an ascent in which he spreads the Good News, while his eyes are fixed on the future and he helps the world in its entirety to evolve toward him and thus toward his God.

Is St. Paul an opponent of the Church year?

A superficial reading of the Letter to the Galatians might lead us to see in St. Paul a convinced foe of Christian feasts: "But now that you have come to know God, or rather to be known by God, how can you turn back again to the weak and beggarly elemental spirits, whose slaves you want to be once more? You observe days, and months, and seasons, and years! I am afraid I have labored over you in vain" (4:9-11).

Christ had said that the Sabbath was made for man, not man for the Sabbath (Mark 2:27).

In a similar vein St. Paul tells the Colossians, in connection with yearly and monthly feasts and Sabbaths: "These are only a shadow of what is to come; but the substance belongs to Christ" (2:17).

Texts such as these do not seem to encourage the celebration of a liturgical year. How, then, has the Church been able to celebrate days and years? Has she fallen back into the fault of which St. Paul speaks? In the beginning the Church celebrated each Sunday; then, in the mid-second century, she chose one Sunday for the special celebration of the Pasch — and chose that Sunday for its relation to the full moon! Then, out of the Easter Vigil developed the fifty days of Eastertide as well as a Lent that gradually reached its present form. Christmas and Epiphany were established, and later on at Rome, Advent.

But the basic issue in this whole development is our deliverance — *that* is the object of all these joyous feasts. If the liturgical celebration were a burden, if it were the yoke of the Mosaic law in a new form, then man would be made for the Sabbath. In fact, however, the Sabbath is made for man, and all the feasts point to our salvation. This is why every day is a feast day for the Christian. The celebration of feasts such as Sunday does not mean that certain days are now not profane like the others, nor does the phrase "keep Sunday holy" mean to make sacral a day that otherwise would be profane. The Fathers emphasized rather the deeper theological dimension of "feast" and insisted that for the Christian every day is a Sabbath. There is a classical text of St. Justin on the subject:

> The new law bids you celebrate an unbroken Sabbath. You, on the other hand [i.e., Trypho and the Jews], remain inactive for a single day and think yourselves pious on that account. . . . No! If a man is a thief or a liar, let him cease to be such; if he is an adulterer, let him change his ways. That is how he will properly celebrate the joyous Sabbaths of God.[8]

Reflecting on Paul's attitude toward feasts, Origen writes:

> I think this is what Paul had in mind when he called the feast that is held on days set apart from the others "part of a feast" [Col. 2:16]; he hinted by this phrase that the life that is continually being lived according to the divine word is not a "part of a feast" but an and continual feast.[9]

The early Church and the patristic writers kept their eyes on the reality of salvation as received in the community that is Christ's Body, and therefore they thought like Origen in this matter. We must bear in mind that until the fourth century the dominant reality was the Pasch of the Lord; that is what was being celebrated. Whether the "day by day" of Acts 2:46 is to be taken literally or loosely, the Christians of the first generation were certainly zealous about the breaking of bread and prayer (Acts 2:42). Each day they broke bread in their homes and praised God (Acts 2:46-47); each day the Lord added to their community those who were being saved (Acts 2:47); each day, they preached the Good News of Jesus Christ (Acts 5:47). The vivid experience of deliverance, and of new life begun in them and progressively reaching out to embrace the whole world, was the basis for the "feast," the Christian's daily celebration.

However, precisely because man enters into the celebration with the whole of his human reality, it was natural to make one or other day the special time for prayer and the gathering of the community; such a day, as we might expect, would be the day on which the resurrection of Jesus had occurred. But this observation by itself is not enough, it seems to me. Precisely because man in his entirety does enter into the celebration, it is not enough for him to celebrate the feast of the resurrection each day, no matter how conscious he may be of the daily passage of the Lord through his life. For he needs special moments; his basic psychology requires it. He needs special actions that will enable him to express, to lay hold of in a more personal and reflective way, the reality of his deliverance. The Christian indeed lives always and at every moment in the end-oriented time of salvation and is no longer enslaved by time as measured in days and years; nonetheless, it is normal that a certain recurrence and repetition should enable him to enter more deeply into his own joy and to unite himself more fully to the deliverance bestowed upon him.

The liturgical year, therefore, is not an iron yoke; it is not an accumulation of memories that have nothing to do with life and that he listens to patiently, as one might listen to an old man who buries himself in the past and repeats the same stories over and over again. On the contrary, the liturgical year brings home both the reality of his new life and the profound value of his daily existence.

The liturgical year: reality or psychological stimulus?

We may ask whether the liturgical year with its Sundays and feasts represents only a psychological need. Does it have stimulus value but no real content?

For an answer to this basic question we must have recourse to Scripture and the Jewish liturgy. Here is how practicing Jews think: "Do not flee the world of space; use spatial realities for your action — but concentrate your love on eternity alone."[10] This would represent at least one Jewish approach to our present question. For the Jew, God is involved in history; but for God, the past, present, and future coexist. God is he who was and is and will be. The Jewish liturgy is envisaged as an act that allows a being whose existence is transitory to come into contact with him who always is; he who always is comes into contact with him whose existence is transitory.

If the Jew at worship were concerned only with past history, his worship would be indistinguishable from the Hellenistic cults. In fact, two attitudes which he regards as supremely important and which, in his eyes, correspond to the real order set his worship apart from other cults. He is contemporary with what was, but also contemporary with what will be. "To commemorate is not to stand afar off from what happened in the past; on the contrary, it is to eliminate the distance between present and past." To commemorate is to give the past a new existence, it is to think that each of us is contemporaneous with historical events whose consequences we still endure or whose effects we still prolong in time.[11] At the same time, the Jewish liturgy is oriented toward a future. The Passover meal is not an imaginary commemoration of the Exodus from Egypt; rather, each participant thinks of himself as now freed from slavery. And he is not thinking in terms of poetry or abstract theology; he means a real deliverance right now. On the other hand, at the Passover meal a place is reserved for the prophet Elias, showing hope and expectation of fulfillment.

Is the Church year simply a psychological stimulus? A kind of imaginative instruction in the faith? Patristic tradition, at least, thought of it quite differently. For the Fathers, the liturgical year is not an edifying commemoration of the past, but a making real in the present for the sake of a future. But, we may ask, was not the fourth century a period that tried to sacralize everything? Did it establish its celebrations in the same spirit that animated the liturgies of the earlier centuries? Some writers scent in the Christian feasts of that period sacralizing, and thus paganizing, tendencies.[12]

Now it is a fact that we find in the Fathers a tendency to imitate at least the vocabulary of contemporary religions. They did this, most of the time, in order to be understood. We can also reproach them for being excessively distrustful of the world. And yet, there is nothing in them of a false kind of sacralization. They had an innate sense of God's involvement in history; events, in their mind, formed a continuous web. To convince ourselves of this, we need only recall their interest in typology: in the typological view, world history as directed by God is not made up simply of successive events or "stories" but forms a unity. A "type" is not simply an example; it is also a starting point that reaches its corresponding end point in the "antitype." For example, the crossing of the Red Sea is not an illustration but a type of baptism; that is, it is the starting point, and our baptism is the continuation of this beginning as we move toward the complete "crossing" in which we shall meet the Lord.

In this view, then, we are part of a history that we both continue and bring to completion. We begin to glimpse what the world meant to the Fathers. In their eyes, every celebration meant an actual presence of the mystery of Christ, who continues the history of the Old Testament in the New and in the ongoing present. We find St. Leo the Great affirming this in categorical fashion and without any effort to be poetic about it: "Although the series of bodily

actions is now past, as ordained in the eternal plan . . .
nevertheless we adore the virgin birth that brings us salvation." [13]

What St. Leo writes with regard to the Nativity, he repeats in greater detail for the Epiphany: "For, although this
day passed, the power of the work revealed on this day did
not also pass away." [14]

St. Leo's intention is to emphasize the effectiveness of
the liturgical celebration as a means of dispensing the past
mysteries of Christ, which we must receive in our own today. He writes:

> Beloved, the remembrance of what the Savior did for
> mankind is most useful to us, provided that what we
> venerate in faith we also receive and imitate. For in
> the communication of the mysteries of Christ to us,
> there is present both the power of grace and the en-
> couragement which teaching gives, so that we may
> follow by our deeds him whom we confess in the
> spirit of faith.[15]

In the mind of St. Leo, "the remembrance of what the
Savior did" is not a simple recall of the past but a remembering that enables us to share in the mysteries of Christ.
The sharing is based on grace, teaching, and example. We
have here a doctrine dear to St. Leo, who likes to insist that
the sacrament (that is, the efficacious sign that gives the action of Christ a here-and-now existence) is for us both an
example and a grace.

Two classic passages from the sermons of St. Leo confirm
what we have been saying about him. One passage relates
to the annunciation:

> The astonishing conversation of the angel Gabriel
> with Mary and the conception that is the work of the
> Holy Spirit and that is as marvelous in the promise of
> it as in Mary's believing acceptance of it do not take
> place simply in our memories but before our very
> eyes, as it were.[16]

The same teaching of the actualization of a past mystery in a present "remembrance" is affirmed of the redemption. This actualization St. Leo calls a "sacrament of redemption" (*sacramentum redemptionis*)[17] and explains elsewhere what he means by these words:

> All that the Son of God did and taught for the reconciliation of the world we not only know through the narration of past events; we also experience the effects of it in virtue of these present deeds [the sacraments].[18]

These texts and numerous others have served as the basis for a theology of the liturgy. Dom Odo Casel, a German monk of Maria-Laach, was a chief pioneer in the elaboration of this theology. His rediscovery was, however, more intuitive than scientifically and exegetically, or even theologically, well founded. It would be out of place for us here to offer a positive and negative critique of his views; in any event, others have done this.[19] But despite some principles that are open to criticism or even simply unacceptable, the pioneers managed to shape a theology of the liturgy that has now been presented to the Church in Vatican II's *Constitution on the Sacred Liturgy*.

The liturgical year: actualization of the past for the sake of the future

The *Constitution on the Sacred Liturgy* offers us a first-rate theology of the liturgy. Three sections give the essentials of this theology.[20] First, there is the redemptive work of Christ; then, the redemptive work as continued by the Church and accomplished in the liturgy; finally, the presence of Christ in the liturgy. These passages have been the subject of so many commentaries that there is no point in our giving the whole text of them. We shall try, in our own way, to explain the vital meaning of the liturgical celebration of the mysteries of salvation, and to do so in a simple fashion.

If we are to understand the liturgy, we must take as our starting point the incarnation of the Word and the later coming of the Spirit. Until the Word became incarnate, man's experience of God was of a philosophical kind: a prayerful reflection, an intellectual and psychological approach to God, with the more or less profound effects this might have on the person's private and social behavior. The Old Testament, in its steadfast monotheism, shows the beginnings of a mediation through signs, for example, the sign of fire, which indicates the presence of the Lord (Exod. 3:2-4; 19:18).

With the incarnation, however, the manner in which man comes into saving contact with God is radically changed, and the flesh becomes the instrument of salvation.[21]

As soon, however, as we say "incarnation," we are bound to take past, present, and future into account.

The past: Christ focuses upon his own person all the expectations and the whole typology of the Old Testament. Moreover, as soon as we think of the incarnation, we recall the whole series of events making up the history of a world that awaits reconstruction and renewal. The Christ who is born according to the flesh represents the fulfillment of the Old Testament types, which are neither simple prophecies nor simple examples, but the starting points of events that are fulfilled in Christ and continue to be fulfilled in the Church. This is the case, for example, with the Exodus and Passover.

The present: Through signs, the first and foremost of which is the Church, we are in contact with Christ, who continues to be present. When Jesus tells his disciples, "It is to your advantage that I go away" (John 16:7) and when he promises them the Paraclete (John 14:16-19), he is emphasizing the continuity of his presence among us. It is good for us that he has gone. Indeed, it was necessary that he go if he was to take the glorified body that would give him an unlimited presence in time and space. Now, through signs, we are in contact with the glorious body of Christ.

Our experience of God is thus a sacramental experience — not a primarily contemplative experience, but experience by real contact with the real person of Christ in his glorified body and by means of signs. It is, then, an experience that is, so to speak, materialist, being both our own and intrinsically bound up with the incarnation. Only because the body of Christ is glorified is it possible for us to enter into contact, here and now, with all his mysteries, mysteries that absorb into themselves their preparation and beginnings in the Old Testament.

Only because God has become incarnate can we be, as we are, in the presence of two facts. On the one hand, for Christ as for every other man, his actions are limited in space and time; think, for example, of his death on Calvary. On the other hand, since Christ is God, none of his actions are limited in space and time; in him there is neither before nor after. Consequently, at the Last Supper he could render already present what would be effectively done later, on Good Friday. For the same reason it is possible for us, in the Eucharistic celebration, to make actual a past event that happened only once: the death of Christ and the whole paschal mystery.

If we apply what has just been said to all the mysteries of salvation, we can see how immensely rich the reality of the liturgical year really is. The celebration of Christmas is not a simple remembering; rather, it actualizes for us the whole mystery of the incarnation. Similarly, to await the incarnation is not a mere poetic fiction, since in awaiting the sign that is the celebration of Christmas, we await the moment when the incarnation of the Lord will be actualized for us. The expectation that characterizes Advent is thus a genuine, not a simulated, expectation of what Christmas makes real.

The future: This dimension is there because Christ is in his glory and the sending of the Spirit creates in the Church a tension toward the full realization of the divine plan of salvation. Experiential contact with the glorious body of Christ is contact with the whole of the Old Testament and

with the mysteries of salvation that are made present now
for the sake of a future which I experience in hope and of
which I already have a pledge. I experience sacramentally
the past, the present, and the future. Thus, in our liturgical
experience of God we are always constructing a future. We
are not simply being drawn toward a future; we are building it together with Christ, who is present through us. The
entire world has the task of reconstructing itself in view of
a future until God's plan is perfectly fulfilled and Christ
comes to gather in the mature fruit of his entire work of paschal reconciliation.

The presence of the Lord

If we can speak so emphatically of the intrinsic value of
the liturgical year, it is because we celebrate it together
with Christ himself. The special nature of the Church year
is entirely due to the fact that the Lord himself presides
over it and that he celebrates his mysteries with the Church
for the glory of the Father. The Second Vatican Council laid
heavy stress on the various ways in which Christ is present
in the liturgical celebration.[22] The highest form of this
presence is the real presence in the Eucharist, and it is the
source and summit of all liturgical celebration because it is
the presence of the paschal mystery. On the other hand,
each Eucharistic celebration, while having the paschal mystery as its basis and background, derives its particular features and coloring from the celebration of the liturgy of the
word. The Eucharistic celebration on Christmas is different
from, as well as the same as, the Eucharistic celebration of
the day when the Pentecostal Spirit was sent. The celebration of the word gives each Eucharistic celebration its special coloring.

We must emphasize, moreover, the presence of the Lord
in the celebration of the word as such, just as in the celebration of the Office. The *Constitution on the Liturgy* asserts
the fact but does not risk an explanation of it. Pope Paul VI
seems to have been struck by the rediscovery of this pres-

ence of the Lord in the proclamation of the Word. The Bible, by itself a dead book, becomes alive and actual when it is proclaimed in the liturgical assembly. The *Constitution on the Liturgy* simply teaches that the Lord himself is still proclaiming his gospel even today,[23] but the Pope seems to go further.

In his encyclical *Mysterium fidei*, in which his chief purpose is to insist on the permanence of the real Eucharistic presence, Pope Paul VI takes the opportunity to say that there is more than one "real" presence and that we must not exclude all presences but the Eucharistic one. This statement is all the more important since it is made in a context where the main point is to insist on the reality and value of the Eucharistic presence. The Pope writes: "This presence of Christ in the Eucharist is called 'real' not to exclude the idea that others are 'real' too, but rather to indicate presence par excellence."[24] This statement represents a step forward and is a very valuable clarification. But we must still try to penetrate its meaning more fully.

The writer who seems to have done this with the greatest depth and clarity is S. Marsili.[25] According to Paul VI, there are several modes of real presence. What distinguishes them is not the realness of the presence but the mode of it; this diversifies them and gives them each its own "level," as it were, but all are real. The real Eucharistic presence presupposes both a "transubstantiation" and a permanence in the sign; other presences, for example that of Christ in the proclamation of the Word, do not have these distinguishing marks.

The important thing is that the presence of the Lord in the proclamation of the Word is not analogical and figurative, as when someone reads the works of a poet at an intellectual gathering and entitles the reading: "The Abiding Presence of. . . ." In the proclamation of the Word there is a real, active presence of the Lord. This notion is still unfamiliar and has not become part of the instinctive habits of mind of our contemporaries, whose attention is still focused exclusively on the real Eucharistic presence. This latter presence does, of course, still represent the supreme form of the Lord's presence.

This last point needs to be emphasized. It is the most important of all, for it gives the celebrations of the liturgical year their full coherence and value.

THE ADVENT MYSTERY

BIBLICO-LITURGICAL REFLECTIONS ON THE ADVENT SEASON

1. WAITING IN HOPE

Is there a Christian way of hoping?

The subject is a complicated one, but it is also of basic importance. For how is it possible to really live without looking forward to someone and something? Can a man breathe if he does not have hope? Can a Christian be a prisoner within a narrow round, knocking his head on the walls of his cage, whether it be the cage of legalism or of some ready-made affair called "the spiritual life"? Does not the Christian, like every other man (though perhaps more than any other), have the duty of cultivating a stern yet joyous discontent with his human condition? Perhaps that is what distinguishes the Christian's hope: though it is fierce and implacable, stern and eager, it is also, paradoxically, full of joy. But isn't that very description just bad poetry and ecclesiastical drivel?

As a matter of fact, hope is an aspect of faith and inseparable from love. The connection with love, however, is not specifically Christian. Anyone who loves another, precisely because he loves him, has unquestioning confidence in him and with great hope expects everything from him. Péguy, in one of his brilliant theological intuitions, saw hope as a little girl who goes off to school between her two big sisters, faith and love, holding each by the hand. He explains his meaning in his *Le porche de la deuxième vertu*: In the eyes of those who see the three sisters passing, little hope is being guided by the other two; in fact, however, little hope is pulling forward the two who seem to be leading her.

If Péguy is correct, then we must recognize that the distinction between these three fundamental attitudes of faith, hope, and love is not easily to be made. The books of the Old Testament show hardly any awareness of a distinction between what would later be called the three theological virtues. The Hebrew texts show how close in meaning are the three terms, whose roots too are closely connected. Some of the terms used seem to mean the fact of hoping, but the meaning is not an exclusive one, and sentiments of faith and love mingle with it.

St. Paul will speak of the three virtues as distinct but closely interwoven (1 Tim. 1:3; 1 Cor. 13:13; Gal. 5:5-6). There is no hope without faith and love. On the other hand, a man believes and loves because he hopes; hope gives strength to faith and love, while faith and love give rise to hope.

Our world is a sad place; it seems to be without hope, precisely because its crisis is a crisis of faith and love. But the crisis is an old one. The whole drama of the Old Testament is focused on hope and its fluctuations. The problem experienced there can shed light on ours.

Through his prophet, who is a human-divine concretization of hope, God gradually led his people to hope for more than earthly blessings. And yet, what he promises them is a land flowing with milk and honey (Exod. 3:8)! It will take centuries before Israel as a people realizes what the hope of salvation entails. To some extent this hope will materialize in the "remnant" that will be saved and become a leaven of renewal (Amos 9:8; Is. 10:19). The basic content of that renewal is revealed by divinely inspired prophets; its outlines are sketched as they stimulate the hope of peace and salvation, light and God's full victory over sin. Their efforts are focused on an objective not easily attained: to push the people of God toward a hope in ultimate righteousness before God.

Is knowing God important? This knowledge becomes the object of hope, but we must give the word "know" the full meaning it has in the Semitic languages. The point is not a metaphysical knowledge but an experiential knowledge: to know God is to touch him, to see him (Is. 11:9). The renewal sought is primarily a renewal of man's heart (Ezek. 36–37). At this point there is quite naturally a call for a perfect, disinterested worship, what we might readily call selfless contemplation (Pss. 63; 84).

However, the people of the Old Testament (in contradistinction to the divinely inspired revelation in the Old Testament) stopped short while still on their journey; their hope was still in means to which they could attach themselves. The result was disillusionment, painful yet often beneficent. The whole tireless work of the prophets had to be done before the people of God finally put their hope in God himself (Is. 60:19, etc.). They had to learn that only the Lord and his reign were worth waiting and hoping for (Pss. 96–99).

This was not all just words. There were some in Israel who were sincere, who really believed what God said, and wanted to live accordingly. These really wanted to find salvation in God (Wis. 5:9); they had a burning desire for immortality (Wis. 3:4), and gradually their hope was purified. But the hope by and large remained an earthly, and often even a material, hope. And so we see willing without real willing, hope without real hope, love without real love — all the unexpected, contradictory movements so deeply rooted in the psyche of man at every stage of human history. God should be the only important one in the life of his peoples; suffering and death should count for nothing (Pss. 73; 49:16); but how difficult it is to look for God alone while expecting everything from his hand!

But is the Old Testament a genuine experience for us as well? Do we really hope for salvation? The ideal we would like to see the Church realize; hope in the realization of this ideal; the vision of what holiness should be; pride in theology for its own sake; detailed and barren criticism of the Church as an institution; hope for the earthly achievement of the ideal of holiness that we dream up for ourselves — all these are subtle barriers to true hope!

Is there, then, a Christian way of hoping? Has Christianity really made a contribution to the idea and reality of hope? The answer is clearly and irremediably disillusioning for anyone who does not believe.

The reason is that, for the believer, his personal hope is inseparably connected with the hope of the entire Church and that when united to the hope of the Church, it is oriented in two directions: toward Christ and toward the renewal of the world.

Christ? We await during Advent the actualization of his incarnation and then we celebrate Christmas, but we still hope and wait for his second coming. This is a hope the non-believer cannot share, for it is contrary to what hope should normally be. This Christian hope is indeed a strange thing; no society of men has ever been able to walk this road, because it seems contradictory and turns any sane philosophy topsy-turvy. Why? Because the Christian hopes for what he already possesses! In the inscription of Pectorius we read: "(You hold) the Fish in your hand."[26]

"Fish" in Greek is *ichthys*, and *ichthys* is the monogram of Christ. Therefore we hold Christ in our hand. But this is either simple stupidity or it is true; if it isn't true, the whole of Christianity is nothing but mystical poetry without real value. It is true enough, of course, that Christians haven't much faith in the privilege that is theirs: with and in Christ they are dead and risen (Rom. 6:1-7; Col. 3:1); they already possess in an invisible but real fashion what the baptismal ritual, in the oldest of its prayers, calls the "rudiments of their own glory," which is invisible[27] but present and real (2 Cor. 3:18–4:6). This is why, according to St. Paul, every Christian possesses the first fruits of the world to come (Rom. 8:11-23).

Christian hope is thus compounded of certainty: that is, we hope for what we already possess. The powerful dynamism that inspires this hope of a reality we already possess and grasp, though we do not see it, is an intense light for faith and a joyful spur to love. We cannot explain in any other way the attitude of the martyrs and the saints. As for ourselves, our glory resides in the Christ whom we possess, and it is so great (2 Cor. 4:17) that it shines through our present life (1 Peter 1:8).

Purged of anxiety, calm, sure, joyous: such is Christian hope — in theory. In fact, we see around us sad-faced Christians who claim, with a pride not wholly devoid of snobbery, that they live in anxiety. They show no sign of that deliberately maintained good humor that is a sign of the genuine hope of those who already possess. We Christians are in an unusual position: we already possess, "as though we were looking on the invisible God," but we still await the face-to-face encounter with him who is promised to us and whom we now possess. Our hope thus consists in waiting for the successive realities that we can already touch and that we already share.

Let the mirror be broken!

How, in the last analysis, can we explain this specifically Christian hope, which consists in waiting for what we already possess?

I think it is possible to express this hope in very concrete terms (though I shall avoid trying to persuade the reader of the theology behind my view). Without realizing it, we hope now for the disappearance of the signs and sacraments through which we lay hold of God and our happiness. At the very moment when we celebrate that happiness, and for the very reason that the celebration thrusts us into the future, we eagerly wait for the disappearance of the whole regime of liturgy and sacrament. We hope that the veil will be rent and the mirror broken. We see now "as in a mirror" (1 Cor. 13:12). We long and hope and wait for the mirror to be broken. To bring that great moment closer to us is one of the purposes of every liturgical celebration. It is in this way that our hope grows more abundant (Rom. 15:13), since all of God's promises to us have been fulfilled in Jesus Christ (2 Cor. 1:20).

If the preceding remarks on hope seem to us nothing but

preacher's jargon, we show that we have not yet begun to live the Christian life nor understood the meaning of our baptism. And that is precisely the situation of the vast majority of the baptized! They live as if they were dead, and their hope seems inspired by bitterness; they hope because they do not see what else they can do. They have not yet been enlightened as to the real object of their hope. They have to stop fixing their hopes on the here and now, on success in this life, on the glory of the institutional Church, or on the splendid flowering of science. Their hope is in fact a stunted, ill-natured thing; it is sour. In its place they need a hope that can embrace mankind and the whole of this world that is passing away and destined for renewal.

Many Christians think they cherish a Christian hope. In fact, however, their hopes are limited to themselves. It is difficult to stop hoping only for one's personal future or for the world's future because one is part of that world. Many hopes are ultimately self-centered. The Church realizes full well how difficult Christian hope is. That is why over the centuries she has fashioned a special liturgy that, beyond other liturgies, is a liturgy of hope, of waiting in hope. But liturgy is never simply a moralizing exhortation, never simply a set of consoling words to restore the energetic outlook and make the patient endure by helping him forget his toothache.

The purpose of liturgy is to put the Christian in contact with a reality that, though spiritual, is fully real. Each year, then, the Church puts the Christian into a situation where his hope can come alive and grow strong: she bids him hope, along with the whole of the Old Testament, for the coming of deliverance. The deliverance has already been accomplished; now he can celebrate it as a deliverance that is present to him through signs, and as he celebrates it, he can reach out for, and make his way toward, that moment when all signs shall vanish. The element of waiting that is part of Christian hope finds sacramental expression as the Christian relives in the present the Old Testament past, lives the incarnation as an event of today, and waits for the return of Christ and the breaking of the mirror on the last day.

Such is the rich life of the Advent season. We must now indicate its major elements and explain the waiting and the present hope that characterize it.

The hope of a sinful people

Hope is impossible unless we sincerely acknowledge what we are, what we ought to be, and what we will have to make of ourselves. The Church and each of us, her members, must be courageous enough to face up to his real condition, in order that he may bring to life once more the energies latent in hope. The prophet Isaiah is not afraid to use harsh words that we do not like to hear these days. He confronts the people of God as their judge and, within the space of a few verses, levels two relentless charges against them.

First of all, he says, the people of God has sinned gravely: God has made the Israelites his sons, but that people does not know God and has departed from him. "The ox knows its owner, and the ass its master's crib; but Israel does not know, my people does not understand" (Is. 1:3). Punishment has been to no avail, and the Lord does not know how to chastise them and make them understand their own state of soul (Is. 1:5-6). The seriousness of Israel's situation is reflected in the devastation of the land, which looks like Sodom after it had been overthrown; the physical scene brings home the perverse moral condition of the people (Is. 1:7). Happily, though, a scanty remnant remains and carries responsibility for the salvation of the people (Is. 1:9).

The second accusation is just as harsh: The people think they can have recourse to their liturgical practices and everything will be fine! No, the important thing is justice toward the neighbor. Without such honest dealing, Israel will continue to be punished (Is. 1:10-18). Prayer must become honest and pure, for only then can it be acceptable to God.

Then the light of hope shines: "Come now, let us reason together, says the Lord: though your sins are like scarlet, they shall be as white as snow; though they are red like crimson, they shall become like wool" (Is. 1:18).

Isaiah repeats the theme in another form: the contrast between the faithful wife and the adulterous wife.[28] The consequences for the city of her sin are evident: she has become the haunt of murderers, and every dweller in the city thirsts for power. But the vision is not one of total darkness, for God will win out over his enemies and then the city will be called "city of righteousness, the faithful city" (1:26). Then comes the marvelous vision of chapter 2, which we should read here:

> It shall come to pass in the latter days that the mountain of the house of the Lord shall be established as the highest of the mountains, and shall be raised above the hills; and all the nations shall flow to it, and many peoples shall come, and say: "Come, let us go up to the mountain of the Lord, to the house of the God of Jacob; that he may teach us his ways and that we may walk in his paths." For out of Zion shall go forth the law, and the word of the Lord from Jerusalem. He shall judge between the nations, and shall decide for many peoples; and they shall beat their swords into plowshares, and their spears into pruning hooks; nation shall not lift up sword against nation, neither shall they learn war any more. O house of Jacob, come, let us walk in the light of the Lord (Is. 2:2-4).

Thus the faithless city becomes the eschatological center for the gathering of the nations in peace and unity. Such is the hope-filled vision set before a people that acknowledges its sinful state.

But there is a serious danger, always present, never wholly exorcized: the danger of religious formalism that gives rise to a false hope, the danger of hope that is not grounded in conversion. Isaiah seems haunted by this danger. There must be no acts of worship to which nothing corresponds in a man's heart;[29] God is fed up with rote prayers.

Here we men are, in darkness, without faith, unable to see. Here we are, irresolute and stupefied, blind and sightless, our eyes shut and our heads covered (Is. 20:10). But once again salvation is on the way, and Isaiah paints a splendid picture of eschatological salvation in the latter part of chapter 29 (vv. 17-24). "In that day the deaf shall hear the words of a book, and out of their gloom and darkness the eyes of the blind shall see" (29:18).

Hopeful waiting in time of conversion

No hope is possible unless we turn to the Lord and wait for him to come to us. This is a theme frequently found in the Gospel readings for Advent as well as in the Old Testament readings.

In the conversion that makes hope possible, we can distinguish three elements: conversion, watchfulness, and God's initiative.

The Old Testament offers the conversion of Ephraim as a model for us.[30] The conversion in this instance was radical. "In that day men will regard their Maker, and their eyes will look to the Holy One of Israel; they will not have regard for the altars, the work of their hands, and they will not look to what their own fingers have made" (Is. 17:7-8). Here conversion is a turning to God, an abandonment of one's own outlook, of the prayers learned by heart and the meaningless gestures of contrition, of the easy worship that is meant to protect man against God. Here conversion means leaving everything else and advancing toward God. (Is. 17:7). John the Baptist will be constantly summoning men to conversion; such will be his basic role and the image we will rightly have of him.[31]

Conversion can be triggered by reflection on what would have happened if we had been attentive to the Lord. "O that you had hearkened to my commandments! Then your peace would have been like a river, and your righteousness like the waves of the sea" (Is. 48:18).[32] The searing vision of lost time, of all that has been missed and destroyed, can lead to hope, conversion, and waiting upon God. Henceforth we must walk uprightly and without stumbling toward the day of Christ, when we shall have in full measure the justice won for us by Jesus Christ.[33] To do God's will in imitation of Christ, and to do it without any of the bigoted hope we find so hard to put up with in pseudo-Christians who shift all their crosses onto the shoulders of others — that is what conversion means.[34] That is the authentic turnabout required by the waiting in hope of which conversion is the indispensable condition. The man who refuses to change his way of life does not possess authentic hope.

More is required, however, than a first, easy act of turning (heroic though we may think it!). We must also persevere. The conversion that gives rise to hope requires vigilance. To be always waiting means that we hope and never rest, simply because we are always expecting the fulfillment of our desires. We must keep watch, therefore, because we know not the day nor the hour of the Lord's coming.[35]

The convert thus faces a great deal of work, which John the Baptist,[36] echoing Isaiah,[37] describes as smoothing the rough ways, filling in the valleys, and preparing the Lord's paths.

The hope that springs from conversion also implies faith. Jesus had harsh words for his people: John the Baptist came to them, but they did not accept him or believe what he told them; but the prostitutes and tax collectors did believe him.[38] Hope, faith, and love — all are required if we are to turn to God.

God's compassion for us

A single cry, and God bestows his favor upon us;[39] as soon as he hears he answers. And straightway our eyes are opened and we discover our true condition: "Then you will defile your silver-covered graven images and your gold-plated molten images" (Is. 30:22). Then the Lord covers us with blessings: "The Lord binds up the hurt of his people, and heals the wounds inflicted by his blow" (Is. 30:26).

Compassion is a response dear to the Lord. In the missionary discourse of Matthew's Gospel, from which the Gospel for Saturday of the first week of Advent is taken, we hear Jesus voicing his pity for the crowd and telling us that he and his disciples are sent "to the lost sheep of the house of Israel."[40] The Lord comes to save us, and our God himself is our salvation.[41] The saving action of God is, in the concrete, identical with his coming, his two comings. What we now hope for in a confused fashion is his coming to meet and save us once and for all.

Waiting in the Spirit

The special characteristic of Christian hope is the unique dynamism that the Holy Spirit instills into it.

We may regard as a special grace of the Holy Spirit in our time the keen, restless desire of our contemporaries for the end and fulfillment of history. They seem to share the chief concern of the early Church in this respect. The present generation seems convinced that the time is short (1 Cor. 7:29); it is deeply sensitive to the present moment of history. This twofold outlook fits in very well with the mindset of the liturgy for the Advent season: a grasp of the provisional nature of the present time and a grasp of the end of time that is coming. Such a grasp is not possible, however, without special attention to the work of the Spirit.

We must recall here the purpose for which the world was created and the manner in which it was created. A careful reading of Genesis shows how God willed to create the world as a unity. At the beginning of God's action, the *ruah*, or breath, which is a type of the Spirit, presided over the process of creating a unified world. Thus, subhuman creatures were created to serve one another and man, and, in the last analysis, to glorify God. Since they were incapable of expressing their own submission to the Lord, they did it through the mediation of man, whose being is bound up with theirs. In Genesis, man is summoned to give these lower creatures their names as a sign of his authority over them.

Man himself is also created as a unity, with his body the outward manifestation of his soul. He is the image of God and, as such, is closely united to God. Sin will consist precisely in the breaking of the unity. Once sin has occurred, God's plan is to reconstruct a world that is united in every respect, as he had willed in his original plan. As the Spirit had presided over the creation of the world, so he will preside over its re-creation.

At the various stages of Old Testament history, we see the Spirit given to leaders — prophets, judges, kings — so that the people might be reshaped and renewed. The failure of the various covenants leads God to make a definitive effort at reconstruction through the incarnation of the Word, which takes place by the power of the Spirit. Here we have the first and long-awaited coming of God among us. Henceforth men are the object of God's good will (Luke 2:14). When the fullness of time comes (Gal. 4:4), the Spirit overshadows the Virgin Mary, and by his power she becomes with child (Matthew 1:18).

This Spirit is closely bound up with the Word who enters Mary's womb at the annunciation. The prayer for December 20, after speaking of the Virgin as the dwelling place of the Godhead, emphasizes the fact that she both received the ineffable Word and was filled with the Spirit. Thus, her response, "Let it be done," led to the coming into her of the Word and of the Spirit who is present in the incarnate Word. At the very moment of the incarnation, which the Spirit effects, the mystery of the Pasch begins. All that is done here will eventually lead to the glorious resurrection in the Spirit, of which the opening prayer for the fourth Sunday of Advent speaks. At the beginning of the Letter to the Romans, St. Paul writes: "[Christ was] designated Son of God in power according to the Spirit of holiness by his resurrection from the dead" (Rom. 1:4). Thus the Spirit shows himself already at work in this first coming of Christ. He continues his action in the Eucharist (which is the Pasch of the Church), as we are reminded in the prayer over the offerings on the fourth Sunday of Advent: "Lord, may the power of the Spirit, which sanctified Mary the mother of your Son, make holy the gifts we place upon this altar."

When the Fathers speak of the time or age of the Church, they think of it as the time of "the Spirit's dispensation." This idea emerges especially in the liturgy of Advent.

To sum up: What we await is the gathering of all peoples, and we find the Holy Spirit at work during this time, doing what is special to him: creating unity.

A twofold expectation

There is a further point that arises frequently in the Advent liturgy, an idea we shall have to delve into more deeply in another chapter. It is the idea that the Advent hope looks to a double coming.

> We proclaim the coming of Christ — not just a first coming but another as well that will be far more glorious than the first. The first took place under the sign of patient suffering; the second, on the contrary, will see Christ wearing the crown of God's kingdom.
>
> Almost everything about our Lord Jesus Christ is twofold. He has two births: one from God before the ages, the other from the Virgin at the end of the ages. He has two comings: the one is hidden and resembles the falling of the dew upon a fleece; the other — the future one — on the contrary, will be manifest. At his first coming, he was wrapped in linens and laid in a manager; at the second, light shall be his robe. In his first coming he endured the Cross, heedless of its shame; at his second coming he will be in glory and surrounded by an army of angels. Let us therefore not stop at his first coming but look forward to the second. We hailed him at his first coming with the words,

"Blessed in he who comes in the Lord's name!" and
shall hail him in the same way at his second coming.
For we shall go out to meet the Lord and his angels,
and, prostrating ourselves before him, we shall cry,
"Blessed in he who comes in the Lord's name!"[42]

Although there was no Advent liturgy in the East in the
fourth century, St. Cyril of Jerusalem was well aware that
the liturgy cannot separate two events that it is its very purpose to render actual and contemporaneous with us. We
must accustom ourselves to these complex superpositions
in which the various levels and stages illuminate one another. We can glimpse here how different an exegetical
reading of the Bible is from a liturgical reading of it. In a
liturgical celebration we cannot proclaim Genesis without
glimpsing the presence of the Apocalypse as well. In each
and every reading we read the whole Bible, from the first
book to the last, and all of it in the light of the paschal mystery. That is why, as we shall see, the liturgical theology
given us on the first three Sundays of Advent relates to the
second coming of Christ as well as to the first; both comings
are envisaged in the chants and readings.

In order, however, to better grasp the specific nature of
the Christian hope that found expression, in the seventh
century, in the Roman liturgy of Advent, we must enter
more deeply into the meaning of the expectation voiced in
Scripture and the liturgy.

2. THE HOPE AND EXPECTATION
OF THE AGES

Advent is a special season in the Church's life, and during it we find her laying heavier stress than at other times
on a basic Christian need: a living faith. Living faith alone

gives coherence to Christian life, and it alone gives the Christian real access to what the Church herself calls "the summit toward which the activity of the Church is directed."[43]

But if we live our faith and our Christian life as modern men, shaped by the cultural ambience of our age and concerned to meet the concrete and very complicated demands that contemporary life makes of us, can we really enter into the mysteries of the Church? Or must we first cut ourselves off from our normal surroundings and set aside our everyday questions and anxieties?

In order to give an honest answer to this question, we must first give a synthetic overview of the biblico-liturgical theology of Advent as the Church of today understands it.

The Church is part of a longer history; she represents a new stage of it that will last until the final day. It should not surprise us, therefore, to find her using the Old Testament as the starting point for her various celebrations. In the Old Testament she discerns attitudes and events that are fulfilled in the New Testament and that continue to be actualized in our liturgical gatherings today and to require acceptance by each of us. Consequently, distant though the hopes and fears of the Old Testament people may seem to be from the questions that concern us here, it is with those hopes and fear that we must begin.

The expectation of Israel

Expectation, waiting, was characteristic of the Israelite people throughout their history. Even a cursory reading of the Old Testament will see in its pages countless traces of a never-failing hope in a deliverer and in the salvation he brings.

It is less easy, however, to discern in this firm belief the nature of the one for whom the Israelites clamor so loudly and the role they expect him to play.

The Old Testament in its entirety looks for the coming of the Messiah, but we must be careful to see how men thought of the Messiah. To foretell the coming of a Messiah is not to foretell the coming of a man-God, especially not one who possesses, so to speak, the theological dimensions that the teaching of Christ, the light of his Spirit, and the Church's long tradition have enabled us to grasp. To project the Christian understanding of the Messiah back into a past that was not yet transformed by the blood of Christ and illumined by Pentecost would be to fail to see the slow process of purification through which Israelite thought had to pass. Contemporary exegetes think they can now make out the progressive stages of Israel's belief in its deliverer. Israel hoped for a Messiah, but its hope was not bold enough initially to glimpse the Messiah as we now know him to have been and as he is for all ages: a King not only of Israel but of the universe, a universal King and a God.

At the same time, it would be a mistake to think that Israel's hope was focused solely on a nationalist goal and limited to the material world. To think this would be to mistake the Semite, who does not neatly separate the spiritual from the material as we do. In his eyes, the material is the sign of the spiritual; the material universe is a gift of Yahweh. The world is a sign of spiritual realities and at the same time an outflow of God's superabundant riches. Spiritual values and material values are thus closely connected, the latter being an emanation, as it were, and a sign of the former.[44]

It would also be an error to separate the hope and expectation of salvation for the people as a whole from the hope and expectation of a personal salvation. That kind of distinction is unknown in the world of the Bible, where knowledge is not ruled by metaphysics but is focused on man in the concrete: man who is body and soul, and is closely linked to the community and the world in which he lives and with which he is in ontological continuity.[45]

What believing Israel waited for was to win out over sin and walk intimately with God. Without explicitly identifying this God with the Messiah, but in the last analysis implicitly assuming their identity, the people of the Old Testament hoped that their God would come. They even knew that their God had already come and yet was still coming, and that these "comings" were a preparation for the final great coming. God "is always coming"!

The reference here is to the theophanies that gave vitality to Israel's hope and made it eager for the day of the final encounter, "the day of Yahweh." The "comings," the "days of Yahweh," were what set in motion the long history of Israel, which stretches from the Fall to the day when God will establish his kingdom on earth. The very name of Yahweh, which means "I am" in Exodus (3:13-15), signifies the only God, God with us, but it also signifies the God who is there, who intervenes on his appointed "days," and by his interventions keeps the world moving toward his "day." The very name of Yahweh has an eschatological meaning.[46] Yet even then he often came into the midst of his people, as the prophets and the psalmist were well aware. The refrain of Psalm 46, for example, expresses this conviction: "The Lord of hosts is with us" (vv. 7,11). Concretely, all the important events of Israel's history, and all the blessings, catastrophes, and chastisements were regarded by God's prophet's as "days of Yahweh," as "comings" of their God. "The Lord of hosts is with us; the God of Jacob is our refuge" (Ps. 46:7).

The "comings" of Yahweh, the "days of Yahweh," the "visitations of Yahweh" are pretty much equivalent expressions. They all point to the ceaseless activity of God in the history of his people. Nothing happens that does not have God for its first cause: "Does evil befall a city, unless the Lord has done it?" (Amos 3:6). This theme of the day of Yahweh is important; we find its real fulfillment in the Gospel theme of Jesus' "hour."

Israel loved to recall the "days" that had shaped and continued to shape its history. The "day of Midian," for example, on which Gideon had won a great victory, was always remembered in the history of Israel (Is. 9:3), since the victory was seen as indisputable proof of Yahweh's personal action in the midst of his people. Isaiah writes: "Behold, the name of the Lord comes from far" (30:27); and later, when the Israelites are carrying the burden of exile: "Be strong, fear not! Behold, your God will come with vengeance, with the recompense of God. He will come and save you" (35:4). Yahweh's coming is thus close at hand; the prophets & Amos, perhaps, even more than the others — usually think of the day as imminent. Yahweh comes — but for the sake of retribution. He is a judge, and "the haughtiness of man shall be humbled, and the pride of men shall be brought low; and the Lord alone will be exalted in that day. And the idols shall utterly pass away" (Is. 2:17-18). This is a judgment of Yahweh that allows Israel to pick itself up and continue its journey.

In a text that has become classical, Zephaniah foretells the terrible intervention by his God:

> The great day of the Lord is near, near and hastening fast; the sound of the day of the Lord is bitter, the mighty man cries aloud there. A day of wrath is that day, a day of distress and anguish, a day of ruin and devastation, a day of darkness and gloom, a day of clouds and thick darkness, a day of trumpet blast and battle cry against the fortified cities and against the lofty battlements. I will bring distress on men, so that they shall walk like the blind, because they have sinned against the Lord; their blood shall be poured out like dust, and their flesh like dung. Neither their silver nor their gold shall be able to deliver them on the day of the wrath of the Lord. In the fire of his jealous wrath, all the earth shall be consumed; for a full, yea, sudden end he will make of all the inhabitants of the earth (1:14-18).

Thus Yahweh multiplies his days and his comings in order to give new life and vigor to his people. That is how the hope of Israel is strengthened. Because of his interventions, Yahweh is a God who is always there, ready to help, to repay, and, in a manner sometimes harsh, to set his people on the right path again. "On the foundation of the past, hope looks forward to the future in the experience of the present moment." [47]

But at the end of days . . .

These many comings of Yahweh will end with his decisive "coming," his decisive "day." After the visitations of Yahweh that are connected with concrete historical events in the life of his people, there will be a coming that is both imminent and yet unspecified in its relation to time, despite its definite character. It is described in vague terms such as "in those days," "at that time," "at the end of days." Prophets and psalmist give enthusiastic descriptions of this day of God's decisive coming to triumph over sin and death. The prophets look upon it as the day of the new covenant that God will freely initiate, despite the incurable sinfulness of his people and their complacency in their infidelity. His coming will be an encounter at which sins will be forgiven, and a people sickened by their own evildoing will be made new again. On this point Ezekiel is the most explicit of the prophets:

> For I will take you from the nations, and gather you from all the countries, and bring you into your own land. I will sprinkle clean water upon you, and you shall be clean from all your uncleannesses, and from all your idols I will cleanse you. A new heart I will give you, and a new spirit I will put within you; and I will take out of your flesh the heart of stone and give you a heart of flesh. And I will put my spirit within you, and cause you to walk in my statutes and be careful to observe my ordinances. You shall dwell in the land which I gave to your fathers; and you shall be my people, and I will be your God. And I will deliver you from all your uncleannesses; and I will summon the grain and make it abundant and lay no famine upon you (36:24-29).

Psalm 130 echoes the prophet: "My soul waits for the

Lord more than watchmen for the morning. . . . O Israel, hope in the Lord! For with the Lord there is steadfast love, and with him is plenteous redemption. And he will redeem Israel from all his iniquities" (vv. 6-8).

According to the prophet Daniel, the Messiah's role will be to purify: "Seventy weeks of years are decreed concerning your people and your holy city, to finish the transgression, to put an end to sin, and to atone for iniquity, to bring in everlasting righteousness, to seal both vision and prophet, and to anoint a most holy place" (9:24).

But there will be only one Servant, the Servant of Yahweh, whose mission will be to bear the sins of his brothers and to establish a lasting covenant:

> Surely he has borne our griefs and carried our sorrows; yet we esteemed him stricken, smitten by God, and afflicted. But he was wounded for our transgressions, he was bruised for our iniquities; upon him was the chastisement that made us whole, and with his stripes we are healed. . . . He shall see the fruit of the travail of his soul and be satisfied; by his knowledge shall the righteous one, my servant, make many to be accounted righteous; and he shall bear their iniquities (Is. 53:4-5, 11).

Then the earth will at last be at peace. Isaiah's vision recalls the first, paradisal days of mankind:

> The wolf shall dwell with the lamb, and the leopard shall lie down with the kid, and the calf and the lion and the fatling together, and a little child shall lead them. The cow and the bear shall feed; their young shall lie down together; and the lion shall eat straw like the ox. The suckling child shall play over the hole of the asp, and the weaned child shall put his hand on the adder's den. They shall not hurt or destroy in all my holy mountain; for the earth shall be full of the knowledge of the Lord as the waters cover the sea (Is. 11:6-9).

To sum up Israel's expectation in a few words, we might say that it is an ardent, restless longing for a definitive, transforming encounter with God, one that makes sin and guilt passé.

The expectation of the Church

There is seemingly an impassable gulf between the outlook of Israel and our own. If the Christian were to enter into the feelings of the Israelite people as they waited for the Messiah, he would be putting himself into a situation that is unreal for him. Undeniably, in the not too distant past, a spirituality filled with good intentions did endeavor to lead us along paths where we felt ill at ease. But there can be no question, really, of our cultivating an expectation of the Messiah such as the Israelites had; we are not called to practice a spirituality based on fiction or to celebrate a liturgy that would in the last analysis be simply playacting! There is no basis in tradition for this kind of thing, and it is difficult to see how it could help make the mysteries of salvation real in us.

In other words, a Christian cannot adopt the psychological viewpoint proper to a time in history when the Messiah had not yet come. He can indeed examine and try to grasp the psychological state of a people who were waiting for a savior-king as the agent of their full development, but he is not justified in trying to live as though that were really his own state, nor has the Church any reason for asking him to make such an artificial journey back in time. We must therefore reject any spirituality of Advent that is based on such an attempt and tries to make us pray as if God had not yet sent his Son among us and as if we had not yet received him. That would be a perverse and destructive misinterpretation of what the Church's liturgy is and is meant to be.[48]

Why, then, should we recall the hope Israel had? Why does Advent remind us of the expectations cherished by the patriarchs, the prophets, and the whole of Israel? Isn't it because their expectation and waiting are an anticipation of ours?

But the expectation of Israel was directed to more than the coming of a Messiah whose person and true role became clear only in a long slow evolution. More radically Israel's messianic expectation took concrete form in the hope of an encounter with God that would eliminate sin and all its obscene implications; with sin totally done away with, God could and would embrace his people and all mankind in loving peace.

For us, the Christ, or Anointed One, has already been born; we have received the Messiah, and all mankind has seen the kind of salvation he brings. We know that in principle we are already within the kingdom, although we also know that God's reign over sin and Satan has not yet reached its full form and is still developing. Our definitive encounter with God has not yet taken place, and we see him now only in mystery and "as in a mirror." The face-to-face meeting is still in the future and will come on the last day when Christ returns; now we wait for it.

The Christian always looks toward this hour of his personal encounter with God; it is also the hour when the world in its entirety will acquire the dimensions of holiness that the Lord intended it to have when he created it. It is in relation to that future that Christian expectation becomes the prolongation of Israelite expectation. We may even say that Israel's longing and waiting finds its completion in the longing and waiting of Christianity for the completion of salvation from sin and guilt and the glorious return of Christ.

There is thus no opposition between Israel's waiting and ours; on the contrary, there is continuity between them and progression from the one to the other. The coming of the Messiah does not effect an unbridgeable break between the two phases in the long waiting, rather it intensifies the ardent longing of the Christian. The Lord's birth does not put an end to Israel's waiting but gives it its full meaning, intensifies it even more, and fills it with an impatient longing for the Lord's definitive coming in his fully established kingdom. With the same fervor as the people of Israel, we follow them in their hopes but make these hopes even richer and bolder. Therefore we can sing with Israel: "The Lord is close at hand; come, let us worship him"; "Tomorrow . . . the sinfulness of earth will be destroyed. The Savior of the world will be our king." [49]

We can see from this the spirit in which we may seek a better understanding of Israel's expectation. There is to be no fictional re-creation of the past, for we are dealing with two successive moments, not with a single identical one. We celebrate the same waiting and longing, but at a higher and more perfect level. Speaking of the Old and New Testaments, St. Irenaeus wrote: "God called his people from secondary concerns to primary, from types to realities, from things temporal to things eternal, carnal to spiritual, earthly to heavenly." [50]

The coming of Christ, his atoning sacrifice on the Cross, and his resurrection were the beginning of eternal life and complete salvation. Yet history continues on in our time and in our midst. Far from stopping the course of history, Christ's coming gave it a new impulse, and the world is moving toward its fulfillment. The Church of our time celebrates her expectation of the end, but her hope is rendered patient and serene because it rests on a past in which God has already shown his wonderful deeds. The *mirabilia*, or "marvelous acts," that God freely accomplished in Old Testament times in order to guide men's hopes toward the kingdom are a pledge that has been confirmed by the first coming of Christ and by the new marvels which Christ performed and which fortell and prepare for the definitive kingdom that will be established at his second coming when "sin and death will be no more."

When the Church of our time applies to her own situation the words of prophet and psalmist, she does not apply them from without to her present circumstances, as though they were images intended to illustrate and explain these circumstances. The point is rather that the prophecies, types, and psalms acquire their full meaning only in Christ and now in his Church. Moreover, they will find their complete fulfillment only when Christ returns at the end of time. The passages borrowed from the Old Testament show that God's plan is a single plan continuously operative in the history of the world, in the history of Israel, and in our own history. We can say of the Psalter, as we can of every book of the Old Testament, that it contains in germ a reality that will develop fully in the future. In a single phrase that reality is redemption from sin — the passover mystery.

The liturgy of Advent, then, does not require the Christian to indulge in fiction. It is in a fully real way that the believer of today shares Israel's hope: the hope of forgiveness, the hope of meeting his God. The Christian, like the Israelite of Isaiah's time, can with complete truthfulness sing the words of the entrance psalm for the first Sunday of Advent: "To you, my God, I lift my soul" (Ps. 25:1). But for the Christian, Christ's coming deepens his desire for the eternal vision of God, and thus this entrance psalm has an even greater depth of meaning and poignancy for him, while it also expresses a limitless confidence based on the first coming of Christ into our world.

The Gospel of the first Sunday brings home to us the full scope of Advent, for it concerns the parousia, or return of Christ on the last day. Here is where our expectation and that of Israel coincide. For us, the Messiah has already come within earthly time; we do not still await that first coming, and it would be foolish for us to try to live, along with Israel, an experience that cannot be ours. On the other hand, with a fervor deepened by Christ's first coming, we can and do await with Israel of old the world's encounter with its Deliverer at his second coming. Israel's expectation bridged the gulf between the fall and the birth of Christ; ours bridges the distance between the coming of the Lord within historical times and his second coming at the end.

The Israelite of old and the Christian today hope for the same thing. Both are summoned to "wake from sleep" and to "cast off the works of darkness and put on the armor of light." That is the point of the Epistle for the first Sunday.[51]

We have noted how the fervor of our hope for encounter with our God has been greatly intensified by the fact of Christ's first coming. Thus our waiting and longing, while linking us to the Chosen People of old, also separates us from them by the fact of the Messiah's birth in time.

There is a further difference between the two hopes, Israel's and ours. Just before his earthly pilgrimage ended, Jesus the Messiah gave us a special bread to eat and a special cup to drink: a divine food, our sustenance on the journey toward the promised land, a Eucharist closely bound up with his death. It is of this food that St. Paul says: "For as often as you eat this bread and drink the cup, you proclaim the Lord's death until he comes" (1 Cor. 11:26). The Eucharist, then, creates in the Christian a state of restless longing for the Lord's return. The Lord himself, through his sacrificial, atoning death for sin and his resurrection, which are present in the Eucharist, nourishes in each Christian and in the world at large the hope of his return; it is he who hastens the maturation process so that the hour of his coming and of our definitive encounter with him may come at last.

We shall have occasion later on to speak again of these essential aspects of Catholicism. What we have already said, however, is enough to help us understand both the longing expectation of Israel and what our own should be as a prolongation of Israel's and by contrast with it.

We cannot understand Advent if we eliminate any of the perspectives we have been analyzing. All make up a single complex totality, and the meaning of the whole is falsified if we isolate one aspect and focus exclusively on it. Two realities must be kept in view and not separated: Israel's waiting, which was a preparation for the historical coming of the Messiah; and our own waiting, which is grounded in the Lord's birth and looks ever more intently for God's complete sovereignty over the world and the full establishment of his reign of holiness and peace.

The two Advent prefaces give an excellent synthesis, in prayer form, of the season's two themes, which overlap and fit perfectly together in God's plan. "When he humbled himself to come among us as a man, he fulfilled the plan you formed long ago and opened for us the way to salvation. Now we watch for the day hoping that the salvation promised us will be ours when Christ our Lord will come again in his glory."

Thus does the first preface, at the beginning of the Eucharistic Prayer, present the two comings of Christ. The second preface bases its description rather on the concrete facts of history. "His future coming was proclaimed by all the prophets. The virgin mother bore him in her womb with love beyond all telling. John the Baptist was his herald and made him known when at last he came. In his love Christ has filled us with joy as we prepare to celebrate his birth, so that when he comes he may find us watching in prayer, our hearts filled with wonder and praise."

The world's waiting

Let us return to the question we started with. Does this whole liturgy, however rich and beautiful it may be, afford any answer to the world's distress?

We have the right to ask whether or not a sound theology of Advent as experienced and "acted out" in our liturgical life can answer the agonizing problems of the modern world and give meaning to man's existence as he seeks his human development.

The generations now alive have had too brutal an experience of the world's frailty not to be ready to downgrade any effort to rebuild that world. The collapse of value systems and of institutions recognized as essential for human life has led men to believe that the end has come, that there is no more hope. The experience of two World Wars has made them think in apocalyptic terms and see the end of the world as imminent; our present experiences and the uncertainty of peace stimulate the same kind of thoughts.

Admittedly, the same thoughts have filled men's minds at every great crisis in history. What is peculiar to our age is a despair, a sense of futility, a keen awareness of the uselessness of human efforts to assure earthly progress. A philosophy is now abroad that springs from the sudden, violent accumulation of catastrophes that men themselves have brought upon mankind. It is perhaps here that we have the most serious of the illnesses now afflicting mankind. It is very important that a clinical analysis be made of the situation, since it is one that endangers important spiritual values.

The illness is complicated and even paradoxical. As perhaps never before, mankind has been discovering more and more ways of raising the living standard, doing away with many forms of material drudgery, and thus making possible a broader and richer use of man's intellectual faculties as well as a greater scope for his spiritual energies. At the same time, however, there is a contrary movement; man has become deeply impressed by the uncertainty of his very existence and has developed a philosophy of despair. Literature and the arts are full of this agonizing awareness. Many, especially among the young — all allowances made for faddism — are obsessed by the brutal discovery of what they regard as a life doomed to failure.

Since, then, we are headed for final annihilation, why try to develop a civilization, a science, or an art? In a way, what we have here once again is the attitude St. Paul blamed in the Thessalonians.[52] It would be a mistake, however, to see a perfect parallel between today and St. Paul's day. The modern attitude is due, in fact, either to a type of atheism or to an erroneous or incomplete theology.

Heidegger's philosophy is still alive and active among us. His atheism admittedly has a certain grandeur about it. Man may be locked into his dread because he is fettered to a world whose very existence is a precarious thing. But he does not therefore have the right, says Heidegger, to give way to discouragement and apathy. On the contrary, having discovered nothingness, he must take hold of himself, confront his lot without flinching, scorn the nothingness he has discovered, and look for ways to improve the lot of his brothers and raise the level of a civilization he knows to be hopelessly doomed to annihilation. Such is the tough, stoic attitude of a proud cynic.

Many believers are ready, perhaps unwittingly, to adopt such an outlook without any significant modifications. In their view when faced with Christ and his word of salvation, man must recognize the nothingness of his present life, and the ineffectiveness and worthlessness of all his human actions, even those done for religious motives. The kingdom of God is simply given to man, and the latter may not for a moment believe that his actions or his virtues prepare for it in any way; there is no connection at all between the virtuous acts men do and the kingdom that is offered to them. Only faith counts — faith in the risen Christ.

On the basis of that faith, salvation is bestowed upon us and we can only accept it; it can in no way be brought to pass within history. The Christian does not work for his salvation in time and in this world, for in the world and time there can be no acquisition of authentic values and no real progress. Consequently, the Christian shares with the pagan a pessimistic view of the world. There is nothing to do but to reject the world, since in it there can be no progress, spiritual or even simply human, that has any relation to the kingdom of God.

Catholics indeed believe that their faith and their works do have a relation to the kingdom of God and to eternity. Despite this, many of them ask whether there is any point in seeking human progress when the world itself is passing away. A certain kind of philosophy and its distrust of technological progress is one of the most distressing signs of a tendency that explains to some extent the unbelief of scientists. In responding to a questionnaire on the reasons for contemporary unbelief, Teilhard de Chardin wrote as follows:

> To those who are not extremely familiar with it, Christianity quite certainly gives the impression . . . of not making up its mind frankly to accept, in their general application and in their spirit, the views on cosmic developments that are universally accepted everywhere except in Christianity. It seems to delight in belittling human hopes and pointing out the weaknesses of our society. It despises or fears progress and discovery; in short, it in no way hallows or magnifies the loftiest and most intensely felt aspirations of modern man.[53]

There is a type of Christianity that admittedly does justify such a criticism. For if we judge by the outlook of one category of Christians (often people very concerned to be authentically Christian), there is no reason for desiring the advancement of our civilization, since the Christian hope has nothing to do with the present world. These people appeal to Scripture and tradition in attempting to justify their rejection of progress: the world is passing and is destined to give way to the kingdom when Christ returns.

I see a usefulness in thus summarizing several views that see no relation between human progress and God's plan, either because they deny that there is any divinely established order or because, while admitting such an order, they see no continuity between men's actions, even virtuous ones, and man's eternal destiny in God's final kingdom, or, finally, because in the name of Scripture and tradition they set up an extreme opposition between the present world and the world to come.

Far from having digressed from our subject, we are now at the very heart of it. We wait for the Lord, and we cherish a sure hope that we shall someday go to meet him. But what should our attitude be to the present world? Do our actions have anything to do with the coming of the kingdom? These are questions of central importance for understanding the Advent that is our lives.

First, let us recall a point made earlier: our culture has become used to compartmentalizing spiritual and material values. If we are to find an answer to the questions we ask in our distress, we must set aside attitudes like that, which are alien to the biblical view of reality. Salvation is meant for the whole of our being, body and soul, and it embraces the whole of creation, including subhuman reality. As we wait, therefore, for the definitive establishment of the kingdom, we may not totally separate the spiritual and the fleshly, soul and body, spiritual values and material values. The world that is to come will restore full value to all these orders of reality and restore a balance in which they are in perfect harmony each with the others.

The contemporary rediscovery of Scripture, of the Fathers who comment on Scripture, and of the liturgy, which actualizes the Scriptures and enables us to "live" them, is helping us develop broader, more balanced, and less fragmented views on the relations between these different orders: the divine, the spiritual, the human, the fleshly.

In his book *Catholicism*,[54] Henri de Lubac has gathered numerous statements of the Fathers of the Church on how creation is to be understood and how it is affected first by sin, then by redemption.

The Fathers are not interested in a scientific explanation of the events recorded in Genesis; their purpose is not to reject or accept the views of the writer of Genesis on creation, in the name of scientific discoveries. Their theological interpretation is not dependent on a scientific knowledge of the world but looks rather to the spirit in which God created the world. He created man in his "image and likeness." God himself is the model for mankind, and the latter derives its unity from the one divine image that is reproduced in each individual.

But man is in turn the center of creation, and everything

about him is created for his sake. Subhuman creatures share in the unity that mankind possesses by God's will, and Adam was put into the world as a cosmic personage; that is, an ontological bond unites him to the rest of creation. He is God's steward; his mediation makes it possible for mute subhuman creatures to express their acceptance of the divine will. Consequently, there is a close bond between the world and men, within each man, between man and subhuman creatures, and among subhuman creatures themselves. The world was created as a completely unified reality, a unity deriving from the fact that it is a reflection of God. The Fathers are unanimous in subscribing to this vision of the world.

They are no less unanimous in seeing Adam's sin as the cause of the dislocation that now marks the world. Adam's sin fragmented the world; a world in which there was no mine and thine has become an aggregation of individuals violently at odds with one another. The fragmentation of the world is the most evident consequence of sin. Origen sums it all up in a few words: *Ubi peccata ibi multitudo*: "Where there is sin, there is fragmentation."[55]

Thus, God has his own conception of mankind, which he created as a unity in which man is called to give subhuman creatures their names (or, in Western terms, to dominate them). To this conception correspond God's efforts, after the Fall and throughout the Old Testament, to renew his intimate relationship with his creation.

The Bible brings before us a drama that begins with the first sin and portrays the unwearying, stubborn effort of a Creator-God to begin his creation anew, rescue it from the fragmentation caused by sin, and restore it for good to the unity that derives from its being his image. The story of Noah and the ark shows how God sought unity for his creation: as he saves man by enclosing him in the ark, he also saves, along with man, a pair from each species of animal. His creation will survive in the form he willed for it; it will be a totality, a whole made up of many parts. The theme of the covenant could be studied with a view to seeing at every point how God aims to restore his creation to a unity that embraces man and subhuman creatures.

The Fathers of the Church go on to show how the incarnation of God, the Cross, and the resurrection affect the material universe. In a single word St. Paul sums up the effect of Christ's activity on the material world when he speaks of redemption as a "restoration" or "recapitulation" of the world. The old Adam, a cosmic personage, was united to the world around him — even the material world — that was to contribute marvelously to the development of the natural man. This first Adam is followed by the new Adam, Christ; like the old Adam, he too is a cosmic personage. His mission is to gather into unity the whole created world, that is, man and the rest of creation, through the victory of the Cross.

How is it possible, in view of God's really taking our flesh to himself, to maintain the impossibility of a connection between human progress and his plan? Christ's mission is to renew God's image in all things; every created thing can appeal to him as the living exemplar in whose likeness it has been made. God's activity in the Old Testament was but a preparation for the decisive moment of the incarnation and for the new period in which the whole of creation would, amid "groans" (Rom. 8:22), gradually reach its deliverance at the moment when it would experience a resurrection and become identified on the last day with God's kingdom.

It is at this point in our effort to gain a vital understanding of the link between human progress and God's plan that we must turn to the liturgy as the Church understands it and as the faithful ought to understand it.

We have briefly sketched God's intervention in the history of the Old and New Testaments. We have done so because this same intervention of God is still being exercised now, today. The liturgy of the Church is far more than ceremony, pomp, and rubrics. Its only real purpose is to render present in our world, to re-actualize for the world of today, God's action in the old covenant and his sending of his Son to die for us and rise from the dead as the foundation of the new covenant. In other words, the Catholic liturgy has for its purpose to continue the gathering of creation into the unity whose basis is the divine likeness, and it does so by raising up before the eyes of the world the sign of the new and everlasting covenant: the Cross of Christ.

There we have the essential function of the Eucharistic celebration: to actualize for us the redemptive work of Christ.

The new Adam, the one St. Paul calls the Head of the Mystical Body, intends his redemption not simply for the spiritual element in men but for the whole of their being, body and soul; he comes to save the whole man. Moreover, he wills to save not only the whole man but the whole of creation over which man is to be king. The entire universe is part of the Mystical Body of Christ, and since the redemptive actions of Christ are actualized for us in the Mass and in the rest of the liturgy, we must think that the whole of creation, like the Mystical Body, is growing and developing.

The re-actualization of the historical events of our salvation, with the mysteries of Christ's life as the climax, is a leaven at work in the world. The new covenant has been given to us only so that we may advance toward a definitive fulfillment. The Eucharist is the goal of the whole Old Testament and of God's efforts to restore the world, but it is also a starting point for a journey leading to the Lord's return at the end of time. In other words, all that is summed up in the term "sacred history" is made real here and now in the Eucharistic celebration, and we really, truly, actually experience the whole of that history.

The Cross of Christ is the goal of all the history that came before it. We may say that the whole of the Old Testament is a movement toward the historical life of Christ on earth. This life in turn is in its entirety a movement toward the Cross; the historical event of the Cross looks to its representation or actualization by the Eucharistic celebration;

and the actualization then initiates a progressive movement toward the return of Christ and the inauguration of the eternal kingdom.

Nor can we limit the reactualization to the Eucharist and the sacraments. The tradition of the Church shows quite clearly that we cannot restrict the representative effectiveness of the liturgy solely to the sacramental order and that we must not subscribe to the narrow definition of liturgy that would make it coextensive with the sacraments.[56] In addition to the sacramental re-presentation that takes place in us and acts in us and influences the whole of creation through us as long as we do not prevent it, there is another way in which our salvation is actualized for us and for the created universe, human and subhuman. This other way is the living celebration of the liturgical mystery.

We Catholics do not reflect enough on this when we participate in the liturgy. And yet, especially at the celebration of the Eucharist, we are commissioned, with and in Christ, to embrace the world and the whole of creation. We are to bear witness that creation in its entirety is the workplace of God. We may say, in consequence, that human thought, art, technology, progress are all moving in the same direction as God and Christianity. For all these things are bringing the world to its maturity and preparing it for its renewal. Would it be an overstatement to claim that Christianity cannot be its full self unless it welcomes progress, not simply with a benevolent smile but with an ardent embrace?

Thus, for the Catholic who reflects on what he is doing, every participation in the Mass and the rest of the liturgy will be seen as a contribution not only to the spiritual development of the world but also to the advancement of the material universe as it moves toward its fulfillment. It has often and rightly been said that the incarnation of Christ sanctified matter by restoring to it its dimension of truthful sign. All matter has now become a sign, a symbol of higher realities. We need but think of the sacraments and the new significance they give to matter: water, oil, bread, wine, fire — all of them material signs whose function it is to prolong in time the incarnation of the Christ, who continues to work in our world.

By means of the liturgy, then, we must rediscover the meaning God gives the world, the meaning he gives to work and progress. There is no question, of course, but that both Scripture and tradition contrast the present world and the world to come. Recall the First Letter of St. John:

> Do not love the world or the things in the world. If any one loves the world, love for the Father is not in him. For all that is in the world, the lust of the flesh and the lust of the eyes and the pride of life, is not of the Father but is of the world. And the world passes away, and the lust of it; but he who does the will of God abides for ever (1 John 2:15-17).

But, given what we have been saying about God's plan and its understanding by the Fathers, we must not be simplistic in our interpretation of this passage and of similar words spoken by Christ; we must not reduce them to a mistrustful moralism. The scriptural tradition does indeed contrast two worlds: the present world and the world to come. It does not however reject creation, since creation is God's handwork and continues to be it even after the Fall. What the Scripture is focusing on is what the evil one is doing in the world. St. John makes this quite clear when he writes that "the whole world is in the power of the evil one" (1 John 5:19).

There is no doubt that the effort to incarnate Christianity in the temporal life of men can and does present dangers. What we have been saying up to this point may lead some to think that by his efforts the Christian can build a paradise on earth and that the apparent slowing down of the advance of Christianity is due simply to the fact that Christians have not made those efforts. But a Christian life that includes an intimate sharing in the Church's liturgical life will not fall victim to that kind of confusion. When a Catholic receives a sacrament, he knows that he now possesses a power that can raise the world to new heights. But his very reception of the sacrament also shows him how he is to conceive such a re-creation of the world.

He knows that after the incarnation and redemption the world cannot again be fragmented and that we, along with the rest of creation, are saved in principle. This truth is the source of his optimism and hope, but he does not let it blind him to reality. He knows that the ever active power of redemption must work against Satan, who continues to be present in the world and can turn human progress into an instrument of warfare against God, against redemption, and against the authentic reconstruction of the world.

When he leaves the liturgical celebration, the Catholic has just borne witness to two facts: *sin* and *death*, which have ravaged the world and caused the death of Christ. When he finishes the celebration in which the sacrifice of the Cross has been actualized for us, he goes forth with the assurance that the world is redeemed and the entire universe lifted up, and that the world is advancing in accordance with the same divine will that decreed its redemption. But he does not forget that this progress on the world's part can only be along the road of the Cross.

The Catholic, then, should seek progress; he should devote himself to lessening the social and economic disorder around him; he should be on the lookout for ways of alleviating men's suffering; he is conscious, as St. Augustine was, that we cannot preach the gospel to men who are starving. At the same time, however, the Catholic leaving Mass also knows that his mission is to display the Cross to the world. He must do all he can to lessen the sufferings of men, but he also has the mission of persuading them to accept suffering as a means of becoming victor over suffering itself and death.

The Catholic, then, does not dream of an earthly paradise or imagine that the struggle will have a definitive happy ending in this world. Sin, suffering, and death will continue to be the world's lot, and Christian hope must not be confused with human success. Redemption, which is rendered constantly present in the world through the liturgy, does indeed have the last word to say in our world, but it does not therefore suppress suffering and death; instead, it makes of them instruments enabling man to better identify himself with the Cross of Christ.[57]

Yves de Montcheuil sums up nicely what we have been saying thus far:

> Although he lives in a sense outside this world and already has his hands upon abiding reality, the true Christian cannot excuse himself from working to transform the world so that someday the dawn of the heavenly city may break over it. He must also realize, however, that the full light of heavenly day will never shine on any earthly creation. Therefore he must keep at a task he knows can never be successfully completed, and yet not scorn it or, at the other extreme, let himself be seduced by the recurring protean myth of possible success. He must set his heart on what lies beyond this world, and yet he has no right to lose himself in the foretaste of it that is given to him here below. There can be no living of true Christianity unless the various elements of the latter are kept in balance or, more accurately, in tension.[58]

This passage sums up exactly what the liturgy tells us about human progress and God's outlook on the world. Redemption actualized over and over again in the liturgy renders the world more worthy of man's efforts and more disposed for genuine progress. But the world that is thus moving toward its fulfillment should be the object of our interest only insofar as our relations to it are in perfect conformity with God's plan.

Such, then, should be our attitude during the Advent that is our earthly lives, lived as they are in the long interim between the birth of Christ and his return at the end of time.

Is the answer to our distress and that of the world now complete? Yes, it is complete objectively and as far as God is concerned. But it will satisfy only those who believe and have entered upon the way of the paschal mystery; those who, enlightened by faith, have come to see that the answer is contained in the mystery of death and resurrection. It is a hard answer, and yet it is, even humanly, a satisfying one for those who have had the sacramental experience of Christ and realized how the Lord of glory made our humanity his own in order to transform it in the fire of suffering. The Church has no other answer to give. If she is to avoid being mistaken for simply another political organization, she must endeavor to transmit to her children and to the world only the one treasure that is hers: the death and resurrection of Christ, as an efficacious sacrament unto holiness and as a model to be imitated.

3. WAITING FOR THE COMINGS OF THE LORD

A point made earlier must be repeated and applied here: There would be no purpose in reading this chapter if we did not have faith. What we shall be saying would seem ridiculous or, at best, lacking in any real content. Catholic liturgy says nothing except to those who believe, but them it can lead to deep peace in the possession of God.

Every liturgical celebration has three dimensions: it recalls the past, in the present, for the sake of what is to come. Advent provides a splendid opportunity to see the intricate interconnection of these three dimensions. Consequently, it is the ideal season for entering fully into a living theology of the Roman Catholic liturgy.

The two dimensions of expectation

The liturgy of Advent gradually took shape in the Church beginning in the fourth century. Toward the end of this century we find in Gaul and Spain a period of preparation for the feast of Christmas. The feast itself had just been established at Rome as a kind of Christianization of the pagan celebration of the victorious sun: *Natale solis invicti* (birth of the unconquered sun) or celebration of the winter solstice, when the sun triumphed over the winter mists. The Church of Rome saw in the natural occurrence a symbol of Christ victorious over the dark powers of evil and took the occasion to celebrate on December 25 the birth of Christ according to the flesh. She saw in this birth the beginning of the mystery of mankind's deliverance from sin and guilt that will culminate in the Pasch of the Lord. It seemed natural, therefore, to prepare for the celebration, just as for the celebration of the Pasch. We will have to ask, however, why it took so long for this period of preparation to be introduced into the Church of Rome, where it appeared in fact only in the middle of the sixth century.

Preparation for the incarnation of Christ supposes a certain faith-inspired outlook, or to put it another way, a specific understanding of the celebration of Christmas. Christmas did not have the same importance in everyone's eyes. St. Augustine, for example, saw in this feast a simple "memorial."[59] From his point of view, the celebration was only a recalling, even though the recall possessed a special spiritual efficacy. In this case the liturgy could not awaken an authentic expectation in its participants, since the event had already taken place and only the memory of it was now being celebrated. We can appreciate the effects of a past event, even if the event remains purely in the past. But how can we prepare actively for its celebration and be filled with a joyous impatience to encounter the event in its concrete reality?

St. Leo has quite a different understanding of the celebration of Christmas. For him it is a "sacrament" and possesses an actuality because it is the first moment in the carrying out of the passover mystery and is closely bound up with the latter.[60] This is why Christmas is efficaciously present across time and space. On the Vigil of Christmas the Eastern martyrology proclaims "A Pasch, a three-day festive holiday."[61]

Against this background we can better understand why the Church decided to introduce a period of preparation for the liturgical actualization of Christ's birth. The Council of Saragossa (380) obliged the faithful to gather daily from December 17 to January 6. In the sixth century, St. Gregory of Tours mentions a penitential period lasting from November 11 to Christmas, during which people fasted three days a week; this is the period that would later be called "St. Martin's Lent."[62] In the sixth century the tendency was to make Advent as long as Lent.

At Rome, it was only toward the middle of the sixth century that an Advent liturgy was celebrated; the season lasted six weeks. On the sixth Sunday, however, there was no liturgy; the introduction of the Ember Days meant that the liturgy was celebrated during the night between the fifth Saturday and the sixth Sunday, the latter then having no proper liturgy of its own. Under St. Gregory the Great, the number of Sundays was reduced to four.

Advent, then, as a special season, came into existence during the period from the fourth century to the middle of the sixth. But while elsewhere it was generally a time of fasting and only gradually developed its special liturgy, at Rome it was seen as liturgical from the beginning and related to the feast of Christmas (first celebrated in 336).

This very summary sketch could give a false impression of the theology at work. As a matter of fact, from the time that Christmas became a feast of major importance in the Roman liturgy, Advent had a twofold significance: it was a preparation for the Lord's birth (this aspect was emphasized especially outside Rome), and it was a time of waiting for the parousia. So interwoven are the two themes that it is difficult to say whether the readings and prayers were chosen to prepare the faithful for Christmas or for the parousia. Reference to the parousia was not missing from the non-Roman liturgies, which had begun to celebrate Advent before Rome did, but it became prominent only after Rome had created its own Advent liturgy.

There are still two questions to be asked concerning the celebration of Advent at Rome.

We know that there is evidence of a celebration of Advent beginning in the fourth century elsewhere than at Rome. How are we to explain the fact that Rome, which had instituted the feast of Christmas, lagged so far behind in introducing the celebration of Advent? Furthermore, how are we to explain the Roman emphasis on the two objects of Advent expectation?

It is difficult, perhaps impossible, to give definitive answers to these questions, but we can at least offer plausible hypotheses, while resisting the temptation to make certainties out of them.

It is possible that Rome viewed Christmas simply as a feast preparatory to the paschal feast. For the Romans, Christmas was a kind of inchoative Pasch; Easter alone was to be dignified by a preparatory season (which from the fourth century on included the catechumenate). Easter alone was to be celebrated in a way worthy of the feast that actualizes the heart of the whole mystery of salvation.

But the biblical and instinctively theological sensibilities of the faithful enriched the feast of Christmas by introducing a time of expectation that focused on a twofold object, as we have already said. Christmas was celebrated in close relation to the paschal mystery, being regarded as the beginning of Christ's triumph over evil. The Fathers of the Church, especially St. Leo, linked the Lord's coming to Bethlehem with his second coming in glory at the end of time. In their eyes, despite the lowly state of the Lord in the crib, Christmas is a victory feast, connected both with the redemptive triumph of the Cross and with the final triumph of Christ at his return.

Quite naturally, then, the preparation for the feast of Christmas took on the same rich dimensions and twofold perspective as the feast itself. *Adventus* was a term borrowed from the pagans and meant "coming"; it was extended from the feast or event itself to the preparation for it, and acquired the meaning "expectation." In other words, "advent" meant first of all the Lord's birth and the anniversary of it, then the time of preparation for the event, and finally the expectation of, or time of waiting for, the second coming of Christ.[63]

Expectation of the second coming

The books of the New Testament are filled with the confident thought of the Lord's coming on the last day; a Christian messianism underlay the theology that the Church lived from the very beginning of its existence. Christ himself often refers to his return, and it was quite natural that the writings closely concerned with him should reflect the promise of that coming, which was always present in the minds of his apostles and disciples.

With the passage of time, the theology and even the very imagery connected with the second coming would be seriously distorted. The catastrophes accompanying the end of the world, and the proximity of that end, would become the chief focus of interest, and the return of the Lord would be cast into the shadow. In modern times, spirituality seemed to have simply lost sight of the end of the world and of Christ's return, and to have concentrated on the individual's encounter with the sovereign Lord and just Judge at the moment of death. Apocalyptic descriptions and paintings of the final judgment and second coming betrayed an erroneous theology.

It is far easier for us today to obtain a proper understanding of the biblical mentality. This, along with the themes of the Advent liturgy, can help Christians grasp the real meaning of the events we await, and the concrete meaning of the waiting itself. But the ground must first be cleared, for Christians have developed attitudes that make it difficult for them really to focus their attention on the end of the world and the return of Christ.

To begin with, it is difficult for us to rid ourselves of a very commercialized and individualistic vision of the history of salvation. Despite the sociological jargon we use and despite our preoccupation (philosophical at best, but most often purely verbal) with the salvation of the community, we tend to see the problem solely from the viewpoint of the individual. The end of the world means *my* end; the judgment is the judgment to be passed on *me*; and the encounter with the returning Christ is *my* encounter with him.

Such a conception of the retribution that Christ brings can hardly rouse enthusiasm. A theology of hope and a real life of hope cannot be focused on the individual, as though he existed as an isolated monad. In fact, a man cannot accept salvation unless other men and the world itself are involved. Only an outlook that is as hopeful for the future of the world as it is for others and for the individual can win a man's enthusiastic assent and become the basis for a whole style of life.

Here, of course, we have entered the domain of faith. We made this point at the beginning of the chapter and must repeat it here: Without faith, all that we have been saying and shall be saying is meaningless. There can be no efficacious liturgical celebration without faith. But we must also repeat something else said earlier: The properly Christian outlook on the future and renewal of the world is of concern even to those "outside" who are allowed to gain a right understanding of it through the scriptural and theologico-moral presentation of Advent.

"He will gather his elect from the four winds"

Christ did not mince words in predicting his return. This is evident from a well-known passage of St. Mark's Gospel:

> But in those days, after that tribulation, the sun will be darkened, and the moon will not give its light, and the stars will be falling from heaven, and the powers in the heavens will be shaken. And then they will see

the Son of man coming in clouds with great power
and glory. And then he will send out the angels, and
gather his elect from the four winds, from the ends of
the earth to the ends of heaven (Mark 13:24-27).

St. Mark is here utilizing a messianic prophecy of the
prophet Daniel: "I saw in the night visions, and behold,
with the clouds of heaven there came one like a son of man,
and he came to the Ancient of Days and was presented before him" (Dan. 7:13).

The theme of gathering is basic. It is interesting to see
that just as on the day of the Fall the world that had been
created in God's likeness was fragmented, so (in the imagery of the apocalypses) the whole world is shaken by the
Lord's return. The first action of the Son of Man will be to
"gather his elect from the four winds." The image will be
very familiar to the early Christians; we find it, for example,
in the attractive prayer of blessing in the *Didache*.[64]

Isaiah foretells the gathering of the nations in the Temple
at Jerusalem for an age of happiness and peace: "He [the
Lord] shall judge between the nations, and shall decide for
many peoples; and they shall beat their swords into plow-
shares, and their spears into pruning hooks; nation shall not
lift up sword against nation, neither shall they learn war
any more" (Is. 2:1-5. *LH*, Monday, first week; Mass, first
Sunday [A]).

Isaiah also sees the remnant of God's people surviving all
the trials and being reunited on Mount Zion (Is. 4:2-6. *LH*,
Tuesday, first week).

St. Matthew puts on Christ's lips a prediction of a gathering for the banquet in God's kingdom: "I tell you, many
will come from east and west and sit at table with Abraham,
Isaac, and Jacob in the kingdom of heaven" (Matthew 8:5-
11. Mass, Monday, first week). Jesus is here foretelling the
fulfillment of Isaiah's prophecy.

In the "apocalypse" of Isaiah (cc. 24–27), there is a prediction of the great universal banquet: "And he will destroy
on this mountain the covering that is cast over all peoples,

the veil that is spread over all nations. He will swallow up
death for ever" (Is. 25:6-9. Mass, Wednesday, first week).

The golden age

The theme of gathering into unity is a favorite of Isaiah's.
He gives it fine expression in his well-known poem on the
golden age:

> The wolf shall dwell with the lamb, and the leopard
> shall lie down with the kid, and the calf and the lion
> and the fatling together, and a little child shall lead
> them. The cow and the bear shall feed; their young
> shall lie down together; and the lion shall eat straw
> like the ox. The sucking child shall play over the hole
> of the asp, and the weaned child shall put his hand on
> the adder's den (Is. 11:1-10. Mass, Tuesday, first
> week, and second Sunday [A]).

What is being foretold here is the restoration of creation
to unity, as envisaged in God's first plan, according to
which all creatures serve one another for the glory of the
Father.

Second-Isaiah describes him whom God has chosen and
sanctified so that he might effect this gathering into unity.
Prisoners will be liberated and captives released; the Lord
will make justice and praise spring up before all the nations
(Is. 61:1-11. Mass, third Sunday [B]).

The prophet Baruch offers a similar vision of the gathering of God's people: "Arise, O Jerusalem, stand upon the
height and look toward the east, and see your children
gathered from west and east, at the word of the Holy One"
(Bar. 5:1-9. Mass, second Sunday [C]).

According to Jeremiah, the new form for oathtaking will
be: "'As the Lord lives who brought up and led the descendants of the house of Israel out of the north country and
out of all the countries where he had driven them.' Then
they shall dwell in their own land" (Jer. 23:5-8. Mass, December 18).

The gathered people will pray and worship together. According to Isaiah, the Lord's house will be called "a house of prayer for all peoples" (Is. 56:1-8. Mass, Wednesday, third week).

If we refer back to what was said earlier on the unity of creation and on the disappointment of God, who then decides to renew the world and even sends his Son to establish a new paschal covenant, we will be struck by the way the liturgical texts of Advent focus on the idea of the regathering of the nations. The theme is both paschal and eschatological. God's plan of renewal will surely succeed — that is a key element in Christian hope during the time of waiting.

St. Cyprian emphasizes the aspect of patient perseverance that must characterize our hope in what we do not yet see:

> Our Lord and Teacher has a salutary warning for us: "He who endures to the end will be saved." And again: "If you continue in my word, you are truly my disciples, and you will know the truth, and the truth will make you free." We must therefore endure and persevere, dear brothers, so that, having been given the hope of truth and freedom, we may be able to attain that truth and that freedom. What makes us Christians, after all, is faith and hope; but if faith and hope are to reach fruition, we must be patient.
>
> It is not a present but a future glory that we seek, as Paul the Apostle reminds us: "In this hope we were saved. Now hope that is seen is not hope. For who hopes for what he sees? But if we hope for what we do not see, we wait for it with patience." Waiting and patience are necessary if we are to complete what we began and if we are to obtain what, by God's inspiration, we believe in and hope for.[65]

In the same spirit, the Liturgy of the Hours has taken as an Advent reading a passage from Vatican II's *Dogmatic*

Constitution on the Church, which speaks of the eschatological nature of the pilgrim Church.

The Church, to which we are all called in Christ Jesus, and in which by the grace of God we acquire holiness, will receive its perfection only in the glory of heaven, when will come the time of the renewal of all things (Acts 3:21). At that time, together with the human race, the universe itself, which is so closely related to man and which attains its destiny through him, will be perfectly reestablished in Christ (cf. Eph. 1:10; Col. 1:20; 2 Pet. 3:10-13).

Christ lifted up from the earth, has drawn all men to himself (Cf. Jn. 12:32). Rising from the dead (cf. Rom. 6:9) he sent his life-giving Spirit upon his disciples and through him set up his Body which is the Church as the universal sacrament of salvation. Sitting at the right hand of the father he is continually active in the world in order to lead men to the Church and, through it, join them more closely to himself; and, by nourishing them with his own Body and Blood, make them partakers of his glorious life. The promised and hoped for restoration, therefore, has already begun in Christ. It is carried forward in the sending of the Holy Spirit and through him continues in the Church in which, through our faith, we learn the meaning of our earthly life, while we bring to term, with hope of future good, the task allotted to us in the world by the Father, and so work out our salvation (cf. Phil. 2:12).

The final age of the world has already bome upon us (cf. 1 Cor. 10:11) and the renewal of the world is irrevocably under way; it is even now anticipated in a certain real way, for the Church on earth is endowed already with a sanctity that is real though imperfect. However, until there be realized new heavens and a new earth in which justice dwells (cf. 2 Pet. 3:13) the pilgrim Church, in its sacraments and institutions, which belong to this present age, carries the mark of this world which will pass, and she herself takes her place among the creatures which groan and travail yet and await the revelation of the sons of God (cf. Rom. 8:19-22).[66]

A constructive judgment

The Christian expectation is not only of a gathering on the last day but of a judgment as well. Consequently, the expectation is accompanied by vigilance.

When Jesus shows his intention of returning among men to gather the fruit that has been ripening there for him, he speaks of two purposes for his return: he returns to judge as well as to renew the world at the stage of maturation it will have achieved. In the Gospel of St. Matthew, return and retribution are connected: "The Son of man is to come with his angels in the glory of his Father, and then he will repay every man for what he has done" (Matthew 16:27).

Later on, in a more detailed description, we see the Son of Man coming in his glory to the assembled nations and separating the sheep from the goats (Matthew 25:31-46). St. Mark also points out, though in a more allusive way, the judgment that will come with Christ's return: "Whoever is ashamed of me and of my words in this adulterous and sinful generation, of him will the Son of man also be ashamed, when he comes in the glory of his Father with the holy angels" (Mark 8:38).

But we must avoid too narrow an understanding of the judgment. The judgment is in fact only a necessary moment in the restoration of a world from which all dross must be eliminated. That is precisely the point of the parable of the weeds that is told in Matthew 13 and that Christ himself then interprets:

> Then he left the crowds and went into the house. And his disciples came to him, saying, "Explain to us the parable of the weeds of the field." He answered, "He who sows the good seed is the Son of man; the field is

the world, and the good seed means the sons of the kingdom; the weeds are the sons of the evil one, and the enemy who sowed them is the devil; the harvest is the close of the age, and the reapers are angels. Just as the weeds are gathered and burned with fire, so will it be at the close of the age. The Son of man will send his angels, and they will gather out of his kingdom all causes of sin and all evildoers, and throw them into the furnace of fire; there men will weep and gnash their teeth. Then the righteous will shine like the sun in the kingdom of their Father. He who has ears, let him hear (Matthew 13:36-43).

This negative phase in the restoration guarantees that the new world abuilding will have no trace of Satan or evil in it. All this will happen when "heaven and earth will pass away" (Mark 13:31). For, Jesus says,

Truly, I say to you, in the new world, when the Son of man shall sit on his glorious throne, you who have followed me will also sit on twelve thrones, judging the twelve tribes of Israel. And every one who has left houses or brothers or sisters or father or mother or children or lands, for my name's sake, will receive a hundredfold, and inherit eternal life (Matthew 19:28-29).

The Twelve will be there with him, Christ promises:

In my Father's house are many rooms; if it were not so, would I have told you that I go to prepare a place for you? And when I go and prepare a place for you, I will come again and will take you to myself, that where I am you may be also (John 14:2-3).

The whole Gospel, therefore, clearly manifests the certainty of a second coming that brings judgment, gathering, and renewal.

The Acts of the Apostles reports what Peter said to the people of Jerusalem and thereby enables us to understand what we might call the early Church's theology of Advent. His sermons also show us what the main lines of our own theology of Advent should be.

> Repent, therefore, and turn again, that your sins may be blotted out, that times of refreshing may come from the presence of the Lord, and that he may send the Christ appointed for you, Jesus, whom heaven must receive until the time for establishing all that God spoke by the mouth of his holy prophets from of old. Moses said, "The Lord God will raise up for you a prophet from your brethren as he raised me up. You shall listen to him in whatever he tells you. And it shall be that every soul that does not listen to that prophet shall be destroyed from the people." And all the prophets who have spoken, from Samuel and those who came afterwards, also proclaimed these days. You are the sons of the prophets and of the covenant which God gave to your fathers, saying to Abraham, "And in your posterity shall all the families of the earth be blessed." God, having raised up his servant, sent him to you first, to bless you in turning every one of you from your wickedness (Acts 3:19-26).

We find here a concept identical with that in Matthew: Christ's return is accompanied by judgment and the renewal of the world. We should note the absence of any apocalyptic imagery and of any preoccupation with the signs of the Lord's coming. The real issue is the understanding of the present age, which was begun by Christ and will reach its climax and end with his return. Repentance and conversion hasten the time of definitive salvation and that restoration of the world that Isaiah had foretold in his prophecy of new heavens and a new earth (Is. 65:17; 66:22). But, though the parousia is certainly kept in mind, it is not the principal focus of attention; the important thing for the moment is to live properly in the present age, which extends from the first coming of Christ to the establishment of the everlasting kingdom.

St. Paul takes up the same theme when he addresses the philosophers of Athens: "The times of ignorance God overlooked, but now he commands all men everywhere to repent, because he has fixed a day on which he will judge the world in righteousness by a man whom he has appointed, and of this he has given assurance to all men by raising him from the dead" (Acts 17:30-31).

He does not mention the renewal of the world, but he does show how a man should view the time that separates him from the unknown day of Christ's return. A day has been set for judgment; we on earth, who are drawn by the risen Christ, must repent. That is what the Thessalonians did, turning away from idols in order to serve the living God and await his Son from heaven (1 Thess. 1:9-10). We know how these men impatiently awaited that great day and the kind of questions they asked about it (2 Thess. 3:10-22). The Second Letter of Peter shows that many were becoming discouraged and bitter.

> First of all you must understand this, that scoffers will come in the last days with scoffing, following their own passions and saying, "Where is the promise of his coming? For ever since the fathers fell asleep, all things have continued as they were from the beginning of creation." They deliberately ignore this fact, that by the word of God heavens existed long ago and an earth formed out of water and by means of water, through which the world that then existed was deluged with water and perished. But by the same word the heavens and earth that now exist have been stored up for fire, being kept until the day of judgment and destruction of ungodly men.
>
> But do not ignore this one fact, beloved, that with the Lord one day is as a thousand years, and a thousand years as one day. The Lord is not slow about his promise as some count slowness, but is forbearing toward you, not wishing that any should perish, but that all should reach repentance (2 Peter 3:3-9).

Christians wait for the Lord. The words *"Marana tha"* (Lord, come!"), which we find in St. Paul (1 Cor. 16:22) and in the liturgical text in the *Didache* (10:6), show the desire of the community, expressed in prayer form, for the coming of the day of the Lord. We would mistake the emphasis in this expectation if we were to reduce it to an expectation of personal salvation. What is awaited is rather the salvation of all mankind and even of all creation.

> For the creation waits with eager longing for the re-vealing of the sons of God; for the creation was sub-jected to futility, not of its own will but by the will of him who subjected it in hope; because the creation it-self will be set free from its bondage to decay and obtain the glorious liberty of the children of God. We know that the whole creation has been groaning in travail together until now; and not only the creation, but we ourselves, who have the first fruits of the Spirit, groan inwardly as we wait for adoption as sons, the redemption of our bodies (Rom 8:19-23).

All creation, then, exists in a perpetual Advent season as it waits to be delivered from corruption by an outpouring of God's glory. In Adam the world was fragmented by sin; the new Adam will restore the whole creation to unity.

Watchfulness: he will come like a thief

No one will be expecting the last day when it comes; it will be upon mankind before men become aware of it. In this respect the Deluge is a good parallel. For those con-temporary with the event, everything had been going on as before, as though nothing extraordinary were imminent: sin, false joy, the struggle for a livelihood and for mastery of others, the quest for importance, eroticism — in short, all that we see going on today in the lives of those who have no sense of permanent values. And it was all still going on when the Deluge took them by surprise.

Christ's warning is clear: "Therefore you also must be

ready; for the Son of man is coming at an hour you do not expect" (Matthew 24:44). Isaiah foresaw this coming. For him, it is not chiefly a day of catastrophe but the day when the Lord will come to gather the nations and to bring them into a kingdom of everlasting peace (Is. 2:1-5). The Church will take the same view and, in response to Isaiah's prophecy, will sing Psalm 122: "Let us go to the house of the Lord!"

We can easily judge from the New Testament the reactions of the newborn Church as a whole and what it considered to be the meaning of man's present life and of the world's historical existence.

St. Paul instructed his brothers, of course, on what their attitude ought to be. He has no teaching on the proximity of the last day. The only thing he has to say on this is what he received from the Lord, who describes his own coming as unexpected and sudden as the coming of a thief. The Letter to Titus offers a program of life for the time between Christ's first coming and his return.

> For the grace of God has appeared for the salvation of all men, training us to renounce irreligion and worldly passions, and to live sober, upright, and godly lives in this world, awaiting our blessed hope, the appearing of the glory of our great God and Savior Jesus Christ (Titus 2:11-13).

The proper use of created things; justice, that is, a life conformed to God's plan; piety, that is, truthfulness in our attitude to God.

The Thessalonians were impatient and were thrown off the true course by an overly human interpretation of the parousia. The two Letters to them likewise describe for us a very practical line to follow. Purity of life, charity, hard work (1 Thess. 4:1-12, 13-22), prayer and, again, hard work (2 Thess. 3) should mark the Christian as he lives in a pagan world. Such should be our life as we await our blessed hope, the glorious coming of our great God and Savior Jesus Christ.

Our ignorance of the moment of Christ's coming should be a spur to us. Taking the same theme as the Gospel of Mark, 13:33-37 (Mass, first Sunday [B]), Second-Isaiah expresses our longing expectation as he says to the Lord: "O that thou wouldst rend the heavens and come down" (Is. 63:16b-17; 64: 1, 3b-8. First Sunday [B]). After the Exile the people of God ardently desires its own complete and lasting restoration, but it knows that God alone can save a nation that has been destroyed and restore its unity. Psalm 80, which is sung in response to the reading from Isaiah, expresses the drama in lyric terms: "Lord make us turn to you, let us see your face and we shall be saved. Give ear, O Shepherd of Israel. . . . Stir up thy might, and come to save us!"

Such is our situation in the Church between the two comings of Christ. But we are not abandoned and left to our own resources: "You are not lacking in any spiritual gift, as you wait for the revealing of our Lord Jesus Christ" (1 Cor. 1:3-9. Mass, first Sunday [B]).

In any event, our redemption is near at hand, and we must be vigilant. This means abandoning vices and attitudes irreconcilable with a genuine expectation of the Lord's coming. This is the warning given by a number of texts used in the Advent liturgy. Be watchful (Matthew 24:37-44, first Sunday [A]; Mark 13:33-37, first Sunday [B]; Luke 21:25-28, 34-36, first Sunday [C]) and prepare the way for the Lord (Matthew 3:1-6, second Sunday [A][Mark 1:1-8, second Sunday] [B]; Luke 3:1-6, second Sunday [C]): these are the themes nost emphasized. We must live as children of the light who have put on Christ, for salvation is now nearer at hand than it was when we first received the faith (1 Thess. 3:12–4:2, first Sunday [C]).

And yet all this does not eliminate optimism, for the end of time will also be a constructive event. The Lord who is coming is "our righteousness" (Jer. 33:14-16, first Sunday [C]). We must ask him to lead us along the right way and to teach us, for he is the God who saves, and the ways of the Lord are love and truth (Psalm 25, first Sunday [C]). May the Lord not permit our concern with present tasks to hinder us as we go to meet his Son; may he grant us the spiritual understanding that will prepare us to welcome him and to share his life (prayer of second Sunday). May he grant his faithful the power to live with courage and justice in his presence, and may he call them at the judgment to take possession of the kingdom of heaven (opening prayer, first Sunday).

Waiting for what is already here

In Israel, even in the time of John the Baptist, waiting meant hoping for what was already possessed. For there were signs which proved that the object of hope was not a poetic abstraction. The object of hope was rather a concrete situation that was already present, even though still awaited.

As we have already pointed out, this paradox expresses what is specific to Christian hope: we wait for what we already possess! The same paradox marks the liturgy of Advent, which stresses the presence, here and now, of what is expected at the end of time. The texts have to be read carefully in their contexts in order to eliminate any ambiguity. But then, Jesus himself, as we know, did not hesitate to speak of the kingdom as already present in our midst. Among the signs of this presence of a reality whose full manifestation we still await, the following are important: the cures, the preaching of the Good News to the poor, and the prefigurations of the messianic banquet.

The blind see

The cures are proof that the reign of God is already present. Christ's answer to the messengers from John the Baptist is unambiguous: "Go and tell John what you have seen and heard: the blind receive their sight, the lame walk, lepers are cleansed, and the deaf hear, the dead are raised up, the poor have good news preached to them" (Luke 7:19-23, Wednesday, third week).

When St. Matthew relates the cures that Christ wrought, his intention evidently is to show that the messianic age has begun. He records Jesus' reply to John in the very same words as Luke (Matthew 11:2-11, third Sunday [A]). Quite naturally, the first reading, chosen to correspond to the Gospel, is a prophecy of Isaiah that lists the signs of the Messiah's coming: "'Be strong, fear not ! Behold, your God will come with vengeance, with the recompense of God. He will come and save you.' Then the eyes of the blind shall be opened, and the ears of the deaf unstopped; then shall the lame man leap like a hart, and the tongue of the dumb sing for joy" (Is. 35:1-19, third Sunday [A]).

In the weekday readings of Advent, there are many accounts of the cures which are signs that the messianic age is here. St. Matthew goes out of his way to emphasize the coming of God's salvation. He has numerous reports of divine actions that show God taking the initiative in renewing his relationship with the world and with men. Jesus invites the afflicted to come to him and be consoled (Matthew 11:28-30, Wednesday, second week). A reading from Isaiah reinforces this theology of the divine initiative in the work of our salvation: it is the Lord who gives strength to the fainting and vigor to the weak (Is. 40:25-31, Wednesday, second week). Jesus takes pity on the crowd and bids his disciples freely give what they have freely received (Matthew 9:35–10:1, 5a, 6-8, Saturday, first week). Isaiah tells us we need only cry out to the Lord and he will have pity on us (Is. 30:19-21, 23-26, Saturday, first week). The Lord's attentive compassion is directed first and foremost to the little ones, whom he does not wish to see lost. At this moment he sees himself as the shepherd in charge of them and therefore leaves the other sheep behind to go in search of the one that has strayed (Matthew 18:12-14, Tuesday, second week). He is the loving Shepherd who collects his lambs and carries them on his breast; he takes care of the sheep that are nursing their young (Is. 40:1-11, Tuesday, second week).

The Lord works many miracles. St. Matthew tells us that

great crowds came to him bringing the lame, the blind, the maimed, the dumb, and many other kinds of sick people; they brought them to Jesus and he cured them (Matthew 15:29-37, Wednesday, first week). He is indeed the Lord of whom the Apocalypse of Isaiah says that he will wipe the tears from every face (Is. 25:6-10a, Wednesday, first week). In particular, he cures two blind men who believe in him. Their cry of faith, "Have mercy on us, Son of David," touched him (Matthew 9:27-31, Friday, first week). We recall that Isaiah saw in the curing of the blind a sign that the kingdom is at hand (Is. 29:17-24, Friday, first week).

But St. Matthew also notes, on several occasions, how unbelief blinds men: they will not listen either to John the Baptist or to the Son (Matthew 17:10-13, Saturday, second week); John the Baptist has come, but they have not believed his message (Matthew 21:28-32, Tuesday, third week).

St. Luke likewise recounts the miracles of Jesus. In Jesus the reign of God is truly present, for he has the power to forgive sins (Luke 5:17-26, Monday, second week).

The cures, then, are not only responses to faith, nor are they worked simply in order to arouse faith. They are also a sign that the kingdom is here.

In a reading chosen for the Office on Wednesday of the second week of Advent, St. Augustine speaks to us in his commentary on the psalms. The central theme of the passage is that God fulfills his promises to us through the mediation of his Son.

> [God] promised divinity to men, immortality to mortals, justification to sinners, and glorification to those brought low. . . .
>
> But, brothers, men deemed God's promise impossible: that out of mortality and corruption, lowliness and weakness, dust and ashes there should emerge men equal to God's angels. Therefore, God did not simply put the promise in writing so that men might believe it. He also gave as pledge of his trustworthi-

ness a mediator who was not a mere prince or even an angel or archangel, but his only Son. He would make known to us through his Son the way in which he would lead us to the promised goal.

It was not enough for God simply to have his Son point out the way to us. He made him be our Way so that you might walk in him who guides you. . . .

All this had to be prophesied and foretold, and its coming made known beforehand, so that men might not draw back in fear at its sudden appearance but look forward to it eagerly because they believed in its coming.[67]

Thus it was through increasingly clear signs that the age to come was proclaimed and is now present.

The Good News is preached to the poor

We have a sufficient grasp by now of what the word "poor" means in the Old Testament. Let us sum up its content briefly.

It is the presence or absence of this poverty that determined the course of Israel's history from its very beginnings as recorded in the first three chapters of Genesis. This poverty, as we have already seen, is not destitution, whether material or intellectual or social, but an attitude of humility and detachment in the presence of the Lord, along with the humble acknowledgment of one's sins. We must note, however, that the "poor" of the Beatitudes are not simply those "spiritually poor," while the material poverty from which the Israelites suffered during their exile stimulated them to "spiritual poverty."[68] It was the "poverty" of the Israelites, with its various components, that moved the Lord to action: "I have seen the miserable state [=poverty] of my people in Egypt. I have heard their appeal to be free of their slave-drivers" (Exod. 3:7 JB).

Their affliction becomes an occasion for the manifestation of God's goodness; he hears the prayers of those who cry out to him (Judg. 3:9; 3:15; 4:3). When God protects the oppressed, this is not simply a companionable act on his part; what he is concerned with, above all, is the restoration of justice, for justice is a reflection of his being. Man must be good as God is good — this is the real basis of the whole legislation in behalf of the poor. Biblical poverty cannot be reduced to material poverty; the Scriptures, after all, consider wealth to be a gift of God. Biblical poverty has a spiritual dimension; the real "poor man of Yahweh" is the man who serves God and his brothers, and he is described for us in the Servant poem of Isaiah 42.

One of the signs Jesus gave to the disciples of John the Baptist was that "the poor have good news preached to them" (Luke 7:19-23, Wednesday, third week). Second-Isaiah had spoken of this sign: "The Spirit of the Lord God is upon me, because the Lord has anointed me to bring good tidings to the afflicted" (Is. 61:2, 10-11, third Sunday [B.]).

The natural response to this prophecy of Isaiah, which Christ was later to read and apply to himself in the synagogue at Nazareth (Luke 4:16-21), is the *Magnificat*, in which the Virgin shows herself to be the humble servant whose role is to give birth to the Messiah: "He has regarded the low estate of his handmaiden" (Luke 1:48).

Zephaniah likewise puts messianic salvation within the reach of the poor: "I will leave in the midst of you a people humble and lowly. They shall seek refuge in the name of the Lord" (Zeph. 3:12; see Tuesday, third week). For "the Lord hears the cry of the poor" (refrain for responsorial psalm, Tuesday, third week). For "the Lord hears the cry of the poor" (refrain for responsorial psalm, Tuesday, third week).

The preaching of the Good News to the poor is a sign that the Messiah is here. The right moment has come: there are men whose hearts humility has opened and who are ready to receive the message that salvation is now given to the nations. Such universalism is a further sign of the messianic age. The Lord cannot forget the poor man but stays with him. Now the Lord comes, preceded by the proclamation of the Good News of his coming.

The messianic banquet

A further sign of the presence of the kingdom is the banquet. Here, as with the poor, we have a basic image of Scripture. A meal is a sign of the restoration of union with God and a sign, too, of the world's renewal. Eating at the Lord's table is a favorite theme of the Bible, and Christ will often use the image of a meal. The ancient liturgies realized how important a theme this was for the period of waiting. Our own liturgy has taken as an Advent reading the multiplication of the loaves, with its several levels of significance (Matthew 15:29-37, Wednesday, first week). Isaiah speaks of the joy of being at the Lord's table (Is. 25:6-10a, same day). The Book of Proverbs uses the same image to describe the joy of the wise man (Prov. 5:1).

The two themes of banquet and the poor are very closely linked, since the banqueters will be all who are hungry; their lack of money does not matter (Is. 55:1). The banquet is essentially an image related to the parousia. Jesus describes it to his disciples as a meal to be shared by all who believe as did Abraham, Isaac, and Jacob (Matthew 8:11). It is the meal at which we shall meet the Lord; therefore we must be wearing a wedding garment (Matthew 22:11-14). The Apocalypse gives a poetic description of the parousaic supper: "Behold, I stand at the door and knock; if any one hears my voice and opens the door, I will come in to him and eat with him, and he with me" (Apoc. 3:20).

Waiting for the incarnation

When St. Mark recounts the first multiplication of the loaves, he apparently wishes us to see the multiplied loaves as a sign of Jesus' word and Jesus' body (Mark 6:30-34). Saint John speaks of Jesus as the real Bread (John 6:32).

The multiplication of the loaves is both an eschatological sign and a sign of the incarnation of the Word, who is Bread from heaven.

We shall not insist further on the "sacramental" character of the Christmas feast as an actualization of the Incarnation. It is this actualization that prescribes the very nature of our waiting. If we are to reach the parousia, we must pass by way of efficacious signs, of which the incarnation is the first. We are capable of sharing in the final banquet at Christ's return because we journey toward him now in the light of his incarnation, which is prolonged through signs and which is the ground sustaining all the other signs of salvation. For now "we see our God made visible" (Christmas Preface I).

The Christian is now in contact with the mystery that is rendered present for him. As he waits each year for the incarnation, he acquires a deeper understanding of the signs of salvation. He discovers anew the Church and its sacred signs; in the body of Christ as signified in the Church and the sacraments, he discovers anew mankind and the world, which are called to undergo the radical transformation that the incarnation effects in all things. To wait for the incarnation is deliberately to enter more deeply into death with Christ so that we may rise with him and take possession of the kingdom with him. Consequently, to wait for the incarnation is also to wait for Christ's return at the end of time.

To accept the law of incarnation is the humble attitude of the believer, the attitude of one who is poor. Man can enter into glory only if he obeys the humbling law of incarnation and learns to discover God through signs that are tailored to man's limitations and thus could easily prevent him from seeing through to the riches they contain. For the Church to celebrate the incarnation, then, is to become aware once again of what she is: both divine and human. She is required to try to make the human in her ever more worthy of the divine. She is forced to examine her conscience, for though she is the instrument of Christ's presence on earth, she is not Christ and must strive at every moment to resemble him more and more. The celebration of the incarnation is also the occasion for the Church to see whether or not her signs correspond sufficiently to the law established by the incarnation, in which they have their roots. According to that law, her signs must serve the sanctification of men and the transformation of the world, as well as the glory of God.

Waiting, even in our day?

All that has been said thus far by way of explanation may leave us still in doubt. Can the kind of ideas we have been developing awaken any chord in our contemporaries?

At first sight the answer might well seem to be no. And yet the minds of many today seems to show two tendencies: a type of despair but also an irresistible desire to build a new future.

Despite this desire, when we look, even as believers, at our present world, the success of Christianity seems dubious. The Christian cannot, of course, believe that Christianity will simply fail. He is, however, tempted to minimize the achievements of the past, and such an attitude will, if his faith is not fed and if it does not send down deeper roots, close his mind to the theology we have been exposing in these pages.

At this point, then, it will be in place to attempt a brief analysis of the difficulties Christians of today find in "waiting for the Lord's coming."

Renewal of the "soul" for a purely future world?

We may well ask whether the basic obstacle is not our progressive estrangement from the Scriptures and their outlook. The estrangement began at least as early as the tenth century. Philosophical systems, applied to the elucidation of Christian dogma, have divided man's soul from his body, and the present world (which is always evil) from the future world (which does away with the present world). Some sense of the destiny proper to the whole of creation may have been preserved, but any notion of ongoing renewal has been limited to the soul, which seeks renewal with a view to a world that is wholly future.

This dichotomy is undoubtedly responsible, in good measure, for the reactions we see today. "Waiting" is at best thought of as the waiting of the soul for perfection — a soul that alone is to be saved and to grow in charity. There is little or no room in this kind of expectation for the human person in his entirety. A "spirituality" thus limited to the soul alone is disappearing, but to the extent that it survives, it has no room for the kind of hopes that move men today.

Once we admit that God intervenes in the world, that he has intervened to the point of entering the world himself, and that he continues to act in the world through his Spirit, we can no longer make the soul alone the focus of properly Christian expectation. No, the expectation embraces the whole human person. Moreover, the expectation cannot focus on a future world, in the sense that the present world must simply disappear and yield place to another. The building of a new world has already begun, and the elements of the present world are contributing to it.

When we think of God intervening, we are too quick to conceive his action after the pattern of ours. How, for example, do we conceive the institution of the sacraments? For many Christians, the institution means that Christ simply created the saving sign in its entirety. There was no background, no religious context we need consider. The signs whose role is to change and renew man by bringing him into contact with God could not (we think) be shaped out of what already existed; there must a new creation and a total contrast with all that had gone before.

This picture is quite false. It is one of the great merits of contemporary theology to have shown, on the basis of history, that Christ, in "instituting" a sacrament, gave new content to a pre-existing form. Here we have a parallel to the manner in which we ought to understand our expectation of a new world. The renewal is not something that belongs to a future, different world; rather, it occurs within pre-existing forms. Consequently, we can say that our expectation of a new world is not purely passive, but that we must ourselves work for the transformation of the content of a world whose structures already exist.

Expectation of the renewal of the human person and of our world is both possible and encouraging to us. It will draw out all our energies and make us share in the common task of building a future whose first fruits are already ours.

Vocation of man and mankind

Such an expectation, if conceived as we have explained, is really an essential element in the vocation both of man and of mankind. But here again we must grasp things correctly. The Christian expectation does not turn our attention from essential changes in ourselves and the world, as though we had to watch these passively and from a distance. On the contrary, as we obey God, we are responsible for such changes taking place. God intervenes in history; the first stimulus to renewal comes from God; man's first activity must be to listen to God. But none of this makes man any less responsible for the future and the great restoration. He may not wait passively for it to come about but must work actively and intelligently to bring it to pass.

Man's contribution, however, is a collective one. He cannot work in isolation or he will fail. It is as part of a community that he actively awaits his own and the world's restoration.

Interior dualism and desacralization

Such a view is, theoretically, able to rouse men and the world to enthusiasm for a future that has already begun. In the concrete, distortions inevitably occur. I regard two deviations in particular as serious and capable of checking all real progress. One is an interior dualism; the other is a desacralization that affects the Christian's own interior life.

Spiritual or interior dualism has always existed. The great

spiritual writers have warned of the danger. St. Paul was convinced of its reality and found fault with himself on account of it: "For I do not do the good I want, but the evil I do not want is what I do" (Rom. 7:19).

At the moment, however, I am not thinking of this dualism insofar as it affects us all because of man's inherent weakness. Weakness, after all, does not destroy the will to seek the good. I see this dualism at work rather in the attitude that would divide a man's religious life off from his ordinary life, as though the religious life were in a sealed compartment of its own and a man could think of religious problems only at certain special moments. In recent times people have become more aware of the unity there must be between what they like to call "spiritual life" and "the political order."

As far as I can see, this subtle but convenient separation of life into compartments is at work every time the Church or an individual Christian stagnates and is content to indulge in purely "spiritual" expectations. My purpose here is not to arraign anybody or to give a course in spirituality. My concern is simply to emphasize the problem; others can go into it in greater detail. I wish only to remind the reader that the attitude I have been describing makes Christian expectation impossible, and makes it impossible, too, to enter into a liturgy whose purpose is to give vitality to that expectation. Fortunately the thirst for authenticity is so strong today that the compartmentalization I have described is, if not impossible (the unconscious and man's weakness are always at work!), at least increasingly infrequent. This is to the credit of today's Church.

The second deviation is an erroneous kind of interior desacralization. We tend to separate the sacred from the profane within us. (In so doing, we find ourselves back in the dualism just described.) Biblical man knows no separation between sacred and profane. For the Bible, the only thing truly sacred is God himself, and creatures cannot exist except to the extent that they are properly ordered to this one sacred reality. Human existence, therefore, would be meaningless if it were not directed to the sacred, even though human existence in itself is profane. There is a right kind of secularization: that which attributes to man and the world their true value; God also is truly sacred; only Christ's redemptive action and the sacraments that continue his work among us can sacralize our world, which is profane. Consequently, man and the world truly have meaning only when they are ordered to the sacred.

In other words, once man and creation become their own end, once they choose for themselves a goal other than the one that God and Christ assign them, we have a false secularization and an erroneous kind of desacralization. Unfortunately these deviations do not remain in the order of ideas alone; they are a rejection of God and destroy his plan.

Faith, action, and expectation

As we can easily see, waiting or expectation is possible only where there is faith. "Faith" here is a wide-ranging virtue. We must not only have faith in God who is Master of history and rules the world and its progress, but also faith in a Church that is the extension on earth of the glorified heavenly body of Christ and that is able to actualize Christ's presence and his mysteries so that they may contribute to the ultimate restoration of the world. Without this faith (which is also indispensable for the reception of the sacraments), the Advent liturgy becomes simply a seductive poetic representation of the path followed by God's people.

At this point we may take up our earlier train of thought and ask: If the believer is one who expects, what can and ought he expect? How is he to wait?

The believer today, like the believer in Old and New Testament days, is not to expect that his life will be humanly happy because he awaits the last day. At the same time, it seems inaccurate to speak of a "spiritual" waiting. After all, as we said earlier, it is man in his entirety that is advancing, together with his world, toward the end of time, and there is no turning back. Now, while such expectation does not have human happiness as its primary result, neither does it exclude such a result. On the contrary, we may say that the awareness of the Lord's real presence in the midst of men in this world is a source of harmony and balance in all the activities of life, whether in the sphere of human love or in scientific research, artistic endeavor, and all else that brings man happiness and well-being.

Consciousness of the presence of the Lord who guides the world and each individual toward the future he wills, gives us a sense of optimism and a constancy that enables us to learn serenity through conflict and to pass unscathed through all situations, foreseen and unforeseen. No circumstances can dismay or lead astray one whose hope is directed by God himself.

We must be honest, however, and admit that these dispositions and such a harmony of mentality and reactions with the mentality and reactions displayed by the Church in the Advent liturgy are not universally found among Christians. We might even be inclined to say that they will be found only in an elite (a cultural elite as well as a chosen body of faithful). That is a false impression. A deep faith is indeed required if we are to enter fully into what the Church proposes to us; on the other hand, the biblical themes, once given a modicum of explanation, have power to lay hold on those who are looking for an authentic Christianity.

We may also say that the liturgy, as we have been describing it, is congenial to the outlook of our contemporaries as they inquire into the meaning of the human person, the sacred, and the world. The Lord already dwells in men and in the world he seeks to restore. Consequently, men and the world are not simply passively undergoing a remaking but are taking an active part in their own renewal. They share the sacredness proper to everyone who is moving toward a future that is wholly focused on a unity that will restore, in a more perfect form, the unity that creation originally possessed.

The demands that such a vision makes are indeed great.

It would be a mistake, however, to believe that a superhuman life of waiting is the only adequate response. Far from it! Once people lead a completely and concretely human life in a human world, but a life that also has for its center the already present reality of the future, they will be capable of giving an authentic response to the demands inherent in waiting and expectation. The human being who most perfectly embodies the expectation of the world to come is one who lives a humanly normal life in a fully normal way. Such a man, when he is a believer, shows in the whole of his life a divine balance between prudence and boldness, peace and conflict, love and reserve.

We prepare, amid waiting, for the future world whenever we sacrifice our selfish interests and accept life as it is and events as they are, that is, as an unpredictable sum total of joys, sufferings and anxieties, brutal separations and painful confrontations. The active acceptance of all this is required of us on our mysterious journey through time to the end the Lord has foreseen. In suffering as in joy (we have little power over either), we are summoned to travel over high mountains, in realms far beyond our normal human condition and at altitudes where, left to ourselves, we could not breathe. Yet we are to journey as though that air were native to us.

STRUCTURE AND THEMES OF
THE ADVENT LITURGY

4. INTRODUCTION

Structure of the Sundays and the weeks

As we have seen, the Church had a twofold expectation in the celebration of her Advent liturgy and had to make both of these clear to the faithful. She could not speak of the one without the other. When the time came, however, for the postconciliar reform of the liturgy, some of those involved wanted to make of Advent simply a time of preparation for Christmas, a time of waiting for the incarnation of the Word. But they forgot that the Church can never celebrate a liturgy without emphasizing the eschatological dimension of her hope. The real need, then, was for celebrations that would accustom the people to seeing (and not just in a theoretical way) both objects of the Church's expectation in their intimate relationship. This would not, of course, make it wrong to lay a greater emphasis on the expectation of the incarnation as the feast of Christmas draws near.

In order to develop more fully the authentic spirit of waiting, some liturgists urged a return to a season of six Sundays and thus to the earlier tradition. It was decided, however, to retain a four-Sunday season. But at the same time the liturgy of the season was notably enriched. In the ancient tradition with its six Sundays, no special readings were provided for the weekdays; this continued to be the case in the later tradition with its four-week season. Now, the general principle that increased use should be made of Scripture in the liturgy has led to an extensive development of the already rich Advent season.

Thus, though Advent still has only four Sundays, there is now a three-year cycle of readings for these Sundays (Cycles A, B, and C). Consequently, from the viewpoint of the use of Scripture, we have twelve different celebrations for the Sundays of Advent. The liturgical reform did not stop there but has also provided readings for each day of the four weeks. The Sundays each have three readings, the weekdays each have two (the same each year). The readings have been so organized that each of the four Sundays emphasizes a different aspect of the mystery; the aspect proper to each Sunday receives several varying expressions in the course of the three-year cycle. The readings on the weekdays are usually related to the theology expressed in the preceding Sunday's liturgy.

Let us look a little more closely at the structure of the Sundays. The first two Sundays focus chiefly on the second coming of Christ; as we have already pointed out, they also express expectation of the incarnation, but the emphasis is not on this. If we wish to give a descriptive title to the three-year cycle proper to each of these first two Sundays, we can say that the first emphasizes the coming of the Lord and the attitude of vigilance that marks our expectation of it; a suitable title for this cycle would be: "Vigilant waiting for the Lord who is coming." The second Sunday concentrates on the preparation for this coming, and the readings naturally refer to the warnings issued by John the Baptist. The title for the cycle of readings proper to the second Sunday would be: "The warning of John the Baptist: Prepare the way of the Lord."

The third Sunday has a special function. It has traditionally given expression to the joy Christians feel at the coming that is now imminent. In the reformed liturgy the third Sunday retains this purpose and tone. It concentrates not only on the future coming but on the signs of the actual presence of the messianic kingdom; in other words, it looks to Christ already present and to Christ who is coming. It is thus a kind of transitional Sunday between the first two, which express a general attitude of expectation, and the fourth and last Sunday, which concentrates clearly on expectation of the incarnation. The cycle for the third Sunday might be entitled: "The messianic age is here. Rejoice!"

There is no difficulty about the interpretation of the fourth Sunday; its celebration is clearly a preparation for "The incarnation of the Word."

A table will be given, a little further on, that contains the title of each Sunday, a list of the readings, and a few words to sum up the content of each reading; a similar table will be given of the weekday readings. To simplify our constant references to the readings, each will be given a number: 1–36 for the Sundays, 37–84 for the weekdays. We shall also provide a table of the biblical readings in the Liturgy of the Hours (nos. 85–112).

Liturgical reading of Scripture

In this section of the book we intend to treat at least each of the Sundays as a well-defined entity. The procedure is justified, because the texts were chosen so as to form a whole, without however forcing them to make all three express the same theme.

In order to understand the liturgical theology expressed in celebrations such as those of the Sundays of Advent, we must, I think, approach them in three different ways. The first is to get a panoramic view of all the Sundays in the series and to uncover the continuity that gives this liturgical season its specific character.

The second approach, and the one that seeks the deepest penetration, requires the most attention, for it has to do with the authentically liturgical reading of the Bible.

What do we mean when we speak of a "liturgical reading of the Bible"? To begin with, it cannot mean the abandonment of all scientific exegesis. A strict exegesis, such as is now practiced in universities and other centers and given to us in books by experts, is an indispensable basis for further study. But, given such a basis, the liturgical reading of Scripture still retains its special character.

Let us explain by taking a concrete example. Usually the general lines of the theology expressed in a celebration of the word are given by the Gospel. Take the familiar passage in which Zacchaeus climbs a tree in order to catch sight of the Lord; Jesus sees him and visits his home (Luke 19:1-10). An exegetical commentary will study each point in the passage and try to situate it in its proper historical and social framework. Now, the Gospel in itself has numerous theological aspects; to develop all of them would be to compose a commentary on the passage, not to do a liturgical reading of it. For, in sheer point of fact, when this particular passage is used on the day of the consecration of a church, the emphasis is on the Lord's coming into the home of Zacchaeus; that is why the passage was chosen, and all other aspects of the passage are secondary in this context.

When we read the same passage on the thirty-first Sunday of the year, what is the main point in it that makes it appropriate to this new context? Well, the first reading, which is from the Old Testament, is intended to correspond to the Gospel passage and therefore can give an indication of why the latter was chosen. The Old Testament passage is from the Book of Wisdom (11:22–12:2) and speaks of God's long patience as he actively seeks the conversion of men. This tells us that the main point in the Gospel is not Christ's coming to the home of Zacchaeus but rather the process leading to faith. Zacchaeus wants to see Jesus and does everything he can to see him as he really is. Christ responds to Zacchaeus's desire, and the latter enters upon the path of conversion, as he shows by telling the Lord how he intends to live as one converted.

Sometimes, though not always, the second reading on the Sundays of the year will add details that confirm the interpretation already made of the Gospel. That is the case here. Paul tells the Thessalonians that God is constantly calling us and endeavoring to make our faith alive and active (2 Thess. 1:11–2:2).

Now, in all this we are not trying to compose a commentary on the Gospel passage, but simply determining how, in the liturgical context, we are to read the Gospel; we are learning which aspect or teaching of the passage we are intended to concentrate on, while treating everything else as secondary. This second approach to the liturgical theology of a given celebration is not always easy, but it is essential.

There is a third approach, a third level of reading, as it were. Here it is a reading of the entire liturgy of the word as it presents itself to us. It may be that the chant that introduces the Gospel will give us the essential point of the day's liturgy. The entrance song, the opening prayer, and sometimes the Communion song that picks up something from the Gospel may also help us determine the essential point that the liturgy of the word as a whole intends to proclaim.

In the following pages we shall be using the threefold approach we have been describing. This does not mean that we will expressly use the three successive methods; for the most part we shall simply present the results reached through the application of the three types of reading.

The earlier chapters of the book have given a general theology of Advent. The last few pages have sketched an overall view of the Sundays of Advent. Now we turn to the themes proper to each of the four weeks.

READINGS FOR THE SUNDAYS OF ADVENT

Sundays	The Prophet		The Apostle		The Gospel	
I. Vigilant waiting for the Lord	1	A The nations gather Is. 2:1-5	4	A The day is near Rom. 13:11-14	7	A Watch! Matthew 24:37-44
	2	B May God come down! Is. 63:16b-17; 64:1, 3b-8	5	B Day of the Lord 1 Cor. 1:3-9	8	B Watch! Mark 13:33-37
	3	C A just shoot Jer. 33:14-16	6	C Day of the Lord's coming 1 Thess. 3:12–4:2	9	C Watch! Luke 21:25-28; 34-36
II. Warning of John the Baptist: Prepare the way of the Lord	10	A The Spirit of the Lord is upon him Is. 11:1-10	13	A Promises fulfilled in Jesus Rom. 15:4-9	16	A Prepare the way Matthew 3:1-12
	11	B Fill in the valleys Is. 40:1-5, 9-11	14	B New heavens and a new earth 2 Peter 3:8-14	17	B Prepare the way Mark 1:1-8
	12	C Every lofty mountain is laid low Bar. 5:1-9	15	C Day of the Lord's coming Phil. 1:4-6, 8-11	18	C Prepare the way Luke 3:1-6

19	A	Cures: Signs of the times Is. 35:1-6a, 10	22	A	Patience until the Lord comes James 5:7-10	25	A	Cures as signs Matthew 11:2-11
20	B	The Good News to the poor Is. 61:1-2, 10-11	23	B	Joy at the Lord's coming 1 Thess 5:16-24	26	B	Christ in our midst John 1:6-8, 19-28
21	C	Rejoice! God is in your midst Zeph. 3:14-18a	24	C	Rejoice! The Lord is here Phil. 4:4-7	27	C	A mightier is coming Luke 3:10-18

III. The Messianic

28	A	A virgin shall give birth Is. 7:10-14	31	A	Of David's line according to the flesh Rom. 1:1-7	34	A	Message to Joseph Matthew 1:18-24
29	B	Your house forever before me 2 Sam. 7:1-5, 8b-12, 14a, 16	32	B	The mystery revealed to all Rom. 16:25-27	35	B	Annunciation to Mary Luke 1:26-38
30	C	She who is to give birth Micah 5:2-5a	33	C	Christ, coming, says: "Here I am" Heb. 10:5-10	36	C	Message to Elizabeth Luke 1:39-45

IV. The incarnation of the Word

READINGS FOR THE WEEKDAYS OF ADVENT

Day	No.	Reading	No.	Reading
Wednesday	53	The Lord is the strength of the weary — Is. 40:25-31	54	Come to me, all who are weary — Matthew 11:28-30
Thursday	55	The redeemer, the Holy One of Israel — Is. 41:13-20	56	John the Baptist, greatest of the prophets — Matthew 11:11-15
Friday	57	Observing the commandments — Is. 48:17-19	58	They listen neither to John nor to the Son — Matthew 11:16-19
Saturday	59	Elias will return[70] — Sir. 48:1-3, 9-11	60	Elias has come and not been recognized — Matthew 17:10-13
3. Monday	61	A star rises out of Jacob — Num. 24:2-7, 15-17a	62	Baptism of Jesus — Matthew 21:23-27
Tuesday	63	Messianic salvation and the poor — Zeph. 3:1-2, 9-13	64	John came, and they did not believe him — Matthew 21:28-32
Wednesday	65	Let the heavens open! — Is. 45:6b-8, 18, 21b-25	66	The kingdom is present — Luke 7:19-23
Thursday	67	The Lord takes back the deserted wife — Is. 54:1-10	68	John prepares the way — Luke 7:24-30

Friday	69	The temple, a true house of prayer Is. 56:1-3a, 6-8	70	John is a lamp burning bright John 5:33-36
December 17	71	The scepter shall remain with Judah Gen. 49:2, 8-10	72	Genealogy of Jesus Matthew 1:1-17
December 18	73	A righteous shoot Jer. 23:5-8	74	Jesus, son of David, born of Mary Matthew 1:18-24
December 19	75	Birth of Samson fortold by an angel Judg. 13:2-7, 24-25a	76	Birth of John the Baptist foretold by an angel Luke 1:5-25
December 20	77	A virgin shall conceive Is. 7:10-14	78	You will conceive and give birth to a son Luke 1:26-38
December 21	79	The beloved comes from the mountains Cant. 2:8-14	80	The visitation Luke 1:39-45
December 22	81	Anna gives thanks for the birth of Samuel 1 Sam. 1:24-28	82	God has done great things for me Luke 1:46-56
December 23	83	Elias will come before the day of the Lord Mal. 3:1-4; 4:5-6	84	Birth of John the Baptist Luke 1:57-66

SCRIPTURE READINGS IN THE LITURGY OF THE HOURS

First week:

85 *Sunday:* Is. 1:1-18
    Exhortation to conversion so as to offer sacrifice. Israel has not acknowledged its God.

86 *Monday:* Is. 1:21-27; 2:1-5
    Israel is unfaithful. Sion is the center of the eschatological kingdom.

87 *Tuesday:* Is. 2:6-22; 4:2-6
    The Lord comes to judge. He will renew the world at the end of time.

88 *Wednesday:* Is. 5:1-7
    The vineyard of the Lord, who sings a song of love for his people; they must change and be converted.

89 *Thursday:* Is. 16:1-5; 17:4-5
    A kingdom of mercy is proclaimed. Sion is a refuge for the Moabites.

90 *Friday:* Is. 19:16-25
    Future conversion of the Egyptians and Assyrians.

91 *Saturday:* Is. 21:6-12
    Fall of Babylon.

Second week:

92 *Sunday:* Is. 22:8b-23
    Pride and punishment of Jerusalem and Shebna.

93 *Monday:* Is. 24:1-18
    The manifestation of the Lord on his "day."

94 *Tuesday:* Is. 24:19-25:5
    The earth quakes. Judgment and reign of Yahweh. Song of the saved.

95 *Wednesday:* Is. 25:6-26:6
    The banquet of the Lord; Moab declared a rebel. Hymn of triumph.

96 *Thursday:* Is. 26:7-21
    The judgments of the Lord. The resurrection.

97 *Friday:* Is. 27:1-13
    The Lord's vineyard. Restoration of Israel. The deserted city.

98 *Saturday:* Is. 29:1-8
    God's judgment on Jerusalem.

Third week:

99 *Sunday:* Is. 29:13-24
    Religious formalism. The Lord threat-
    ens. Salvation on the last day.

100 *Monday:* Is. 30:18-26
    Conversion of the people. Promise
    of future happiness.

101 *Tuesday:* Is. 30:27-33; 31:4-9
    Coming of the Lord and punishment
    of Assyria.

102 *Wednesday:* Is. 31:1-3; 32:1-8
    The reign of justice.

103 *Thursday:* Is. 32:15-33:6
    Restoration. Hope in the Lord.

104 *Friday:* Is. 33:7-24
    Future salvation.

Fourth week:

105 *December 17:* Is. 45:1-13
    The salvation of Israel.

106 *December 18:* Is. 46:1-13
    The Lord rejects the idols of
    Babylon.

107 *December 19:* Is. 47:1, 3b-15
    Lament over Babylon.

108 *December 20:* Is. 48:1-11
    God is sole master of the coming
    age.

109 *December 21:* Is. 48:12-21; 49:9b-13
    The new exodus.

110 *December 22:* Is. 49:14-50:1
    The restoration of Sion.

111 *December 23:* Is. 51:1-11
    Promise of salvation to the child-
    ren of Abraham.

First Week of Advent

5. WATCH AND PRAY

Vigilant waiting for the Lord

The words "vigilant waiting" capture the mood of the first Sunday of Advent. Each year the Gospel reading is a passage from the Synoptics that speaks of the last day and the need to be vigilant [7, 8, 9]. The prayers and chants chosen for this day all focus on this expectation of the Lord. The deeply meaningful and traditional entrance antiphon expresses the attitude of the entire Church on this day — a trusting, fervent prayer and a hopeful expectation that will not be disappointed: "To you, my God, I lift my soul, I trust in you; let me never come to shame. Do not let my enemies laugh at me. No one who waits for you is ever put to shame" (Ps. 25:1-3).

This song and the opening prayer in the liturgy of the word show that foremost in the Church's mind is the expectation of the last day and the judgment that it will bring. The faithful must advance courageously to meet the Lord; they are called to enter into the kingdom of heaven at the judgment. Here we have the Church's intention clearly expressed, as well as the key for interpreting the readings of the liturgy.

(A) The Lord proclaims his return. Let us be vigilant. The nations are gathering. The day is near.

The Lord's proclamation of his return for judgment, in the Gospel of St. Matthew [7], can undoubtedly give rise to a pessimism that may obscure for the listener the teaching in the other two readings. The suddenness of his coming is disturbing. And yet the perspectives opened up for us by the prophet Isaiah convey a deep sense of optimism and peace [1].

There is no real opposition between the two tonalities. The end of the world and the return of Christ are indeed sudden and calculated to arouse a certain fear. It is no less true, however, that the return presupposes a great success, namely, the gathering of the nations. Isaiah presents us with a vision of the created world being restored to unity, and this is an aspect of the judgment that is often overlooked. "The mountain of the house of the Lord shall be established as the highest of the mountains, and shall be raised above the hills; and all nations shall flow to it . . . nation shall not lift up sword against nation" (Is. 2:2, 4). The responsorial psalm likewise makes the point that the last day is the day on which we shall enter the Lord's house: "I was glad when they said to me, 'Let us go to the house of the Lord!'" (Ps. 122:1).

In this context Psalm 122 becomes first and foremost a psalm of expectation. We should advert to the broadening of perspective that such a vision of the last day effects. Individualism has been eliminated, for I shall be part of a universal gathering that embraces all the nations. A kind of moralism and an overemphasis on the particular judgment have to some extent made the Latin Church lose sight of the social aspect of the last day.

Isaiah urges us to walk in the light of the Lord. St. Paul, for his part, when warning us that the last day is close at hand, urges us to emerge from the darkness and to arm ourselves for the struggle on behalf of the light [4]. He makes his exhortation very concrete, reproaching the faithful for carousing and drunkenness, sexual excess and lust, quarreling and jealousy. The Liturgy of the Hours likewise exhorts us to be converted [85]. "The ox knows its owner, and the ass its master's crib," but Israel has not known its Lord. The important thing is, not to offer sacrifices the Lord does not want, but to be converted, to cease from evil, and to seek justice. Then the Lord will pardon us, even if our sins be like scarlet (Is. 1:1-18).

(B) We must be vigilant, since we are waiting for the Lord Jesus to manifest himself. If he comes, everything — the world and each of us — will be restored.

In the Gospel passage read on this Sunday, St. Mark does not refer to the tragic circumstances that will mark the end of time, but he does urge us to be vigilant, since we do not know precisely when the Master will come [8]. On the other hand, our attitude toward his coming is not to be one of pure fear; we must also hope for that coming and petition it with loud cries. The coming is the coming of a father; he is a potter, and we are all of us the work of his hands [2]. If we hope in him, live justly, and are mindful of him in all we do, he will come to meet us. The vision of the return is thus optimistic, even if it makes strict demands of us.

St. Paul repeats the optimistic note. God has enriched us with speech and knowledge, and the Christ who is coming will enable us to be steadfast to the end, so that he will have nothing to reproach us with on the last day [5]. This is the kind of realism that encourages us. We may be constantly searching and not allowed to settle down anywhere, but we are always under the protection of the Christ who is coming to meet us, and there is no place for anxiety.

(C) Be vigilant and ready to appear before the Son of Man. A righteous branch will spring up on the last day, a day for which we must always be ready in holiness.

Luke depicts the majestic coming of the Son of Man. He touches on the terror that the end of time will strike in men's hearts, but he evidently gives greater importance to the coming of the Son of Man in majesty on the clouds. His advice is that we look up and raise our heads, because our salvation is drawing near. The end of time is thus presented here as a necessary stage, but it points to the coming of redemption [9]. Justice will be established, Jerusalem will dwell in security, and the name given her will be "The Lord is our righteousness" [3].

Here justice is once again seen as something primarily

positive: it justifies man and builds him up rather than destroys him. St. Paul asks the Lord to establish us solidly in blameless holiness against the day when the Lord will come. He offers the same advice that he gives in his First Letter to the Corinthians [5], referring to the way we must conduct ourselves if we are to please God. He has elsewhere listed the attitudes a Christian must avoid as he keeps in mind the day of the Lord's coming [4].

Psalm 25, which provides the response for this first Sunday (C), shows us how we should pray during this time of waiting: "Make me to know thy ways, O Lord; teach me thy paths. Lead me in thy truth, and teach me, for thou art the God of my salvation." We have a shepherd to lead us: "Give ear, O Shepherd of Israel . . . thou who art enthroned upon the cherubim, shine forth. . . . Stir up thy might, and come to save us!" (Ps. 80, response for first Sunday, B).

The whole orientation of the first Sunday of Advent is thus clearly eschatological. It provides an opportunity for us to ask ourselves what place the "last day" and the meeting of the whole people of God with its Lord has in our real lives. We are challenged, not to forget our personal meeting with the Lord and the need of making ready for it, but rather to broaden our vision so as to embrace the entire world, and to set our sights on the rebuilding of that world against the day of the Lord's coming.

Such a broadening of perspective will also affect our sense of urgency with regard to conversion and a moral life. We will be able to see how our personal decisions and our efforts to live as God would have us live do not simply affect us as individuals but contribute to the reconstruction of creation as a whole. The object of our faith-inspired hope will likewise become far more vast, and we will forget the paltry expectations we cherished when we thought merely of our own narrow life.

In all this there is a theology to be found and lived by (since it is concrete in character and makes demands of us). A Christianity inspired by such a theology will be so open and all-embracing that it will force itself upon the attention of all, even those who do not yet believe but are searching. It is a theology that can also knock down the barriers that too often still separate the brothers of the Christ who came to save the world and will come again at the end of time.

Characteristics of our messianic age

The weekdays will express in greater detail the theology contained in the liturgy of the first Sunday and show us the characteristic traits of the messianic era that has begun and of our expectation of the last day.

The special signs of the hidden presence of God's reign are the cures of the blind [45, 46], the Lord's compassion for the crowds [47, 48], and the multiplication of the loaves, which symbolizes the joyous messianic banquet [41, 42]. We shall know the Lord who will reveal himself in the Son by the power of the Spirit [39, 40]. The last day will be a day on which unity is made perfect [37, 38]. In the interim period, which is that of our lives, we must do the Father's will and live righteously [43, 44].

The readings of the Old and New Testaments complement each other admirably during this first week. We must now go into the various themes a bit more fully; as we do, we shall meet numerous points that have now become more familiar to us.

Cure of the blind who believe

There can be no doubt that the real point here for us is the spiritual blindness of which physical blindness is an eloquent symbol. But as we reflect on spiritual blindness, we are once again (as in the earlier pages of this book) confronted with the problem of faith. There are two ways of attacking the problem, and they seem contradictory.

On the one hand, the cure, the light, the "knowledge," gives rise to faith. Certain "lights" that the Lord gives us through men or events or some intellectual and spiritual development or some important experience have the power to open us to faith and make us more receptive to the gift given us. The gift is an invitation to be more attentive to persons and things, to circumstances and events, and to judge them with greater circumspection. The habit of judging more spiritually the events that impinge upon us and sometimes condition our whole lives henceforth can give our faith a scope and range we would not have suspected. The search for the meaning of an event or for the place of a human being, friend or enemy, in our life is a properly Christian activity, and quite difficult to carry out. It is likely that lukewarmness in faith originates in extensive negligence or pride in the way we evaluate the circumstances and people among whom we live our lives. Expectation of the last day should arouse us to renew our sensitivity to surroundings we too often think of as dangerous or, even more often, as a burden.

But the problem has its other side, because the gift of faith is what enlightens us. Because we believe, we understand more perfectly, and our vision of the environment in which we are placed acquires a special character that we can make intelligible to the non-believer only with great difficulty. The understanding of the Christian paradox is entirely dependent on this gift of light. It is a simple fact that we more often experience this to be true than otherwise. The gift of faith opens new perspectives to the believing mind.

But are we cured because we believe, or do we believe because we are cured? There is no set, definitive answer to this question, and we must therefore be very attentive. Faith in all its dimensions is thus to the fore during the season of Advent, which is intended to be a stimulus to the faith of the Church and to faith in the Church. We can understand how in some liturgies, for example the Gallican, Advent, like Lent, was a period in which catechumens were prepared for baptism (on Epiphany). Advent is a time both of faith and of healing.

The Lord's compassion

There is a kind of theology that worries about the "precise moment" when Christ "instituted" the sacrament of the forgiveness of sins. Unfortunately those who practice such a theology are not sufficiently concerned about finding and teaching the countless passages of Scripture in which the Lord seeks out the sinner and, in response to the sinner's first cry to him, tries to convert and cure him. We have grown accustomed to a juridical conception of forgiveness and have set down conditions God must observe, although he himself set only one condition: we will be pardoned in the way that we ourselves pardon others.

Advent seems to be a good time to recall how God's mercy is not limited by my deficiencies, be they great or small, nor measured by my spiritual pulse-beat, but extends to the whole world. It becomes intelligible only when we realize that he intends a new creation that is to be formed out of our old world, which must be renewed by accepting and cooperating in its own redemption. It is to the entire people that the Lord stoops when he hears its cry; it is to the entire people that he shows the way; and at the end he will bind up his people's hurts and heal their wounds [47]. God's mercy embraces both the world and me individually. It is true enough that the Lord heals the broken hearted (Ps. 147; response for Saturday of first week), but we must not limit his mercy to our personal troubles. If he keeps them in mind — and he does — it is because our healing is part of the reconstruction of the world.

The Gospel repeats this aspect of God's mercy [48]. Jesus is fulfilling the prophecy of Isaiah, to which we have already alluded: he has mercy on the crowds and sends out his disciples to work cures. These cures in turn will be a sign that the kingdom is already here. The basic point, I think, is this: God's mercy on the Church today, on the world today, on me at this very moment, is first and foremost a sign that the reign of God is here. His mercy is a deliverance, such as is petitioned in the opening prayer for the first Saturday of

Advent: "Grant that those who call to you from the depths of their heart may be free to love you." [71] The prayer shows that God's mercy is exercised not so much to cure us as to liberate us, and that the liberation is granted not for its own sake or to make us more balanced creatures but so that we may be able to love God. These few words from a simple prayer at the beginning of the first Saturday's liturgy surely provide a remarkable approach to penance and forgiveness.

Joy at the table of the Lord

The emphasis on the multiplication of the loaves [42] and on the meal taken with the Lord at the end of time [41] is in full accord with the eschatological orientation established on the first Sunday of Advent. The opening prayer for the Wednesday celebration likewise emphasizes the eschatological aspect: "so that on the day when your Son comes, he may judge us worthy to sit at his table and receive from his hand the bread of heaven." [72]

We may leave aside the literary aspect of this prayer. (It is difficult to see how Jesus can give us the bread of heaven, since all signs will have lost their point once we are in the direct presence of Christ; it is also difficult to understand in what sense the Eucharist would continue to exist.) The important thing is the emphatic link between eating and eschatology. The salient aspect of this meal will be its joyousness. God will have taken away the veil of sorrow that covers the nations and will have wiped away the tears from all faces, Isaiah tells us. He also makes clear to us what it is that we are really hoping for: "Lo, this is our God; we have waited for him, that he might save us. This is the Lord; we have waited for him; let us be glad and rejoice in his salvation" [41].

Psalm 23, "The Lord is my shepherd," had a privileged place in the rite of Christian initiation and has been perhaps the most popular of the psalms in our time. It serves as a very apt response to the above reading from Isaiah on the first Wednesday of Advent.

Cures of the sick, multiplication of the loaves [42], and eating with the Lord on the last day [41] — these are the signs of God's reign that is already here and is still coming.

From this viewpoint, the Church's Eucharist once again acquires dimensions unknown in the narrow presentations sometimes made of this sacrament, even today. The Eucharistic celebration should awaken all these resonances in us. More than that, every Christian meal is evidently an anticipation of the messianic joy. Many monasteries, thank God, have advanced beyond the rediscovery of a rather superficial kind of "brotherhood" and have maintained the ancient tradition of the meal taken in silence and recollection and consciously linked with the joyous, eschatological Eucharistic banquet. The Eucharist is the most fraternal of meals as far as reality and depth of expression are concerned.

Revelation of the Father in the Son through the Spirit

We spoke of faith when commenting on the cure of the blind. The Father reveals himself to us lowly creatures, provided we accept his Son [40]. When we thus accept him, the Spirit acts, and we know the Father in the Son. Then the secret of the kingdom is revealed to us, a secret having to do essentially with the Trinity.

The Gospel of the first Tuesday of Advent is undoubtedly one of those best suited to help us enter more easily into the mystery of the Trinity. It speaks of God loving the world enough to send his Son as its Savior, and of the Spirit effecting in us the image of the Son who reveals the Father. Each time the Father gazes upon us he finds in us his own Son, and each time we come in contact with the Son we discover the Father. That, basically, is what it means to enter the kingdom of God, and our entry has already begun. The opening prayer of the Mass for this first Tuesday emphasizes this point: "May the presence in our midst of him who is to come give us courage." [73]

The Spirit of the Lord rests upon Christ with his gifts of

wisdom, understanding, and counsel, and the same Spirit
rests upon us. This same text of Isaiah [39] is used in the
rite of confirmation at the moment when the laying on of
hands symbolizes the coming of the Spirit upon us. We are
thus committed to help bring about the definitive reign of
God, wherein we shall live in the company of Father, Son,
and Spirit, sharing their Trinitarian life.

Unity restored

Here we can observe once again that the focus of this first
week is eschatological, for in these readings we are bidden
to contemplate the unity that the world will possess when it
is reconstructed.

This is another of the very meaningful themes of Advent.
Unity is indeed a basic thrust of Christianity: unity between the elements of the world, unity between us and
them, unity within ourselves, unity with other men, and,
above all, unity with God. Unity is also an object of Christian hope. Yet how petty and narrow our view of the purposes of human life too often is! There is no doubt, of
course, that our salvation is important, but are we justified
in concentrating on it apart from its proper context? Is it
really possible to conceive of a salvation that is separable
from the restored unity of the world as a whole? Our hope,
then, must be essentially missionary, and any concern for
personal salvation must be incomplete and even illegiti-
mate if it is not accompanied by concern for the salvation of
other people in the world. In this regard, Advent proves
once again to be a fine school of Christian formation and a
basis for broadening the perspectives that guide such a
formation.

We should note that in the Gospel for the first Monday of
Advent [38] Christ once again uses the image of the messianic banquet. And he sees even pagans seated at God's
table in the kingdom! Here is indeed a single vision of the
world and salvation, and one to which the Advent season
should make us receptive.

The will of the Father

These various considerations cannot remain a matter of merely passive contemplation; we must also do the Father's will. The opening prayer for Thursday of this first week suggests a point with which we are not very familiar; it emphasizes the social aspect of salvation and our responsibility for it: "Support us by your power so that the salvation that our sins have delayed may be hastened by your merciful grace."[74] We are hardly accustomed to think of salvation as being delayed by our faults!

The responsorial psalm for this same day echoes the reading from Isaiah [43] by using Psalm 118, "His steadfast love endures for ever!" It is upon this love that we must rely, and not on men, for the Lord is able to bring the just into his kingdom and give them victory and salvation.

Entry into the kingdom has a prerequisite: we must do the Father's will. If we are to enter the kingdom, it is not enough to call upon the Lord's name; we must also live as he bids us live. If we hear this word and put it into practice, we act as prudent men who build their houses on a solid foundation [44]. Thus does Jesus speak to us in the Gospel for this first Thursday. The activity that should fill the time of waiting is the doing of the Father's will.

Overview

The Eucharistic liturgies throughout the first week, along with the readings from the Liturgy of the Hours, provide us with very important indications as to how we are to understand and live the first stage of Advent. Let us try to summarize and synthesize these indications in a few words.

The whole of this first week is focused on the end of time and the return of Christ on the last day. We must be vigilant [7, 8, 9]. But this vigilant waiting is not passive. The day is close at hand, and we must do the Father's will by living a life based on love of the Lord and on righteousness [4, 5, 6, 43, 44]. The readings in the Liturgy of the Hours lay a heavy emphasis on conversion [85, 88, 89, 90], especially in the splendid canticle of the vineyard [88]. Conversion is rightly shown to be essential, and far more important than the offering of sacrifices [85]. The emphasis is meant to put us on guard against falling back (as we easily can) into a ritualism that would excuse us from living the true Christian life of love. A Christian must do more than "practice"; he must truly *be* a Christian.

Our Christian life of waiting is entirely concentrated on one object: the Lord's return to gather his people. The perspective that controls our lives, our searching, and our action is therefore broad indeed, for we disdain religious egocentrism and embrace the entire world. To reach the goal is beyond our unaided powers, and we can achieve it only through faith: a faith that is stimulated in us by the light God bestows upon us through men and events, but also a faith that in turn enables us to judge events as God himself does [45, 46].

The light and the grace to advance on the paths that lead to Christ's return have been given us by a merciful God. His compassion embraces each of us and the world in its entirety, since it is the world as a whole that is to reach a state of righteousness and peace [47, 48]. In faith and by the limitless mercy of God, we are able to know the Father even now, for the Son reveals him to us through the Spirit [39, 40].

As we move toward the last day, fortified by the signs that proclaim the presence of the kingdom among us, we glimpse the era of justice and peace [3, 43] that lies ahead. Sion is the center of this eschatological expectation [86]; we know that all of creation will be restored to the unity that God originally intended. That is how God wins his victory over evil [1, 37, 38, 87].

Here and now, while we are still on earth, we know that we already have pledges of the reality to come. The cure of the blind — ourselves! — the multiplication of the loaves, and the Eucharist are signs of the eschatological banquet that we already celebrate with joy as an efficacious symbol of the gathering that will take place on the last day [41, 42].

Second Week of Advent

6. PREPARE THE WAY

The Gospels chosen for the second Sunday of Advent all have as their theme the preparation of the way of the Lord [16, 17, 18]. John's urgent warning has echoed throughout the world ever since he spoke it, and as it reaches us today it has a twofold reference: prepare for the Lord's coming at Christmas, but prepare also for his return on the last day. The opening prayer of this Sunday can be understood as referring to both comings, but if we set it alongside the other prayers of the day and the readings, it is in fact more concerned with the Lord's return. "Let not our preoccupation with present tasks hinder us from going to meet your Son, but give us an understanding heart that will prepare us to welcome him and enter into his life." [75]

If we look closely, we will see that the first part of this prayer looks to the parousia, while the second is concerned rather with Christ's coming in the flesh, where we can meet him and share his life through the sacraments.

The entrance antiphon, on the other hand, though it too can be referred to either coming, is readily understood of the saving incarnation of the World: "People of Zion, the Lord will come to save all nations, and your hearts will exult to hear his majestic voice" (Is. 30:19, 30).

(A) Prepare the way for the Lord. The Spirit is upon him, and in him the promises are fulfilled.

The voice crying in the desert will echo until the end of time [16], since conversion will always be necessary, and the work of conversion will never be finished. It is not enough to belong to a Christian people, just as it was not enough to have Abraham for a father. We must produce the fruits in which conversion finds expression. This conversion leading to the forgiveness of sins is closely connected with baptism: both the baptism of John, which led to conversion, and the baptism of Christ, which is a baptism in fire and the Spirit, giving a divine rebirth and gathering together the people of God.

John uses uncompromising words to emphasize the need of conversion and of purifying baptism: "His winnowing fork is in his hand, and he will clear his threshing floor and gather his wheat into the granary, but the chaff he will burn with unquenchable fire" [16].

The image is harsh, its meaning inescapable; it is difficult simply to ignore John's warning and close one's ears. Preparing the way for the Lord requires a constant effort at conversion: "Even now the axe is laid to the root of the trees; every tree therefore that does not bear good fruit is cut down and thrown into the fire."

But what is involved in "being converted"? St. Paul suggests the starting point of every conversion: the patient courage to live in harmony with one another according to the spirit of Christ Jesus [13]. That was the point Paul emphasized in a Church that was still new and very young. He was speaking of a love that is open and in accordance with the spirit of Christ; we are to accept one another as we ourselves have been accepted by Christ. Starting with that, we can go on to achieve a second objective of our conversion: the possibility of giving glory to God, that is, of finding the essential motive for the creation of the world and of man. Christ, who came as a servant, guarantees the fulfillment of the promise made to the patriarchs: that, because God is merciful, even the pagan nations, once converted, will be able to glorify God. Conversion means we are able to sing to the Lord: "I will praise thee among the Gentiles, and sing to thy name" [13].

Jesus is, then, according to Romans, the guarantor of our salvation, that is, of our ability to give glory to the Father. That is our hope, and we go forward sustained by the lessons of patience and words of encouragement found in the Scriptures. We hope for the salvation of all men, that is, that all will be made capable of glorifying God.

We can see here why the sacrament of penance is an act of worship. As an efficacious sign of conversion, it is thereby a hymn of praise to God for his mercy in sending his Son, who has accomplished the work of our salvation by making us capable of praising the glory of God. Conversion, then, is not only a cure and the regaining of a certain psychological balance; it gives, above all, the possibility of taking our place once again in the concert of praise that rises from creation to the glory of the Father.

He who makes possible the conversion of the world and of man is the Messiah upon whom the Spirit of the Lord rests: "Righteousness shall be the girdle of his waist, and faithfulness the girdle of his loins" [10]. Singled out by the Spirit of the Lord for the bestowal of his gifts of wisdom and understanding, counsel and strength, knowledge and fear of the Lord, the Messiah will restore justice and unite the world. The passage is a poem on the "golden age"; we commented on it, from this point of view, in Chapter 3. The responsorial psalm (Ps. 72) expresses a wish for the Messiah: "May his name endure for ever, his fame continue as long as the sun! May men bless themselves by him, all nations call him blessed!"

Despite external appearances, we are already living, through faith, in this golden age, which has already begun. But appearances are our problem! How can we see the golden age in a world that is adrift, a world in which virtue and vice are so mingled? We can only respond by pointing to the fact that the Good News is being preached to the poor, the blind see, and the dead rise — since the Church accomplishes all these miracles in the spiritual order. The outlook of faith and a hope grounded in faith — these alone can enable us to see the presence of the golden age in its beginnings. Advent is the season of Christian optimism.

(B) To prepare the way is to prepare for a new world, a new earth.

The Good News of Jesus Christ, the Son of God, begins,

in St. Mark's Gospel, with the exhortation of John the Baptist: "Prepare the way of the Lord, make his paths straight" [17].

The Good News is thus the news of our conversion and the possibility of our meeting the Lord as he comes. John the Baptist was simply repeating the words of the prophet Isaiah: "Every valley shall be lifted up, and every mountain and hill be made low; the uneven ground shall become level, and the rough places a plain. And the glory of the Lord shall be revealed, and all flesh shall see it together, for the mouth of the Lord has spoken" [11].

Every Christian, by his conversion, is a preacher of the Good News of the Lord who comes and gathers his sheep. It is Good News for us as it was for Jerusalem, because our sins are forgiven and we have received double punishment at the Lord's hand for all our faults [11].

The Lord wishes that we all be converted, but we must also make the effort to be worthy preachers of a new earth. And even though the Lord does not consent to the loss of some but wills that all have the opportunity for conversion, he will come nonetheless like a thief. Such is the teaching of St. Peter, who follows in this the teaching of the Gospels [14]. Peter is aware that a new heaven and a new earth are coming, but his concern is to remind us of what such a renewal requires of us: "what sort of persons ought you to be in lives of holiness and godliness, waiting for and hastening the coming of the day of God. . . . Therefore, beloved, since you wait for these, be zealous to be found by him without spot or blemish, and at peace."

(C) See the salvation of God, don the cloak of justice, and wear the mitre of glory.

When we read the third set of texts for the second Sunday, it is hard not to feel that, while charming, they foster illusions and seek to lull us in distress by softening the pain of suffering. It would, of course, be blasphemous to agree that this impression is justified. Our real problem is that we have difficulty in believing what lies ahead for us: that all mankind shall see the salvation of God, once the crooked ways have been made straight [18].

Baruch's prophecy, however, goes beyond this rather general statement, and we may well find it amazing. He shows us the Church at the end of time clad in God's own splendor, wrapped in the cloak of justice that comes from him, and wearing on her head the mitre that displays the glory of the eternal name. Jerusalem is told to look and see her children being gathered, from east to west, by the word of the holy God. We should read this entire poem of Baruch, which describes the victory of Jerusalem and Israel. It is encouraging. In fact, it may even stir in us a kind of triumphalism. That is a temptation that the Church, as we know, has not always resisted. But to yield to it would be to show that we had not grasped the difficult road the people of God must travel in order to reach the Day of Christ.

St. Paul, addressing the Philippians and now us, does not hide the problems and difficulties the Christian must face [15]. Yet he is not pessimistic but finds that the work has been well begun by God himself, who will bring it to completion. Each of us, however, must do his part and make continual progress in true understanding and in that clarity of mind that enables us "to approve what is excellent."

The last admonition of St. Paul is astonishingly relevant today. At a time when the world is being renewed, and when one civilization is coming to an end and another, it seems, is beginning, we are well aware that it is no simple matter to discern what is really important as we live our lives. And yet it is absolutely necessary that we advance upright and without stumbling toward the Day of Christ. The problem of our age is to acquire a right vision of reality, so that we can hold on to the essential without imperiling it by an imprudent neglect of the secondary; this is a burning issue in the world today. To draw back from the problem is to condemn ourselves to mediocrity and even to death. We must take the risk, but we must make sure that in taking it we are guided by a higher vision of what is necessary. The crisis now facing institutions can be summed up as the task of choosing what is most important. Today's task is to refuse to get trapped in the past, while also refusing to jettison secondary things that are so interwoven with the essentials that they cannot be separated without infinite patience. Experience has already shown that impatience and getting bogged down in the past are alike the result of a lack of deep faith and of a blindness that refuses to see that everything in this world, even the most traditional institutions, has meaning only with reference to what will abide when the Day of Christ has come [15].

John the Baptist, greatest of men

The readings of the season have brought us into continual contact with the personality of Isaiah the prophet. Now, on the second Thursday, we hear Jesus speaking of John the Baptist as the greatest among men [56]. The Gospel for this day sings the praises of the Precursor. But Christ then goes a step further and speaks of the children of God's kingdom as superbeings: "he who is least in the kingdom of heaven is greater than he [John]." And yet only the violent will be part of that kingdom!

Isaiah seeks to give us a foretaste of this kingdom of heaven by his description of the restoration of the world: "I will make the wilderness a pool of water, and the dry land springs of water. . . . I will set in the desert the cypress, the plane and the pine together; that men may see and know, may consider and understand together, that the hand of the Lord has done this, the Holy One of Israel has created it" [55].

Psalm 145 sings of these great deeds of the Lord in response to the reading of the prophecy of Isaiah: "All thy works shall give thanks to thee, O Lord, and all thy saints shall bless thee! They shall speak of the glory of thy kingdom, and tell of thy power."

Elijah has come, but they have not recognized him

In the Gospel for the second Thursday, Christ said: "If you are willing to accept it, he [John] is Elijah who is to come" [56]. The Gospel of the second Saturday picks up this theme. John had been imprisoned and has now been beheaded. The disciples inquire of Jesus concerning the coming of Elijah, who is to precede the Messiah. Jesus' answer is clear: Elijah has already come in the person of John the Baptist, but they failed to recognize him, just as they will fail to recognize in Jesus the suffering Messiah [60].

The Book of Sirach the sage foretold the coming of Elijah at the end of time; in so doing, it was repeating what had already been written. Elijah's function would be "to turn the heart of the father to the son, and to restore the tribes of Jacob" [59]. In other words, he was to unify men.

The failure to recognize Elijah's coming is a permanent lesson for us, and a hard one. More frequently than we think, God comes to us through things and events, in order that he might restore the world. Recognizing and accepting these "prophecies" is no simple matter, since there are so many false prophecies around today. The criterion by which we will recognize them is, of course, their fruits.

The strength of the weary

Expectation is always long, even if life is short, because waiting is made up of suffering and contradictions. That is the experience of each of us, and that will be the world's experience until the moment of its definitive meeting with the Lord on the last day. It is difficult not to be sluggish; sluggishness seems quite legitimate, being part of human life, stuck to it like a vile garment. And yet faith can completely eliminate the glumness from our lives. Many of the Scripture texts read on the weekdays of this second week call our attention to the presence of God at our side as we pursue our difficult way under skies that are often overcast.

The Lord is coming to save us: "Be strong, fear not! Behold, your God. . . . He will come and save you" [49]. The world will at last be made one with the unity God wants, and our efforts will prove not to have been in vain. Psalm 85, which supplies the response to the above reading of Isaiah on the second Monday, voices the joy a man experiences when he waits calmly in faith: "Yes, the Lord will give what is good, and our land will yield its increase. Righteousness will go before him, and make his footsteps a way."

In addition, Jesus is not niggardly with his wonders. The cures he effects are connected with the forgiveness of sins, for he has within himself the very power of God. The paralytic has his sins forgiven and walks, and everyone praises God: "We have seen strange things today" [50]. This cry is not an exclamation proper only to the past; it can well be ours today, and in fact it should be ours. Is there any truly believing Catholic who has not seen, through faith-enlightened eyes, things really extraordinary: healings of the soul, unexpected transformations of people we thought lost, miracles of friendship in God, limitless charity for the wretched of the world, complete and life-long commitments to God and one's fellows? We do see extraordinary things that are signs of the kingdom already present and signs that we are advancing toward the great meeting with Christ. Such things are the joys the life of faith brings.

A despairing spirit of criticism is abroad in our day and has "seen through" all the enthusiasms. Everything has been dirtied: religious life, married life, any life of commitment. Criticism that is wholly negative has discredited everything pure. There are people whose greatest talent is to leave dirty marks on all the white things they touch. In the process, a wellspring of strength has dried up. The past was indeed not perfect, but it showed tremendous energy and deserves to be praised for it. It is the easiest thing in the world to laugh at past and present, but in doing so we close eyes that might have seen extraordinary things. The proud have had their momentary triumph. But have they not often been soon confounded?

God, who comes to renew mankind [51], does not want his little ones to be lost, and so he watches over them and leads them as a shepherd does his flock [52]. He is present to help the afflicted [54] and the weary [53]. True enough the words of Christ sometimes sound like idle poetry: "My yoke is easy and my burden is light," but that is because only the ears of faith can understand them. Nonetheless, they are addressed to all of us — just as we are. At moments when we are tempted to give up, we should repeat these words of Christ over and over, like an obsessive melody. If we do, they will, through faith, effect in us what they signify. For even if depression is a psycho-physical fact, it also originates in the fear of commiting ourselves unreservedly to the life of faith. Making ourselves drunk on these words of Christ might be the best remedy for our depression and the strongest stimulus to stride forward with the Church as she advances toward her Lord.

They listen neither to John nor to the Son

They did not see that Elijah had come in the person of John, nor did they recognize the Son when he came. "For John came neither eating nor drinking, and they say, 'He has a demon'; the Son of man came eating and drinking, and they say, 'Behold, a glutton and a drunkard, a friend of tax collectors and sinners!'" [58].

It is easy to find specious reasons for rejecting God's messengers and refusing to face the questions they put to us. Entire generations of Christians have chosen this alternative, building a wall of pretexts lest they see and hear and understand. The present generation wants to avoid this kind of hypocrisy that shelters behind tradition as a way of avoiding all questions. Will it succeed? Yes, to the extent that in the questions it asks it is not simply looking for itself; to the extent that it does not decide on its own what the questions are to be, thus unwittingly assuring that it will find only itself, but accepts the questions God wants to ask.

There is a kind of snobbery possible when it comes to problems (especially false problems!), and it is easy to fool ourselves in this matter. We think we are looking for objective solutions, but we are really standing before a mirror and indulging in a spiritual narcissism that is hard to cure because it springs from what is blindest and more irradicable in us: egotism and pride.

And yet the Gospel of the second Friday tells us, for our joy, that God's wisdom is revealed precisely by what he does.

If we wish to hear and answer the questions God puts to us, we need but follow a modest, yet difficult method: *obey his commandments* [57]. Perhaps because of the narrow way in which the commandments are often presented to us, we mistakenly think of Isaiah's advice as mere moralism, as though the commandments were not meant to be the work of love and the way to build up and restore both man and his world. We often look at the commandments through the wrong end of the telescope and with a feeling that we are humiliating ourselves, theologically, by focusing our attention on them. Perhaps, however, concentration on the commandments will be the beginning of a lowly journey on which we will learn to see the true meaning of the things of this world and to acquire a love of what is eternal (see the prayer after Communion on the second Friday of Advent).

Overview

The second week of Advent is still focused in good measure on the last days. All the Communion antiphons, except for Monday's, should be interpreted as referring to the second coming of Christ, which has already begun for us through our reception of the Eucharist. It is to be expected that Communion antiphons generally should relate in a special way to the parousia. Take for example the antiphon for Saturday of this second week: "I am coming quickly, says the Lord, and will repay each man according to his deeds." Or the Friday antiphon: "We are waiting for our Savior, the Lord Jesus Christ; he will transfigure our lowly bodies into copies of his own glorious body."

The opening prayers of this week's Masses, on the contrary, are not thus clearly oriented to the second coming. Those of Monday and Tuesday clearly have the incarnation in view: "Lord, free us from our sins and make us whole. Hear our prayer, and prepare us to celebrate the incarnation of your Son" (Monday). The opening prayers on the other days can be understood as referring to both comings. "All-powerful Father, we await the healing power of Christ your Son. Let us not be discouraged by our weaknesses as we prepare for his coming" (Wednesday).

The readings, however, as we have already seen, focus on the expectation of the last day. The Scripture readings in the Liturgy of the Hours for the second week have likewise been chosen solely with the second coming in mind: manifestation of the Lord on the last day [93], quaking of the earth and reign of the Lord [94], banquet with the Lord and victory song [95], judgment of the Lord [96, 98], resurrection [96], and gathering at Jerusalem [97]. All these passages immediately turn our thoughts to Christ's return.

If we go back now to the readings at Mass during the second week, we find that they adopt the same perspective and are concerned to show us how we should wait for the return of Christ. We are to try to recognize and accept the comings of the Lord in the person of his messengers and to listen to them [59, 60; 58]. To accept these comings means concretely to fall in with the plan of reconstruction they offer us [57]. The Lord's will is our source of strength [50, 53, 54]; in his work of renewing the world he passes over no one, not even the lowly [52].

Isaiah, a model for those who wait

The readings for Advent have brought us into frequent contact with Isaiah. It will be worth our while to reflect briefly on his personality.

The Gospels say nothing directly about Isaiah as a person, but they do cite him, and we may glimpse his presence in the mind and even on the lips of Christ. He is the great prophet of the time of waiting; he is surprisingly close to us, he is one of us, a man of today. What makes him this is his longing for deliverance and his desire for the absolute, that is, for God. He belongs to us by the implacable logic of his life, which is a life of struggle and combat. He is of our time by his literary art, in which our century can see reflected its own preference for images that are bare yet powerful to the point of being harsh. He is one of the violent to whom Christ has promised the kingdom of God. No obstacle can halt this visionary gripped by the splendor of the future kingdom that a prince of peace and justice will inaugurate. In Isaiah we find the serene, unshakable power of a man who is possessed by the Spirit, a man who has no choice but to proclaim what the Lord tells him, even if the proclamation goes against his own grain.

This prophet is hardly known to us except through his actions, but these are so characteristic that through them we glimpse and love him as a person. How amazingly close to us is this figure from the eighth century B.C.! He seems to be part of our daily lives, though as one whose spiritual stature makes him tower over the rest of us.

Isaiah lived in a brilliant and prosperous age. Rarely had the kingdoms of Judah and Samaria felt so optimistic, for their political stability allowed them to dream ambitious dreams. Men of religious conviction attributed this political good fortune to God; their very religion led them to expect that success would be unbroken. Then the bubble of happiness burst, as Isaiah came forward courageously to carry out his mission of showing the people the disaster that lay ahead, brought on by their own negligence.

Isaiah probably belonged to the aristocracy of Jerusalem. His mind was shaped by the writings of his predecessors, especially Amos and Hosea. God inspired him, like them, with a prevision of what his nation's history was to be. He looked beyond the present sitaution, with all its criminality and compromises, and saw the coming chastisement that would once again make the crooked ways straight.

Lods writes of the prophets: "Thinking perhaps that they were calling for a return to the past, they in fact made a gigantic leap forward. These reactionaries were also revolutionaries."[76] Such a one was Isaiah, on whom the Lord laid his hand "in the year King Uzziah died," that is, around 740, and whose lips the Lord purified in the temple with an ember broght by a seraph (Is. 6:1-3). From that moment on, Isaiah was no longer his own man. This did not mean that he became a purely passive instrument in the hands of Yahweh; on the contrary, his every power was put at the service of his God, whose messenger he became. But in this case the messenger roused terror, for he told how Israel would be stripped naked and left barely alive.

Isaiah's early prophecies (one of which has given us the background for the ox and the ass at the crib of Jesus) showed what his thinking and his role were to be. He tells his people that while Yahweh wishes to be everything to his people, Israel ignores that God and proves itself far more stupid than the ox, which at least recognizes the cowman who cares for it. "Hear, O heavens, and give ear, O earth; for the Lord has spoken: 'Sons have I reared and brought up, but they have rebelled against me. The ox knows its owner, and the ass its master's crib; but Israel does not know, my people does not understand'" (Is. 1:2-3).

Then the prophet's curse is uttered:

> Ah, sinful nation, a people laden with iniquity, off-spring of evildoers, sons who deal corruptly! They have forsaken the Lord, they have despised the Holy One of Israel, they are utterly estranged. Why will you still be smitten, that you continue to rebel? The whole head is sick, and the whole heart faint. From the sole of the foot even to the head, there is no soundness in it, but bruises and sores and bleeding wounds; they are not pressed out, or bound up, or softened with oil. Your country lies desolate, your cities

are burned with fire; in your very presence aliens devour your land; it is desolate, as overthrown by aliens. And the daughter of Zion is left like a booth in a vineyard, like a lodge in a cucumber field, like a besieged city. If the Lord of hosts had not left us a few survivors, we should have been like Sodom, and become like Gomorrah (Is. 1:4-9).

A virgin shall bear a child

But Isaiah did not confine himself to the role of preacher of morality. Instead, he became for all generations the great prophet of the parousia, of Yahweh's coming. As Amos had risen up to protest the lust for domination that had been stimulated by the flourishing economic situation of Judah and Samaria in the eighth century, so Isaiah predicted the disaster that the day of Yahweh would bring (Is. 2:1-17). The day of Yahweh was to be a day of judgment upon Israel. In Isaiah's view, as later in Paul's and John's, the coming of the Lord would mean the triumph of true justice.

Chapters 7 to 11 describe for us the prince who would rule in peace and justice. In chapter 7 there is an extremely important passage:

Again the Lord spoke to Ahaz, "Ask a sign of the Lord your God; let it be deep as Sheol or high as heaven." But Ahaz said, "I will not ask, and I will not put the Lord to the test." And he said, "Hear then, O house of David! Is it too little for you to weary men, that you weary my God also? Therefore the Lord himself will give you a sign. Behold, a young woman [a virgin] shall conceive and bear a son, and shall call his name Immanu-el. He shall eat curds and honey when he knows how to refuse the evil and choose the good. For before the child knows how to refuse the evil and choose the good, the land before whose two kings you are in dread will be deserted. The Lord will bring upon you and upon your people and upon your father's house such days as have not come since the day that Ephraim departed from Judah — the king of Assyria" (Is. 7:10-17).

It is important that we familiarize ourselves with the twofold meaning of this text. For unless we grasp the ambiguous reality of which it speaks, we shall always be unable to understand the Scriptures, including certain passages of the Gospel, and to experience the full impact of the liturgy. The Gospel for the first Sunday of Advent, which deals with the two perspectives of Advent — the end of the world and the parousia — is an example of the same specifically biblical phenomenon in which one and the same event points to two different realities.

The kingdom of Judah must undergo devastation and ruin. The contemptuous infidelity of King Ahaz must be punished. Nevertheless, God's promise to David by the mouth of Nathan the prophet will not be cancelled out. The sign given to Ahaz and the house of David is the certain destruction to come upon Jerusalem and the royal dynasty. But Yahweh will remain true to his word; and "Emmanuel" will indeed bless Israel with his presence. In the meantime, however, the sign given to Ahaz will have long been fulfilled in the destruction of his house and kingdom.

The golden age

Moreover, the literary form of the oracle and the manner in which Isaiah speaks of the birth and early years of this child, hint to us that the prophet is looking beyond the political situation of his time and seeing the child as one who will save the entire world. In later oracles Isaiah will describe the characteristics of this Messiah. Here he is content simply to note them incidentally, reserving their detailed description for later. Here is how he describes this just king:

> There shall come forth a shoot from the stump of Jesse, and a branch shall grow out of his roots. And the Spirit of the Lord shall rest upon him, the spirit of

wisdom and understanding, the spirit of counsel and might, the spirit of knowledge and the fear of the Lord. And his delight shall be in the fear of the Lord. He shall not judge by what his eyes see, or decide by what his ears hear; but with righteousness he shall judge the poor, and decide with equity for the meek of the earth; and he shall smite the earth with the rod of his mouth, and with the breath of his lips he shall slay the wicked. Righteousness shall be the girdle of his waist, and faithfulness the girdle of his loins. The wolf shall dwell with the lamb, and the leopard shall lie down with the kid, and the calf and the lion and the fatling together, and a little child shall lead them. The cow and the bear shall feed; their young shall lie down together; and the lion shall eat straw like the ox. The sucking child shall play over the hole of the asp, and the weaned child shall put his hand on the adder's den. They shall not hurt or destroy in all my holy mountain; for the earth shall be full of the knowledge of the Lord as the waters cover the sea (Is. 11:1-9).

In the past, the attribution of this passage to Isaiah was called into question, but no one today openly challenges its authenticity. The reader will, of course, have recognized it as the source of the traditional doctrine of the seven gifts of the Holy Spirit.

The prophecy describes the ideal judge, who is also a warrior, a priest, and a prophet. The restoration of justice and order turns a world of strife into a true earthly paradise, in which beasts we know as ferocious live side by side with the meeker animals. The prince of justice reconstitutes the unity that had been lost.

Here again, a twofold interpretation may be called for. Ezechias is about to take the throne, and the poem is written — if we are to believe certain critics — in praise of him. But how can a weak human being possess so many eminent qualities? Is Isaiah not seeing here, behind Ezechias, the figure of the Messiah? That, at least, is how the Church understands the passage; she assigns the reading to the second Sunday of Advent (A).

We have already heard Isaiah, in the second chapter of his book, prophesying a parousia that would also be a judgment. In chapter 13 he describes the fall of Babylon when it was captured by Cyrus. Once again, we are invited to look beyond this historical event to the coming of Yahweh on his "day." The description of the cataclysms that will occur are repeated by Joel and again in the Apocalypse.

> Behold, the day of the Lord comes, cruel, with wrath and fierce anger, to make the earth a desolation and to destroy its sinners from it. For the stars of the heavens and their constellations will not give their light; the sun will be dark at its rising and the moon will not shed its light. I will punish the world for its evil, and the wicked for their iniquity; I will put an end to the pride of the arrogant, and lay low the haughtiness of the ruthless (Is. 13:9-11).

At his coming Yahweh will crush the one who had willed to become God's equal (Is. 14). St. John, in his Apocalypse, will use similar images to describe the overthrow of the devil.

Beginning on Monday of the second week of Advent, the Church has us read lengthy passages from the "Apocalypse" of Isaiah (cc. 24-27) in the Office of Readings. Modern critics propose that these chapters did not come from Isaiah; the poems, however, are certainly expressive of his outlook. They depict the day of Yahweh and the parousia; that is why the Church reads them during this season. The overall choice of readings from Isaiah is a further proof that the liturgy of Advent is concerned with the two comings of Christ, for the readings are sometimes from the passages on Emmanuel, sometimes from those that speak of the parousia.

At Mass on the third Sunday of Advent (A), we find Isaiah

describing the coming of Yahweh: "The burning sand shall become a pool and the thirsty ground springs of water" (35:7). We see here a reference to the curse that had come upon creation as the result of man's sin (Genesis). Yahweh is coming, however, and will restore everything to its proper form. At the same time Isaiah foretells the healings that Jesus will use as a way of proclaiming God's reign: "Then the eyes of the blind shall be opened, and the ears of the deaf unstopped; then shall the lame man leap like a hart, and the tongue of the dumb sing for joy" (35:5-6). Jesus will allude to this passage when he sends the messengers back to John in prison [25].

We can summarize the whole of the prophet's work by relating it to two objectives. The first was to deal with a present historical situation, by struggling against it and by providing a remedy for it. That very remedy necessarily involved his second objective: the more distant messianic future and the restoration of men to Yahweh's good grace. Isaiah comes before us as the messenger of a God whom he has seen face to face. As though hypnotized by this God, Isaiah speaks of him in every line he writes. Yet his very descriptions also bring home to us the fact that Yahweh is the Holy One, the one who is apart from us, and the one whom, therefore, we cannot fully understand. He is the one who refuses to let us know him. Or, more accurately, we can know him only through his works, which concentrate above all on holiness or justice. To establish justice, Yahweh intervenes constantly in the course of history. The prophet may give a literary form to his description of these interventions, but they are nonetheless really historical, both in fact and in the prophet's conception of them. At the same time, however, as we read Isaiah we are constantly looking beyond the historical interventions of God to the coming age of the Messiah.

How attractive a person Isaiah is: a man awed by the greatness of his God, a man convinced that God is constantly intervening in his creation through specific, historical, even contemporary actions, yet also a man who has his mind fixed on the greatest of all these interventions, the final realization of the divine redemptive plan in the Messiah.

The Messiah will be born of a woman and thus be part of the dynasty of David, as Matthew reminds us at the beginning of his Gospel. But the Messiah's coming is not the end. Isaiah bids us look beyond him to the Day of Yahweh, a day that is all-decisive and terrible for man, yet also a day of justice and peace when the world will find itself once again ordered and at one with its Maker.

Thus we find in Isaiah the two great perspectives of the Advent season and liturgy.

Third Week of Advent

7. THE MESSIANIC AGE

The third Sunday of Advent has traditionally been marked by the note of joy. As we shall see, the joy has two causes: the proximate coming of the Lord in the incarnation and his return at the end of time. The opening prayer for this Sunday speaks of "your people, who look forward to the birthday of Christ," while the opening prayer for Wednesday of this week asks: "May the coming celebration of the birth of your Son bring us your saving help." In fact, the prayers on the whole are clearly inspired by joyful expectation of the Nativity. Moreover, this week thinks of the kingdom as already present [66].

(A) God is coming to save us; his coming is at hand; the cures are signs of his presence.

The cures in the Gospels are always presented as signs of the messianic age. This point is emphasized in both the first reading [19] and the Gospel [25] for this third Sunday. The focus is on the presence now of the messianic age. Nothing could be simpler or more impressive than the answer Jesus gives to the messengers sent by John the Baptist; both John and his messengers are, of course, well aware of Isaiah's prophecy [19]. As we observed earlier, the capacity we now have for seeing, understanding, and living a new kind of life is a sign that God's reign has begun and that we now await its definitive establishment in us and the world.

St. James exhorts us to patience as we wait for the day not too far distant when God's kingdom will be fully established [22]. He compares the patience we must have to that of a farmer. Like him, we plant the seed and then must await the harvest. The exhortation is one by now familiar to us: Wait in patience and mutual love. Christian hope is compounded of patience and love, and St. James offers us as a model the sufferings and persevering patience of the prophets.

(B) In our midst is one we do not recognize. Rejoice in the presence of him who bears the Spirit's mark.

After identifying himself in a negative way, John the Baptist directs his hearers' attention to one who is among his people but unrecognized by them: "Among you stands one whom you do not know, even he who comes after me, the thong of whose sandal I am not worthy to untie" [26]. Observe that John denies that he is Elias, and yet Christ says that John was indeed Elias but no one recognized him [56]. The presence of the Messiah makes conversion necessary so that a man may enter the kingdom that is now here.

Isaiah foretells the coming of the Messiah and gives us an attractive picture of this man whom the Spirit has consecrated [20]. The one on whom the Spirit rests will preach the Good News to the poor and heal the brokenhearted. He will establish justice in the presence of all the nations. We have already had occasion to emphasize these characteristic traits of the Messiah. The new element on this third Sunday, the element that gives the day its special tone, is the joy that fills him who has been sent to proclaim salvation: "I will greatly rejoice in the Lord, my soul shall exult in my God; for he has clothed me with the garments of salvation, he has covered me with the robe of righteousness" [20].

This poem of Isaiah evidently parallels the *Magnificat* of the Blessed Virgin. The Church therefore uses the latter as a responsorial psalm after the reading from Isaiah: "My soul magnifies the Lord, and my spirit rejoices in God my Savior."

St. Paul, in his First Letter to the Thessalonians, gives advice on how we are to await the Lord's coming. Three things, he says, are essential: joy, constant prayer, and thanksgiving in all circumstances. These are what should basically characterize the life of the Christian. But there is another virtue that is extremely important: not to quench the Spirit. This means not to grow content, even with our joy or prayer or thanksgiving, but to be flexible enough to accept the questions raised by a brother whom the Spirit has moved. In all things, however, we must exercise discernment.

There is a thought that will prove very strengthening to us as we wait. It is that the God who calls us is faithful and will do all that he has promised.

(C) A mightier than John the Baptist is coming. Rejoice, for he is here! Now is the time of brotherhood and justice.

As soon as they realized that the messianic age was at hand, all — crowds, tax collectors, soldiers — had to ask themselves: "What then shall we do?" [27]. The same question arises at times in our own minds: "What ought we to do?" Unfortunately, the question, as we ask it, refers too exclusively to practices that we hope will be sure ways of reaching eternal life. John's answer is simple. No matter who asks the question of him, he answers: "Be just in the work you do. Live as you should, being righteous and conscious of the needs of others." That is, in fact, the only valid answer. The Christian should always be a man of joy, and his serenity should be evident to all. He cannot be a disturbed man but must in all circumstances pray and thank God, while also addressing his petitions to him. That, for the believer, is the source of the peace "which passes all understanding" [24].

John tells us that the Messiah's coming is imminent; he is at hand. And in a joyful poem Zephaniah assures us: "The King of Israel, the Lord, is in your midst. . . . The Lord your God is in your midst, a warrior who gives victory" [21].

The kingdom is here

The blind see, the lame walk, the lepers are cleansed, the deaf regain their hearing, the dead rise, and the Good News is preached to the poor [66]. Always the same signs of the same presence. We must be always interpreting them and seeing how they apply today, in our lives. They are disturbing signs, because they confront us with a demanding choice, but they are also reassuring, because they are a sign of victory. Isaiah is very positive on this last point: "For I am God, and there is no other. By myself I have sworn, from my mouth has gone forth in righteousness a word that shall not return: 'To me every knee shall bow, every tongue shall swear'. . . . In the Lord all the offspring of Israel shall triumph and glory" [65].

In chapter 31 Isaiah describes the final victory in another fashion, by recalling the Lord's triumphs over his enemies. The passage is read in Office on Wednesday of this third week [102].

The Office also contains a text of St. Irenaeus of Lyons, who comments on the coming of Christ and the possibility of our seeing God:

> Man shall not by his own power see God, but God, if he wishes, shall be seen by men — by whom, and when, and as he wills — for he is all-powerful. He was seen in the prophetic mode through the Spirit; he was seen, according to the mode proper to adoption, through the Son; and he will be seen in his very fatherhood in the kingdom of heaven. The Spirit thus prepares man in advance for the Son of God; the Son leads man to the Father; and the Father gives man the incorruptibility and eternal life that flow from the vision of God to those who see him. For just as those who see the light of day are within the light and perceive its rays, so those who see God are in God and share in his radiance. The radiance of God, however, is life-giving. Therefore those who see God will share in his life.[77]

A star shall arise

The proclamation of Jesus the Messiah becomes ever clearer. In the Book of Numbers, which is read on the third

Monday of Advent, the pagan prophet Balaam says: "I see him, but not now; I behold him, but not nigh: a star shall come forth out of Jacob, and a scepter shall rise out of Israel" [61].

In the Gospel of the same day, Jesus has no desire to hide the source of his authority, but because the chief priests are unwilling to admit the authority by which John baptized, neither will Jesus tell them by what authority he himself teaches: "Neither will I tell you by what authority I do these things" [62].

The entrance antiphon on this day proclaims the coming of the Messiah in the words of Jeremiah and Isaiah: "Nations, hear the message of the Lord, and make it known to the ends of the earth: Our Savior is coming. Have no more fear" (see Jer. 31:10; Is. 35:4).

But we must look for and discover this Lord who has already come. It is of this that the opening prayer at Mass on this Monday speaks: "Let the light of the coming of your Son free us from the darkness of sin."

John prepares the way for the Lord. That is why he was sent. "What then did you go out to see? A prophet? Yes, I tell you, and more than a prophet. This is he of whom it is written, 'Behold, I send my messenger before thy face, who shall prepare thy way before thee'" [68].

The Office for Thursday of the third week, in order to highlight John's prophetic function, emphasizes the role of Christ himself. For this purpose it uses a text of Vatican II on revelation:

> After God has spoken many times and in various ways through the prophets, "in these last days he has spoken to us by a Son" (Heb. 1:1-2). For he sent his Son, the eternal Word who enlightens all men, to dwell among men and to tell them about the inner life of God. Hence, Jesus Christ, sent as "a man among men," "speaks the words of God" (John 3:34), and accomplishes the saving work which the Father gave him to do (cf. John 5:36; 17:4). As a result, he himself

— to see whom is to see the Father (cf. John 14:9) — completed and perfected revelation and confirmed it with divine guarantees. He did this by the total fact of his presence and self-manifestation — by words and works, signs and miracles, but above all by his death and glorious resurrection from the dead, and finally by sending the Spirit of truth. He revealed that God was with us, to deliver us from the darkness of sin and death, and to raise us up to eternal life.[78]

This revelation is given because the Lord loves his people and is calling them back to himself like a wife that had been abandoned. This is what Isaiah tells us in the reading for the Mass of the third Thursday. God in his anger had hidden his face for a moment, but his eternal love won out and he took pity on man. His love will be unchanging, and his covenant of peace shall never be shaken [67].

John, a lamp burning bright

With increasing clarity Jesus asserts that he is the Messiah who has come among men. "He [John] was a burning and shining lamp, and you were willing to rejoice for a while in his light. But the testimony which I have is greater than that of John; for the works which the Father has granted me to accomplish, these very works which I am doing, bear me witness that the Father has sent me" [70].

He is the Christ who brings salvation and gathers men into unity. The reading from Isaiah at Mass on the third Friday emphasizes this fact once more: "For soon my salvation will come, and my deliverance be revealed." The universal scope of the salvation that the Messiah brings becomes increasingly clear in the prophets. Even foreigners will come "to my holy mountain," and the Lord will make them happy in his "house of prayer" [69]. His house shall be called "a house of prayer for all peoples."

Here the gathering of all mankind and their meeting with

the Lord are thought of as taking place in a "house of prayer." And indeed the desire to meet the Lord is to some extent identical with prayer. St. Augustine develops this theme in commenting on Psalm 37:13-14, and the passage has been taken into the Office for the third Friday of Advent. Here is a short extract from it:

> Your desire itself is your prayer, and if your desire is continuous, so is your prayer. It was not without reason that the Apostle said: "Pray without ceasing." We cannot be constantly genuflecting or prostrating ourselves or lifting our hands, can we? It is not with reference to such actions as these that we can speak of "praying without ceasing."
>
>   There is however another prayer that is really ceaseless: it is interior and consists in desire. . . . If you do not wish to leave off praying, then do not leave off desiring.[79]

Expectation, then, means desire based on faith, and is a form of prayer. John came, but they did not believe him [64]. Now the salvation brought by the Messiah has been preached to the poor [63], but we must actually accept that salvation. If we are to accept it, we must desire it, and to desire it is to pray for it. Such is the attitude to which we have been exhorted on several occasions during this season.

Overview

The readings in the Office for this week always concentrate on the Lord's return at the end and on future salvation [99-104]. The readings at Mass, however, emphasize rather the presence among us of the messianic age and the kingdom. We are at a critical point in the time before Christmas, and the liturgy is beginning to focus more on the fact of Christ's coming in the flesh.

We are bidden, in the Office, to meditate on a subject by now quite familiar, and we might easily think of ourselves as marking time while we do it. Salvation on the last day

[99], the pressing need of conversion and the future happiness we can now glimpse [100], the coming of the Lord to punish the Assyrians, a prefiguring of the Messiah's triumph over evil [101], the establishment of the reign of justice [102], a restoration of the world that should be the subject of our hope in the Lord [103] and turn our thoughts to our future salvation [104] — such are the themes proposed to us in the Office of Readings. True, they are not new, but there is certainly room for us to enter more deeply into them.

The Scripture readings at Mass are more concerned with the prediction of the Messiah and with his presence among us; meanwhile, the person of John the Baptist and his mission as Precursor are also emphasized. For this reason it will be good to reflect a bit on his personality.

John the Baptist, a man of expectation

If we limit the close relationship between John the Baptist and Isaiah to a mere matter of literary borrowing, we show that we have not understood either John or Isaiah. As a matter of fact, it is difficult to separate these two men; between them there is a continuity of thought, message, and role. Isaiah is present to us in John the Baptist, just as John is present in him whose way he prepares and who will say of him: "Truly, I say to you, among those born of women there has risen no one greater than John the Baptist" [25].

We know Isaiah only through his writings. For John, on the contrary, we have the Gospel to inform us of his origins, his words, and his attitudes.

St. Luke reports in detail the announcement of the birth of the Baptist (Luke 1:5-25). The miraculous entry on the scene of a person who will represent a very important milestone in the execution of the divine plan is quite in the Old Testament tradition. All living beings were to be wiped out by the Deluge, but Noah and his family were saved in the ark. Isaac was born of Sarah when she was too old to have children. David, a young boy without experience in battle, laid Goliath low. Moses, the future leader of the Israelites, was found in a basket (the word in Hebrew also means "ark") and saved from death. In all these occurrences God was making it clear that he was taking the initiative in the salvation of his people and choosing for himself the instruments he would use as he saw fit.

The announcement of John's birth is a solemn one that occurs within the framework of the temple liturgy. Everything about the child, including his name, which means "Yahweh is gracious," is part of God's careful preparation of the instrument he has chosen. John's birth will not go unnoticed but will be a source of joy for many (Luke 1:14). He will be one consecrated to the Lord and therefore, as prescribed in the Book of Numbers (6:1-21), he will drink neither wine nor strong drink. This Nazirite vow points ahead to John's calling to be an ascetic and one in whom the Holy Spirit has dwelt since he was in his mother's womb.

In addition to being an ascetic, John is to be a leader of his people (Luke 1:18) and will go before the Messiah, a role that Malachias (3:23) assigns to Elias. At John's circumcision, the fact that God is setting him apart is made clear in a new way: he is given a name that no one among his kinsfolk has borne (Luke 1:61); despite custom, God wishes him to be named John. The Lord has chosen this child; the Lord is controlling events and leading his people.

"Blessed be the Lord God of Israel"

John's birth is the occasion for a splendid poem that is both a song of thanksgiving and a description of the child's future role. The Church recites this poem daily at the end of Morning Praise, expressing through it her praise of God for the salvation he has given her, and her gratitude for John who continues to show her "the way of peace."

> Blessed be the Lord God of Israel, for he has visited and redeemed his people, and has raised up a horn of

salvation for us in the house of his servant David, as
he spoke by the mouth of his holy prophets from of
old, that we should be saved from our enemies, and
from the hand of all who hate us; to perform the
mercy promised to our fathers, and to remember his
holy covenant, the oath which he swore to our father
Abraham, to grant us that we, being delivered from
the hand of our enemies, might serve him without
fear, in holiness and righteousness before him all the
days of our life.

And you, child, will be called the prophet of the
Most High; for you will go before the Lord to prepare
his ways, to give knowledge of salvation to his people
in the forgiveness of their sins, through the tender
mercy of our God, when the day shall dawn upon us
from on high to give light to those who sit in darkness
and in the shadow of death, to guide our feet into the
way of peace (Luke 1:68-79).

John the Baptist is a sign that God is again intervening in
his people's history. The Lord is visiting them, saving
them, and bringing about the covenant he had promised.
The Precursor's role is clearly defined: it is to prepare the
way for the Lord (see Is. 40:3) and to bring his people
"knowledge of salvation."

The exclusive subject of Israel's speculation and contemplation was precisely the knowledge of salvation and of
God's marvelous plan for his people. Such knowledge it
was that prompted the thanksgiving, blessing, and proclamation of God's benefits that we find in Zachary's canticle.
"Blessed be the Lord God of Israel" was in fact the traditional formula Israel used in expressing its gratitude and
wonder at God's plan. Abraham's servant uses the words
when he thanks Yahweh (Gen. 24:26). Jethro, father-in-law
of Moses, uses them in his response to the amazing story of
what Yahweh had done in rescuing Israel from the hands of
the Egyptians (Exod. 18:10).

The salvation that John will make known consists in the
forgiveness of sins and is the work of God's tender mercy

(Luke 1:77-78). John's role will be to announce a baptism in the Spirit that will effect the forgiveness of sins. But this baptism will not be purely negative in its effects; it will also bring enlightenment. For the tender mercy of God will send us a Messiah who, according to two passages of Isaiah (9:1; 42:7) to which Christ alludes (John 8:12), will "give light to those who sit in darkness and in the shadow of death" (Luke 1:79).

John's mission will be to go before the Lord to prepare straight paths for him. He is aware of this and speaks of himself, in Isaiah's words, as "the voice of one crying in the wilderness, 'Make straight the way of the Lord'" (John 1:23). He will act in an even more positive way by making known the one who is already there but unrecognized (John 1:26) and pointing him out when he comes: "Behold, the Lamb of God, who takes away the sin of the world!" (John 1:29).

John wishes to, and does, live up to what had been foretold of him, namely, that he would bear witness to the Messiah's presence. The way in which he speaks of the Messiah shows what the latter meant to him: the Messiah is "the Lamb of God." John knew, of course, the fourteenth chapter of Leviticus, which describes the immolation of a lamb in expiation for legal impurity. When he read it, he thought of the Servant of Yahweh, whom Isaiah had described in chapter 53 as carrying the guilt of all Israel. In pointing Christ out to his disciples, John already has a vision of him as the true Passover Lamb whose death will be far more effective than that of the Passover lamb in Exodus (12:1) and will bring salvation to the whole world.

The greatness of John the Baptist is due to his humility and self-forgetfulness. He is bathed in the radiant light of the Messiah, whom he is so anxious not to hide from others: "He must increase, but I must decrease" (John 3:30).

"All flesh shall see the salvation of God"

John's role and his determination to be self-effacing have made him a vital figure down the centuries. We cannot speak of him without speaking of Christ, but the Church has also reversed that relationship and never recalls Christ's coming without also recalling his Precursor. The Precursor is linked not only to Christ's coming but to his work as well, for John announces that work as being the redemption of the world and the rebuilding of the world through the years until the parousia. Each year the Church reminds us of John's testimony and of his attitude toward the message he preaches.

In consequence, John is present at every point in the Advent liturgy. As a matter of fact, the Church should constantly have his example before her eyes, since it is her mission, and that of each of us, to prepare the way for the Lord and to proclaim the Good News. Fulfillment of this mission, however, requires a conversion. If one is really to be the instrument of Christ, one must be divested of self. Without such an asceticism on our part, Christ can be in the midst of the world and go unrecognized (see John 1:26). Like John, the Church and her members have an obligation not to stand between men and the light but rather to bear witness to the light (John 1:7).

The Bride, who is the Church, must yield place to the Bridegroom; she is a witness and must let attention be focused on him to whom she bears witness. It is difficult to be present in the world, present to the point even of suffering martyrdom, and yet not to focus attention on some "institution" instead of on Christ himself. "He must increase, but I must decrease." It is difficult to proclaim the Good News and not this or that spirituality or religious order or special form of Catholic Action or parochial interest. It is difficult to act like John and show our disciples where they can find the "Lamb of God," and not keep them for ourselves as though we were their light.

This lesson is always valid and always necessary, as is the lesson of John's desert asceticism and of a loving inwardness for the sake of being a better witness. The eloquent silence of the desert is the foundation for any genuinely effective proclamation of the Good News.

In his commentary on St. Luke's Gospel, Origen writes: "For myself, I think that the mystery of John is still being fulfilled in the world, even today."[80] The Church is continuing the work of the Precursor, showing Christ to us and directing us to the coming of the Lord.

During Advent the great figure of the Baptist is a living reality for us twentieth-century men as we advance toward the Day of Christ. Christ himself, referring to Malachias 3:1, speaks of John as a "messenger" [25], and John speaks of himself in the same way [26]. St. Luke describes John as a preacher who calls for an unqualified conversion and a renewal: "Every valley shall be filled, and every mountain and hill shall be brought low, and the crooked shall be made straight, and the rough ways shall be made smooth; and all flesh shall see the salvation of God" (Luke 3:5-6). The words are from a poem of Isaiah (40:4-5) that Luke uses in order to describe John's work. John is calling for a renewal, a shake-up, a conversion that consists chiefly in the effort to practice love of neighbor.

> The multitudes asked John, "What then shall we do?" And he answered them, "He who has two coats, let him share with him who has none; and he who has food, let him do likewise." Tax collectors also came to be baptized, and said to him, "Teacher, what shall we do?" And he said to them, "Collect no more than is appointed you." Soldiers also asked him, "And we, what shall we do?" And he said to them, "Rob no one by violence or by false accusation, and be content with your wages" [27].

Luke sums up the whole of John's activity in a short sentence: "He preached good news to the people" [27]. John's role then was to prepare the way for the Lord and to preach the Good News. He exhorts us to do the same.

It is no simpler a task today than it was in John's time, and it is incumbent on each of us. John was martyred, in the last analysis, because he was frank and honest in his denunciation of sin. Christians today often compromise, under the pretext of being more open to the world; in the end, they are in danger of becoming like Herodias and strangling the voice. What a contrast! An age that is all for authenticity also tries to drown out the voice of anyone who makes demands on it! This is not the only paradox in human life, of course, but it is one of which we must be aware.

John the Baptist announced the Lamb of God. He was the first to give this name to Christ, anticipating the Apocalypse, which invites us to the marriage feast of the victorious Lamb after he has shed his blood for the redemption of the world. This is why we cannot participate in the Eucharistic banquet, which is the wedding feast of the Lamb on earth, without at the same time proclaiming the death and resurrection of the Lord and the demands made upon us who have been baptized into that death and resurrection. This is the inexorable logic of Christian life; John lived by this logic and bore witness to it with his blood.

We must quote here the beautiful preface recently introduced into the liturgy for the feast of the martyrdom of St. John the Baptist; it is a fine summation of his life and his role.

> His birth brought great rejoicing: even in the womb he leapt for joy, so near was man's salvation. You chose John the Baptist from all the prophets to show the world its redeemer, the lamb of sacrifice. He baptized Christ, the giver of baptism, in waters made holy by the one who was baptized. You found John worthy of a martyr's death, his last and greatest act of witness to your Son.

Fourth Week of Advent

8. THE ANNUNCIATION OF THE
MESSIAH'S COMING

The liturgy of Advent now turns its full attention to the coming birth of the Lord. The antiphons concentrate on it; for example, the entrance antiphon for the fourth Sunday: "Let the clouds rain down the Just One, and the earth bring forth a Savior" (Is. 45:8), and the Communion antiphon for the same day: "The Virgin is with child and shall bear a son, and she will call him Emmanuel" (Is. 7:14). The prayers, too, increase our awareness of the coming that is at hand; for example, the opening prayer for the fourth Sunday: "you revealed to us by an angel the coming of your Son as man."

We are making a definite transition, therefore, to the other major theme of the Advent liturgy: expectation of the incarnation of the Word.

(A) The annunciation to Joseph. A virgin shall conceive the Son of God, Jesus Christ, who is of David's line.

St. Matthew's Gospel describes the dramatic situation that St. Joseph finds himself in when he learns of his fiancée's state [34]. The narrative indicates three points that are extremely important for the history of salvation: the incarnation of the Word as a member of David's line; the intervention of the Spirit; the role of the one to be born, whose name "Jesus" means "The Lord saves," since it is he who will save the world from its sins. All this the angel announces, and Joseph's response is an act of faith.

The story may strike us as very unsophisticated. As a matter of fact, nothing changed as a result in the life of the times; life went on as it always had, the sun shone as before, men worked or played, did good or evil — nothing changed. Nor was there apparently any change in the outward lives of Joseph and Mary. This fact should put us on guard against thinking of the events of salvation as theatrical in character. They are not. They respect and do not disturb the course of events, and for that very reason we sometimes minimize their importance. Here we are, for example, at the very turning point of world history, for history will be changed and take on an entirely new meaning. Yet nothing of this appears on the surface. Joseph goes on as before while he waits; he is caught up in the drama, but he is at peace ever since he accepted God's will in faith.

This is the sign the Lord gives: "The Lord himself will give you a sign. Behold, a young woman (virgin, LXX) shall conceive and bear a son, and shall call his name Immanuel" [28]. The responsorial psalm chosen for this reading brings out the divine rank of him who is to be born: "Let the Lord enter; he is king of glory. — The earth is the Lord's and the fulness thereof, the world and those who dwell therein; for he has founded it upon the seas, and established it upon the rivers" (Ps. 24:1-2). The psalm goes on to specify what is required of those who wish to draw near to this king: "He who has clean hands and a pure heart, who does not lift up his soul to what is false."

St. Paul has no greater news to give the Romans than this. In fact, it is precisely to proclaim this Good News that he has been set apart as an apostle. It is the Good News concerning the Son of God, "who was descended from David according to the flesh and designated Son of God in power according to the Spirit of holiness by his resurrection from the dead, Jesus Christ our Lord" [31]. Paul is here pointing to the close link between the incarnation and the paschal mystery. It is this link that makes possible the actualization of the mystery of Christ's birth in the liturgy.

In the Eucharistic Prayer he suggests for the day of a bishop's consecration, St. Hippolytus of Rome speaks in a way that is strange to us, but one that brings out the importance of the incarnation. He says of Jesus: "He became incarnate and was manifested as your Son."[81] The Son is, of course, eternally the Son. Hippolytus has in mind, however, the fact on which John the Evangelist lays so much stress: the Son's essential role is to do the Father's will. Hippolytus thinks, therefore, that the Son truly merits his name of Son when he obeys the Father and does his will by giving his life for the redemption of the world. To do the Father's will in this fashion, the Son had to become man.

This idea of Hippolytus, which at first glance seems opposed to faith (since the Son is eternal), as a matter of fact throws light on the role of the incarnation in the history of salvation. We can never overremphasize the reality of Christ's humanity and of his birth from a virgin in accordance with the prophecy [28].

(B) The annunciation to Mary. The throne of David will last forever. God is now revealing the mystery hidden through the ages.

To this account of the annunciation to Mary, which has so often been the subject of literary treatment and pictorial representation, our response should be one inspired by faith alone, as Mary's was at the time. The account, like all great things, is simple; we have trouble conceiving the event and get ourselves twisted up when we try to explain it. There is God's choice, the intervention of the Spirit, Mary's faith-inspired acceptance, and the conception of God's Son by a woman [35]. In straightforward fashion the angel says that the promise made to David by the prophet Nathan is being fulfilled. The first reading records this promise: "I will make for you a great name, like the name of the great ones of the earth. . . . And your house and your kingdom shall be made sure for ever before me; your throne shall be established for ever" [29].

Psalm 89 was a natural choice to provide a response to such a reading: "I have made a covenant with my chosen one, I have sworn to David my servant: 'I will establish your descendants for ever, and build your throne for all generations!" (Ps. 89:3-4).

The mystery that has been hidden through the ages is

now revealed. St. Paul cannot hide from the Romans his wonder at the execution of God's plan of reconstruction that was announced at the very moment of the Fall in the promise made to Eve and that was being implemented in silence down the centuries. "Mystery" here is not what we habitually take it to be: that which we can neither see nor understand. For Paul, it is something revealed to all, for the salvation of all. "My gospel . . . according to the revelation of the mystery which was kept secret for long ages but is now disclosed and . . . made known to all nations, according to the command of the eternal God to bring about the obedience of faith." He concludes with a shout of enthusiasm: "To the only wise God be glory for evermore through Jesus Christ! Amen" [32].

(C) The annunciation to Elizabeth. From Judah shall come forth one who shall rule Israel. He comes to do God's will.

John the Baptist leaps for joy in his mother's womb as he meets the Lord, who is concealed in the Virgin's womb. Elizabeth's words to Mary are a profession of faith: "Blessed are you among women, and blessed is the fruit of your womb! And why is this granted me, that the mother of my Lord should come to me?" [36].

The first two readings, which tell what the child will be, stand in contrast and yet are in profound harmony. The first, from the prophet Micah, speaks of the Messiah as one who shall shepherd his flock by the strength of the Lord. In his person, "he shall be great" [30]. After a time of seeming abandonment, the Lord will send the Savior.

The responsorial psalm sings of this mighty Shepherd: "Give ear, O Shepherd of Israel, thou who art enthroned upon the cherubim, shine forth. Stir up thy might, and come to save us!" (Ps. 80:1-2).

The Letter to the Hebrews, for its part, already has its eye on the paschal mystery and the obedience unto death of the Messiah who comes among us. The coming of Christ as

man does away with all the other sacrifices, which the
Father had not wanted. Jesus offers himself in expiation for
sins. His sacrifice is first and foremost a spiritual sacrifice,
which consists in doing the Father's will; his giving of himself to the point of bloodshed and death is a sign of that
inner sacrifice. The author of the Letter takes us fully into
the paschal mystery when he adds: "And by that will [of
the incarnate Word] we have been sanctified through the
offering of the body of Jesus Christ once for all" [33].

Jesus, son of David

Nothing could be more impressive than the genealogy of
Jesus and its magnificent ending: "Jacob [was] the father of
Joseph the husband of Mary, of whom Jesus was born, who
is called Christ" [72]. This entrance of God into the world
as one of us is the event that towers over the whole history
of mankind. In point of fact, however, it does not control
our personal lives. Our faith is so weak that our attitudes do
not befit the dignity proper to men in the ages after the Son
entered the world. The opening prayer for December 17
seems to be that of one moved to tears by the mystery:
"Father . . . you decreed, and your Word became man, born
of the Virgin Mary. May we come to share the divinity of
Christ, who humbled himself to share our human nature."
Thus, the scepter will not pass from Judah; God will keep
his promise [71].

The Gospel for December 18 concentrates once again on
the birth of the Savior as a man. His birth is from a virgin,
and his mission will be to "save," as his name, Jesus, indicates. Thus the prophecy of Isaiah concerning the birth of
Emmanuel will be fulfilled. He who is to come is both son
of David and Son of God [74]. He will bring right and justice into the world [73].

The birth of John the Baptist

The event, an important one, and is spoken of twice in
the readings of the final week of Advent. On December 19

the Gospel recounts the announcement of John's birth to his father. It is an announcement resembling that made to Mary, but it is received in a very different way, leading to the punishment of Zachary for his lack of faith. The power of God who alone chooses, and chooses as he wishes, is very much accentuated in this account. The Old Testament saw the impossible birth of Isaac, the handing over to Jacob of the rights proper to the first-born son, and the saving of Moses from the waters. The New Testament now sees the birth of John and will soon see that of Christ. God uses the means, and the men, that he chooses [76].

The first reading, from the Book of Judges, offers the announcement of Samson's birth as a parallel, for an angel told his barren mother that the boy would be conceived and born. He would be a man consecrated to God from his conception until his death [75]. When the Lord is determined to save, nothing can stop him — that is the message of Psalm 71, which supplies the response for this day. "Be thou to me a rock of refuge, a strong fortress, to save me, for thou art my rock and my fortress" (Ps. 71:3).

At John's birth, Zachary recovers his speech. "'What then will this child be?' For the hand of the Lord was with him" [84]. John's birth precedes that of the Savior. That is why a parallel for the Gospel of December 23 has been sought in Malachias who speaks of Elias the prophet being sent "before the great and terrible day of the Lord comes" [83]. We will recall how Jesus pointed to John as the Elias who was to come.

A Virgin shall conceive

The Church has already voiced this idea several times during these days, always with the same sense of wonder and the same faith. Now, on December 20, with Christmas so near, she recalls it once more [77]. Yesterday, on the 19th, we heard of the birth of John; today's Gospel is of the announcement of Jesus' birth [78]. On December 21 the liturgy will feature the account of the visitation [80] and a reading from the Song of Songs in which we see the beloved, Jesus, coming across the hills [79].

The facts recounted are familiar to us, but there is an air of enthusiasm and triumph about the liturgies of this week. The antiphons and responses are becoming increasingly joyful. "Cry out with joy to the Lord, you holy ones; sing a new song to him" is the refrain used with Psalm 33 on December 21. And the entrance antiphon for December 22 shouts out: "Gates, lift up your heads! Stand erect, ancient doors, and let in the King of glory" (Ps. 23:7).

"He who is mighty has done great things for me"

To the successful execution of God's plan that had been hidden since the beginning of history, the Virgin's response, like that of Anna at the birth of Samuel [81], is a cry of astonished praise of God [82]. It was impossible to let Advent pass without recording her glorious hymn, and in fact the Church presents it to us in the Gospel for December 22.

We have seen Isaiah as a model for those who wait and John as a man of expectation and proclamation. We must turn now to the Blessed Virgin.

Our Lady, the woman who waits

The Masses of this season do not fail to present Mary to us for remembrance and praise. It is, however, the Liturgy of the Hours above all that contains many texts in praise of the Virgin.

First of all, there is daily an antiphon at Terce, Sext, and None that refers to the Blessed Virgin. "This is the good news the prophets foretold: The Savior will be born of the Virgin Mary" (Terce). "The angel Gabriel said to Mary in greeting: Hail, full of grace, the Lord is with you; blessed are you among women" (Sext). "Mary said: My soul is deeply troubled; what can this greeting mean? Am I to give birth to my King and yet remain a virgin for ever?" (None).

At Vespers on the first Sunday of Advent the antiphon for the *Magnificat* is taken from the Gospel of the annunciation: "Do not be afraid, Mary, you have found favor with God; you will conceive and give birth to a Son, alleluia." At Vespers on Monday of the first week the antiphon is: "The angel of the Lord brought God's message to Mary, and she conceived by the power of the Holy Spirit, alleluia." For Thursday Vespers it is: "Blessed are you among women, and blessed is the fruit of your womb." At Vespers for the second Sunday of Advent: "Blessed are you, O Virgin Mary, for your great faith; all that the Lord promised you will come to pass through you, alleluia."

At Lauds for Wednesdays, the reading is from chapter 7 of Isaiah: "The virgin shall be with child, and bear a son, and shall name him Immanuel. He shall be living on curds and honey by the time he learns to reject the bad and choose the good." There is no point in continuing a list that would quickly become boring. The short list we have given here indicates the presence of the Virgin in the Advent Office, whether the emphasis is on the first coming of her Son or on his return at the end of time.

We will remember that the feast of the Immaculate Conception is celebrated during Advent. It fits in quite readily with the theme of Christ's birth, but it would be a mistake to think of that as the only theme of the feast. This celebration, like the others of the season, contains Old Testament perspectives as well as New; we are made aware that we are moving toward the end of time. "The events recorded of the people of God in the Old Testament lead up to Mary, and those of the New and Eternal Testament start from her. In this twofold aspect, she proclaims, prefigures, and realises, in a wholly unique manner, all the sanctity to be attained ultimately by the Church, when it shall have reached its perfection."[82] The virgin "without spot or wrinkle" (Eph. 5:27) who is to be presented to Christ at the end of time is the Church. Mary, consequently, is the promise already fulfilled and the pledge already given to us of what all of us together are to become.

What Origen said of John the Baptist can also be said of Mary: "The Mystery of Mary is still being fulfilled in the world, even today." During the Advent season the Church helps us see our Lady, the Mother of God, who is constantly present among us.

Respect is surely due to a devotion that has benefited many people past and present. Yet it must be said, I think, with all due qualifications, that despite the biblical and liturgical renewals, the Marian devotion of too many is characterized by an outmoded sentimentality and by excesses in language, attitude, and even devotion itself.

The Church undoubtedly has the right and even the duty to welcome new forms of piety. Undoubtedly too, her concern for the spiritual needs of men at each stage of history leads her to develop certain types of devotion as a way of meeting a lack. We must assert uncompromisingly that it is unjust and imprudent to advise people against a devotion on the pretext that it is not scripturally or liturgically inspired, and without having first provided the faithful with a more solid spiritual food.

That having been said, it does not seem out of place to contrast the great attention given to the "month of May" with the almost total neglect of the Marian season of Advent. We must respect the efforts made during "Mary's month," but we cannot allow a tradition as old as the veneration of Mary during Advent to be overshadowed or even completely unknown. Many Christians are so unaware of the presence of God's Mother during Advent that they celebrate the Immaculate Conception as though it were an isolated feast, closely connected with Lourdes but unrelated to the rest of the Advent liturgy!

There is a lot of scope here for pastoral effort. The point is not to do away with a devotion that the Church has encouraged, but rather to establish a hierarchy of values and to become conscious that a liturgical celebration such as that of Advent has a rightful priority over other forms of Marian devotion, however much more developed they may be.

For any mother, the birth of her child is a festive day she will never forget. But the time before birth, during which she is developing a special intimacy with her child, is also a privileged period. For Mary, Christmas is the supreme feast day of her motherhood, but the season of Advent that prepares for it is also a precious time. (For comment on the readings proper to the feast of the Immaculate Conception December 8, see page 327).

Overview

While the scriptural readings in the Masses of the final week concentrate on the incarnation, those in the Office continue our meditation on the prophecies of salvation, victory, and punishment [92–98]. The patristic readings afford a wealth of teaching on the period through which we are now living in the liturgy. On December 17, a passage from a letter of Pope St. Leo the Great presents Christ's birth as sacrament of our reconciliation.

> Unless the new Man had been made in the likeness of the flesh of sin and thus had assumed what is "old" in us, and unless, while continuing to be consubstantial with the Father, he had deigned to become consubstantial with his Mother and, as the only man free of sin, had made our nature his own, mankind would have continued to be a captive under the devil's yoke. Nor could we profit by the victory of the triumphant Christ if that victory had been won in a nature not ours.[83]

The letter adds that we share in this "sacrament of our reconciliation" only if we are born of God.

On December 19, the Office has a text of St. Irenaeus that sums up the economy of salvation. He emphasizes our inability to save ourselves and, on the basis of the incarnation, asserts that the God who is with us effects our salvation.

> This is why the Lord himself has given us as a sign of

our salvation the Emmanuel born of the Virgin: because the Lord himself was to be our Savior when we had no power to save ourselves. For this reason Paul says when preaching of man's weakness: "I know that nothing good dwells within me, that is, in my flesh." He means that the good which is salvation comes not from ourselves but from God. And again: "Wretched man that I am! Who will deliver me from this body of death?" Then he points to the deliverer: "The grace of our Lord Jesus Christ."[84]

The purpose of this fourth week of Advent is to prepare us for the final moments before the birth of Christ. For we know that we are not celebrating a fiction but an authentic presence in our own time.

The "O" antiphons

Using a particular form that was very important in the Middle Ages, the Liturgy of the Hours speaks of the coming of Christ in a poetic form of which many people are unaware. We refer to the series of antiphons for the *Magnificat* that begins on December 17; each antiphon starts with an exclamation: "O Wisdom!" "O sacred Lord!" etc. These antiphons, seven in number, seem to have originated at Rome. In Germany and at Liège and Paris, two similar antiphons were added to the traditional seven; at times we find as many as twelve antiphons. The form must have been felt to be a very appropriate one. Later on, antiphons for the Doctors of the Church or for the feast of the ascension were cast in the same format.

The singing of the "O" antiphons during Advent was a very solemn affair in cathedrals and monasteries. In some places the solemnity has been preserved; the Liturgy of the Hours has kept at least the antiphons themselves. In them, as elsewhere, we are reminded of the two comings that give Advent its basic theme.

First antiphon, December 17

O Wisdom, O holy Word of God (Sir. 24:3), you govern all creation with your strong yet tender care (Wis. 8:1). Come and show your people the way to salvation (Is. 40:3-5).

The antiphon is addressed to the Son. We may recall here the Prologue to the fourth Gospel: "In the beginning was the Word, and the Word was with God, and the Word was God." He is the Word who comes from the Father's mouth and creates the universe. Here we call upon him, and the invocation shows the two dimensions of our expectation: we need his coming so that he may teach us the way of salvation, and we need it so that we may be able to travel this road that will lead us to the end of time.

In the last analysis, "Come" is man's only valid prayer; it sums up all of his need of God. It is the ceaseless cry of mankind ever since the expulsion from paradise. Man remembers that he chose evil; how, therefore, is he now to know the "way to salvation," or the "way of justice," as Scripture often phrases it? In the Old Testament, justice and judgment go together. "Justice" there is not an abstract ideal but something personal and concrete: it is the state of innocence proper to a man who is faithful to this indescribable ideal.[85] Isaiah, from whom the third part of the antiphon is taken, is the prophet who perhaps saw most clearly the role of the Messiah in relation to justice. "The essential role of the Davidic Messias is, for Isaias, the establishment of justice."[86] He comes to David's kingdom "to uphold it with justice and with righteousness" (Is. 9:7).

"Justice" here is still conceived in somewhat material terms, that is, as a social justice that does away with favoritism, corruption among judges, and so forth. The concept of justice is gradually deepened, however, since the vision of Isaiah cannot become a reality except in an atmosphere of guiltlessness in which each person does the Lord's will. It is impossible, however, for the world to reach this state of peace and moral purity unless Yahweh himself intervenes. Therefore he will destroy the sinner (Is. 5:3-15) and then bring a new world into being; Sion will be cleansed of its filth, and the bloodstains shall be washed from Jerusalem (Is. 4:3-5).

God's intervention in judgment is thus far from being merely condemnatory; both in intention and in fact, it leads to a reconstruction. Here we are confronted once again with the two dimensions of the parousia. Christ is to come, and we call upon him to lead us in this way of justice or salvation, that is, the way that leads to the complete renewal of the world on the day of judgment.

Second antiphon, December 18

> O sacred Lord of ancient Israel (Exod. 6:2, 3, 12), who showed yourself to Moses in the burning bush (Exod. 3:2), who gave him the holy law on Sinai mountain: come, stretch out your mighty hand to set us free (Exod. 6:6).

The Lord made himself known to Moses by telling him his name. For a Semite, to tell another your name is to give him power over you. It is clear, of course, that the God of Israel cannot hand himself over to the power of men like a pagan god whose devotees invoke him with the idea that they can coerce him by magical practices and will therefore be heard. But the name "Yahweh" will always remind Israel of the great deeds God has done for her deliverance.[87]

This antiphon puts us in the context of the paschal mystery, since the coming of the Son is directly related to his redemptive mission.

The last part of the antiphon contains a profound thought to which we rarely attend. The words "come . . . to set us free" express, of course, the purpose of the incarnation and are a short statement of the theology of the incarnation that was current at the end of the sixth century. The rest of the words, however, namely "stretch out your mighty hand," say something more, at least if we translate the Latin words literally: "come to redeem us with outstretched arm." The phrase "with outstretched arm" is scriptural and occurs, for example, in Exodus 6:6. The Hebrew root *zr'* means "to sow, to pour out or spread, to make fruitful." From this root two different nouns derive. One, *zera'*, means "time for sowing, vital seed, posterity, stock, stump, shoot"; in Isaiah it has a precise messianic significance. The other word, *zeroa'* means "arm, power, virility, violence, support, help." The phrase "with outstretched arm" is thus complex and rich in meaning.

He who is to come is the "shoot from the stump of Jesse" (Is. 11:1); he is the Messiah; he is also the one who comes in order to restore life to his people; he is power, support, and help. We must, of course, avoid pushing these juxtapositions too far, but it is at least worth noting that several times in his work *Against the Heresies* (*Adversus haereses*) St. Irenaeus uses the expression: "He stretched out his hand when he suffered [his Passion]."[88] This phrasing is rarely found elsewhere, but it does occur in the Eucharistic Prayer in St. Hippolytus's *Traditio Apostolica* (beginning of the third century): "He stretched out his hands when he suffered in order to deliver from suffering those who believed in him."[89]

Here, then, we call on Christ, and we expect him to continue his work of redemption in our world until the end of time.

Third antiphon, December 19

> O Flower of Jesse's stem, you have been raised up as a sign for all peoples (Is. 11:10; Rom. 15:12); kings stand silent in your presence (Is. 5:15); the nations bow down in worship before you. Come, let nothing keep you from coming to our aid (Hab. 2:3; Heb. 10:37).

This antiphon draws its main inspiration from chapter 11 of Isaiah. The prophet there sees the Messiah coming "as an ensign to the peoples." We are reminded of Jesus' words and St. John's comment: "'I, when I am lifted up from the earth, will draw all men to myself.' He said this to show by what death he was to die" (John 22:32-33). This death will be a victory that will silence the proud of this world. Even the pagan nations will call upon the Savior: "In that day the root of Jesse shall stand as an ensign to the peoples; him shall the nations seek, and his dwelling shall be glorious" (Is. 11:10).

Fourth antiphon, December 20

> O Key of David, O royal Power of Israel, controlling at your will the gate of heaven (Is. 22:22; Apoc. 3:7): come, break down the prison walls of death for those who dwell in darkness and the shadow of death; and lead your captive people into freedom (Is. 42:7; Ps. 107:14; Luke 1:79).

It is the Messiah's prerogative to open or shut the gate into the kingdom. We call out to him. Let him come to rescue us, because the dark-shadow of death will lie upon us until the kingdom of Satan is forever destroyed.

Fifth antiphon, December 21

> O Radiant Dawn (Zech. 6:12), splendor of eternal light (Heb. 1:3), sun of justice (Mal. 4:2): come, shine on those who dwell in darkness and the shadow of death (Luke 1:78-79; Is. 9:2).

The picture is that of Christ returning at the end of time, when his radiant light will once and for all dispel the darkness that still lies on hearts and souls. The end of the antiphon recalls the end of Zachary's *Benedictus* (Luke 1:78-79).

Sixth antiphon, December 22

> O King of all the nations, the only joy of every human heart (Haggai 2:8); O Keystone (Is. 28:16) of the

mighty arch of man (Eph. 2:14): come and save the creature you fashioned from the dust (Gen. 2:7).

The antiphon speaks of the Son as having already effected the gathering ("of the mighty arch of man" would read, in a literal translation, "who make the two one," an allusion to Ephesians 2:14). The Church begs him to come and save man, whom God has fashioned in his own image but whose features sin has distorted. We await the return of Christ, who is the Keystone, or, in a somewhat different image, the Cornerstone upon which the Church, as the definitive ingathering of mankind, is built.

Seventh antiphon, December 23

O Emmanuel (Is. 7:14, 8:8), king and lawgiver (Is. 33:22), desire of the nations (Gen. 49:10), Savior of all people, come and set us free, Lord our God.

The theme here is the same as in the preceding antiphon. Our real lawgiver is Christ, who has liberated us from the yoke of the Law. Jews and pagans together await him as King and Savior.

These antiphons express the theology of Advent and are the season's brightest jewels. The incarnation of the Son, salvation, the pursuit of our redemption until the end of time — these are the constant themes of Advent theology. From them we can see that the celebration of Advent, like that of Christmas, has its true center in the paschal mystery, wherein the death and resurrection of Christ accomplishes our salvation.

9. ADVENT IN THE LITURGIES
OF THE PAST

This short inquiry into the celebration of Advent in the past is motivated neither by simple curiosity nor by an interest in things ancient for their own sake. A theological study could certainly be made of the material we present, and it would very likely bring to light largely unsuspected elements in the Advent celebration. But such a study would not fit in with the purpose of this book. We shall restrict ourselves to brief indications, almost in the form of notes.

1. Advent in the Early Roman Liturgy

The readings

During one week of December, the Roman Church kept a fast on Wednesday, Friday, and Saturday. These three Ember Days were not, however, the seed out of which the whole season developed. On the contrary, the Ember days were integrated into the season.

Before the Würzburg epistolary, there is no text that alludes to any preparation for Christmas at Rome. The Würzburg Lectionary contains an epistolary and an evangeliary, but they date from different periods and are not necessarily in harmony. The list of Epistles is regarded as dating from 602.[90]

The Advent Epistolary in the Würzburg Lectionary

First Sunday	Rom. 13:11-14
Second Sunday	Jer. 23:5-8
Third Sunday	Rom. 15:4-13
Fourth Sunday	1 Cor. 4:1-5
Fifth Sunday	Phil. 4:4-7
Sixth Sunday	*Vacat*

Ember Day Readings

Wednesday	Is. 2:1-5
	7:10-15
Friday	Is. 11:1-5
Saturday	Is. 19:20-22
	35:1-7
	40:9-11
	42:1-9
	45:1-8
	2 Thess. 2:1-8

It will be clear from the above list that the two themes of waiting for Christ's return and of waiting for his first coming are (probably unintentionally) intermingled.

The Würzburg Evangeliary

	Earlier Form	Later Form
First Sunday	John 6:5-14	Matthew 21:1-9
Second Sunday	Matthew 21:1-9	Luke 21:25-33
Third Sunday	Luke 21:25-33	Matthew 11:2-10
Fourth Sunday	Matthew 11:2-10	John 1:19-28
Fifth Sunday	John 1:19-28	

The "earlier form" here is a hypothetical reconstruction. John 6:5-14 was supposedly read on the first Sunday; if so, then the four Sundays of the "later form" must all be pushed back one, so that there would have been five Sundays, not four.[91]

The reader will observe that this lectionary makes no provision for weekday readings.

The selection of John 6:5-14 as a Gospel reading is very meaningful, since the multiplication of the loaves is a double prophecy. It points both to the messianic banquet at the end of time and to the Eucharist, in which Christ is already present among us. As we shall see in a moment, a preface in one of the early sacramentaries speaks of "the birth of the eternal bread."

The Murbach Lectionary

This lectionary was composed in Murbach, France, toward the end of the eighth century. It later on acquired authority at Rome, and the Missal of Pius V made extensive use of it.[92]

In the following table, the asterisk indicates readings taken over into the lectionary of 1570 (Pius V), while the plus sign indicates readings taken from the Würzburg Lectionary.

First Sunday	Jer. 23:5ff. +	John 6:5ff. +
Wednesday	2 Thess. 1:3-10b	Luke 10:3-13
Friday		Mark 13:33-37
Second Sunday	Rom. 13:11-14a*+	Matthew 21:1ff. +
Wednesday	James 5:7-10	Matthew 3:1-6
Friday		Luke 3:7-18
Third Sunday	Rom. 15:4-13 *+	Luke 21:25ff. *+
Wednesday	Mal. 3:1-18; 4:6a	Matthew 11:11-14
Friday		Matthew 1:1-16
Fourth Sunday	1 Cor. 4:1-5 *+	Matthew 11:2-10 *+
Wednesday	Is. 2:2-5 *+	Luke 1:26b-38 *+
	Is. 7:10-15 *+	
Friday	Is. 11:1-5 *+	Luke 1:39ff.*
Saturday	Is. 19:20b-22 *+	
	Is. 35:17a *+	
	Is. 40:9b-11b *+	
	Is. 45:1-8 *+	
	2 Thess. 2:1-8 *+	
	Dan. 3:47-51 *+	Luke 3:1-6*
Fifth Sunday	Phil. 4:4-7 +	John 1:19b-28 *+

The Murbach Lectionary is much enriched by the addition of readings for the weekdays. There are five Sundays; readings are provided for Wednesdays and Fridays and for Ember Saturday. Only a Gospel reading is noted for the first three Fridays.

The Lectionary of the 1570 Missal

St. Pius V decided to reform the liturgy in its entirety. As a matter of fact, the rubrics in the Missal promulgated in 1570 for the whole Church were those of the Missal of the Roman Curia from the preceding century (except for a few changes, most of which were no better than what they replaced). The readings were taken from the Murbach Lectionary, but the special readings for Wednesdays and Fridays were eliminated except for Ember Week. The Gospel for Ember Saturday is repeated the next day (fourth Sunday). Historically, the Mass of Ember Saturday had been celebrated during the night between Saturday and Sunday, and there was no Sunday liturgy.

The 1570 lectionary was thus poorer than its predecessors. Compare it with the lectionary issued after Vatican Council II, and see how rich a treasure of scriptural readings we now have for Advent. The season now constitutes an inexhaustible source of Christian spirituality.

	Advent in the Missal of 1570	
First Sunday	Rom. 13:11-14	Luke 21:33-35
Second Sunday	Rom. 15:4-13	Matthew 11:2-20
Third Sunday	Phil. 4:4-7	John 1:19-28
Wednesday	Is. 2:2-5	
	Is. 7:10-15	Luke 1:26-38
Friday	Is. 11:1-5	Luke 1:39-47
Saturday	Is. 19:20-22	
	Is. 35:1-7	
	Is. 40:9-11	
	Is. 45:1-8	
	Dan. 3:47-51	
	2 Thess. 2:1-8	Luke 3:1-6
Fourth Sunday	1 Cor. 4:1-5	Luke 3:1-6

The prayers

The sacramentaries contained prayer formulas for the various celebrations. The *Verona Sacramentary* is a collection of *libelli*, or booklets of formulas, to be used on various feasts and occasions. At one time their composition was attributed to St. Leo the Great, and the whole book was therefore called the *Leonine Sacramentary*. In fact, however, the prayers came from various sources. In the collection there are prayers for the Ember Week Masses in December.[93]

Among them we find these beautiful words: "so that we may not only enjoy the fruitfulness of the earth but may also receive with purified hearts, the birth of the eternal bread."[94]

Another sacramentary that is of far greater importance for Advent is the *Gelasian Sacramentary*. According to some scholars, this was composed at Rome and later copied in France, where local Mass formularies were also inserted.

Other scholars, however, believe that the sacramentary was composed elsewhere than at Rome.[95] The manuscript dates from 750 and contains the first formularies we have for the Advent season. The texts have become disordered, however; we give here, using the numbers in Mohlberg's edition, the order of texts as proposed by A. Chavasse.[96]

	1	Collect 2	3	Secret	Preface	Post-communion
First Sunday	1120	1121	1125	1122	1123	1124
Second Sunday	1126	1127	1128	1129	—	1130
Third Sunday	1136	1131	1132	1133	—	1134
Fourth Sunday	1140	1135	1137	1138	—	1139
Fifth Sunday	1141	1142	1143	1144	—	1145

A number of these prayers have been taken over into our present sacramentary: First Sunday, opening prayer, 1139; second Sunday, opening prayer, 1153. From the beginning of Advent to December 16: First Monday, opening prayer, 1128; first Wednesday, opening prayer, 1154 and 1140; second Friday, opening prayer, 1136; third Friday, opening prayer, 1126. From December 17 to December 24: December 17, prayer over the gifts, 1175, and prayer after Communion, 1134; December 20, prayer after Communion, 1352; December 21, opening prayer, 1145; December 23, prayer after Communion, 996.

We shall indicate here a few interesting prayers that have not been taken into the new sacramentary. "Lord, stir up your power and come, and in your mercy do as you promised your Church you would, until the end of time."[97] Alongside this beautiful eschatological prayer we may set a postcommunion that exhorts us to move beyond earthly things toward the everlasting kingdom: "We have been filled with spiritual nourishment. We beg you, almighty God, that you would teach us, through our sharing in this mystery, to disdain earthly things and love those of heaven. Free us from the bonds of deadly desire and bring us into the kingdom of everlasting freedom."[98] Note here the very close connection between reception of the Eucharist and entrance into the kingdom.

A preface offers an interesting theology of the time of waiting and of Christ's birth. "Answer our prayers and show your Church the mercy in which she believes. Manifest to your people the marvelous sacrament of your only-begotten Son so that the nations of the earth may receive what you promised in the gospel of your word, and your adopted children may possess that to which the Truth bore witness." [99]

2. Advent in the Ancient Liturgy of Milan

We know what the readings for Advent were in the Ambrosian liturgy of the Middle Ages.

Readings in the Ambrosian Mass in the Middle Ages

First Sunday	2 Thess. 2:1-14	Matthew 24:1-42
Second Sunday	Rom. 15:1-13	Luke 3:1-18
Third Sunday	Rom. 11:25-36	Matthew 11:2-15
Fourth Sunday	Heb. 10:35-39	Matthew 21:1-9
Fifth Sunday	Gal. 4:22–5:1	John 1:15-28
Sixth Sunday	*Bergamo*: Philippians 4:4-9	Luke 1:39-45
	Biasca: 1 Corinthians 1:4-9	

A couple of points are specific to this liturgy: the reading of Hebrews 10:35-39; on the first Sunday the reading refers not only to the coming of the Lord but to what will precede it, namely, Antichrist, apostasies, and the signs that proclaim the coming of the Lord at the end of time. The Milanese Advent had six Sundays; it also placed a great deal of emphasis on the Blessed Virgin, Isaiah, and John the Baptist. The chief liturgical books from which we derive our knowledge of this liturgy are the Sacramentary of Bergamo and the Sacramentary of Biasca.[100]

The Milanese liturgy provides us with some fine prayers. Here are three examples.

In the Sacramentary of Bergamo, the first Sunday takes us straight into the paschal mystery and thus gives Advent a very characteristic tone. "God, in your Son you made us a new creature for yourself. Look graciously on the work of your merciful hands, and by the coming of your Son cleanse us from all the corruption of our old selves."[101]

Two prefaces deserve to be generally known. On the second Sunday the preface speaks of the two comings of Christ.

> Through Christ our Lord, whose incarnation saved the world and whose Passion brought redemption to every man. Let him lead us, we pray, to our eternal reward who redeemed us from the darkness of hell. Let him justify us at his second coming who redeemed us at his first.[102]

The sixth and final Sunday of Advent concentrates entirely on the Blessed Virgin. Its preface reads as follows:

> From her womb came the fruit that nourished us with the bread of angels. What Eve destroyed by her sin, Mary restored for our salvation. The deeds of the serpent and the Virgin were opposed: from him came the poison of division, from her the mystery of the Savior; through him the creature fell, through her the Creator rose. Since then human nature has no longer been captive but has been restored to liberty and has received from Christ, the Author of life, what it had lost through Adam, its father.[103]

3. Advent in Merovingian Gaul

Several lectionaries give us insight into the rich Advent liturgy of Merovingian Gaul, although we can speak of it only briefly here. The table below is taken from Pierre Salmon's book on the Luxeuil Lectionary.[104]

If the reader takes the time to read the Scripture passages listed in the table, he will note, especially in the Bobbio Missal, both the emphasis on the paschal aspect of Advent and the theology of the last days and the return of Christ.

The prayers in the liturgy of Merovingian Gaul are of

some interest, but we must again limit ourselves to a few examples. The Angoulême Sacramentary has some quite original prayers.[105] For instance: "Almighty God, purify our consciences by your daily visitation so that when your Son, our Lord, comes, he may find in us a dwelling prepared for him."[106] Or the following, which is somewhat baptismal in character: "Let our souls, we beg you, be inflamed by your Spirit so that we may be filled with the divine gift and be brightly shining lamps when your Son comes."[107]

We should recall that in Merovingian Gaul, Advent was thought of as "St. Martin's Lent." The Bobbio Missal contains a special Mass for St. Martin.[108]

4. Advent in Spain

The surviving manuscripts are quite numerous. We have them from Toledo, though in mutilated or fragmentary condition.[109] The Silos Lectionary,[110] the Léon Lectionary of 1065–71,[111] and the San Millán de la Cogolla Lectionary of 1073[112] fill out the picture. It seems that Advent came into existence in two stages, with the passages from Isaiah being chosen in their order within the book, and the passages from the Gospels being made to harmonize with Isaiah.

Note below the structure of the readings for the third Sunday. The reading from Ezechiel proclaims the coming of the Lord. The Gospel reading tells of Jesus' entry into Jerusalem, when he is acclaimed as the one who comes in the name of the Lord. St. Paul relates it all to the Christian's life: When Christ is manifested, our own glory shall be revealed; but if that is to happen, we must live in a certain way now.

The Spanish liturgy was especially rich in prayers, rich enough to merit a whole book on the subject. We find them in the *Liber mozarabicus sacramentorum*; most of these prayers date from the years 400–450.[113] The prayers frequently juxtapose the two comings of Christ. There is, for example, this prayer before the Our Father on the first Sunday of Advent: "O Word of the Father, you who became man and dwelt among us, grant that we who believe you have already come and hope you will come again may be freed from all stain of sin."[114]

Then there is the opening prayer for the Mass of the third Sunday. It recalls the cures as the signs that the kingdom is here:

> Let the hearts of your faithful be fortified by your coming, I pray, Lord Jesus Christ, and the knees of the weak be strengthened by your name. May your visitation heal the wounds of the sick, your rule make strong the feet of the lame, and your mercy untie the bonds of sin. Grant that those who accept you at your first coming may joyfully greet you when you come again for judgment, and lead them to the delights of paradise where they may live forever in gladness.[115]

First Stage
(No indication of readings from the Letters)

First Sunday	Is. 11:1-5; 4:2-3	Matthew 3:1-11
Second Sunday	Is. 28:16-17; 29:17-24	Mark 1:1-8
Third Sunday	Is. 35:1-2	Luke 3:1-8

Second Stage

First Sunday		
Is. 2:1-5; 4:2-3	Rom. 11:25-30	Matthew 3:1-11
Second Sunday		
Is. 28:16-17; 29:17-24	1 Cor. 4:1-5	Matthew 11:2-15
Third Sunday		
Ezek. 36:6-11	Col. 3:4-11	Matthew 21:1-9
Fourth Sunday		
Mal. 3:1-4	1 Thess. 5:14-23	Mark 1:1-8
Fifth Sunday		
Is. 35:1-2	Phil. 5:14-23	Luke 3:1-18

Sunday	W	S	S¹	V	B	P
First Sunday	Rom. 15:9-13 Matthew 20:29–21:3	Is. 6:1-10		Rom. 1:1	Mal. 3:1-6 James 5:7-12, 19, 20	John 1:35-51
Second Sunday		Is. 35:1-10		(8:3)	Matthew 11:2-5 Rom. 8:3-6	Matthew 24:15
Third Sunday		Is. 62:10-12; 45:8	Rom. 11:30-36	Rom. 11:25	Matthew 3:1-12	Matthew 11:2
Fourth Sunday		Is. 54:1-5	1 Thess. 3:9-13	Rom. 15:4	Matthew 15:8-13	Luke 3:2
Fifth Sunday		Is. 49:1-10	1 Thess. 3:9-13	Phil. 4:4	Matthew 24:27-44	
Sixth Sunday		Is. 11:1-10	Col. 1:23-29			Matthew 3:1
Seventh Sunday			Phil. 4:4-9		Phil. 4:4-7	Matthew 21:1
Vigil					Luke 12:35-37	

W = Wolfenbüttel Palimpsest, ca. 500. It seems to indicate readings for the first Sunday of Advent, but some take them as meant for the feast of the circumcision. Edited in Alban Dold, *Das älteste Liturgiebuch der lateinischen Kirche* (Texte und Arbeiten 26–28; Beuron, 1936). See Vogel, *op. cit.*, p. 290.

S = Merovingian Lectionary, ca. 700; originally from northern Italy. Partial edition in Germain Morin, "Un lectionnaire mérovingien de Sélestat avec fragments du texte occidental des Actes," *Revue bénédictine* 25 (1908), pp. 161–66; idem in *Études, Textes, Découvertes* 1 (Maredsous, 1913), pp. 440–56. See Vogel, *op. cit.*, p. 292.

S¹ = Fragment of a lectionary from Sélestat, indicating the readings from the third Sunday of Advent on. Edited in G. Morin, *art. cit.*, p. 166. See Vogel, *loc. cit.*

V = Vatican manuscript giving the "Bobbio List" or "Bobbio Epistolary," which indicates the pericopes from Paul; from Northern Italy. See Vogel, *loc. cit.*

B = The eighth-century Bobbio Missal, preserved at Paris. Edited by E. J. Lowe and J. W. Legg, *The Bobbio Missal* 1: *Facsimile*; 2: *Text* (Henry Bradshaw Society 53 and 58; London, 1917–20). See Vogel, *op. cit.*, p. 293.

P = Marginal notations in the seventh-century evangeliary of Saint-Dénis. Edited by P. Salmon, "Le texte biblique de l'Évangéliaire de Saint-Dénis," *Miscellanea Mercati* 1 (Rome, 1946), pp. 103–106. See Vogel, *op. cit.*, p. 295. The texts in the Luxeuil Lectionary start only with the Vigil of Christmas.

THE CHRISTMAS MYSTERY

BIBLICO-LITURGICAL REFLECTIONS

ON CHRISTMAS

10. CHRISTMAS: A Charming Memory?

Is the incarnation a myth?

Our aim here is not apologetics, and we have no intention of using the methods proper to apologetics. Our aim is rather to enter into the concerns of some among us today — perhaps some of the best among us — who are still looking for Christ and wish to meet him in a personal way. In present-day doctrinal teaching and catechetics, we do not hear much about the person of Christ. Everyone is interested in religious anthropology and religious sociology; eloquence lags when it comes to presenting Christ himself. Even the young are objecting to this failure and are beginning to feel the emptiness of a Christian religion that no longer gives Christ first place.

At the same time, however, contemporary critical study, especially in the area of comparative religion, is suggesting new difficulties and creating problems for faith. One of man's oldest desires, after all, is that God should come to earth to meet man. In the classical religions it is often not easy to decide whether the appearance of a god on earth is an object of real belief or simply a consoling myth that may give men hope amid the distress of their earthly lives.

It may perhaps be said that Christianity, more than other religions, has developed a cult of God-as-a-child and accepted all the artistic, romantic, and affective repercussions of such a cult. But we must immediately add that this cult of the manger was a late development in the Church and that Christmas originally laid no such heavy emphasis on the infant condition of Jesus. On the contrary, the coming of the

Word as man was closely connected with the paschal mystery. In fact, this connection is characteristic of the specifically Christian idea of God's incarnation. Incarnation means not only that God is with us but also that we are redeemed and with God. Fallen mankind is redeemed and shares the very life of God.

In the truly traditional thinking of the Church, there is nothing poetic about the incarnation. In fact, the emphasis is, if anything, on a rather brutal fact: The Word came to do God's will, even to the point of dying on a Cross. Another element in the specifically Christian view of the incarnation is that God became man, not so that he might be with us, but so that we might be with him. In other words, the incarnation is the starting point of our divinization. But even this "divinization" is not an end in itself. It comes about so that, having become in a sense "divine," we may be capable of effectively working with Christ to rebuild the world for the glory of the Father. We are thus not passive bystanders at the incarnation. The incarnation radically transforms the history of the world and the personal history of each of us. Because of it, each of us must measure up to God's plan and play his proper role in it.

Now, for many, all this sounds rather unreal. But the problem that people have with it today is not the problem of Christ's one person in two natures that preoccupied the Christians of the fourth century; what men question today is rather the usefulness of such a coming of God among us.

The bewilderment that the divine method of assuring man's salvation causes in the minds of many is due, I think, to the fact that the incarnation is looked upon too much as an isolated fact. It is not seen in continuity with the whole history of salvation and as the beginning of the final and supreme stage, the new and eternal covenant. We think of Christ's birth (and many other events recorded in the Bible) as an isolated "story," an event that belongs to folklore or as being mysterious. We forget that Christ's birth, and every biblical event, is linked to past, present, and future. The incarnation is seen in a new light as soon as we connect it with the paschal mystery and the covenant.

The incarnation as conceived by a Christian is quite different from the incarnations of the gods in pagan myth. Even so, it is something accepted on faith. Faith, of course, can and should be an enlightened faith. These days, indeed, we are more aware of the need of doing justice to the reality of the incarnation by avoiding too limited a view of it, without at the same time denying that God could legitimately use man's sensibilities, art, and affectivity in order to draw mankind at various periods of its history into the living mystery of the Word made flesh.

The point, however, that we must emphasize here, and later on, is that the feast of Christmas originates in a celebration of radiant splendor. I am referring to the celebration of the sun's victory over the cold and storms of winter, a victory won at the very moment when Christians would be celebrating the birth of the Word as man. In its origin, then, the celebration of the incarnation was a paschal celebration of the Lord's triumph.

It is here that we can see the depth at which the Church's faith in the incarnation operated. This faith is of such a kind that some of the early writers exaggerated its importance and expressed themselves clumsily. For example, in the Eucharistic Prayer that St. Hippolytus of Rome, in his *Apostolic Tradition*, suggests for the use of a newly consecrated bishop, he has a strange but very meaningful expression: the Word became flesh and "was shown as a son to you" (*filius tibi ostensus est*).[116] We might think that this language is not quite in keeping with Christian faith, since the Son is eternally the Son. But, in Hippolytus's view, the birth of the Word as man is so important because it allows the Son to prove that he is truly the Son. Why? Because what makes a son a son is that he does his father's will. If the Word was to do the Father's will, he had to become a man.

What we really have here is the theology of the Fourth

Gospel, with its sensitivity to Christ's mission as consisting in the doing of his Father's will. St. Hippolytus was well acquainted with the writings of St. Irenaeus of Lyons, who had been a disciple of Papias, who in turn had known St. John. The important thing for us about Hippolytus's viewpoint and manner of expressing himself is that it shows us how closely the early Church connected Christ's birth and his paschal mystery.

But there are similarities, are there not, between Christ's birth and death and those of the gods in pagan myth? In saying this, however, we are forgetting certain things that are absolutely unique about the Christian faith. The incarnation is indeed the first step toward Christ's sacrifice and death, but we misunderstand that death if we think of it in isolation and as being an end in itself. The Scriptures are constantly emphasizing the uselessness of external sacrifices in themselves and insisting on the importance of the spiritual offering, that is, of self-giving. This holds for Christ as well. The entire value of his death derives from its being the sign of an interior submission to the Father's will. In his dying, the physical death is the outward sign of a spiritual sacrifice. The spiritual sacrifice, in turn, derives its whole worth from the fact that it is the sacrifice of a God-man, whose death becomes the sign and embodiment of an offering worthy of the Father.

Christ's death is, therefore, a sign. If it were merely a death, we could not be saved by it, since God has no more use for human sacrifices than he has for animal sacrifices. At the same time, however, Christ's death is necessary, especially and precisely because it is the sign of the God-man's submission to his Father's will and an act of love directed to the Father's glory.

It must also be said that if this death had not taken place, we would not have been saved. Why? Because there would be no way for us to verify and come into contact with the interior reality of self-offering on Christ's part. That self-offering finds its expression precisely in his death. Moreover, the sign by which we are united to each other would

be lacking, a sign which is now sacramentally signified and made available to us in the ever-repeated Supper
we call the Mass. In all of this the incarnation has supreme
consequences that no myth ever envisaged.

Let us repeat: In saying what we have said, we have not
been engaging in apologetics. Our whole appeal is to the
faith of the person who meditates on the mystery of the incarnation.

The celebration of Christmas — a folklore survival?

If people today, so anxious to be authentic, are to sur-
mount the obstacles to a genuine celebration of Christmas,
we must briefly summarize the history of this feast. Knowing its history, we will be in a better position to understand
its theology and appreciate its realism.

As is generally known, December 25 was the day on
which pagans celebrated the feast of the *Natalis solis invicti*, "the birth" — or rebirth — "of the unconquered sun."
The "Chronographer of A.D. 354," the anonymous compiler
of an almanac for Roman Christians, mentions this pagan
feast on December 25 in one of his lists. Was it the
Church's intention to counteract the influence of this solemn festival of the solar cult that had been supplanting the
hitherto popular mystery religions such as the cult of
Dionysos during the third century?

There can be no doubt that the worship of the sun had
won an important place in contemporary life. St. Leo and
St. Augustine were both concerned about the practice of
this cult, toward which Christians at times showed excessive sympathy. Not surprisingly, then, we find in a Christian treatise, *De solstitiis et aequinoctibus* (On Solstices
and Equinoxes), dating from the end of the third century,
that Christ is presented to us as the true and always victorious Sun, while his birth is regarded as the only true birth of
the only unconquered Sun.[117]

There is, then, a relation between the *Natalis solis invicti*
and Christmas, but the relation has been explained in vari-

ous ways. Some scholars, relying on the sermons of the fourth-century Fathers, have thought that conjectures on the date of Christ's birth led to the choice of December 25 as the day of celebration.[118] But the arguments showing the Fathers inquiring into the date of Christ's birth are value-less. What caused December 25 to be chosen for the cele-bration seems rather to have been the influence of the festi-val of the *Natalis solis invicti*. Among Christians, *natalis* had long meant "the anniversary of death," but through contact with pagans, the word also came to have for Chris-tians the sense of "birthday."[119] This seems to show that there was a real relation between the pagan and the Chris-tian feast.

Some see in the establishment of Christmas a counter-feast. Popular enthusiasm for the celebration of the pagan feast was to be diverted to a feast that was clearly Christian in character, an opposition feast that was in no way con-taminated by the pagan feast.

It may also be admitted, however, that the Church simply decided to christianize the pagan feast of the winter sol-stice. There was little difficulty in doing so. Light and darkness were themes dear to St. John, as they were to the entire biblical and Christian tradition. It was a simple mat-ter to make use of them in this new context and to focus on them the attention of the faithful, who were already used to them from reading Scripture and hearing sermons. Moreover, people at this period liked to assign dates in the annual cycle to the events of salvation; the equinoxes played a role in the determination of such dates.[120] Quite possibly, then, the Church simply took over and chris-tianized the pagan feast of the *Natalis solis invicti*.

Is it possible to say just when this infusion of Christian doctrine into pagan forms took place? The anonymous Chronographer of 354 provides both a civil and a religious calendar. In his civil calendar he mentions, under De-cember 25, *N(atale) invicti*. Then, at the head of the list of the bishops of Rome, whose date of death he gives, he notes, as occurring on December 25, the birth of Christ at

Bethlehem in Judah.[121] This list seems to have been compiled in 336, so that the celebration of Christmas at Rome goes back at least to before that year.[122]

The fact that Christ's birth is mentioned in a list of dates for commemorating the anniversaries of the martyrs (dates always fixed and invariable) emphasizes the historical dimension of Christmas. Christmas relates to an event; the birth of the Lord, his appearance among us as a man, is a precise, concrete datum; it took place at a definite moment. While Easter is a movable feast, the birthday of the Lord is celebrated on a fixed day in the annual cycle. This fact suggests certain reflections to which we must now turn.

Christmas: Anniversary or mystery?

St. Augustine seems to have been so struck by the fact that Christmas is celebrated on a fixed day that he regards it simply as an anniversary or *memoria*. It is, though, a very special *memoria*, for the Creator himself picked this day for his coming: "Born of the Father, he determines the courses of all the ages; born of his Mother, he consecrates a particular day: today." [123]

But, when all is said and done, Christmas is only an anniversary or *memoria* for Augustine. From our viewpoint today, we might be tempted to think of it, not as indeed a mere folkloric memorial, but as a memorial of a great moment, a great turning point in the history of the world and our own personal history. Thus, it would be the kind of memorial around which we build up a folklore.

If St. Augustine thinks of Christmas as a simple memorial, the reason is that he also knows of celebrations that are *sacramenta*. He speaks of these *sacramenta* in two letters. Around 400, Januarius, a layman, had asked him a series of questions about liturgy, and he gave his answer in the two letters. One of these (Letter 54) is fairly short; the other (Letter 55) turns into a treatise that gives us insight into Augustine's mind and contains his theology of the liturgy.

In Letter 54 he says that the Lord endowed his new society with a small number of *sacramenta* that are easy to carry out and whose meaning is marvelous indeed.[124] Augustine is here using the word *sacramentum* in a very broad sense. What is included among these *sacramenta* that are few in number and characterized by great simplicity? In his view, all the signs that are bearers of salvation, however varied they may be (and they include more than our seven sacraments), are *sacramenta*. Baptism and the Eucharist are *sacramenta*, but so is the celebration of Easter. It is not just the seven sacraments that make present again the mysteries of salvation. Every liturgical celebration makes present the mystery celebrated. This is teaching that will be repeated in Vatican II's *Constitution on the Liturgy*.[125]

But how can such efficacy be attributed to every liturgical celebration? St. Augustine explains in Letter 55: "A celebration is a 'sacrament' when the commemoration of a past event presents itself to us as the sign of a reality that must be received in a holy manner."[126]

Easter is a "sacrament" because we do not simply call to mind what Christ did for us (his death and resurrection). Rather, the celebration makes present to us, under a veil of signs, the sacred reality of that death and resurrection, and we must really receive it as the pledge of our own passage from death to life. The celebration is thus based on a sacred sign, but, through and by means of the sign, the celebration takes us into the reality signified. Every sign representative of Christ's, and our, passage from death to life is a sacred sign, and any celebration using this type of sign is a "sacrament."[127]

St. Augustine draws the conclusion that Christmas can only be a simple memorial, not a sacrament. The celebration of Easter is sacramental because it is a sign of Christ's death and resurrection; these events of our redemption find expression in the Easter solemnities, in baptismal initiation, and in the Eucharistic liturgy. The feast of Christmas, however, contains no such signs and is therefore simply an imaginative re-creation, a memorial or anniversary. On that feast we simply recall the fact of Christ's birth.[128]

Is Christmas, then, what Anton Baumstark liked to call a "Feast of Idea"?[129] (Baumstark was motivated by a desire to give centrality and absolute primacy to the paschal mystery and its representation in the liturgical celebration.) It is true enough that Christmas did give expression to a basic truth about the two natures of Christ, which had been the subject of so much controversy. Some of the Christmas antiphons restated in poetic form the definition proclaimed by the Council of Chalcedon in 451, and the liturgy was an occasion for teaching the faithful how to think of the divine Person and two complete natures, human and divine, of Jesus.

Perhaps St. Augustine believed that December 25 was actually the date of Christ's birth; perhaps this impressed him so much that he could think of the feast only as a *Natale*, even though a very special one, since it was that of the Lord. But, as we have seen, it is impossible to connect the choice of December 25 with the historical date of Christ's birth or even with an inconsistent tradition about the date.

The choice of December 25, which was the time of the winter solstice, did establish a link between the biblical symbolism of light and darkness, and Christ as the victorious, invincible Sun that dispels the darkness. Augustine was well aware of the pagan feast of the *Natale solis invicti*, for he mentions it in one of his sermons: "Let us celebrate this day, brothers, not because of the visible sun, but because of him who made this day."[130] It is surprising that Augustine was not struck by the connection between the winter solstice and the lightness-darkness symbolism, especially since, in writing to Januarius, he discoursed at length on the connection between the date of Easter and the lunar cycle. Augustine's attention was focused on the one mystery of our passage with Christ from death to life, and he was not sensitive to the elements of this mystery that were to be found in the feast of Christmas. Had he been sensitive to them, he would have seen that Christmas, too, by his definition, was a "sacrament."

Christmas, a mystery of salvation

Pope St. Leo the Great will maintain the position St. Augustine did not reach. We will hear him using phrases in his sermons that Augustine would not have tended to use: *sacramentum Natalis Christi,* "sacrament of the day of Christ's birth," or *Nativitatis dominicae sacramentum,* "sacrament of the Lord's birth." He writes that the words of the Gospels and prophets teach us "to think of the Lord's birth, wherein the Word became flesh, not as a past event which we recall, but as a present reality upon which we gaze."[131]

This is not to be taken as mere literary embellishment. In the preceding sermon St. Leo makes his thought even clearer: God became man "so that, by turning to that ineffable divine act of merciful condescension whereby the Creator of man deigned to become a man, we might be found in the nature of him whom we adore in our own."[132]

In this celebration of Christmas, then, Christ takes an active part, since through the "divine act of merciful condescension" we will acquire "the nature of him whom we adore in our own." In other words, in this celebration the grace implied by the re-presentation is actively at work. That is why St. Leo can say, just before the words quoted above, that "today . . . the sacrament of the Lord's birth shines more brilliantly before our eyes."[133]

The Church of our day certainly intends to celebrate Christmas as a mystery that is present in her liturgy. This outlook likewise justifies the celebration of Advent as a time of waiting not only for Christ's return on the last day but also for his first coming at his incarnation. We shall see this theology at work in the prayers of the Christmas season when we examine these later on.

Since, however, Christmas, like Easter, renders present the mystery of our passage from death to life with Christ, are the two feasts identical? Is Christmas simply a useless duplicate? St. Leo, after all speaks of Christmas in the same terms he could have used in speaking of Easter: "the day chosen for the sacrament of man's restoration."[134]

St. Leo is not exaggerating, and Christmas is indeed a sacrament of salvation, but it is not therefore strictly a celebration of the paschal mystery as such. There is only one sacrament of salvation, but it is celebrated according to its various aspects. What Christmas renders present is the starting point of our salvation; it is ordered toward our redemption, which it already contains.[135]

The introduction of the crèche and all the Christmas folklore has been a good thing, and neither can nor should be simply rejected. We must admit, however, that the injection of these elements, especially at a time when both the liturgy and the knowledge of Scripture were in decline, has turned Christmas, for many, into the feast of tender pity; midnight Mass is the most important thing to these Christians, and the feast has no further influence on their lives. The mistake is to have focused the celebration too much on the birth at Bethlehem and to have turned the object of the feast into a moving story.

Rome was the place where this feast, with its clearly paschal theology of the Sun's victory, was created. How ironic, then, that Rome should also be the home, even today, of the folklore that has almost completely obscured the deeper meaning of the celebration! And yet, all that would be needed in order to bring out once again the full meaning of the feast would be to connect with the crèches (often quite beautiful from an artistic viewpoint) a representation of the victorious sun. "His birth at Bethlehem is rather the occasion than the object of the feast. The object is the total mystery of Redemption, the already announced Paschal Mystery."[136]

The incarnation: Today? For me?

Through the liturgical sign the incarnation of the eternal Word is therefore present, today and for me. But what can such a "presence" mean for me? What purpose does it serve? Does not Christmas seem to be an example of the wearisome redundancy to which theology succumbs when it tries to prove too much or when it exerts itself to make us feel at every moment a total dependence on God? Isn't it enough to celebrate Easter as present? Must we also turn the beginnings of the redemptive mystery into something present? We are not denying the incarnation, of course, but isn't it just a springboard? Why dwell on it? In what way can this feast be a source of inspiration and energy for modern man? In fact, isn't Christmas really a kind of forced celebration, comparable to so many celebrations and commemorations we must put up with in civic life? What can we gain from it? Or, if that be too utilitarian a viewpoint, what point of contact does Christmas have with the contemporary world that gets its back up at the thought of tender religious feelings?

I do not regard such questions as unprofitable, for they touch the very foundations of our Christianity. Admittedly, a man can become holy without knowing why the Church thought it good to actualize not only the paschal mystery but its beginnings as well. But we cannot on that account refuse to try to get clear the importance of actualizing the incarnation.

We will have occasion in the course of this book to see how the liturgy seeks to relate to our everyday lives the present graces of the incarnation. But even before seeing what the liturgy's view is, we shall not be wasting our time if we seek an overall view of the values inherent in the actualization of the incarnation.

Today, as in the past, the God-man is a cause of wonderment; he has also radically changed the course of history. And yet, in terms of the impact made on mankind, the most eye-catching thing has not been the paschal mystery of Christ but the birth of the Word according to the flesh. The myth of a divine human being is to be found everywhere in mankind, but when has the union of two complete natures in one divine person been studied with the same sense of wonder as by those who have set themselves to scrutinize the mystery of Christ's person?

This fact, however, does not yet tell us why the union of two complete natures in Christ at his incarnation should be of primordial importance for us. In this context, we must recall that redemption would have been impossible if Christ had not become fully a man and thus head of the human race and a counterweight to Adam, while at the same time being fully God. His action of self-offering would have lacked the perfection of love.

Today we are perhaps struck even more by the fact that Christ's incarnation was necessary for the understanding of all the sacraments, especially the celebration of the Last Supper and now the Mass.

How could there be a real contact with God if the incarnation had not occurred? If we can now know and touch God, it is because the Word became incarnate. Our relationship is with this incarnate Christ whose glorified body is now really present in the Eucharistic celebration, although without being subject to the limitations of space and time. The Eucharistic presence that is so essential to the Church's life is unintelligible without the presence of the glorified body of the risen Christ. The incarnation thus involves our humanity; it is our humanity that is divinized. How then can the incarnation fail to concern us? It is not a matter of indifference to us whether or not we celebrate the intimate union of two natures in Christ on the day when the Word was born according to the flesh.

We may indeed be indifferent, of course, if we have not grasped in a progressively deeper way the heights to which our nature has been raised by the incarnation, and if we do not enter ever more fully into the mystery of the new life that comes to us through rebirth in water and the Spirit. These two births go together: the human birth of the Word as Prophet, Messiah, King, and Priest, and our rebirth, through water and Spirit, as adoptive sons, when we too become prophets, priests, and kings, sharing the one priesthood of Christ in the measure proper to baptism.

The fact that the Word has become incarnate should, then, unsettle all my present attitudes. The human nature I have inherited is not human nature as it was before the incarnation. Far from being in any way diminished by the in-

carnation, human nature has gained a dignity which faith
alone can properly appreciate but which is by any accounting extraordinary. It is not only human nature "in itself," as
it were, that acquires this divine dimension from the incarnation but all its activities as well, and especially its worship.

Because of the incarnation of the Word, we can boast of
offering a worship that no other religion has ever been able
to offer. The reason is that, according to Catholicism, Christ
himself celebrates our liturgy and draws us into his self-
giving to his Father. And if the reader thinks these various
considerations to be only pious maunderings, he should
realize that he lacks essential elements of the faith and that
his religion is very impoverished.

These important themes will be developed in the pages
that follow. We had to present them succinctly here as justification for the creation of the feast of Christmas in the
fourth century. We offer them also as evidence of the irre-
placeable, always contemporary value of a celebration that,
we hope, will gradually acquire once again its real and essential paschal meaning.

II. GOD AND MAN, KING
AND SERVANT

In the Office of Readings on December 24, the invitatory,
which will be repeated as the entrance antiphon of the
Vigil Mass, reads thus: "Today you will know the Lord is
coming, and in the morning you will see his glory."

In two passages of the Book of Exodus, we find similar
phrasing used to announce a miraculous deed that is a sign
of God's extraordinary good will. "At evening you shall
know that it was the Lord who brought you out of the land
of Egypt, and in the morning you shall see the glory of the

Lord" (Exod. 16:6-7). And again: "At twilight you shall eat flesh, and in the morning you shall be filled with bread" (Exod. 16:12). It seems quite clear that these passages, like the liturgy, refer to two moments within a single act. God is miraculously present to serve mankind, and the "today" and "tomorrow" refer to two moments of this one presence.

John the Evangelist was using words in the most realistic possible way when he wrote in his Prologue: "We have beheld his glory" (John 1:14).

For Israel, to see the Lord's "glory" was the most miraculous of all events, for God's glory is the manifestation of his presence. The column of cloud and the column of fire were both manifestations of the divine presence (Exod. 13:22), while the "glory" of God will also be said to be enclosed in a cloud. In this respect, the majestic theophany recorded in Exodus 19:16-25, with its storm and trumpet blasts and heavy cloud, gives a good idea of what Israel had in mind when it spoke of God's "glory" being manifested. God's "glory" is that awesome majesty no mortal eyes can see. But the prophet Ezekiel depicts that glory in human form in his vision of the "Chariot of Yahweh":

> And above the firmament over their heads there was the likeness of a throne, in appearance like sapphire; and seated above the likeness of a throne was a likeness as it were of a human form. And upward from what had the appearance of his loins I saw as it were gleaming bronze, like the appearance of fire enclosed round about; and downward from what had the appearance of his loins I saw as it were the appearance of fire, and there was brightness round about him. Like the appearance of the bow that is in the cloud on the day of rain, so was the appearance of the brightness round about. Such was the appearance of the likeness of the glory of the Lord. And when I saw it, I fell upon my face (Ezek. 1:26–2:1).

God's glory is also his might, the power he brings to bear upon his enemies: "In the greatness of thy majesty thou overthrowest thy adversaries" (Exod. 15:7). When the psalms sing of the Lord's glory, they will have their eye especially on the day of his definitive coming.

"That which we have touched with our hands"

This glory no one can see: "You cannot see my face; for man shall not see me and live" (Exod. 33:20), and yet St. John says that we have indeed seen it. Why? Because "the Word became flesh and dwelt among us" (John 1:14). The incarnation has thus overturned the old order of things. John wishes to show that God no longer limits himself, as under the old covenant, to an invisible presence in a place where he manifests himself (as in Genesis 12:7 and especially in the theophanies at Mount Sinai, the "mountain of God"). To this end, he speaks in his First Letter of his own experience:

> That which was from the beginning, which we have heard, which we have seen with our eyes, which we have looked upon and touched with our hands, concerning the word of life — the life was made manifest, and we saw it, and testify to it, and proclaim to you the eternal life which was with the Father and was made manifest to us — that which we have seen and heard we proclaim also to you (1 John 1:1-3).

After reporting the miracle at the wedding in Cana, John says of Jesus: "This, the first of his signs, Jesus did at Cana in Galilee, and manifested his glory; and his disciples believed in him" (John 2:11). Later on, just as he is about to raise Lazarus, Jesus himself says to Martha: "Did I not tell you that if you would believe you would see the glory of God?" (John 11:40). The glory of Jesus is seen in his mighty signs; it leads to faith when a man has seen it, but faith is needed in order to see it. The Gospel of John frequently speaks of this double relationship.

This glory that the Apostle John has contemplated and the whole world could have seen is also a judgment on this world. "'Now shall the ruler of this world be cast out; and I, when I am lifted up from the earth, will draw all men to myself.' He said this to show by what death he was to die" (John 12:31-33). When Christ is raised up on the Cross, he is also raised up to heaven; he rises from the dead and receives his reward at the Father's right hand. His death, his resurrection, and his triumph form a single mystery, a point so well made in John 12, "The hour has come for the Son of man to be glorified. Truly, truly, I say to you, unless a grain of wheat falls into the earth and dies it remains alone; but if it dies, it bears much fruit" (John 12:23-24).

The glory of God that we have seen is also Christ's triumph when he returns on the last day. "In the morning you shall see the glory of the Lord." Morning is the time of radiant light, and the light here is the light of Christ's return on the last day to judge the living and the dead. Between now and then, "of the increase of his government and of peace there will be no end, upon the throne of David, and over his kingdom, to establish it, and to uphold it with justice and with righteousness" (Is. 9:7).

From the Vigil on, then, Christmas evidently celebrates a threefold mystery: the coming of Christ to earth, the mystery of his death and resurrection (the redemptive act for which he comes), and his return for judgment. The opening prayer of the Christmas Vigil Mass pulls this theology together: "God our Father, every year we rejoice as we look forward to this feast of our salvation. May we welcome Christ as our Redeemer, and meet him with confidence when he comes to be our judge."

The glory of God that St. John saw and the Word of life that he touched is the Lord who has come, who comes today, and who will come again. He is the King of peace, but a King who dies in order to save us, then triumphs and takes his seat at the Father's right hand, whence he shall come again to judge the living and the dead.

Of the invitatory for Matins and the entrance antiphon, derived from Exodus 17:7, St. Bernard writes:

These words belong to a specific place and time in Scripture, but Mother Church has not unfittingly applied them to the Vigil of the Lord's Nativity. . . . When she modifies or applies a text taken from the divine Scriptures, her accommodation is weightier with meaning than the text was in its original context, as the truth is weightier with meaning than the prefiguration of it, the light than the shadow, the mistress than the handmaid.

In my view, the text clearly speaks to us of two days. The first runs from the fall of man to the end of the world. . . . The second will be the day that lasts forever amid the splendors of the saints. . . . Our [true] knowledge is to know that the Lord will indeed come, though we know not when. . . .

Today, the coming of the only-begotten Son lights in us the lamp of true knowledge, that is, the knowledge that the Lord will come again.[137]

We ourselves are fully involved in this mystery that is both one and threefold. The Lord comes, and we must welcome him, that is, we must go out of ourselves so as to suffer and die with him for our own redemption. Then we enter with him into glory and be henceforth united to the "King of glory." Then, forever and completely, "we shall see the Lord"; man, expelled from paradise, shall see his God once more.

"We see our God made visible"

When the Church celebrates the feast of Christmas, she cannot but connect it with the paschal mystery in its entirety. But she dwells upon one aspect of the total mystery: the God-man himself.

The God whom John saw and touched is the same God the Church claims to know now. She proclaims it to the Christian assembly: "We see our God made visible." Chapter 40 of Isaiah had foretold this: "And the glory of the Lord shall be revealed, and all flesh shall see it together" (Is. 40:5).

During the night of Christmas, the Church presents her Christ to us: he is the eternal Word, the Lord among his people, but he is also a Lord who has become man and dwelt among us. In the entrance antiphon of the Midnight Mass, she makes use of one particular psalm to express her faith-tradition: "The Lord said to me: You are my Son; this day have I begotten you" (Ps. 2:7).

When we read this psalm in the Bible and connect it with Psalm 45:8, Isaiah 9:6, Jeremiah 23:5, and Micah 5:2, we may well wonder what is the real meaning of the messianic prophecy to be found there. Is the text really speaking of a Messiah who is God? The exegetes have defended divergent interpretations. Around 1900 some claimed that the Messiah of whom the prophets spoke was indeed God. But even these exegetes distinguished between the thinking of the prophet himself and the thinking of his contemporaries. The latter, at least, did not think of the Messiah as being strictly divine.

> The prophecy concerning the Messiah has proved to be completely true, and this, like so many other prophecies, in a far more perfect way than the contemporaries of the prophet would have thought possible. They did not know the mystery of the Holy Trinity, and so when they distinguished between the future Messiah and Yahweh himself, they did not think of the Messiah as possessing the divine nature.[138]

Modern exegetes agree with the contemporaries of the prophets. They interpret Psalm 2:7 as referring, not to the eternal generation of the Word and thus his divinity, but to a purely adoptive sonship. If we set the verse of the psalm in its historical context, we see that it alludes to a promise of God in the Second Book of Samuel (7:14) that he will adopt as a son each king in the Davidic line, thus assuring David's dynasty of an eternal duration.

These quite different interpretations of the prophetic texts are due to the way in which prophecy as such is approached. If a prophecy is regarded as an exact report of what is going to happen, the interpreter will tend to take the Old Testament text exactly as it stands and pay no attention to the historical context of the prophecy. But is this approach legitimate? Is prophecy reducible to that sort of thing, so that it lacks any historical and psychological dimension? Can we imagine men perceiving such an immense religious revolution for mankind and yet not having at least an initial experience of a way so utterly new for them? Israel awaits both a Messiah and a meeting with its God, but does it connect in any way the "day of Yahweh" that it awaits and the Messiah who is to restore Israel?[139]

It should be clear to us, then, that when Church reads anew the prophets and the psalms in her liturgy, she elicits from them their full meaning and truth. To think that anthropomorphism in the Bible represents contamination by idolatrous paganism would be simplistic and even wrong. It was through such concrete descriptions of himself that God gradually made himself known. St. Irenaeus of Lyons said that the through the Old Testament theophanies, the Word was gradually habituating himself to living among men. The anthropomorphisms of Scripture were slowly preparing mankind to receive a God who would also be a man and able to experience hunger and thirst, physical and moral suffering, and even death.

A concrete theology

The God-man theme could not fail to receive a vibrant theological form in the liturgy. Rarely, in fact, do we find a theology more concrete in its expression; it is based on contrasts that the liturgy, like the Fathers and commentators, delights in emphasizing.

The hymn *A solis ortus cardine*, attributed to Sedulius, which used to be sung at Christmas Lauds, developed its thought by means of such contrasts: "The blessed maker of the world assumed a servant's form. . . . He deigned to have hay for a bed, and did not refuse the shelter of a manger. He does not suffer even a bird to hunger, and yet He was fed with a little milk."[140] Some of the responsories in the older Office also reflected this realistic theology, as the following examples show:[141]

The fourth responsory for Christmas: "What a great mystery, what a wonderful sign, that animals should see the Lord, new-born, lying in a manger!" The eighth responsory at Matins on the Sunday within the octave of Christmas: "O King of heaven, to whom such homage is given! He who contains the universe dwells in a stable. He is laid in a manger and reigns in heaven." The sixth responsory at Matins on January 1: "He lay in the manger and shone in heaven." And the seventh responsory on the same day: "For you carried in your womb the One whom the heavens cannot contain."

St. Paul, when attempting to give the Athenians the essentials of Christianity, said to them: "They [every nation of men] should seek God, in the hope that they might feel after him and find him. Yet he is not far from each one of us, for 'In him we live and move and have our being'; as even some of your poets have said, 'For we are indeed his offspring'" (Acts 17:27-28). And in the Letter to the Colossians he writes: "He is the image of the invisible God, the firstborn of all creation; for in him all things were created, in heaven and earth. . . . For in him all the fullness of God was pleased to dwell" (Col. 1:15-16, 19). The Word made flesh is the masterpiece and crown of creation.

It is with this God that we are now in contact: we see him and we touch him. The second reading for the Mass during the Day on Christmas says that "in many and various ways God spoke of old to our fathers by the prophets; but in these last days he has spoken to us by a Son" (Heb. 1:1-2). In the Old Testament theophanies God spoke to the leaders of his people; in the New Testament he gives men the privilege of seeing him as well as hearing him: "Philip . . . he who has seen me has seen the Father" (John 14:9). The older liturgy of Christmas used to give very concise expression to this wonderful shift from the hearing of God's word to the presence of the Word among us, for in the third lesson for Matins in the older Breviary, she read Isaiah 52:1 in a Latin that departed slightly from the original and had God saying: "I spoke to you of old, and lo! here I am!"

Christ as God-man and revealer of God — such is an essential to the vision early Christianity had. "The knowledge of God (in the biblical sense of the phrase) was the supreme grace in the eyes of the early Christians."

The wonderful deeds of God

The last statement may seem rather strange to a "Christian" mentality that is unfortunately still widespread, despite the return, now well under way, to Scripture and tradition. Our redemption has been given an important place in our religious life, and rightly so; but at times it tends to exclude concern about knowing the God who sends the Savior to us, and this is inexcusable. What it means in practice is a "spiritual life" that is focused not on God primarily but on our own salvation.

To know God and the one whom God sent, Jesus Christ, is more than an intellectual activity comparable to the study of philosophy. Knowledge of God in the Old Testament and in Christianity goes far beyond metaphysics. In fact, the point is not so much to know what God is in himself as to know his "wonderful deeds," the extraordinary, amazing things he has done for us, or the divine plan of our salvation as God has implemented it through the centuries. These "wonderful deeds of God" are the basis and object of the "eucharists," or prayers of blessing, that we find scattered through the Old Testament.[142] The Christian is even more aware of what God has done to gather his people and make them one again. It is now the whole of this divine activity that the Christian sees through Christ, the revealer of God.

When the prayer in the *Didache* thanks God for "the knowledge you have given us through Jesus your Servant," it is referring to the whole of God's activity: the "wonderful deeds of God" in the Old Testament and the incarnation, death, and resurrection of the Son in the New Testament. For it is through God's "wonderful deeds" that have become tangible in Christ that we men are able to "know God."[143]

St. Clement of Rome, in his Letter to the Corinthians, takes up the same theme: "through his beloved Son, Jesus Christ, who has called us from darkness to light, from ignorance to the knowledge of the glory of his name."[144] We should note, in the light of our earlier reflections, how St. Clement continues to use Old Testament terminology: the "knowledge" of "the glory of his name."

At the moment of martyrdom, St. Polycarp addresses God in a great prayer that is very like the ancient anaphoras (Canons, Eucharistic Prayers) and again harks back to the *Didache*: "O Lord, omnipotent God and Father of your blessed child Christ Jesus, through whom we have received our knowledge of you."[145] Finally, the Anaphora of Sarapion voices the same theology: "We praise you, who are known by the only-begotten Son and by him announced and explained and manifested to the saints."[146] These texts — and there are many others like them — give evidence of vital Christology, in which the central theme is the Word made flesh as revealer of the Father.

For God to give such "knowledge" of himself means that he wishes to share his own life with men. Such an offer requires a response from us. "The grace of God has appeared for the salvation of all men, training us to renounce irreligion and worldly passions" (Titus 2:11). Thus begins the second reading at Midnight Mass on Christmas. Similarly, St. Paul reminds the Galatians of what they are committed to by the knowledge they now have of God: "Formerly, when you did not know God, you were in bondage to beings that by nature are no gods; but now that you have come to know God, or rather to be known by God, how can you turn back again to the weak and beggarly elemental spirits, whose slaves you want to be once more?" (Gal. 4:8-9).

A liturgical catechesis

The liturgy provides a very careful catechesis on the two natures of Christ that we celebrate at Christmas. An antiphon at Lauds on the Solemnity of Mary, Mother of God (January 1), besides being beautifully harmonious, graceful, and lucidly clear, offers a perfect theological statement of the mystery of the incarnation. Research has dated the Latin text as composed at Rome at the end of the sixth or during the seventh century. It is in fact a translation of a troparion that was introduced into the Byzantine liturgy by a poet of the fifth century and is still sung in that liturgy on December 26. The poet in turn was inspired by a sermon that St. Gregory Nazianzus had preached at Constantinople on January 6, 379, and his composition is a succinct résumé of that sermon.[147] It reads: "Marvelous is the mystery proclaimed today: man's nature is made new as God becomes man; he remains what he was and becomes what he was not. Yet each nature stays distinct and for ever undivided."

There is an echo here of the ancient controversies concerning Christ and of the reactions these evoked. The author of the text knew what the Council of Chalcedon had said:

> . . . one and the same Christ, son, Lord, only-begotten; acknowledged in two natures unconfusedly, unchangeably, indivisibly, inseparably; the difference of the natures being in no way removed because of the union, but rather the property of each nature being preserved, and [both] concurring into one person and one hypostasis.[148]

The feast of Christmas (Epiphany in the East) served, like many other liturgical feasts, to rectify the faith of the community and to preserve it from deviations. The *Gloria* of the Mass, originally a Greek hymn for the Office of Ma-

tins, entered the Roman liturgy as a song before Midnight
Mass on Christmas. It contained, however, some Arian in-
terpolations that showed the Son as inferior to the Father.
St. Cyril of Jerusalem gave his catechumens the true explanation of the mystery of the two natures in Christ:

> The incarnation was not merely a rumor or something
> men imagined; it took place in very truth. The Word
> did not pass through the Virgin as through a channel
> but was really made flesh out of her body; he really
> ate as we eat, and drank as we drink. For if his as-
> sumption of human nature had been only a pretense,
> so would our salvation be only a pretense. Christ was
> twofold: a man as far as men could see, but also God,
> though hidden from the eye. As a man, he ate as we
> do and had the same fleshly experiences as we do, but
> as God he fed five thousand men with five loaves. As
> a man he really died, but as God he called a man four
> days dead back to life. As a man he really slept in the
> boat; as God he walked on the water.[149]

And St. Leo, in one of his Christmas sermons, likewise
gives an accurate exposé of the Church's Christology:

> One and the same Son of God existed in both natures,
> taking what belongs to us without losing what was his
> own, and thus as man renewing man, while remaining
> unchanged in himself. For the divine nature that he
> has in common with the Father suffered no loss of
> omnipotence, nor did the nature of a servant dishonor
> the nature of God, since the supreme and eternal es-
> sence that stooped to save mankind raised us up to
> share its own glory but did not cease to be what it
> was. Therefore, when the only Son of God professes
> himself to be less than the Father, yet also asserts his
> equality with the Father, he proves that both natures
> are real in him: the inequality shows the human na-
> ture, the equality the divine.[150]

In a like manner the Christmas liturgy presents us with

the God made man in whom "all the fullness of God was pleased to dwell" (Col. 1:19) and of whose "fullness have we all received" (John 1:16).

King and Servant

Nothing is more charged with meaning in the Old Testament than the words "king" and "glory." We have already met the theme "glory of Yahweh": the kingly glory, wrapped in cloud, that no man can look upon and live. The prophet Isaiah recorded his vision of it:

> In the year that King Uzziah died I saw the Lord sitting upon a throne, high and lifted up; and his train filled the temple. Above him stood the seraphim; each had six wings: with two he covered his face, and with two he covered his feet, and with two he flew. And one called to another and said: "Holy, holy, holy is the Lord of hosts; the whole earth is full of his glory." And the foundations of the thresholds shook at the voice of him who called, and the house was filled with smoke. And I said: "Woe is me! For I am lost; for I am a man of unclean lips, and I dwell in the midst of a people of unclean lips; for my eyes have seen the King, the Lord of hosts!" (Is. 6:1-5).

The cloud that here veils Yahweh's glory is the smoke that fills the temple. Anyone dwelling among a people with impure lips cannot see the King in his glory.

Christmas introduces to us a God-man, a visible God who is also a King. The Christmas crèche and the application to it of Isaiah's inspired imagery that includes ass and ox were unthinkable in the early Christian period. Yet if such imagery had begun to develop then as it did later in the time of St. Francis of Assisi, it would not have become a kind of opaque screen that keeps many a Christian at an unconsciously or unavowedly infantile level and causes him to develop a religious sensibility out of touch with real, concrete life. On the contrary, for in the early Christian centuries, the representations of the stages of Christ's earthly life were not fragmentary, episodic, and isolated from one another, and far from constituting a barrier, they led to the knowledge of God by helping to touch the Word of life and thus to know the Father better. In and by means of the imagery of the crèche, the early Christians would immediately have seen God the King.

"He will be called wonderful"

The Roman liturgy of Christmas sings, in the first antiphon for Vespers, of "the King who is our peace; the whole world longs to see him." The first antiphon in the Office of Readings, an antiphon also used as entrance antiphon at Midnight Mass, shows the Messiah who is King: "The Lord said to me: You are my Son, today I have begotten you" (Ps. 2:7). Finally, all the liturgies use this passage from Isaiah: "For to us a child is born, to us a son is given; and the government will be upon his shoulder, and his name will be called 'Wonderful Counselor, Mighty God, Everlasting Father, Prince of Peace'" (Is. 9:6).

This passage was chosen more for its description of the child's kingship than for its mention of his birth; it was chosen for a liturgy to celebrate what was regarded as a feast of glory. The Vulgate changed the text a bit, and in the older liturgy the passage read: "He will be called wonderful, counselor, God, mighty, Father of the world to come, Prince of peace."

The passage has been the object of many commentaries, and the Roman liturgy has used it at several points. Formerly it was the first lesson at Christmas Matins and appeared again in the Christmas Mass at Dawn and as the fifth antiphon at Lauds. In the new liturgy it is used at Midnight Mass and as the third antiphon at Lauds.

The Vulgate translation, which the liturgy used to follow, gives the child six titles or attributes, but it nonetheless respects the spirit of the original. The Fathers took the word "wonderful" as a reference to Christ's birth from the Virgin, a miracle no one had anticipated. The text of the Septuagint was at one time reflected in the translation of the passage; the Septuagint has "Angel of the Great Counsel" rather than "Wonderful Counselor." Not all commentators interpreted this in the same way. Most concentrated on the idea of "angel" or "messenger," looking on Christ as the envoy sent to announce the divine plan of salvation and coming in order to make known the mystery hitherto hidden from men.

Along with Isaiah 9, the Letter to the Hebrews was also read in most liturgies for Christmas. The Roman liturgy now reads Hebrews 1:1-6 at the Christmas Mass during the Day and Hebrews 1:1-2 as a short reading at Lauds.

The Son of God has been made "heir of all things" (Heb. 1:2). To him God has said said: "Thy throne, O God, is for ever and ever, the righteous scepter is the scepter of thy kingdom" (Heb. 1:8). Thus Christ is a King, and a King who distinguishes between good and evil. He is Master of the universe, which he created from the beginning. The Letter to the Hebrews cites at this point a number of psalms (2:7; 103:4; 45:7, 8; 102:25-27) as witnesses that the Son of God is indeed King of the universe.

"We have beheld his glory"

The Christmas liturgy also gives an important place to the Prologue of the Fourth Gospel. If we dwell on this passage, it is not to focus on the Word as Creator of the world and eternally living with the Father, but to emphasize the final verse of the pericope (short form) as used on Christmas at the Mass during the Day: "We have beheld his glory." This is the standpoint from which St. John likes to view the incarnation, and it is the standpoint the Church takes in the liturgy. The most important thing the incarnation reveals to the world is the glory of the Word's Godhead. In other words, the incarnation gives us access to the eternal kingship of Christ. This is not a viewpoint customary among us today, for we are more sensible of the self-abasement of the Son in becoming man than of the possibility given of reaching to the divine royalty of the Lord through his humanity.

Our new Roman liturgy has reconsidered especially the Scripture readings, and its choice makes it clear that the Christmas Child is indeed a King. The entrance antiphon, from Isaiah 9, which is used at the Mass during the Day, points in this direction, as we indicated earlier. In addition, there is a group of psalms for Christmas that have traditionally been used in all the liturgies (especially Psalms 2, 19, 45, 89, 93, 98, 110, 130, 135), and the choice of these again shows the Church's emphasis on the royal and glorious side of Christmas. The new liturgy continues to use some of these psalms.

Various non-inspired compositions of the Church likewise stress the royal character of the Christmas feast. The traditional Vespers hymn, *Christe, redemptor omnium*, describes the royal privileges of Christ: "Jesus, Redeemer of all men, You were begotten by the mighty Father, before light was created, as His equal in glory. Do You, the Father's light and radiance and man's unfailing hope, accept the prayers of Your servants the world over." [151]

The antiphon for the *Magnificat* at First Vespers announces the coming of the King of kings: "When the sun rises in the morning sky, you will see the King of kings coming forth from the Father like a radiant bridegroom from the bridal chamber." The opening prayer at Midnight Mass, for its part, sees all in terms of light, the light that is God's royal splendor: "Father, you make this holy night radiant with the splendor of Jesus Christ our light. We welcome him as Lord, the true light of the world. Bring us to eternal joy in the kingdom of heaven."

The responsory in the Office of Readings follows the same theological line of emphasis on the kingship of Christ: "Today, for our sake, the King of heaven chose to be born of his virgin mother," while the third antiphon at Morning Prayer sings: "A little child is born for us today; little and yet called the mighty God, alleluia."

Evidently, then, it is indeed a King that the liturgy presents to us, and even when it shows us Christ in his human condition, it does so in order to bring us to him as King. This King is also a Servant. This is an idea with which perhaps we are more at ease, an idea to which our century is more responsive. It, too, of course, is a New Testament concept, for St. Paul's focus is always on this God who took "the form of a servant" (Phil. 2:7).

The antiphons that recall the lowly manger stand side by side with those that sing the King's glory. We already find the same juxtaposition in Luke's account: "'. . . you will find a babe wrapped in swaddling cloths and lying in a manger.' And suddenly there was with the angel a multitude of the heavenly host praising God and saying, 'Glory to God in the highest . . .'" (Luke 2:12-13). The Gospels for the Christmas Masses at midnight and dawn tell how Christ came in lowliness, and they stand in contrast to the second reading and Gospel of the daytime Mass, where we contemplate the kingship of the newborn Child.

Thus, at the moment when God is manifesting himself ("the goodness and loving kindness of God our savior appeared" — Titus 3:4), all that anyone sees is a little child! But every time that the liturgy reminds us of the lowly condition of the newborn Christ, it relates this, at least implicitly, to the divine will that through Christ's lowliness we should receive adoptive sonship.

The third of the Christmas Masses especially emphasizes the paradox of the King who is a Servant. The entrance antiphon strikes the tone: "A child is born for us . . ."; we have already noted the messianic and royal resonances of this text from Isaiah.

"A child is born for us"

We can go a step further in our examination of this text, which reads in Latin: *Puer natus est nobis. Puer*, "child," also means "servant," and this meaning emerges here all the more clearly inasmuch as the *nobis*, "for us," has overtones of the paschal mystery that lies ahead. A "servant" is born for us and for our sake; he comes to carry out a mission that concerns not only his Father but us as well. He is the favored Servant, the Son with whom the Father is well pleased. "Through your Servant Jesus" was a formula the early Christians loved, and we find them using it in many of their prayers.

The word "servant" quite naturally brings to our minds the four Servant Songs in Isaiah (42:1-9; 49:1-6; 50:4-11; 52:13–53:12), and it is right that it should do so, since the New Testament recognizes in the Servant the person of Jesus Christ. The Greek word *pais*, which likewise means both "child" and "servant," enables the Scriptures and the liturgy to express the full meaning of Jesus. He is the Son whom the Father sends; he is also the Servant who comes to do the Father's will. When St. Matthew tells us of Jesus hearing the Father's voice at his baptism, the words recorded are: "This is my beloved Son, with whom I am well pleased" (3:17). Jesus is the favored Servant, but he is also the Son whom the Father sends. As early as the Acts of the Apostles, we find the expression "servant Jesus," which was such a favorite of the early Christian generations: "The God of Abraham and of Isaac and of Jacob, the God of our fathers, glorified his servant Jesus" (3:13). Later on, when the eunuch, the official of Queen Candace of Ethiopia, reads Isaiah 53:7-8, the Apostle Philip tells him that the lamb led to slaughter is Jesus (Acts 8:26-39).

The suffering Servant, a theme dear to Isaiah and a personage in whom the New Testament and the Church see Christ reflected, was God's answer to the infidelity and disobedience of Adam, who was to have been the first of God's servants. He was God's favorite, his beloved, and God had created him after his own image. But because of his infidelity, he lost his identity as servant and became a slave. The Letter to the Galatians alludes to Adam and his fall, in the second reading at Mass on the Sunday within the octave of Christmas: "But when the time had fully come, God sent forth his Son, born of woman, born under the law, to redeem those who were under the law, so that we might receive adoption as sons" (Gal. 4:4-5).

Commenting on this passage from Galatians, Cerfaux writes:

> He is so much with us that he becomes the child of a woman and accepts the lowly state of ordinary men. He would push his lowliness and likeness to us to the point of joining us in sin if his dignity as Son of God were not incompatible with sin. He is born a Jew, "a servant to the circumcised" (Rom. 15:8). Consequently, he spends his earthly life observing the Law. By doing so, he fulfilled it perfectly but also put an end to it. The Law had to be thus perfectly fulfilled before it could disappear.[152]

By sinning, men became "slaves to the elemental spirits of the universe" (Gal. 4:3). The Lord therefore had to take "the form of a servant" (Phil 2:7) in order to rescue men from enslavement.

Evidently we are constantly in touch with the paschal mystery as we meditate on these texts from the Christmas liturgy. Thus, when the Church asks, in the opening prayer for Mass on the sixth day in the octave of Christmas, that we might be freed "from our former slavery to sin," she is thinking of the newborn Child as the King and Servant who comes into the world so that he might be obedient unto death and thereby serve his Father and do his will. But the Cross, though a torment reserved for slaves, will also be the means whereby Christ is exalted and all creation is gathered into unity after sin and guilt and death have been done away with.

12. THE CHRISTMAS PASCH

In the preceding chapter we were constantly reflecting on paschal themes. What is "King and Servant," after all, but one expression of the paschal mystery? The Fathers of the Church are always reminding us of a point they evidently consider absolutely basic: "The Son of God became a man in order that men might become God," and this, of course, is a theme both of Christmas and of the paschal mystery. The world has been renewed, and we have become new creatures, but the coming of the Son of God in the flesh is the starting point of these transformations. St. Irenaeus writes: "The Word of God became a man, and the Son of God became a Son of Man, so that man, united to the Word of God, might through adoption become a son of God." [153]

We would be mistaken if we tried to find in the liturgy a metaphysics of the incarnation, and especially one that would be offered for its own sake. Scripture does not take such a narrow approach to Jesus. It sees the incarnation as part of the mystery of our redemption. Paul does not even dwell on the earthly life of Jesus: "Even if we did once know Christ in the flesh, that is not how we know him now" (2 Cor. 5:16, JB). He is aware, of course, that the earthly life of Jesus is the necessary starting point, but it is precisely that — a starting point — and derives its meaning from the goal, which is our salvation and our transformation as new creatures.

If, then, Christ became a man, he did so in order to redeem us. "When the time had fully come, God sent forth his Son, born of woman, born under the law, to redeem those who were under the law" (Gal. 4:4-5). He came in order to offer the sacrifice that would ransom us: "And being found in human form he humbled himself and became obedient unto death, even death on a cross" (Phil. 2:8). The Letter to the Hebrews gives clear expression to this theology of the incarnation as directed to sacrifice: "Sacrifices and offerings thou hast not desired, but a body hast thou prepared for me; in burnt offerings and sin offerings thou hast taken no pleasure. Then I said, 'Lo, I have come to do thy will, O God,' as it is written of me in the roll of the book" (Heb. 10:5-7).

While directed toward sacrifice, the incarnation must lead

ultimately to resurrection and victory, or it would be a ven-
ture that had failed. Everyone knows, at least from the
liturgy, St. Paul's words in his Letter to the Philippians:
"Therefore God has highly exalted him and bestowed on
him the name which is above every name, that at the name
of Jesus every knee should bow, in heaven and on earth
and under the earth, and every tongue confess that Jesus
Christ is Lord, to the glory of God the Father" (Phil. 2:9-
11).

On January 1, the Solemnity of Mary, Mother of God, the
Church sings in the first antiphon for Vespers: "O marvelous exchange!" In her eyes, this exchange is the intended
issue of the incarnation. Of all the Fathers, St. Cyril of
Alexandria and St. Gregory the Great have given perhaps
the clearest expression to the nature of this "marvelous exchange." To bring the meaning home to Christians is one of
their main concerns.

St. Cyril writes: "The Son who was truly begotten of the
Father, the Word of God who is Life, set out upon the way
to death and became a man like us. He did not introduce
into his earthly nature any change emanating from his divine nature (for he did retain his divine nature entire with
all its attributes), but simply assumed an earthly body and a
rational soul." [154] In another passage, after describing the
"exchange," St. Cyril points out its ultimate consequences:
"He who exists eternally was born according to the flesh,
taking to himself what is ours, so that the offspring of the
flesh, that is, we who are subject to corruption and damnation, might abide in him who made his own what is ours
and made ours what is his." [155]

The thoughts of Scripture and of the Fathers on the incarnation have found vital expression in the liturgy. It is
striking that in the East the feast of Christmas should be
announced as "A Pasch, a three-day festive holiday." [156]

The West does not have any such explicit title for
Christmas, but we need only run through the Scripture
texts and liturgical compositions of the Christmas liturgy to
see that the West shares the idea. It took a long time for

theologians to turn back to Scripture, the Fathers, and the liturgy, and to stop limiting themselves to speculation and to engage in the study of the mysteries as parts of the divine plan of salvation. Moreover, the change of attitude in Western theology is something quite recent. Here we have evidence of the extent to which the liturgy had been carried out without being truly experienced or becoming part of life. The liturgy had become simply a ceremony in the course of which texts were read and antiphons were sung; Christians seemed to have lost any sense of the value that these texts and antiphons had for Christian life.

From the Vigil of Christmas on, the liturgy of the season has a clearly paschal character. Three stages in God's plan of salvation are mentioned several times. In the entrance antiphon, the Lord's coming is linked to salvation, and salvation in turn to the Lord's glory. We have already seen the messianic and eschatological significance of that "glory." "Today you will know that the Lord is coming to save us, and in the morning you will see his glory." The choice of text (cf. Exod. 16:6-7) reveals the theological outlook of a whole age.

The second reading presents Christ, the Son of David, as Savior of Israel (Acts 13:16-17, 22-25), while the Gospel, taken from St. Matthew, contains the illuminating sentence: "She will bear a son, and you shall call his name Jesus, for he will save his people from their sins" (Matthew 1:21). The opening prayer of the Mass dispels any doubt: "We look forward to this feast of our salvation. May we welcome Christ as our Redeemer. . . ."

The first coming of Christ, at his human birth, is thus closely bound up with our salvation, and precisely because it is a step toward the paschal mystery, it must have as its ultimate goal the last day and the second coming of Christ. There are several temporal stages involved here and we cannot consider them all simultaneously, but we must bear in mind that the liturgy always celebrates the totality of these mysteries. Rightly so, for they are indeed inseparable.

The Liturgy of the Hours also brings out the redemptive

finality of the incarnation. Thus, the first responsory in the Office of Readings says: "Tomorrow the wickedness of the earth will be destroyed, and the Savior of the world will rule over us." And the third antiphon at Lauds (in the Latin Office): "Tomorrow salvation will be yours, says the Lord of hosts."

Thus, beginning on the Vigil of Christmas, we have a clear statement of the finality of the incarnation and its connection with our salvation.

Redemptive incarnation

As we have already had occasion to remark, we should not go to the liturgy for a treatise on dogma; as a matter of fact, there is always danger of attempting to impose too much of a systematic structure on what we do and experience in the liturgy. Nonetheless, for the sake of greater clarity, we shall recall here the paschal themes taken over by the Roman liturgy for Christmas; we must be on guard, however, not to force the texts.

The theology of the incarnation that is to be found in the Offices and Masses of the season can be expressed as follows. Christ came to earth and assumed our nature in order to deliver us from the guilt of sin. Salvation consists above all in our being forgiven and given a new life, becoming sharers in the divine nature. Because of and through that sharing, we bear in ourselves, once again, the image in which we were originally created. In the final analysis, then, the unity of mankind and the renewal of all creation will depend on the incarnation of the Word. At the end, when the new creation achieves its mature perfection, Christ will come again as supreme Judge, and the definitive entry into the promised land will take place. Mankind will return to the paradise from which the first man was expelled because of sin.

There are many texts which tell us that the purpose of the Son's incarnation was our salvation. Thus the third antiphon at First Vespers on Christmas confronts us with the fact of redemption: "The eternal Word, born of the Father before time began, today emptied himself for our sake and became man," while the ancient hymn "Christ, Redeemer of mankind" puts the same thought in more lyrical form: "The present day, as it comes round every year, bears witness to this — that You, the only-begotten of the Father, have come to be man's salvation. The heavens, the earth, the sea and every creature under heaven greet Him with a new song as the author of new salvation." [157]

In the Office of Readings, St. Leo the Great tell us: "All have the same reason for rejoicing, since our Lord, destroyer of sin and death, found no one guiltless and therefore came to free all." [158] The first responsory in the same Office of Readings reminds us that "today, for our sake, the King of heaven chose to be born of his virgin mother, to reclaim lost men for the heavenly kingdom."

One of the hymns for Morning Prayer, the ancient "From where the sun rises" (*A solis ortus cardine*) sings of the same deliverance: "The blessed maker of the world assumed a servant's form so as to free man by becoming man and not to lose those whom He had created." [159]

The liturgy thus reflects the theology of the Fathers and affirms that our salvation has already been effected in the birth of Christ. Such a statement means, for these writers, that Christ's birth is an intrinsic part of the work of redemption, to the point that it is not simply a condition or indispensable beginning but already contains our deliverance in germ.

In a passage from his ninth sermon on the Nativity, St. Leo the Great explains the concrete significance for Christian life of the mystery that is being celebrated. The salvation inaugurated by Christ's birth is a salvation that is always of this present moment:

> [The prophets] teach us not so much to recall the Lord's birth, in which he became flesh, as though it were past, but to gaze upon it as present to us. . . . We retain in the ears of our heart, as though they were

spoken at today's celebration, the words of the angel:
"I bring you good news of a great joy which will come
to all the people; for to you is born this day in the city
of David a Savior, who is Christ the Lord."[160]

A new creation

The birth of Christ destroys the effects of death and
causes new life to be reborn in us; man is regenerated by
Christ's coming as man. This new life consists in our sharing the divine nature.

Here again, the Church in her liturgy has been guided by
the theology of the Fathers. In the patristic reading for the
Office of Readings on Christmas, St. Leo bids us thank God
through his Son, in the Holy Spirit, because "in his loving
mercy he took pity on us, and when we were dead because
of sin, he gave us life with Christ so that in Christ we might
be a new creation, a new work of his hands." He then utters
the well-known exclamation: "Christian, recognize your
true dignity, and now that you have become a sharer in the
divine nature, do not return to your earlier degradation
through evil ways."[161]

The liturgy links the birth of Christ with a *renovatio*, or
renewal, with our *generatio*, or birth, and with a *novitas*, or
newness of life, as opposed to a *vetustas*, or decrepitude
(the state of one who is worn, decayed, old, and feeble).

The liturgy uses these terms because they were current
in the language and writings of the Fathers, who themselves had found them implicit in Scripture. Thus St. Paul
says that we have become "a new creation" (2 Cor. 5:17).
On the octave of Christmas, a passage is read from the Letter to the Galatians in which Paul explains that we have
become adopted sons of God, being interiorly transformed
to the point where we can say "Abba! Father!" (Gal. 4:4-7).
Many of the Eastern litrugies use this passage in the one
Mass they celebrate on Christmas. The popularity of the
pericope shows how the Christian world has understood
Christmas as the celebration of a renewal and an adoption.

Christmas anticipates Easter and the paschal mystery. Just above, we heard St. Leo saying that in Christ we are "a new creation, a new work of his [God's] hands." Such language, we repeat, was current among the Fathers.

In the Missal of Pius V, there used to be interesting traces of that language in the opening prayer and secret for the Christmas Mass during the Day. In these prayers the expression *nova nativitas,* "new birth," occurred. In the collect there was a contrast between the *nova,* the new, that which renews, and the *vetusta,* the old, the earlier; the *nova nativitas,* the new birth of Christ that makes new, was opposed to the *vetusta servitus,* the ancient slavery of mankind due to original sin. The birth of Christ in our flesh liberates us who had been captive under the yoke of sin.

The postcommunion prayer for the Mass at Dawn, again in the Missal of Pius V, is to be found for the first time in the Gelasian Sacramentary. In the meantime, however, it had been rewritten.[162] In its original form it read: "Lord, may the newness of this mystery of birth constantly restore us, for its singular nobility has cleansed mankind of all decrepitude."

In his fifth sermon for Christmas, St. Leo had used almost identical language: "The Word of God . . . through his birth called mankind back from its decrepitude to a new beginning."[163]

A new world

The birth of Christ shares with the paschal mystery the power to bring the created world together in unity.

St. Ambrose saw the Church as coming into existence at the very moment of Christ's birth: "Christ is born and the shepherds begin their watch, gathering into the Lord's house his flocks, that is, the nations that hitherto had been living like beasts."[164] The second antiphon at Morning Prayer makes use of Luke 2:13, putting the words of the heavenly host into the mouth of a single angel: "The angel said to the shepherds: I proclaim to you a great joy; today

the Savior of the world is born for you, alleluia." The antiphon for the *Magnificat* at Second Vespers has angels,
archangels, and the just of the earth joining together in
song.

The renewal that Christ's birth effects is not to be
thought of as restricted to intelligent beings. The whole of
creation benefits from the re-creation that is the fruit of
Christ's suffering and resurrection and that is already implicitly contained in his birth. St. Paul told the Ephesians
that the aim of God's love-inspired plan was "to unite all
things in him [Christ], things in heaven and things on
earth" (Eph. 1:10).

But Christ's coming also contains an element of eschatological judgment. That is how St. Ambrose sees it
when commenting on Luke 2:34, "Simeon prophesies that
the Lord Jesus Christ has come for the downfall and resurrection of many, that is, in order to distinguish the deserts
of the just and the unjust, and, as a true and just Judge,
decree punishment or rewards as our deeds deserve."[165]

A new Jerusalem

Finally, Christ's birth is linked to man's return to
paradise. The Office of Readings on Christmas alludes to
this idea in the first responsory: "Today, for our sake, the
King of heaven chose to be born of his virgin mother, to
reclaim lost men for the kingdom of heaven."

In the patristic reading, St. Leo speaks of the angels' joy
as they see the heavenly Jerusalem being formed of all the
nations of the earth. He bids the Christian "remember that
you have been rescued from the power of darkness and
brought into the light of God's kingdom."[166] St. Gregory the
Great, commenting on Luke 2:1 in his eighth sermon on the
Gospel of Luke, explains the reason for the census taken by
Caesar Augustus: "Why is a census of the world made just
when the Lord is about to be born, except to show that he
who was coming in the flesh would enroll his chosen ones
in eternity?"[167]

Evidently, then, the subheading to this section is not an exaggeration, but rather brings out the unity permeating the Church's entire liturgy, centered as it is on the mystery of death and life.

In the Byzantine liturgy for the Vigil of Christmas, there is a processional antiphon that brings out quite clearly the paschal character of Christmas: "Rejoice, Jerusalem! All you lovers of Sion, share our festivities! On this day the age-old bonds of Adam's condemnation were broken, paradise was opened for us, the serpent was crushed, and woman, whom he once deceived, lives now as Mother of the creator. . . . Let all creation dance and thrill with joy, for Christ has come to call it home and to save our souls."[168]

Incarnation and cosmos

In one of his visions that are, surprisingly, favorites even today, Isaiah writes: "And one [seraph] called to another and said: 'Holy, holy, holy is the Lord of hosts; the whole earth is full of his glory'" (Is. 6:3). This theme, which has become part of the Eucharistic liturgy, is the best expression we have of the glorification of the cosmos. The whole of creation, and not man alone, experiences the regenerative power of the incarnation.

The "unconquered Sun" idea, as we pointed out earlier, is at the origin of the feast of Christmas. In a sermon that often used to be attributed to St. Ambrose, St. Maximus of Turin wrote: "The people are quite right, in a way, when they call this birthday of the Lord 'the new sun.' . . . We gladly accept the name, because at the coming of the Savior not only is mankind saved but the very light of the sun is renewed."[169]

Toward the end of the third century, an anonymous writer, intent on showing the perfection of Christian worship as compared with the pagan cults, gave us this important text:

> They call [this day] "the birthday of the unconquered [sun]." But is the sun so unconquered as our Lord

who underwent death and overcame it? Or they say it is "the birthday of the sun." But is our Lord not the Sun of righteousness of whom the prophet Malachi said: "For you who fear my name, the sun of right-eousness shall rise, with healing in its wings"?[170]

A renewal of the world takes place, and it begins with the incarnation of the Word. As a matter of fact, the choice of a cosmic phenomenon as a reference point for determining the date of the feast of Christ's birth suggests that we con-sider the repetition of the Christmas cycle as intimately linked with creation itself. The feast we celebrate does not interest man alone, but the whole created world. We should not be surprised, therefore, that the Fathers often mention the connection between the birth of Christ and the cosmic renewal that takes place at the winter solstice. We may well feel some regret that the readings chosen for the Christmas Offices have not given sufficient attention to this aspect of the feast, especially since it is both important in itself and one to which our generation is quite sensitive.

It is easy to see in the emphasis on the renewal of the sun's light a connection with the primal light at the creation of the world. How beautifully Genesis brings out the har-mony that marks God's creation of the world! We can sense the writer's deep emotion in the face of so many splendid things: the earthly paradise that forms the setting, the bodily beauty of man and woman, the light of the stars; he is overwhelmed by it all and tries to give us a glimpse of the beauty he sees. Then the catastrophe comes and puts an end to this marvelous harmony.

Christmas, linked as it is with the winter solstice, comes as the re-creation of the world according to the original plan and its original beauty. The coming of the Word and his entry into the world were not geared, as it were, to sheer efficiency; they were not dull and prosaic. God's plans are never narrow. The Word-made-man will indeed live his life in a particular region of the world, among a particular kind of men, in the climate of the country where he was born; he will speak one human language and submit to the rhythm and laws that govern human life. At the same time, however, we must realize that his presence is a consecration of the world. The world was of course already consecrated to a degree, since God was the one who had made it, but the presence of the Word within the cosmos restores its dignity and gives it the possibility of rebuilding itself with the elements already at its disposal.[171]

It was of this consecration that Isaiah was speaking when he reported his inaugural vision. In the opening prayer of Mass during the Day on Christmas — one of the oldest Christmas prayers we know of, now restored to its proper place — the Church bids us say: "Lord God, we praise you for creating man, and still more for restoring him in Christ. Your Son shared our weakness: may we share his glory."

If we were to think of this restoration as applying only to man, we would be forgetting the context and framework of the celebration. The world too is being restored. A sermon of St. John Damascene on the transfiguration brings this out clearly:

> The benevolent will of the Father united all things in his only-begotten Son. Man is already a microcosm who unites in himself all things visible and invisible. The Lord, whose good will created and governs all, determined that in his only-begotten consubstantial Son, divinity and humanity, and therewith all other created things, should be united, so that God might be all in all.[172]

The Greek Fathers have much more to say on this subject than do the Latin Fathers. They are also more interested in the restoration of the entire world as part of redemption, and they see the incarnation as the first step to the restoration. Here is another text, a magnificent one from St. Gregory of Nyssa:

> Today the darkness begins to grow shorter and the light to lengthen, as the hours of night become fewer. Nor is it an accident, brothers, that this change occurs

on the solemn day when divine life is manifested to men. Rather, to those who are attentive, nature manifests through visible things a hidden reality. . . . I seem to hear her saying: "Realize, man, as you observe these phenomena, that the invisible is being manifested to you through the visible. You see, do you not, that night has reached its greatest length, and since it can advance no farther, comes to a halt and withdraws? Think, then, of sin's deadly night that was lenghened by every evil act and had reached its highest pitch of wickedness, but on this day was cut short and allowed to creep no farther; it is now being forced to lessen and will finally be completely eliminated. Do you see that the beams of light are more intense and the sun higher than it has been? Realize that the true light is now here and, through the rays of the gospel, is illumining the whole earth." [173]

An ambiguous longing

Everyone without exception wants to be free. Such a yearning is exalting, it possesses beauty and grandeur, but it is also ambiguous. For what does "freedom" mean? There is no point here in dwelling on the false interpretations of freedom. A married man is not totally "free" where his wife and children are concerned. A friend is not totally "free" where his friend is concerned. A Christian is not totally "free" as regards the Body of the Church of which he is a member. No individual is totally "free." Certainly man, who has been redeemed from the bondage of sin, is not totally "free" from God.

If freedom is to be an authentic, that is, genuinely liberating freedom, it must make room for the other, for fidelity to men and even more to God. A free man must have respect for himself as well as others. Consequently, we must say that there is a yearning for freedom that is infantile or unbalanced, stupid or even perverse, a yearning that is just literary romanticism or unwitting egoism.

But there is also a yearning for freedom that is a desire to escape both servitude and false freedoms. Christmas is an efficacious celebration of this freedom, which might also be called peace.

Once again, it is impossible to speak of this authentic freedom to anyone who is unwilling to look at things through God's eyes, that is, through the eyes of faith.

Freedom through humble obedience

The incarnation was a self-humbling for the Word of God, and the first step toward the death that would be his sign of acceptance and self-giving to the Father. The incarnation thus represents more than the now real possibility of redemption; it is in itself an event that liberates. Karl Rahner once wrote on this point: "The incarnation is the acceptance of the flesh of sin; in its passible state, which itself is an expression of human guilt, the flesh is destined for death. . . . Thus the incarnation is already a soteriological event in the proper sense of the term, and not simply a condition for the possibility of redemption." [174]

The second preface for Christmas in the new Sacramentary gives succinct expression to this and the previous point: "He has come to lift up all things to himself, to restore unity to creation, and to lead mankind from exile into your heavenly kingdom." Moreover, because of the Son's obedience we become so free that we will live forever, as the third of the Christmas prefaces tells us: "Your eternal Word has taken upon himself our human weakness, giving our mortal nature immortal value. So marvelous in this oneness between God and man that in Christ man restores to man the gift of everlasting life."

Eternal life — that is what we are promised in the incarnation of the Word. It is an idea that deeply impressed the earliest Christian writers. One of the earliest of whom we have knowledge, St. Ignatius of Antioch, wrote a letter to the Ephesians that contains a whole theology of our liberation. It is cast in a literary form that is somewhat alien to us, but the message is clear:

> A star burned in the sky more brightly than all the others; its light was indescribable, its newness marvelous, and all the other stars, along with the sun and the moon, formed a chorus around this star, the light of which reached farther than that of any other. . . . Then all magic was destroyed, and every bond wrought by wickedness was broken, and the ancient kingdom was razed. When God appeared in human form to bring the newness of eternal life, his counsel began to be fulfilled.[175]

In his second Christmas sermon, St. Leo the Great develops the same theme. We were fallen, expelled from paradise, and living in an exile that would never end. Life was hopeless, but suddenly everything changed:

> Of old you were cast off and driven from your thrones in paradise. You were dying in your long exile and turning to dust and ashes; you had no hope of life. Then, through the incarnation of the Word, you received power to return from afar off to your Creator and to acknowledge your Father, to become a free man instead of a slave, a son and no longer a stranger.[176]

Our freedom is the effect of the Son's obedience as a lowly man. The continuous reading of Isaiah during Advent has familiarized us with the theme of liberation. We will recall this passage brimming with enthusiasm: "Shake yourself from the dust, arise, O captive Jerusalem; loose the bonds from your neck, O captive daughter of Zion" (Is. 52:2).

Perhaps it is not a simple matter, even for someone baptized, to believe that he has been liberated. The more we learn of human physiology and psychology, the more man seems subject to pressures that stifle freedom. It remains true, nonetheless, that we can achieve genuine freedom, but only by a dramatic effort that brings much suffering.

The incarnation liberates us, but it does not work by magic; the incarnation is the origin of the Christian's sacramental life, but the sacraments are not magical ways of avoiding a struggle. They are efficacious means, if properly used, of entering into the boundless kingdom of freedom and peace.

Such is the experience of the saints. We cannot claim that our age is not having the same experience. The violence that has become habitual will provide for it, if it wishes, the chance to get beyond the simplistic challenges and the overfacile means of drowning out the inner feeling of enslavement. The artificial means of oblivion as a way of escaping moral struggle and moral obligation have never yet had results that were not far more disastrous than what the users were trying to evade. Escape is really impossible. Once a man has the courage to enter on the path to freedom offered him by Christ and his incarnation, he will become certain that liberation is indeed to be won through suffering and humiliation.

This takes an act of faith. No apologetics can convince someone that entry upon the path of liberating humility that the incarnation has opened to men is indeed an effective means to freedom. We are confronted here with the mystery of God's gift. But there are perhaps moments of abrupt dislocation and keen suffering when God can suddenly lay hold of a man and bring him, amid continued suffering that is however permeated with a certain sweetness, into the way already traveled by the Son in his redemptive incarnation; then a man will experience a hidden joy as he goes.

The Christmas Virgin

Nothing is more frequent in the Fathers than the parallel between Eve and Mary; at times this seems so important to them that it becomes somewhat forced. Their excuse is that they had discovered, and were intensely aware of, Mary's special part in the liberation of mankind.

The Church Father who has perhaps placed the greatest emphasis on the parallel is St. Irenaeus of Lyons (2nd cent.), as he endeavored to show how the Virgin collaborated in her Son's redemptive work:

> Eve disobeyed, and did so while still a virgin. But while Eve, wife of Adam but still a virgin . . . disobeyed and became the cause of death for herself and the whole human race, Mary, spouse of a predestined man but still a virgin, obeyed and became the cause of salvation for herself and the whole human race.[177]

It is odd that the Roman liturgy has not developed the Eve-Mary parallel or contrast, which was such a favorite of patristic tradition. A good occasion for it would have been January 1, now that the feast concentrates once more on its original object: Mary, Mother of God. Other liturgies, like the Ambrosian, as we shall point out later on, made good use of the striking contrast between Eve and Mary in their celebrations. A splendid preface in the Ambrosian liturgy expresses it with vigor and balance; we quoted it in our brief remarks on Advent at Milan.[178]

In addition to the parallel between Eve and Mary in the Christmas liturgy, we occasionally find the Fathers confronting, rather than paralleling, the Virgin with Adam. St. Ephraem, for example, writes: "Mary wove a garment of glory and gave it to her father, Adam, who was naked among the trees. He donned this chaste robe and became beautiful. His wife led him to a fall; his daughter supported him; he arose to be a hero."[179]

All these texts endeavor to state the collaboration of the Blessed Virgin in the work of redemption; the incarnation provides an occasion for doing so. Mary's *Fiat* made it possible for Christ to be born as a man and thus to restore Adam, via the new Adam, to his original dignity. Mary made it possible for the Savior to be the new man who gives the rest of mankind a share in his status. Mary obeyed in order to save us; by her obedience she made up for the harm done by the first disobedience.

The texts are prudent in their expression, but they are nonetheless significant of the devotion the Fathers had to

Mary within the context of the Christmas celebration. The Roman liturgy at a very early date chose rather to establish a special feast in honor of the Virgin Mother of God. Its date was January 1; it was soon turned into the feast of the circumcision, but its original object and purpose have now been restored. This was the oldest feast of Mary in the West. In fact, we should note that the Church chose January 1 well before this day was designated as the first day of the year. In her celebration we hear again the accents of the Fathers. Thus the opening prayer of the Mass emphasizes Mary's role in the incarnation: "God our Father, may we always profit by the prayers of the Virgin Mother Mary, for you bring us life and salvation through Jesus Christ her Son."

The preface of this same Mass likewise speaks of Mary's part in the work of salvation: "Through the power of the Holy Spirit, she became the virgin mother of your only Son, our Lord Jesus Christ, who is for ever the light of the world."

STRUCTURE AND THEMES OF THE CHRISTMAS LITURGY

13. THE INCARNATION TODAY

The appointed time has come (December 24)

The Advent season is at its end, and the Church, which is responsible for the expectation of the world and men, and knows their weakness and impatience (for all creation groans as its awaits its redemption, Rom. 8:22-23) — the Church cries out: "Come, Lord Jesus, do not delay; give new courage to your people who trust in your love."

Thus does the Church speak in the opening prayer at Mass on the morning of December 24. If we are at all familiar with the Roman liturgy, we will be surprised to hear a prayer addressed, not to the Father, but to Christ himself, in the manner of the Spanish or Frankish liturgies. Why did the new Missal choose this mode of prayer, which is alien to Roman usage? Perhaps those who composed the new Mass realized that the celebration of Advent has by now made the faithful impatiently desirous of liberation: "O that thou wouldst tend the heavens and come down" (Is. 64:1).

In proclaiming the Gospel on this day, the Church speaks through the mouth of John the Baptist's father, Zachary. The latter is filled by the Holy Spirit, recovers his lost powers of speech, and prophesies concerning Christ and his own son (Luke 1:67-79). The Lord has "visited" his people, says Zachary, using a familiar Old Testament way of expressing God's interventions.[180] The New Testament also uses the term in other passages besides the present one, and it is especially dear to Luke, who alone seems to use it in this precise Old Testament form (see 7:16; 19:44).

READINGS FOR THE FEASTS AND SUNDAYS OF THE CHRISTMAS SEASON

	Prophet	Epistle	Gospel
Vigil of Christmas	The Lord takes delight in you Is. 62:1-5	Paul testifies that Christ is son of David and Son of God Acts 13:16-17, 22-25	Genealogy of Jesus Matthew 1:1-25
Christmas: Midnight	A son is given to us Is. 9:2-7	God's grace has been revealed to all men Titus 2:11-14	Today a savior has been born for you Luke 2:1-4
Christmas: Dawn	Your savior is born Is. 62:11-12	God's compassion has saved us Titus 3:4-7	The shepherds find Mary, Joseph, and the child Luke 2:15-20
Christmas: Day	The world shall see God's salvation Is. 52:7-10	God has spoken to us through his Son Heb. 1:1-6	The Word became flesh and dwelt among us John 1:1-18
Holy Family	Fear of God and love of parents Sir. 3:2-5, 12-14	The life of a Christian family Col. 3:12-21	A. The flight into Egypt Matthew 2:13-15, 19-23 B. Jesus grew in age and wisdom Luke 2:22-40 C. Jesus among the doctors Luke 2:41-52

Mary, Mother of God January 1	I will bless Israel Num. 6:22-27	The Son of God, born of a woman Gal. 4:4-7	The child is named Jesus Luke 2:16-21
Second Sunday after Christmas	The wisdom of God in our midst Sir. 24:1-2, 8-12	We are predestined to be adopted sons in Jesus Eph. 1:3-6, 15-18	The Word was made flesh John 1:1-18

READINGS FOR THE WEEKDAYS

December 29	Brotherly love and the light within us	The light that enlightens the nations
December 30	Doing God's will 1 John 2:12-17	The witness of Anna Luke 2:36-40
December 31	We are anointed in Christ and have all knowledge 1 John 2:18-21	The Word was made flesh John 1:1-18

SCRIPTURE READINGS IN THE LITURGY
OF THE HOURS

Vigil of Christmas	Is. 51:17–52:2, 7-10
Christmas	Is. 11:1-10
Holy Family	Eph. 5:21–6:4
Mary, Mother of God January 1	Heb. 2:9-17 Heb. 2:9-17
December 29	Col. 1:1-14
December 30	Col. 1:15–2:3
December 31	Col. 2:4-15
January 2	Col. 2:16–3:4
January 3	Col. 3:5-16
January 4	Col. 3:17–4:1

The Lord's "visit" here refers to his active intervention as he comes to free the house of David by raising up within it a liberating force. The prophecies are being fulfilled, and the Lord's mercy is taking concrete form as he shows his fidelity to the covenant. Evil will have no more power over us, and for the rest of our days we will be able to sing of our liberation and our covenant with the Lord, in prayer and in celebration of his worship. And we shall worship, not in slavish attachment to external rites, but "in holiness and righteousness."

This last expression occurs only twice in the New Testament to signify the attitude we should have of complete devotion to the Savior during this time of our salvation. Like Luke, Paul uses it in his Letter to the Ephesians (4:24) to characterize the outlook of the new man. Plato, in this a true Greek, defines holiness as the knowledge of the right behavior toward the gods. The New Testament, however, considers holiness to be an effect of rebirth in God through water and the Spirit.

John the Baptist will tell mankind of its liberation, thus preparing the way for Jesus to reveal to his people that they are saved and that their sins are forgiven. Such is "the tender mercy of our God."

In all this the Lord himself has taken the initiative. The first reading for Mass on December 24 emphasizes the point: "I took you from the pasture, from following the sheep, that you should be prince over my people Israel" (2 Sam. 7:8). The Lord then goes on to say (still speaking through Nathan the prophet): ". . . I will give you rest from all your enemies. Moreover the Lord declares to you that the Lord will make you a house" (2 Sam. 7:11). God is here setting David's line apart, for in it the Christ will be born.

Psalm 89 is a response of awed jubilation to these wondrous things the Lord is doing; in it God now speaks in the Church to the assembled faithful: "I have made a convenant with my chosen one, I have sworn to David my servant: 'I will establish your descendants for ever, and build your throne for all generations.' . . . He shall cry to me, 'Thou art my Father, my God, and the Rock of my salvation.' . . . My steadfast love I will keep for him for ever, and my covenant will stand firm for him."

The Eucharist we celebrate is the tangible proof that God has indeed intervened; the Communion antiphon gives a sacramental reference to the words we just heard in the Gospel: "Blessed be the Lord God of Israel, for he has visited and redeemed his people."

"In the morning you shall see the glory of the Lord" (Vigil Mass)

The Vigil Mass on December 24 stands between the end of Advent and the coming of Christ in the flesh. In what better way could we spend these final moments of waiting than by meditating on his genealogy? How moving this list of Christ's ancestors is! How vividly it shows him to be a member of our race, truly one of us, a son of David (Matthew 1:1-25)!

At the same time, the Church seems to have feared thaat the simple proclamation of the genealogy might have fostered too human a view of Christ. She therefore goes on and tells the faithful of the words the angel spoke to Joseph, who was disturbed by his financée's condition: "That which is conceived in her is of the Holy Spirit; she will bear a son, and you shall call his name Jesus, for he will save his people from their sins" (Matthew 1:20-21). Jesus is Emmanuel: "God with us." With these words added to the genealogy, we have Christ presented to us according to his full reality: he is the God-man.

With the coming of Christ a long history is ended. And yet is this really an end? Or is it not rather the beginning of a new history, the history of a world that is renewed and of men who find a new life and move on toward the definitive fulfillment? The Israel that had been chosen, the Jerusalem that had been preferred — these are now to be identified with the Church to which we now belong and to which all belong, at least in desire, who honestly seek the right way.

The first reading at this Vigil Mass (Is. 62:1-5) shows us this Jerusalem, that is, the Church of yesterday, today, and tomorrow. She is "a crown of beauty in the hand of the Lord, and a royal diadem in the hand of your God," and her names are "My Delight" and "Married." Such is the reality brought into being by the incarnation and God's visitation. The Lord himself rejoices at it in the responsorial psalm (Psalm 89), "He shall cry to me, 'Thou art my Father, my God, and the Rock of my salvation.' . . . My steadfast love I will keep for him for ever, and my covenant will stand firm for him."

Today, as once in the synagogue at Antioch, St. Paul presents the Lord Jesus to us: "Of this man's [David's] posterity God has brought to Israel a Savior, Jesus, as he promised. Before his coming John had preached a baptism of repentance to all the people of Israel" (Acts 13:23-24).

The Alleluia verse sums up the spirit of the Vigil celebration: "Tomorrow the wickedness of the earth will be destroyed: the Savior of the world will be our king." Christmas is part of the paschal mystery.

"Today I have begotten you" (Midnight Mass)

We must not mistake the real spirit of the account of Christ's birth that is read in the Gospel at Midnight Mass (Luke 2:1-14). It can be read simply as a moving story, and many have so read it. Think of all the tender poems, all the paintings, whether realistic or abstract! But the real meaning of the Gospel is indicated by the two readings that precede it: Isaiah 9:2-7, which tells us that a son is given to us, and Titus 2:11-14, which tells us that God's grace has been revealed for the salvation of all mankind.

The central theme of the celebration is also expressed in the Alleluia song that accompanies the procession with the Gospel: "Good News and great joy to all the world: Today is born our Savior, Christ the Lord." The same message may also be sung after the first reading, in place of the "new song" (Psalm 96) to which the good news in the first reading gives rise. The whole earth sings a new song to the Lord; his glory must be proclaimed to the nations and the peoples, "for he comes to judge the earth" (Ps. 96:13).

Oddly enough, the Communion antiphon for this Midnight Mass does not use a verse from the Gospel, but instead takes a verse from St. John's Prologue in order to comment on the reading from Luke and to draw attention to the real mystery being celebrated: "The Word of God became man; we have seen his glory."

The preface, for its part, says: "In him we see our God made visible" (first Christmas preface). This holy night marks the beginning of the Church's and the Christian's sacramental life. Henceforth we experience God through signs, and the signs are efficacious because of the incarnation of God, who thereby allowed himself to be seen and touched. We see his glory. The Eucharist we celebrate, the bread we eat and the wine we drink are the signs through which we touch God. Because the Word became a man, he

was able to give his life for us. Thus there came into existence those sacred signs of the paschal mystery, which enable us to live henceforth in sacramental union with the
Lord.

There might be value in commenting on this passage of
Luke with the help of all the recent studies on its authenticity, its sources, Luke's objectivity, the value of the information he provides, etc. The scientific literature on the passage is indeed extensive. We shall not cite it, however, for
we can surely understand that while it is of great importance, it has nothing to do with Luke's attitude of faith and
with the Church's attitude of faith at the moment of this
celebration.

"A light will shine on us this day" (Mass at Dawn)

The solemnity of the texts and chants at Midnight Mass
are followed by a full vision of life-giving joy in the Mass at
Dawn. This Mass sings of the light that radiates from the
newborn Savior. St. Luke continues his account by telling
us of the shepherds who hasten to find out what has happened and what the Lord would have them know. They
want to see, and to see in this context means to verify God's
love for men. The glory of God is somehow linked to the
peace on earth that originates in the good pleasure of the
God who has come to save mankind. The joy that fills the
message to the shepherds is foretold in Isaiah (62:12), "And
they shall be called The holy people, The redeemed of the
Lord; and you shall be called Sought out, a city not forsaken." The responsorial psalm echoes this joy: "Light dawns
for the righteous, and joy for the upright in heart" (Ps.
97:11).

The good will of God toward the men he has determined
to save is the theme of the second reading (Titus 3:4-7).
Here the true basis for the Christian's behavior finds expression: we live not by law but by the fact of the incarnation and the gift of renewal that has been given to us. Renewal through water and the Spirit is the foundation of the

Christian's action and of the baptized person's value judgments on men and things. Having become just, that is, having been made just by the Lord's grace, we now live in hope of eternal life. But all this has for its foundation the incarnation of our God, for the incarnation is the starting point of a new history for mankind.

In living this new history that moves to fulfillment every day and especially every time we celebrate the Eucharist as an efficacious sign of our liberation and as a pledge of our salvation, we experience a joy that the Communion antiphon tries to express: "Daughter of Zion, exult; shout aloud, daughter of Jerusalem! Your King is coming, the Holy One, the Savior of the world."

A newborn child, our messenger from God (Mass during the Day)

It is in these terms that the entrance antiphon for this Mass presents Jesus to us: "A child is born for us, a son given to us; dominion is laid on his shoulder, and he shall be called Wonderful-Counsellor."

After such an entrance antiphon, no better Gospel passage could be chosen than St. John's Prologue (1:1-18). For this little child that is born for us is the Word of God, the incarnate Word of the Lord himself. This is the one John the Baptist proclaims. Now that this Word has become a man, the whole world will see the salvation of our God. Such is the theme of the first reading (Is. 52:7-10). The Letter to the Hebrews then specifies that after speaking in many other ways, God has finally spoken through his Son whom he has sent among us (Heb. 1:1-6).

The whole liturgy of the word at this Mass focuses on the message of God, that is, on the knowledge of his saving plan that he makes known to us in his Son. Henceforth, the "mystery" will be, not what we do not understand, but, on the contrary, what God has revealed to us about his plan of salvation through the Son he has sent among us (Col. 1:25-29). The child just born is a messenger "who publishes peace, who brings good tidings of good, who publishes salvation"; in the person of this child "the Lord has bared his holy arm before the eyes of all the nations; and all the ends of the earth shall see the salvation of our God" (first reading).

As the Church meditates on this astonishing yet ever present and wonderful fact, she sings her enthusiastic response in Psalm 98, "All the ends of the earth have seen the victory of our God. . . . The Lord has made known his victory, he has revealed his vindication in the sight of the nations."

All this marks the final stage of a very long history. It reaches its climax in the sending of God's own Word, after God's fruitless attempts to enter into a dialogue with us through other messengers. God did doubtless speak to our fathers through the prophets, in fragmentary and varied ways; but now, in the final age, literally "at the end of these very days," he has spoken to us through his Son (Heb. 1:1-2). "At the end of these very days": we should take these words quite as they stand. God speaks now, to us, today: to us who celebrate Christmas as a "today" that is part of the paschal mystery. This is not poetry nor simply a "manner of speaking." God speaks to us now through his Son and reveals to us, now, his plan of salvation.

Encountering Christ

Christmas, then, is far from being just a feast of tender love or a marvelous poem of childhood. What it really means for the world and for us is that we encounter Christ in person, with all the specific consequences such an encounter involves. Christmas puts an end to the mythological notion of a far-off God who has no experience of our lives. It puts an end to the God-of-the-gaps, to whom men have recourse in the difficulties of life. It puts an end to the idea of God as a refuge, the God who comforts us and solves our riddles.

Our God is indeed God, but he is also a man who is all that we are, except that he is not a sinner. The Church at an early date had to deal with the Nestorian tendency to regard Jesus as simply a man, even though a very special man whose mere presence sanctifies things human. Such a view would have meant that Christianity aimed, not at transforming man's life into a divine life, but at "divinizing" the lives of men without really changing them in any significant way. Mankind saved would be mankind "transformed" in Christ, in the sense that the mystery of Christ would cast an aura over mankind without making it different interiorly.

In modern terms, Nestorianism is a form of "horizontalism." It is enough to see God and the sacred in one's neighbor. Social love is salvation. Why do we really need anything else — for example, sacramental signs, especially sacramental signs that are not exact duplicates of what we do in our everyday lives? The ideal Eucharistic celebration is simply an ordinary meal at which the whole emphasis is put on the brotherhood of those present. But in this view, of course, people forget that the Supper was never at any time an ordinary meal, for it was chosen by Christ because it was already a ritual meal actualizing the first Passover and the departure from slavery.

At the other extreme from Nestorianism is Eutychianism: the tendency to deny the humanity of Christ and to see in him only God, whose presence among us rouses us from our torpor. Consequently, those sacred signs, the sacraments, should be as remote from us as possible and be completely esoteric, since they are, after all, the signs of an encounter with the inaccessible God. Everything in the liturgy should be different from our everyday lives: the language should be unintelligible, the garments strange, the gestures unusual and inexplicable. It is essential that all these should be alien to us. Moreover, we should maintain the most extreme possible view of the institution of the sacraments, namely, that Christ instituted them without taking any human context into account and without paying any heed to anthropology and history. In this view, it approaches heresy to think that Christ could have used preexisting forms and filled them with a new content, thus putting himself into the stream of history.

These two very ancient tendencies are always around; we meet them today in many fervent Christians who are hardly conscious of them. Have such people ever understood the liturgy of Christmas? Have they ever had any inkling that their views have nothing in common with a valid conceptual theology of the person of Christ and with a theology expressed in a more vital fashion through the liturgy?

According to St. Leo the Great, in his well-known first sermon for Christmas, the fact of the incarnation has completely changed man's life. The joy a Christian experiences on this feast is deep-rooted, for the Lord has come to destroy sin and death; he finds no one free of sin and comes to set everyone free. The holy person should rejoice, because his reward is near; the sinner should rejoice, because forgiveness is offered to him; the pagan should take courage, because he is being called to true life.[181]

The most famous passage of the sermon is, however, the following: "Christian, recognize your true worth, and, having once become a sharer of the divine nature, do not again live an evil life and thus return to your former base condition. Remember who your Head is and of whose body you are a member."[182] This is the sermon we read in the Office of Readings on Christmas Day. Our encounter with Christ, then, transforms us. It is not merely a psychological encounter, such as may be achieved in prayer, but ever since the incarnation, it is a sacramental encounter through the Church and her signs. Through these, "we see our God made visible."[183]

14. Meditative Celebrations of Christmas

The Byzantine liturgy

The Byzantine liturgy, to which we have ready access these days, contains some truly meditative celebrations of Christmas.

The calendar notes that the Sunday before Christmas is dedicated to "the memory of all the Fathers who pleased God, from Adam to Joseph, the spouse of the most holy Mother of God." Moreover, the five days before Christmas are, as it were, an extended "eve" of the feast. Then, finally, the calender for December 25 says: "Birth according to the flesh of our Lord, God, and Savior, Jesus Christ. Passover."

It is rather striking that despite St. Francis and the Franciscan missions in the East, the celebration of Christmas there never incorporated the folklore of the Christmas crib. In addition, the feast (which includes the birth, the adoration of the shepherds, and the adoration of the Magi) is focused on the Word rather than on the lowly condition he accepted in order to carry out the Father's will. In private, personal prayer, the Western Christian likes to concentrate on Jesus, the Son of Mary; the Eastern Christian prays rather to the only Son of God.

First Vespers contains a series of *stichera*, each with its own melody; these are *troparia*, or sung poems, that are intercalated between the final verses of the psalms at the end of Vespers or between the four last verses of Psalm 150 at the end of Matins. Then come eight readings from the Old Testament. The third and sixth of these readings are followed by another *troparion*.

The list of readings is an interesting one: Genesis 1:1-13; various verses from Numbers 24; Micah 4:6-7 and 5:1-3; and Isaiah 11:1-10; Baruch 3:35 and 4:4; Daniel 2:31-36, 44-45; Isaiah 8:3-6; Isaiah 7:10-16; 8:1-4, and 8:9-10. These are followed in turn by New Testament readings: Hebrews 1:1-12 (with an Alleluia) and Luke 2:1-20.

On the vigil of a great feast such as Christmas, a further Office called a "Vigil" is celebrated between Vespers and Matins. This additional Office consists of *troparia* and numerous other hymns, with their own melodies, that sing of the mysteries associated with the nativity.

In Matins, the psalms are from the Ordinary, but they are accompanied by nine odes, each containing its own *heir-*

mos (a model strophe at the beginning of an ode or group of *troparia*) and *troparia*.

Here are some of these texts. From the first song of the Vigil Office: "Heaven and earth today rejoice with a prophetic joy. We men, and the angels, should rejoice spiritually, since God has been born of a woman and has appeared in the flesh for the sake of those who sit in darkness and the shadow of death." "Heaven and earth are one today, for Christ is born. Today God has come to earth, and man has returned to heaven. Today he who is by nature invisible is visible in the flesh — for man's sake!"

In Matins, the second *heirmos*, or model strophe, of the fourth Ode: "In his songs the prophet Habakkuk of old predicted the new creation of the human race, for he was judged worthy to contemplate its ineffable image. The little Child who has come forth from the mountain that is the Virgin is the Word, who comes to restore the nations."

During the liturgy (i.e., the celebration of the Eucharist), the *Trisagion* (the triple "Holy," i.e., the *Sanctus*) is replaced by these words: "All you who have been baptized in Christ have put on Christ." The words indicate to us the kind of theology that characterizes this rich liturgy. The readings for this same Mass are Galatians 4:3-7 and Matthew 2:1-12.

The Holy Family of Christ

Devout Christians wanted a special celebration for the Holy Family of the Lord, though it is highly probable, of course, that the conditions of the times also played an important role in the insistence of Pope John XXIII on this feast. The feast concentrates on the three persons whose life together should be an influential model for all families today. Each of the three lived for God and for the others, with that true heroism that is always simple and unassuming. The opening prayer of the Mass shows the Church's main concern on this feast, which is a prolongation of the feast of Christmas: "Father, help us to live as the holy family, united in respect and love."

At first sight, such a celebration may seem somewhat childish and of value only to the simple; hardly a celebration for educated Christians! But it would be a mistake not to see in it a new manifestation of the fact that Jesus has come among men and entered into the kind of life we all live. And it would be a sign of superficiality if we failed to grasp the importance of the unpretentious behavior of Mary and Joseph for the unfolding of that sacred history that will reach its climax in the paschal mystery.

The new lectionary has provided a three-year cycle of Gospel readings for this feast. All three focus on the way the parents of Jesus act in regard to him: the flight into Egypt and the return to Nazareth, with Joseph's docility to the Lord's commands and his care to protect the child (A: Matthew 2:13-15, 19-23); the child's growth in age and wisdom, and his parents' surprise at what others say of their child, especially when the old man Simeon tells prophetically of the significance of his life (B: Luke 2:22-40); Jesus discovered among the teachers as he listens and asks questions (C: Luke 2:41-52).

In the reading of Cycle A, we will note the parallelism between the two passages (vv. 13-15 and vv. 19-23). We need only read them carefully and we will find a striking similarity of literary structure. We may note especially the emphasis on the fulfillment of prophecy. In the first section (vv. 13-15), the prophecy is that of Hosea: "Out of Egypt I called my son" (11:1). In the background there is also the account in Genesis 46:2-5, where God bids Jacob set out for Egypt: "Do not be afraid to go down to Egypt; for I will there make of you a great nation. I will go down with you to Egypt, and I will also bring you up again." Note, too that, while in the genealogy Jesus is called "son of David" (1:1), here he is called Son of God: "Out of Egypt I called my son."

For the Israelites, Egypt was the land of slavery; they had experienced it and the Lord had delivered them. Now Jesus is the deliverer. There is a striking parallelism between Exodus 4:19-20 and verses 19-21 of this Gospel reading, with Jesus appearing as the new Moses. Joseph probably did not grasp all that we are now able to see, but he was nonetheless a faithful servant, faithful to the Lord's commands and determined to carry out the Lord's plan of salvation.

In Cycle B, the Gospel passage from Luke (2:22-40) shows us the presentation in the Temple and the meetings with Anna, the prophetess, and with the elderly Simeon, who points to Jesus as Savior, Light of the world, Glory of Israel, and Deliverer of Jerusalem. Yet salvation will in fact be given only to those who believe (Luke 20:17-18). As believers, Simeon and Anna are able to recognize and proclaim the Messiah. Mary receives from Simeon a revelation of her Son's role in the salvation of all mankind, but at the same time she learns of his tragic destiny as he comes to save Israel but is not received with faith. At this point Joseph and Mary take over the rearing of the child who is to save the world.

Luke 2:41-52, the reading for Cycle C, speaks of the relationship between Jesus and his parents. The passage does more than preserve an anecdote, for it reveals the wisdom of Jesus as he shows us how he understands God's will. The divine will is not simply something he learns; rather, his whole life is focused on devotion to his Father's affairs. His parents respect this mystery of their son that will be fully revealed in the paschal mystery, when hidden things become clear in Christ.

The first two readings for this feast are the same every year. The first is an exhortation to respect our parents: "Whoever glorifies his father will have long life, and whoever obeys the Lord will refresh his mother" (Sir. 3:2-6, 12-14). Psalm 128 then sings of the happiness of a family that worships the Lord. Finally St. Paul, in his Letter to the Colossians, exhorts his hearers to the domestic virtues (3:12-21): mutual love and forgiveness, a spirit of thanksgiving, submission of wives to their husbands, love of husband for wife, obedience on the part of the children. This may seem to be an idyllic vision of the Christian family, but it is in fact realistic, since the Holy Family gives us an example of it, and the Lord enables us to imitate that example in our daily lives.

Mary, Mother of God (January 1)

On January 1, the octave day of the nativity, we have the oldest celebration of the Virgin in the Roman Church. The modern Church has decided to revive that celebration of Mary, the Mother of God, without however forgetting either the beginning of the new year or the circumcision of Jesus or his reception of the name Jesus. The entrance antiphon expresses briefly the focus of the Church's thoughts during this liturgy: "Hail, holy Mother! The child to whom you gave birth is the King of heaven and earth for ever."

The Gospel is the same passage as is read in the Mass at Dawn on Christmas. Here again we can observe how the Gospel must be interpreted in connection with the first and second readings of the feast being celebrated. On Christmas, the Gospel was emphasizing the coming of the Word as man; in this new context, the emphasis is on the role of the Virgin Mother of God. For this reason the second reading is taken from St. Paul's Letter to the Galatians (4:4-7), where we read that God sent his Son to be born of a woman. The preface for this day also celebrates the motherhood of Mary, who conceived her Son when the Spirit overshadowed her. "We celebrate at this season the beginning of our salvation." [184]

The Church also remembers today the giving of the name Jesus to the Virgin's child (in the Gospel). It is a powerful name when invoked over the beginning of the new year; that is the point of the first reading, Numbers 6:22-27.

The Word and Wisdom among us

The second Sunday after Christmas continues the Church's contemplation of the mystery of the nativity. The

Gospel is that read at the Mass during the Day on Christmas. The other readings emphasize two aspects of the coming of the Word among us. One is that with his coming the Wisdom of God has now taken up its abode in its own people (Sir. 24:1-2, 8-12). The other is that we are predestined to become children of God through Jesus (Eph. 1:3-6, 15-18). Both aspects are important.

We can hardly believe that in the eyes of the Old Testament writers, Wisdom was a person. The liturgy nonetheless uses this text to describe the person of Jesus. The reading acquires its full Christian meaning once we identify the incarnate Son of God with the Wisdom that comes to dwell among men. Such a re-reading and an identification of Christ with Wisdom is possible and legitimate in a liturgical celebration, although a strictly exegetical reading could not justify such an interpretation.

The second reading unveils to us God's plan of salvation. We were chosen before the creation of the world to become holy and blameless in the Lord's sight; we were predestined in advance to become children for God through Jesus the Christ. It is the Spirit who now makes us discern God's wisdom and conforms us to the image of the Son. We thereby learn how, through the mystery of the incarnation, we enter into the life of the Trinity. From all eternity God has loved us; he never gets discouraged but, despite our sins, loves us so much that he sends his Son. This Son dies for us and redeems us, while the Spirit creates in us the image of the Son so that when the Father sees us, he can see his Son in us.

This marvelous plan of God rouses Paul's wonder and admiration. He prays that the Spirit may open our hearts and that we may be able to grasp the hope that springs from the invocation of the Father, and the priceless and glorious heritage that we share with all believers.

15. CHRISTMAS IN THE LITURGIES
OF THE PAST

1. Christmas in the Early Roman Liturgy

Readings

There is a wide variety of readings for the Christmas season to be found in the lectionaries of earlier times. We must, however, limit ourselves to a selection of these, since too long a list would be cumbersome and less useful. In addition, there are many similarities between the various lectionaries. The reader can peruse the table that follows; there is no need for us to comment on it.

There are other lectionaries from the Roman tradition that we might also have noted; for example, the Chartres Lectionary, compiled around 740,[185] or the Epistolary of Corbie,[186] or the Verona Lectionary.[187]

Prayers

The wealth of prayers in the sacramentaries, and especially in the Verona, or "Leonine," Sacramentary, is truly remarkable, and a whole book would be required for an adequate study of the material. The Verona Sacramentary, for example, contains eight formularies of Masses for Christmas.[188] St. Leo the Great is a chief source of these formularies, which show a close similarity to his other writings.

Some prayers from the Verona Sacramentary have been taken over in the new Missal of Paul VI. There is, for example, a collect for Christmas in the Verona Sacramentary that in the past served in the Roman Rite (and still does, though in modified form) as a blessing of the water to be added to the chalice at Mass, but has now also been restored to its proper function as the opening prayer for Mass on Christmas Day: "Lord God, we praise you for creating man, and still more for restoring him in Christ. Your Son shared our weakness: may we share his glory."[189] Another prayer from the Verona Sacramentary serves as the post-communion of Midnight Mass.[190] A number of other prayers in the new Missal have been inspired by those of the Verona Sacramentary.

We shall limit ourselves here, however, to some especially interesting prayers of the Verona Sacramentary that have not been taken over into the new Missal. The post-communion prayer in the first Christmas Mass is important for a theology of the liturgy as actualization in time of the mysteries of Christ: "Lord, grant your servants a deeper faith and a greater freedom from anxiety, so that your children, who rejoice at the birth of your Son, our Lord, may through your providential governance not experience the opposition of the world and may enjoy in eternity what they yearn to celebrate in time."[191]

The mystery of Christmas is regarded as a paschal renewal: "Lord, you have restored human nature to a more wonderful condition than that in which you first created it. Complete what the divine generation of your Word created in us and what his glorious birth as man has now made new."[192]

The prayers taken over into the new Missal from the older sacramentaries are also quite rich. The Masses for Midnight and Dawn emphasize the theme of light in relation to the meaning of Christmas. Thus the opening prayer of Midnight Mass: "Father, you make this holy night radiant with the splendor of Jesus Christ our light. We welcome him as Lord, the true light of the world. Bring us to eternal joy in the kingdom of heaven." This prayer is taken from the Gelasian Sacramentary,[193] where it is likewise used as the opening prayer of Midnight Mass; it brings out the paschal aspect of the feast, since the grace of the latter is an intensification of the illumination received in baptism.

The first of the Christmas prefaces in the new Missal likewise stresses the theme of light: "In the wonder of the incarnation your eternal Word has brought to the eyes of

	1	2	3	4	5	6
Vigil of Christmas		Is. 62:1-4 Rom. 1:1-6	Matthew 1:18-21		Rom. 1:1-6 Matthew 1:18-21	Rom. 1:1-6 Matthew 1:18-21
Christmas Midnight	Titus 2:11-15	Is. 9:2-7 Titus 2:11-15	Luke 2:1-14		Is. 9:2-7 Luke 2:1-14	Titus 2:11-15 Luke 2:15-20
Dawn	Titus 3:4-7	Titus 3:4-7	Luke 2:15-20		Is. 61:1-3, 62:11-12 Titus 3:4-7 Luke 2:15-20	Titus 3:4-7 Luke 2:15-20
Day	Heb. 1:1-12	Heb. 1:1-12	John 1:1-14		Is. 52:6-10 Heb. 1:1-12 John 1:1-14	Heb. 1:1-12 John 1:1-14
Mary, Mother of God, January 1	Gal. 4:1-7	Rom. 12:6-16	Luke 2:21-32		Titus 2:11-15 Luke 2:21-32	Titus 2:11-15 Luke 2:21
Sunday after Christmas				Matthew 2:19-23	Gal. 4:1-7 Luke 2:33-40	Gal. 4:1-7 Luke 2:33-40

1 = The Würzburg Epistolary (ca. 560–590). Edition: G. Morin, "Le plus ancien lectionnaire de l'Eglise romaine," *Revue bénédictine* 27 (1910), pp. 41–74. For its history, see Vogel, *op. cit.*, pp. 309–10, 313–14, 321–25.

2 = The Comes or Epistolary of Alcuin. The manuscript is from the ninth century, but it is thought to represent a Roman lectionary of the year 626, which Alcuin simply modified. Edition: A. Wilmart, "Le lectionnaire d'Alcuin," *Ephemerides liturgicae* 51 (1937), pp. 136–97. See Vogel, *op. cit.*, pp. 310–12.

3 = The Würzburg Evangeliary (ca. 645), a pure Roman document. See Vogel, *op. cit.*, pp. 313–14.

4 = A pure Roman evangeliary of around 740, described in Vogel, *op. cit.*, p. 314.

5 = The Murbach Lectionary, composed at Murbach, France, toward the end of the eighth century; it is later followed at Rome, and the Missal of Pius V makes extensive use of it. Edition: A. Wilmart, "Le Comes de Murbach," *Revue bénédictine* 30 (1913), pp. 26–69. See Vogel, *op. cit.*, pp. 318–19.

6 = Missal of Pius V.

faith a new and radiant vision of your glory." The second preface concentrates more on the sacramental aspect of the incarnation: "We recognize in Christ the revelation of your love. No eye can see his glory as our God, yet now he is seen as one like us." The third preface emphasizes the wonderful exchange that has taken place: "Your eternal Word has taken upon himself our human weakness, giving our mortal nature immortal value."

The prefaces in the Verona Sacramentary were of great theological depth. We cannot cite them all, but we may at least note how the first of them makes Christmas the basic celebration of the Christian year: "All that a devout Christian faith celebrates has its origins in this feast and is already contained in the mystery we celebrate in this liturgy."[194]

2. The Celebration of Christmas at Milan

We shall simply list the readings given in the Sacramentary of Bergamo[195] and in the present Ambrosian Missal:

	Sacramentary of Bergamo	Ambrosian Missal
Vigil of Christmas	Heb. 10:37-39 Matthew 1:18-25	Heb. 10:38-39 Matthew 1:18-25
Christmas: Midnight	Gal. 4:4-6 John 1:9-14	Gal. 4:4-6 John 1:9 14
Dawn		1 Cor. 9:13-23 Luke 2:15-20
Day		Is. 9:1-7
	Heb. 1:1-12 Luke 2:1-14	Heb. 1:1-8 Luke 2:1-14
Sunday after Christmas		Is. 8:10-18
	Rom. 8:3-11 Luke 4:14-22	Rom. 8:3-11 Luke 4:14-22

Octave of		Bar. 6:1-2, 4-6
Christmas		Jer. 51:47-48, 58
(January 1)		Phil. 3:1-8
	Luke 2:21-32	Luke 2:21-32

The Sacramentary of Bergamo contains no prayer that is unusually rich in content that is not also found elsewhere.

3. The Celebration of Christmas in Merovingian Gaul

The celebration of Christmas in Merovingian Gaul provides us with some interesting readings. We may note, for example, the custom of reading a passage from a Father of the Church during the Vigil Mass (see the Lectionary of Luxeuil). Another point worth noting is the originality shown in the choice of readings from Scripture; this may be seen by comparing them with those of Rome, Milan, and Spain.

4. The Celebration of Christmas in Spain

Christmas	January 1
Is. 7:10-16; 9:1-7	Gen. 21:1-8
Heb. 1:1-12	Rom. 15:8-13
Luke 2:1-20	Luke 2:21-40

For Christmas Day the Spanish *Liber sacramentorum* has a prayer that is of special interest:

Lord, in fidelity to your gifts and your precepts, we place on your altar holocausts of bread and wine. We ask you, in your loving mercy that is given so abundantly, that the undivided Trinity would consecrate these gifts by the power of the same Spirit through whom the spotless Virgin conceived you in the flesh. Then, when we have received these gifts with fear

	L	S	S¹	B	P
Vigil of Christmas	Is. 41:26-42 Is. 44:23-46 Sermon of Augustine Is. 54:1-56 Mal. 3:1-4, 6 John 1:1-14	Is. 9:1-7	Gal. 3:24-4:7	Is. 9:6-7 Heb. 1:1-5 Matthew 1:1-2, 6	
Christmas Day	Is. 7:10-9:7 Heb. 1:1-12 Luke 2:1-20	Is. 9:1-7	Gal. 3:24-4:7	Is. 9:1-7 Heb. 1:1-5 Matthew 1:1-2:6	Luke 2:1-20
Sunday after Christmas	Ezek. 43:18-44:4 Eph. 1:3-14		2 Cor. 6: 12-18		
January 1	Is. 1:10-18 1 Cor. 10: 14-31 Luke 2:21-40	Is. 45:18-24	1 Cor. 10: 17-31		

L = Lectionary of Luxeuil. P. Salmon (ed.), *Le Lectionnaire de Luxeuil* (Collectanea Biblica 7 and 9; Rome, 1944 and 1953). See Vogel, *op. cit.*, p. 291.

S = Lectionary of Sélestat. A Merovingian lectionary, ca. 700; originally from northern Italy. Partial edition by G. Morin, "Un lectionnaire mérovingien de Sélestat avec fragments du texte occidental des Actes," *Revue bénédictine* 28 (1908), pp. 161–66. See Vogel, *op. cit.*, p. 292.

S¹ = Fragment of a lectionary from Sélestat, indicating readings from third Sunday of Advent on. Edited in G. Morin, *art. cit.*, p. 166. See Vogel, *loc. cit.*

B = The eighth-century Bobbio Missal, preserved at Paris. Edited by E. J. Lowe and J. W. Legg, *The Bobbio Missal* 1: *Facsimile*; 2: *Text* (Henry Bradshaw Society 53 and 58; London, 1917–20). See Vogel, *op. cit.*, p. 293.

P = Marginal notations in the seventh-century Evangeliary of Saint-Dénis. Edited by P. Salmon, "Le texte biblique de l'Évangéliaire de Saint-Dénis," *Miscellanea Mercati* 1 (Rome, 1946), pp. 103–106. See Vogel, *op. cit.*, p. 295.

and reverence, whatever militates against the soul will be destroyed, and whatever has been destroyed will not gain power over us again.[196]

Noteworthy, too, is the preface of the Mass for the beginning of the new year:

God our Father, he who was born of you before time began and who with you and the Holy Spirit created time, has deigned to be born within time from the womb of the Virgin Mary. Yet he is eternal and fixed the course of the years through which the world goes its way. . . . Fill the earth with fruits; free our souls and bodies of sickness and sin; eliminate scandals; crush our enemy. . . .[197]

THE EPIPHANY MYSTERY

BIBLICO-LITURGICAL REFLECTIONS ON THE EPIPHANY

16. THE EPIPHANY: A Mystery of Plenty

Two celebrations of the same mystery?

The Ephiphany may at first sight seem to be a superfluous feast, one that originates in the desire to emphasize the dogma of the incarnation. As a matter of fact, there is a certain validity to this view, since the Epiphany certainly did owe its existence to the desire of making the mystery of the incarnate Word better appreciated and of relating it to Christian life.

The purpose of the feast, however, is not to dwell on the details of stories from the life of Jesus, but to highlight his incarnation and manifestation. The folklore surrounding the crèche since the time of St. Francis, the medieval Christmas legends, and an excessive curiosity about the details of Christ's life have all contributed to a loss of the vision of the overall mystery of Christmas and Epiphany. The feasts of Christmas and Epiphany depend for their proper understanding on the paschal mystery, the incarnation of the Word being the first stage in the carrying out of the work of our redemption. The opening prayer for the Mass on Christmas Day, taken from the Verona Sacramentary, is significant in this respect; its whole atmosphere is that of the paschal mystery.[198]

The best way to grasp the connection between Christmas and Epiphany, and at the same time their different objects, is by a comparison of the Roman prefaces for the two feasts.

The Verona Sacramentary contains eight Mass formularies and eight prefaces for Christmas. The sixth of these prefaces sums up the object of the feast in a luminous way:

> It is truly right and proper, fitting and conducive to salvation that we should always and everywhere give you thanks, holy Lord, almighty Father, eternal God, for the magnificent exchange that restores our nature has now been manifested. From the old man a new man arises and from mortality immortality, as the human condition is healed with a remedy wrought from that same human condition; and from a race subject to sin a child innocent of all sin is born. Not only is undying honor done our weak nature when your Word makes it his own, but through his marvelous sharing with us we ourselves become eternal.[199]

This beautiful preface should be compared with the prayer, mentioned just above, that is likewise found in the Verona Sacramentary and now appears in the Mass for Christmas Day. Christmas brings with it the gift of a new nature; so intimate now is our communion with the Word that "we ourselves become eternal." The incarnation is presented as the start of the process of redemption, since the restoration of our nature consists essentially in this, that "from the old man a new man arises."

The mystery of Christmas is seen essentially in the perspective of the paschal mystery:

> It is truly right and proper, fitting and conducive to salvation that we should always and everywhere give you thanks, holy Lord, almighty Father, eternal God, as we offer you the unceasing sacrifice of praise. Abel the just man prefigured it with his sacrifice; the lamb prescribed by the law was its type; Abraham celebrated it; and the priest Melchisedech showed it forth, but only the true Lamb and eternal priest, the Christ born this day, made it a reality.[200]

Finally, the three prefaces now used for Christmas likewise make our transformation their theme.

Since our restoration comes about through intimate contact with the Godhead, the nuptial theme was felt to be appropriate. The sixth preface of the Verona Sacramentary suggests it, as we saw above. The first of the Verona prefaces makes it its major theme as it speaks of our present union with Christ, that is, the union of Christ and his Church that is to deepen and reach its fullest form at the end of time:

> All that a devout Christian faith celebrates has its origin in this feast and is already contained in the mystery we celebrate in this liturgy. It was made known even to the parents of the human race, as the Apostle tells us when speaking of the first human beings: "This is a great mystery, and I mean in reference to Christ and the church." The patriarchs pointed to it in various words and deeds; the observance of the law prefigured it; all the prophets foretold it in their oracles. In it the ancient ceremonies are brought to their perfect form. In it heavenly grace is now bestowed upon us and the promise of blessings to come. For since what was predicted is evidently fulfilled in it, we may rightly and surely expect that what was promised will also come to pass.[201]

The Christmas prefaces, then, speak of our restoration through the incarnation and our resultant close communion with the incarnate Word.

In the Mass for the Vigil of the Theophany (a frequent Eastern name for our Epiphany), the Gelasian Sacramentary has a preface that appears later on in the Gregorian Sacramentary as the preface for January 6; it was also the preface for the Epiphany in the Roman Rite until the recent reform and still forms part of the new preface for the Epiphany: "For, when your only-begotten Son appeared in the reality of our mortal nature, he restored us by the newly manifested radiance of his immortal being."[202]

The theme of renewal or restoration evidently is basic in this preface, but in one respect it is new, inasmuch as it is through an illumination or enlightenment that we are made new. Christ comes as the light that sheds light into our darkness and makes us new. The theme is clearly Johannine.

The other prayers in this Gelasian Mass develop the same theme. Thus the opening prayer reads: "Lord, let the radiance of the coming feast enlighten our hearts, so that we may be liberated from the darkness of this world and reach the fatherland where eternal light shines."[203] The postcommunion prayer continues in the same vein: "Lord, enlighten your people and inflame their hearts with your radiant grace so that the birth of the world's Savior, heralded by the star, may be ever revealed to their minds, and that the understanding of it may grow in them."[204]

On the feast day itself, January 6, the same Gelasian Sacramentary has a preface that aptly highlights the meaning of the feast:

> It is truly right and proper, fitting and conducive to salvation, that we should praise you, our God, who are marvelous in all the works by which you have revealed the mysteries of your kingdom. A star announcing the virginal birth shone in advance of this feast and told the wondering Magi that heaven's Lord was born on earth. Thus God was manifested to the world by a heavenly sign, and he who was born in time was revealed to men through temporal signs.[205]

The preface is supplemented by a *Communicantes* prayer: "In union with the whole Church we celebrate the sacred day on which your only-begotten Son, who shares your eternal glory, appeared as one truly born of our flesh. . . ."[206]

The star is a focus of attention in the liturgy, insofar as it manifests the incarnate Word. In other words, the eternal generation of the Word is revealed by earthly manifestations. The preface quoted above tells us that earthly, temporal signs pointed to him who is born in time. The temporal, earthly signs that thus manifest the birth of the Word are the star, but especially the baptism in the Jordan and the marriage feast of Cana.

The feast of Christmas, then, celebrates the incarnation of the Son of God, while the feast of the Epiphany emphasizes the earthly manifestations of his eternal birth. In the one feast we celebrate the birth in the flesh; in the other we concentrate on the earthly manifestations of the eternal generation of the Word. At Christmas we begin with the eternal generation of the Word and go on to celebrate his earthly incarnation. On Epiphany we recall and celebrate the earthly manifestations which tell us that the newborn child is the eternally begotten Word.

The same theology will be at the center of the liturgical celebrations that follow the Epiphany, and we shall find it especially emphasized on February 2, the feast of the Presentation or, as the Eastern Church calls it, the Meeting of the Lord.

"Three mysteries"

The feast of the Epiphany is truly a feast of plenty, especially in the East, where the *tria miracula*, the "three mysteries" of Christ's life, are celebrated together, with the emphasis on the wealth of teaching they contain. The antiphon for the *Magnificat* at Second Vespers on Epiphany speaks of these three mysteries that are the object of the day's liturgical celebration: the star that leads the Magi to the crib; the miraculous wine at the marriage feast of Cana; the baptism of Jesus in the Jordan.

We shall see in some detail just what these three events of our salvation mean to us. First, however, in order better to grasp the way the various Churches celebrate Epiphany, we must review, even if only briefly, the history of the feast.

The Epiphany in history

St. Paul uses the word "epiphany" (*epiphaneia*) three times in his letters. He uses it of the first coming of Christ:

". . . the grace which he . . . now has manifested through the appearing (*epiphaneias*) of our Savior Jesus Christ, who abolished death and brought life and immortality to light through the gospel" (2 Tim. 1:9-10). The other two texts speak rather of Christ's triumphant return to his own: ". . . awaiting our blessed hope, the appearing (*epiphaneian*) of the glory of our great God and Savior Jesus Christ" (Titus 2:13); "And then the lawless one will be revealed, and the Lord Jesus will slay him with the breath of his mouth and destroy him by his appearing (*epiphaneia*) and his coming" (2 Thess. 2:8).

The Greek words *epiphaneia* and *theophaneia* signify the coming of a king or emperor; the Latin word for this "coming" is *adventus*. The same words are also used, however, for the self-manifestation of a god or for his miraculous intervention. The words were perhaps applied first to the gods and later to sovereigns.

For a better grasp of the history of Epiphany, we should look at it first in the East, then in the West.[207]

In the East, the feast of Epiphany (January 6) was instituted before the feast of Christmas was. At the end of the fourth century, the object of the feast of the Epiphany at Jerusalem was the birth of Christ.[208] Christmas seems to have been introduced around 430, but only for a while, since a sixth-century document shows that at Jerusalem Jesus' birth was celebrated on Epiphany, while December 25 was the feast of SS. David and James. During the years 567–78 the feast of Christmas was reintroduced and set alongside Epiphany.

At Constantinople and in Asia Minor there is no trace of Epiphany before the end of the fourth century. When Epiphany was introduced, it was called *Ta Phōta*, the feast of "lights," and it celebrated the birth of Christ. Once Christmas was also introduced, the feast of lights took for its object the baptism of Christ.

In Syria, January 6 continued to be the feast of the incarnation until around 486, when St. John Chrysostom introduced the feast of Christmas at Antioch. From then on,

Epiphany became the feast solely of the baptism of Christ.

The feast of Christmas thus originates in Rome and is adopted everywhere throughout the East during the fifth century, except perhaps in Armenia. Once Christmas is introduced, the baptism of Jesus becomes the most important and, in some instances, the only object of the celebration on January 6.

Why was January 6 chosen as the date for Epiphany? A letter of St. Epiphanius suggests that in various cities of Egypt and Arabia a feast was celebrated on January 6 in honor of the birth of *Aiōn*, daughter of the virgin *Korē*, and in connection with the winter solstice. In addition, pagan writers like Pliny and Christian writers like St. Epiphanius and St. John Chrysostom report certain wonders connected with January 5: spring water changed into wine; water that never turned foul, because it had been drawn on that day. It looks, then, as if the Church wanted to christianize both the pagan feast and the prodigies.

In the West, the feast of Christmas was celebrated at Rome as early as 336, but there is no trace of Epiphany. Throughout the rest of Italy, Epiphany was being celebrated around 383, but not everywhere; and where it was celebrated, it was not regarded as being of the same importance as Christmas. As for Gaul and Spain, the feast of Epiphany seems to have been introduced there around 384 and 400 respectively.[209] In fact, it may have been celebrated in Gaul before Christmas was, whereas in Rome and in Africa the feast of Christmas antedates that of Epiphany.

Though Epiphany came from the East to the West, it has a threefold object in the West — the visit of the Magi, the baptism of Christ, and the marriage feast of Cana — whereas in the East today, Epiphany is the feast only of the baptism of Jesus.

The Epiphany and ourselves

Despite all this background and explanations, we may well continue to think that Epiphany is simply a feast that sheds further light on Christmas, a continuation of a meditation that is already rich but is now enriched still more. The questions we must ask ourselves are evidently these: What are the Magi to us? What meaning can Christ's baptism have for us today? How can we relate to the marriage feast of Cana? It is difficult for us to overcome the impression that the Church is simply expanding our view of Christmas and spreading before us treasures that further enrich her catechesis of the incarnation.

Even if we have no further need of proofs and no difficulty in admitting both the full divinity of Christ and the integrity of his human nature, we may retain the impression of an Epiphany liturgy that, for all its richness of detail, has more to do with poetic evocation than with any new concrete demands made upon us as soon as we seek to participate in the celebration in an authentic way. Liturgical development under the influence of varied cultures may seem to have turned the feast into a great theatrical display.

The difficulty we may feel, then, is not so much with the general problem of the actualization of the mysteries being celebrated; by what has been said already, we may have been convinced that such actualization is indeed important. Our problem with the Epiphany may not be the "today" aspect in the abstract, but the "today" relation of this particular feast to our daily lives. It is easy to see the relevance of Christmas, but what are we to make of the "three mysteries"?

17. THE MAGI OF OLD AND THE "MAGI" OF TODAY

St. Matthew's Gospel was the one the early Christians liked best. For all its variety, it possessed a profound unity, and readers saw this. There can be no doubt, of course, that this Gospel, like John's, is shaped by the intention of teaching and defending a point of view, or, in other words, that it has a "thesis." But to admit this does not mean, for Matthew any more than for John, that we are to be suspicious or doubtful about the authenticity of the facts recorded in the narrative. Research and discoveries have shown that John's Gospel, often called the "spiritual" Gospel, is perhaps the most accurate of the four in its localization of events.

Exegetes universally see in the First Gospel, the Gospel of the kingdom. That is Matthew's "thesis": the establishment of the kingdom in our world. Within this framework, however, the point that Matthew emphasizes most forcefully is that the teaching and works of Jesus prolong and "fulfill" the Old Testament.[210]

Whether we see the Gospel as a seven-act play[211] or as five books with a prologue (the infancy narrative, chapters 1–2) and an epilogue (the resurrection, chapter 28),[212] the doctrinal unity of the whole work is evident. Not for a moment does St. Matthew forget his essential concern, which is to show the Jews that the Old Testament has been fulfilled. The formula, "All this took place to fulfill what the Lord had spoken by the prophet" (Matthew 1:22), occurs ten times or more.

Cerfaux points out that the infancy narrative

> is a perfect prelude to the Gospel, while the solemn apparition of Jesus on a mountain in Galilee . . . is a very fitting conclusion: the apostles are now sent out to the nations (and not just to the towns of Israel, as on their first mission); they are to teach all of Jesus' commandments, and he will be with them until the end of the world.[213]

Now we have the context and perspective in which we must read the story of the Magi's visit (chapter 2). Their coming fulfills the prophetic proclamation that the nations will acknowledge the God of Israel.

The Book of Numbers had spoken of a leader who would emerge from the midst of Israel and assert his power:

I see him, but not now;
   I behold him, but not nigh:
a star shall come forth out of Jacob,
   and a scepter shall rise out of Israel;
it shall crush the forehead of Moab,
   and break down all the sons of Sheth.
Edom shall be dispossessed,
   Seir also, his enemies, shall be dispossessed,
   while Israel does valiantly.
By Jacob shall dominion be exercised (Num. 24:17-19).

The power and divinity of the king here predicted are signified by a star, which, in the East, was a sign of divinity. St. Matthew, always bent on his apologetic purpose of showing the continuity between the Old and New Testaments, gives us the genealogy of Jesus and stresses the connection between him and his ancestors, Abraham and David. The star, therefore, may, in Matthew's view, be the Davidic monarchy to which he has linked Jesus in the genealogy.

The evangelist here emphasizes once again that a prophecy has been fulfilled (he is only beginning the second chapter of his Gospel, yet this is the second prophecy he sees being fulfilled!). The prophecy in this case is a prophecy of Micah: "But you, O Bethlehem Ephrathah, who are little to be among the clans of Judah, from you shall come forth for me one who is to be ruler in Israel" (Micah 5:2; Matthew 2:6).

Matthew is aware, however, of other prophecies that are even more decisive, and he alludes to these in the course of his story. Thus, the Magi prostrate themselves before Jesus. In so doing, they fulfill a prophecy of Isaiah: "Kings shall be your foster fathers, and their queens your nursing mothers. With their faces to the ground they shall bow down to you, and lick the dust of your feet. Then you will know that I am the Lord; those who wait for me shall not be put to shame" (Is. 49:23).

Chapter 60 of Isaiah, which will play an important part in patristic commentaries on the Epiphany and in the liturgy of the feast,[214] is also alluded to by Matthew:

> Arise, shine; for your light has come,
>   and the glory of the Lord has risen upon you
> For behold, darkness shall cover the earth,
>   and thick darkness the peoples;
> but the Lord will arise upon you,
>   and his glory will be seen upon you.
> And nations shall come to your light,
>   and kings to the brightness of your rising.
> Lift up your eyes round about, and see;
>   they all gather together, they come to you;
> your sons shall come from far,
>   and your daughters shall be carried in the arms.
> Then you shall see and be radiant,
>   your heart shall thrill and rejoice;
> because the abundance of the sea shall be turned to
>   you,
>   the wealth of the nations shall come to you.
> A multitude of camels shall cover you,
>   the young camels of Midian and Ephah;
>   all those from Sheba shall come.
> They shall bring gold and frankincense,
>   and shall proclaim the praise of the Lord (Is. 60:1-6)

The prophecies of Psalm 72 (Vulgate 71) are likewise fulfilled according to Matthew's narrative. This psalm is another passage that the Fathers and the liturgy make great use of; it provides the responsorial psalm for the feast of Epiphany in the new Missal:

> May the kings of Tarshish and of the isles
>   render him tribute,
>   may the kings of Sheba and Seba bring gifts!
> May all kings fall down before him,
>   all nations serve him!
> For he delivers the needy when he calls,
>   the poor and him who has no helper.

He has pity on the weak and the needy,
and saves the lives of the needy.
From oppression and violence he redeems their life;
and precious is their blood in his sight.
Long may he live,
may gold of Sheba be given to him!
May prayer be made for him continually,
and blessings invoked for him all the day!
(Ps. 72:10-15).

He wished to be known by all

St. Leo the Great fully comprehended the theological meaning of the event. The real issue is the founding of the kingdom throughout the world, the preaching of the gospel, the establishment of God's kingdom, the healing of the sick, the working of miracles.

> It was important to all mankind that the Mediator between God and men should be made known to the whole world, even while he was still a child and living in a small town. For though he had chosen the people of Israel and, within that people, a single family in which to make his own the nature all men share, he did not wish his birth to pass unnoticed within the narrow confines of his mother's house. Rather, he wished to be known straightway by all, since he had deigned to be born for the sake of all.[215]

Later in this same sermon, St. Leo points out the symbolism of the Magi's gifts (a theme dear to the Fathers): "To God they offer the incense, to the man the myrrh, and to the king the gold. They are conscious of honoring the divine nature and the human nature as united in a single being. For what was proper to each nature was not divided in the exercise of power."[216]

St. Leo's second sermon on the Epiphany emphasizes the proclamation to the entire world of the Savior's coming:

> Thus the heavens were already proclaiming the glory

of God, and the voice of truth was being heard over the whole earth when the army of angels told the shepherds of the Savior's birth, and a star went on ahead to guide the Magi as they came to worship him. Thus from east to west the birth of the true King was splendidly manifested, since the kingdoms of the east learned the truth through the Magi, while it was not hidden from the Roman empire.[217]

Further on in this second sermon, St. Leo cites Genesis 49:10 and comments:

"The scepter shall not depart from Judah, nor the ruler's staff from between his feet, until he comes to whom it belongs; and to him shall be the obedience of the peoples." With regard to these peoples: the blessed patriarch Abraham had been given the promise of a countless posterity, begotten not by the flesh but by a fruitful faith. This posterity was compared to the stars, in order to show that the father of all the nations hoped for a heavenly, not an earthly, posterity. When the time came for the birth of the promised posterity, the heirs signified by the stars were alerted by the rise of a new star; thus he to whom the heavens had borne witness received from heaven homage and service.[218]

Manifestation to the world

St. Gregory the Great likewise saw that the point of the Magi's visit was the recognition by the entire world of the Savior's kingship. He goes a step further, however, and sees not only men but the very elements acknowledging their Lord:

All the elements bore witness that their Maker had come. In terms customary among men, we may say that the heavens acknowledged this man as God by sending the star; the sea acknowledged him by turning into a solid support beneath his feet; the earth ac-

knowledged him by quaking as he died; the sun acknowledged him by hiding its rays; the rocks and
walls acknowledged him by splitting at the moment of
his death; hell acknowledged him by surrendering
the dead it held.[219]

The Epiphany as understood by the Fathers and the
liturgy is truly what St. Matthew meant it to be: a manifestation to the world. As we shall see, this aspect of manifestation is equally important in the other two events of Jesus'
life that are commemorated by this feast: his baptism and
the marriage feast of Cana. The whole world is already enlightened by the manifestation of the Savior at these three
moments of his human life, even before he enlightens it by
his preaching.

St. Matthew, who so much likes to emphasize the fulfillment of prophecy, evidently has in mind (as we have already pointed out) the prophecies of Isaiah. And in fact it
seems clear that Isaiah was the first of the prophets to
foretell unambiguously "the extension of eschatological
salvation to the entire world."[220] The will of Yahweh, who
is concerned with the whole world, is made clear as early as
chapter 14:

The Lord of hosts has sworn:
"As I have planned —
    so shall it be,
and as I have purposed,
    so shall it stand,
that I will break the Assyrian in my land,
    and upon my mountains trample him under foot;
and his yoke shall depart from them,
    and his burden from their shoulder."
This is the purpose that is purposed
    concerning the whole earth;
and this is the hand that is stretched out
    over all the nations (Is. 14:24-26).

By destroying Assyria, Yahweh crushes the peoples who

form the empire of Sennacherib, that is, for practical purposes (in the author's view), the whole earth.

But an oracle in chapter 2 (which is almost identical with
one in Micah 4:1-3) gives even better expression to Yahweh's action in relation to the whole world, and not simply
to Israel or the "small remnant":

> It shall come to pass in the latter days
>   that the mountain of the house of the Lord
> shall be established as the highest of the mountains,
>   and shall be raised above the hills;
> and all the nations shall flow to it,
>   and many peoples shall come, and say:
> "Come, let us go up to the mountain of the Lord,
>   to the house of the God of Jacob;
> that he may teach us his ways
>   and that we may walk in his paths."
> For out of Zion shall go forth the law,
>   and the word of the Lord from Jerusalem.
> He shall judge between the nations,
>   and shall decide for many peoples;
> and they shall beat their swords into plowshares,
>   and their spears into pruning hooks;
> nations shall not lift up sword against nation,
>   neither shall they learn war any more.
> O house of Jacob,
>   come, let us walk
>   in the light of the Lord (Is. 2:2-5).

Doubt has been cast upon the authenticity of this passage
from Isaiah. The presence of the same text in both Isaiah
and Micah is good reason for judging the prophecy to be of
eighth-century origin. But it seems that Micah, usually a
pessimist, is here dependent on Isaiah, one of whose favorite themes is the universal power of Yahweh.[221] Furthermore, Isaiah 2:2-5 is paralleled by Isaiah 11:1-9; 32:1-5,
and 32:15-20, all of which express the same idea that peace
is the fruit of the knowledge of Yahweh.[222]

We may be surprised that St. Matthew, like the Fathers of

the Church after him, has taken nothing from Amos, even though this prophet was so open to universalism. The reason for this is that Isaiah, though not slavishly repeating his predecessor, is nonetheless deeply influenced by the latter's teaching. At the same time, he is influenced by the prophet Hosea, with his greater sensitivity to the special covenant that Yahweh had made with Israel. It is to be expected therefore that Isaiah, synthesizing as he does the tendencies of both Amos, with his universalism, and Hosea, with his greater interest in Israel, should be a favorite of the Fathers and the liturgy.

The Magi of today

The Church's evident intention is to show us the Magi of yesteryear so as to make of us in turn the Magi of today. St. Leo the Great makes this point clearly in his second ermon on the Epiphany:

> Beloved, let us therefore recognize in the Magi who adored Christ our forerunners in calling and in faith, and with great joy let us celebrate in them the blessed beginnings of our own hope. For it was at that time that we began to enter into our everlasting inheritance; it was at that time that the mysterious passages of Scripture relating to Christ opened their meaning to us, and the truth that the Jews in their blindness did not accept shed its light on all the nations.[223]

In his third sermon on the Epiphany (now the second reading in the Office of Readings for Epiphany), St. Leo recalls the prophecies of Isaiah and concludes:

> All this was fulfilled, as we know, when the star led the three Magi from their distant land to know and adore the King of heaven and earth. The service rendered by the star is a pressing invitation to us to imitate it and to be servants, as far as we can, of the grace that summons all men to Christ. For who-

ever . . . preserves in himself the brightness of a holy life, like a star shows many the way to the Lord.[224]

It is in his fifth sermon for Epiphany, however, that St. Leo becomes most insistent:

> This star that shone before the eyes of the Magi but not before those of the Israelites signifies the enlightenment given to the Gentiles and the blindness of the Jews. Thus, beloved, the mystical content of those events continues to exist, and what began in symbol becomes authentic reality. The star of grace shines in heaven, and in every nation the three Magi, summoned by the brilliant light of the gospel, hasten to adore the power of the supreme King. . . .
>
> Keep the lamps of your souls ever burning, and let no darkness dwell in your hearts, for, as the Apostle says, "once you were darkness, but now you are light in the Lord; walk as children of the light." Make real in yourselves what you see in the figures of the Magi, and "thus let your light shine before men, so that, seeing your good deeds, they may glorify your heavenly Father."[225]

In a sixth sermon, St. Leo adds:

> The gifts of God are multiplied, and we in our time experience all that the first believers did. For though the Gospel account tells us only of the days when three men, untaught by prophetic preaching or the testimonies of the Law, came from the distant East in order to know God, yet we see the same thing happening now even more clearly and on a far larger scale in the enlightment of all who are called.[226]

These long quotations from Pope St. Leo are valuable. Better than many other commentaries, they tell us what the Church aims to accomplish in us when she celebrates the three Magi and their coming. For in them we are to see "our forerunners in calling and in faith." To them, the star is the sign of the great King. As the third antiphon at First Vespers for Epiphany expresses it: "The star burned like a flame, pointing the way to God, the King of kings; the wise men saw the sign and brought their gifts in homage to their great King."

The departure of the Magi from their homelands, as soon as they saw the star, has always been a symbol of the response of faith. The Magi very early acquired a place in Christian iconography because they were seen as models for the faithful; as soon as they were called, they responded with faith. A fresco in the cemetery of St. Priscilla (early second century) at Rome shows the Magi in Persian dress. This is rather odd, since the gifts the Magi bring seem to come rather from Arabia, where they were typical offerings. But just as the Fathers of the Church, without any serious historical basis and in dependence rather on Psalm 72:10-11, think of the Magi as kings, so too, for no special historical reason, they think of them as being Persians.

The immediate response of the Magi to the call mediated by the star is rewarded by an illumination, which is an anticipation of our faith. The hymn for Second Vespers in the Latin *Liturgia Horarum* shows the light of the star helping the Magi to find the true Light they seek: "The Magi went on their way, following the lead of the star they had seen. By its light they go in search of the Light and their gift of incense owns Him to be God."[227]

Recall the passage in which St. Leo emphasizes the present actuality of the "mystery" of the Magi: "The mystical content of those events continues to exist, and what began in symbol becomes authentic reality." In the sixth sermon he makes the same point even more strongly: "That day has not so completely passed away that the power, then revealed, of God's action has passed with it or that the only thing to have reached us is the report of what happened so that faith might accept it and memory honor it. No, the gifts of God are multiplied, and we in our time experience all that the first believers did."[228]

The feast of the Epiphany, then, draws us into a journey

toward the Lord whereby we may more fully acknowledge his divinity and fulfill our creaturely task by an offering to our God.

The prayer over the gifts in the Mass of the Epiphany mentions the gifts offered by the kings of Arabia and Seba as they prostrated themselves before the Lord. Our own gifts of bread and wine become the body and blood of the Lord — a mysterious transformation prefigured by the wine at Cana. But our offering, which replaces the gold, frankincense, and myrrh of the Magi, must also be an offering of our very selves as human beings grafted onto Christ, who alone can make an efficacious offering. The prayer over the gifts gives expression to this theology, according to which the action of the Magi is perpetuated through time by Christ, who himself acknowledges the sovereign power of the Father: "Lord, accept the offerings of your Church, not gold, frankincense and myrrh, but the sacrifice and food they symbolize: Jesus Christ, who is Lord for ever and ever."

Here, once again, we find, in the Epiphany, the paschal mystery of Christ. The light that shines at the Epiphany has renewed our souls; it enables us, as a people fed with the body and blood of Christ, to journey toward the meeting with our God, who is sovereign Master of all things.[229]

A difficult role

Every Christian, we have learned, is to be a "wise man" for his own day, as he seeks the Light and is guided by it in his life of faith, while drawing the nations in his train.

As we meditate on these truths, it is difficult not to feel a painful distance between what ought to be and what is. The Magi were the first in a procession of countless people who have journeyed toward the Lord. But we must always be asking ourselves: Are we really Magi for today? We ought to be, since the light, once received, cannot be hidden under a basket but must be set upon the lampstand! What a heavy responsibility every Christian bears!

The Christian must let the divine light within him shine through to others. He has sought the light and has been guided by it; now, because of the light that is in him, the world must in turn go in quest of the Light. The apostles were Magi for their own time, and the apostles of every age become Magi in their turn: men called by the star, led by it, leading the nations in turn to the King. Many Christians do not believe in their role, and therefore they cease to be lights amid the world's darkness; yet it remains their duty to point to the star.

The Christian role has undoubtedly become a difficult one, yet was it ever anything but foolishness in the world's eyes? It consists, after all, in showing the world "the sign of the great King,"[230] that is, the Lord's Cross! *That* is the sign we must show the world and toward which we must lead the world so that through it the world may find true life. The Cross is the paschal mystery, the central mystery of Christianity, which no baptized person can evade; it promises no earthly success in this life, not even apostolic success, but it does lead to the glory of risen life with Christ.

The individual Christian is not the only one called to point out this sign to men. The Church of every age, illumined by the Spirit of her Christ, has likewise as her essential role to show this light to men. Christ "manifested" himself, and the Church, as his spouse and the agent of his continuing work on earth, also "manifests" him. For her as for the Magi, the most effective way to manifest him is to worship him. It is Epiphany, we may say, that assigns to the Church, once she has been gathered by the Spirit of Pentecost, her activity of unending contemplation. Pentecost is the feast of the Church, because on that day she receives the Spirit of Christ; but Epiphany, too, is in a sense the feast of the Church, because it is the annual celebration of the Lord's self-manifestation to his kingdom. Like the Gospel of St. Matthew, the feast of the Epiphany asserts that the prophecies concerning the kingdom have been fulfilled. To this self-manifestation of Christ corresponds the Spouse's adoration of her Lord.

Her essential act of adoration is to offer bread and wine, Christ's body and blood. But in this very act that embodies her adoration, the Spouse also exercises most effectively her apostolate of showing Christ to men. For in eating the bread and drinking the cup, she proclaims to the world the Good News of the death and resurrection of the Lord — and thus of our salvation — until he comes again.

The Church of our day, then, is prefigured by the Magi. At the same time, the nations that come and acknowledge the Church are also "Magi" who become aware of the self-manifestation of Christ and journey toward his Cross so that they may rise to new life and meet the Lord face to face.

18. THE JORDAN: "Our Jordan"

We have just seen that the feast of the Epiphany, like that of Christmas, is a paschal feast. One object of the Epiphany commemoration, the baptism of Christ (which has now become the object of a special celebration of its own), leads us even more deeply into the paschal mystery. For the baptism of Christ in the Jordan manifests the fact that salvation is now given to all men: sin is destroyed and adoptive sonship is bestowed upon the living who have been rescued from sin. At his baptism Christ is proclaimed God's Son and the Lamb of God who removes the world's sin; and he is anointed as messianic King. These themes, which are developed by the Eastern Fathers and the Eastern liturgy, make Christ's baptism the focal point of the theophany.

If we study Christian baptism in the New Testament, we soon realize that the basis for the tradition concerning baptism is the account of the baptism of Jesus himself. The Synoptic Gospels all record it (Matthew 3:13-17; Mark 1:9-11; Luke 3:21-22); St. John presupposes the event and refers back to it (John 1:33-34). The scene at the Jordan is also one of those most frequently found in Christian iconography.[231]

It is not a matter of indifference that the Jordan was the place where John baptized. In sheer point of fact, of course, it is the only river in Palestine, yet the Fathers saw in it, as they did in the Red Sea, a type of baptism. Origen writes:

> That we may be convinced of this interpretation of the Jordan as the river that appeases thirst and is full of grace, it will be useful to recall Naaman the Syrian who was cured of leprosy. . . . Just as no one is good but one, namely God the Father, so among rivers none is good but the Jordan, which is able even to cleanse from leprosy anyone who with faith washes his soul in Jesus.[232]

Origen thus connects the purifying power of the Jordan with Old Testament events. St. Luke had already referred to the same incident in the Second Book of Kings (5:14) and had written: "And there were many lepers in Israel in the time of the prophet Elisha; and none of them was cleansed, but only Naaman the Syrian" (Luke 4:27). In his homilies on the Third Gospel, Origen pursues the same line of thought when he comes to comment on this verse of Luke.[233]

Origen's attention is also drawn by Elijah's and Elisha's crossing of the Jordan (in 2 Kings 2:8).

> We must note that at the moment when Elijah is to be taken up into heaven by the whirlwind, he takes his cloak, rolls it up, and strikes the water, which parts and allows the two men, Elijah and Elisha, to pass between. Elijah was better prepared for his being taken up by being baptized in the Jordan; "baptized," because Paul, as we saw above, calls the miraculous passage through the water a baptism.[234]

The crossing of the Red Sea and the crossing of the Jordan were two traditional figures of baptism.[235] The New Testament, however, does not mention the parallel when it comes to speak of the baptism of Jesus, as it does when speaking of Elijah. The Fathers nonetheless saw in Joshua's crossing of the Jordan the same idea of deliverance that finds expression in the crossing of the Red Sea. As Joshua was a figure of Jesus (Joshua–Jesus), so his crossing of the Jordan became a type of baptism. In his address on baptism, St. Gregory of Nyssa writes:

> You have been for a long time wallowing in the mud: hasten to the Jordan, not at the call of John, but at the voice of Christ. In fact, the river of grace runs everywhere. It does not rise in Palestine to disappear in the neighboring sea; but it envelops the entire world and plunges itself into Paradise, flowing against the course of the four rivers which come down from thence, and carrying back into Paradise things far more precious than those which came out. For those rivers brought sweet perfumes, and the cultivation and semination of the earth: but this river brings back men, born of the Holy Spirit. Imitate Jesus, the son of Nave. Carry the Gospel as he carried the Ark. Leave the desert, that is to say, sin. Cross the Jordan. Hasten toward life according to Christ, toward the earth which bears the fruits of joy, where run, according to the promise, streams of milk and honey. Overthrow Jericho, the old dwelling-place, do not leave it fortified. All these things are a figure (*typos*) of ourselves. All are prefigurations of realities which now are made manifest.[236]

The Jordan here represents the baptism of which Joshua's crossing is a type.

A baptism that led to the forgiveness of sins

The Gospel of St. John does not tell the story of Jesus' baptism; it simply alludes to it, but the allusion is highly significant. We may note, in passing, that the reference to "Bethany beyond the Jordan" (John 1:28) has been the sub-

ject of much debate. Such a "Bethany beyond the Jordan"
is simply unknown. Father Abel, in his discussion of the
place venerated as the spot where Christ received baptism,
thinks it must have been known to Israelites around the
time of Christ as *Beth 'Abarah*, "place of passage," in
memory of the crossing of the river by the Hebrews.[237]

In practicing baptism, the Precursor was using a rite totally new to his contemporaries. Jewish tradition was familiar with washings intended as ritual purifications. The
Books of Leviticus, Numbers, and Deuteronomy speak
often of "clean" and "unclean" and of the regulations gov-
erning these two states. The "cleanness" or purity in question was of the ritual order, that is, it was achieved by the
performance of a rite, usually a washing.

When, however, Isaiah tells the people of Israel, "Wash
yourselves; make yourselves clean," he adds: "Remove the
evil of your doings from before my eyes; cease to do evil,
learn to do good" (Is. 1:16-17). Here there is evidently no
question of a real ritual bath; the latter simply provides an
image of something deeper. The ritual washing could give
only a ritual purity, and the Israelite did not expect anything more of it. The intention was to symbolize a purity of
heart, but not to try to effect it by an outward rite. In their
struggle with Judaism, the Fathers of the Church made
much of this distinction, seeing in it the essential difference
between Jewish ritual washing and Christian baptism.[238]

Among the Essenes there was an increased emphasis on
ritual purification, with daily ritual washings being practiced. The Qumran finds show that the Community Rule
prescribed many ritual purifications. Yet it was clear to all
that these washings could not bring about an interior purification. For that, men must await the day of the Lord's
visitation, when he would breathe upon them a spirit of
holiness.[239]

The baptism practiced by John was quite different from
these ritual washings. It aimed at interior purification: "Repent, for the kingdom of heaven is at hand" (Matthew 3:2).
Many Jews were willing to be baptized by John, "confess-

ing their sins" (Matthew 3:6). And when Pharisees and
Sadducees came forward for baptism, John spoke to them
very frankly: "You brood of vipers! . . . Bear fruit that befits
repentance" (Matthew 3:8). There could no longer be question of evading God's anger by mere outward ritual; men
must produce fruits of genuine repentance if they were not
to be cut down and thrown into the fire (Matthew 3:10).
John's baptism was thus one of "repentance for the forgiveness of sins" (Mark 1:4; Luke 3:3), or, as John puts it in
Matthew's Gospel, "I baptize you with water for repentance" (3:11).

Three marks thus distinguish John's baptism from other
ritual washings practiced by the Jews. The first of these
marks is external: the Jews purified themselves, but John
baptized others (and he must have done a great deal of baptizing, since his contemporaries named him "the Baptist").

A second distinguishing mark was that when John administered his baptism, he acted as a prophet who proclaimed the coming of the Messiah: "He who is coming
after me is mightier than I, whose sandals I am not worthy
to carry" (Matthew 3:11). The Messiah's coming would
bring judgment with it: "Even now the axe is laid to the
root of the trees; every tree therefore that does not bear
good fruit is cut down and thrown into the fire" (Matthew
3:10).

The third and final mark of John's baptism is that while it
is a baptism that is a sign of conversion and leads to the
forgiveness of sins, it is also a preparation for a further baptism: "I baptize you with water for repentance, but he who
is coming after me is mightier than I. . . . He will baptize
you with the Holy Spirit and with fire" (Matthew 3:11;
Luke 3:16).

Purification by fire is already used in the Old Testament
as an image of God's intervention,[240] and judgment by fire
is a frequent theme.[241] As for purification by the Spirit, John
knew that this had been promised: ". . . until the Spirit is
poured upon us from on high" (Is. 32:15); "A new heart I
will give you, and a new spirit I will put within you; and I

will take out of your flesh the heart of stone and give you a heart of flesh" (Ezek. 36:26); "And it shall come to pass afterward, that I will pour out my spirit on all flesh; your sons and your daughters shall prophesy, your old men shall dream dreams, and your young men shall see visions. Even upon the menservants and maidservants in those days, I will pour out my spirit" (Joel 2:28-29).

We have thus dwelt on John's baptism in general because it will enable us better to grasp the meaning of the baptism Jesus will receive at the hand of his Precursor.

The sign of the Spirit

Given this background, however, we cannot but be surprised by Jesus' receiving baptism from John. John himself felt exactly the same way: "I need to be baptized by you, and do you come to me?" (Matthew 3:14). Jesus' answer soothes him: "Let it be so now; for thus it is fitting for us to fulfill all righteousness" (3:15). St. Matthew is the only one to record the Baptist's hesitation, but the whole first Christian generation must have been puzzled by Jesus' baptism.

Jesus' answer is that the "righteousness" he is fulfilling is that proper to the messianic kingdom. In fact, the baptism that Jesus will receive will be the outward sign of his investiture as Messiah: "Behold, the heavens were opened and he [Jesus] saw the Spirit of God descending like a dove, and alighting on him; and lo, a voice from heaven, saying, 'This is my beloved Son, with whom I am well pleased'" (Matthew 3:16-17; Mark 1:9-11; Luke 3:21-22).

John the Evangelist does not report the scene, but he does bring out its theological meaning: "The next day he [John] saw Jesus coming toward him, and said, 'Behold, the Lamb of God, who takes away the sin of the world! This is he of whom I said, "After me comes a man who ranks before me, for he was before me." I myself did not know him; but for this I came baptizing with water that he might be revealed to Israel.' And John bore witness, 'I saw the Spirit descend as a dove from heaven, and it remained on him'" (John 1:29-32).

What happened at Jesus' baptism completed John's enlightenment. He had indeed known that the Spirit would descend upon, and remain in, the Messiah, who in turn would baptize in the Spirit: "I myself did not know him; but he who sent me to baptize with water said to me, 'He on whom you see the Spirit descend and remain, this is he who baptizes with the Holy Spirit.' And I have seen and borne witness that this is the Son of God" (John 1:33-34).

It was from Isaiah that John would know the Spirit was to descend and rest on the Messiah: "There shall come forth a shoot from the stump of Jesse, and a branch shall grow out of his roots. And the Spirit of the Lord shall rest upon him" (Is. 11:1-2). John the Evanglist must have had this passage of Isaiah in mind as he wrote his first chapter. This is confirmed when, in verse 34, he has the Precursor say: "And I have seen and borne witness that this is the Son of God." These words are undoubtedly an allusion to Isaiah 42:1, "Behold my servant, whom I uphold, my chosen, in whom my soul delights; I have put my Spirit upon him, he will bring forth justice to the nations."

The fact that the Synoptics have replaced "servant" with "Son" does not cause any real problem. We have already had occasion to note that the Greek word *pais* can mean both "servant" and "son."

This is not the place to go into the content of the word "Spirit," which in the Old Testament means the "breath" of Yahweh. At the beginning of creation itself, we see the "Spirit" at work, sweeping over the waters, and his action continues to be felt throughout all subsequent history. The sign of the Spirit serves to make Messiah Jesus known to John the Baptist and all the disciples. Once this sign has been given, no further doubt is possible: "And I have seen and borne witness that this is the Son of God" (John 1:34).

"My beloved Son"

The Synoptics report the words heard from heaven at the moment after Jesus' baptism: "This is my beloved Son, with whom I am well pleased" (Matthew 3:17 and parallels). Though John the Evangelist does not cite these words, he has the Baptist say their equivalent: "This is the Son of God."

The Synoptic statement is of tremendous importance for the Jewish people, since it concerns the divine sonship of an individual human being. The Old Testament had often spoken of God as a Father, but only in relation to the Chosen People as a whole. In this fatherhood of God, moreover, the Old Testament saw a favor bestowed with complete freedom by God.

Jeremiah makes Yahweh speak of himself as a Father: "I am a father to Israel, and Ephraim is my first-born" (31:9). Again, when Yahweh speaks to Israel, his unfaithful spouse, he says to her: "Yet you have a harlot's brow, you refuse to be ashamed. Have you not just now called to me, 'My father' . . . ?" (Jer 3:3-4). In Isaiah we find a similar expression: "For thou art our Father" (Is. 63:16), and again: "Yet, O Lord, thou art our Father" (64:8).[242]

The Book of Deuteronomy implies that if we are to have God for our Father, we must imitate his holiness and become like him in some fashion: "You are the sons of the Lord your God . . . and the Lord has chosen you to be a people for his own possession, out of all the peoples that are on the face of the earth" (Deut. 14:1-2).[243]

In all these passages, however, it is always the people that has God for Father. At the baptism of Jesus, on the other hand, the heavenly voice addresses a single individual as "Son." Jesus is the chosen One, the Servant, the Son. In fact, St. John will give the name "Son" to no one but Jesus and will speak of him as the "only begotten"; the rest of us are called only "children."[244]

The baptism of Jesus consecrates him in the world's eyes as the "Son," as we listen to the first of those dialogues between the two divine Persons, Father and Son, that provide the essential framework of the Gospels, and especially of the Fourth Gospel. Later, as the final Passover draws near and Jesus foretells his glorification, he addresses the

Father once again, and once again, as at the baptism, a voice is heard from heaven: "I have glorified it [my name], and I will glorify it again" (John 12:28).

At the baptism, the Spirit too is present. His special role is to show the world who Jesus is. He anoints Jesus as Messiah and Son of God. The Son and the Father meet in the Spirit, and the Spirit unites them in love: "This is my beloved Son, with whom I am well pleased" (Matthew 3:17 and parallels).

The Lamb of God

The Spirit has descended and remained on Jesus, the Messiah; now Jesus can in turn transmit the Spirit to others. He will be able to do so, however, only after his death and resurrection. Consequently, we find once again, this time in connection with the baptism of Jesus, the paschal theme being voiced. The Precursor himself has already alluded to it, when, on seeing Jesus coming toward him, he exclaims: "Behold, the Lamb of God, who takes away the sins of the world!" (John 1:29).

The word "Lamb" has not been easy for the exegetes to handle. Some of them suggest that the Evangelist has put the word into the Baptist's mouth. The word calls to mind the Passover lamb, whose annual immolation not only reminded the Israelites of Exodus 12 but, by the time of Christ, also had an expiatory function. If this is what John the Baptist had in view, he was thinking of Jesus as one who comes to make expiation, like a Passover lamb. But the word also calls to mind the prophecy of Isaiah about the suffering Servant of Yahweh. In Isaiah 53:7 we have a comparison intended to emphasize the resignation shown by the suffering Servant.

Since the baptism of Jesus was also his anointing as Messiah, we may choose to think that "Lamb" (a term often used of Jesus in the Apocalypse of St. John) was a messianic title used by the Precursor.

A third hypothesis has been proposed. An original

Aramaic text referred to the "servant of God" of Isaiah's prophecy. In Aramaic, however, the word *talia* meant both "lamb" and "servant." Under the influence of Christianity and the typology of the Passover lamb, the Greek translator of the Fourth Gospel translated *talia* as "lamb" rather than as "servant." According to this interpretation, then, the Gospel gives a Christian coloring to John's words; but this is the doing, not of the Evangelist, but of his translator.[245]

We must also observe that the Greek verb *airein* in John 1:29 can mean either "carry" or "take away." It is possible, therefore, to interpret the words as referring to Isaiah 53:4 and the lamb who "bears" our infirmities; or to Exodus 12:23 and the Passover lamb, whose blood, in the Christian interpretation, "takes away" sins. Pursuing this double interpretation, we might claim that John the Baptist interpreted his own words in the light of Isaiah, while John the Evangelist read into them a further Christian reference to the Passover lamb. Such a double meaning for a word is quite in accordance with John's methods. Recall, for example, the use of the verb "lift up" (in John 3:14 and 12:32), which may mean both to be lifted up onto the Cross and to be lifted up or exalted in victory.

"I have a baptism to be baptized with"

How, then, can we sum up the theology of Jesus' baptism as seen by the evangelists? They see in the baptism a clear statement of his messiahship and the solemn, public reception of both his title and his mission. Henceforth Jesus can baptize men in the Spirit which he himself has received: the Spirit who gives men the strength to walk in the right path and who takes sin away.

Thus, when all is said and done, the baptism of Christ confronts us with the Cross and the paschal mystery. The Fathers of the Church were not caught up in the problems of exegesis and did not doubt that the "Lamb" signified Jesus offering his life in order to expiate the sins of the world. They grasped the close connection between the baptism of Jesus and Cross, and in fact between every baptism and the Cross. Their spiritual insight made them see in the account of Jesus' baptism a prediction of his Passion and redemptive role. The Latins interpreted the text in the light of the Passover lamb typology, the Greeks in the light of Isaiah's prophecy of the suffering Servant. Both Latins and Greeks, however, think of the baptism of Jesus as closely connected with his Cross.

At his baptism, Jesus is annointed Messiah and Redeemer, and his answer to the Precursor who is surprised to see him coming is highly meaningful: ". . . for thus it is fitting for us to fulfill all righteousness" (Matthew 3:15). Commentators have often remarked on the explicit juxtaposition of the baptism and the Passion in Mark and Luke. "Are you able to drink the cup that I drink, or to be baptized with the baptism with which I am baptized?" says Mark 10:38. St. Matthew records the same conversation but mentions neither cup nor baptism (20:20-23). In St. Luke, the linking of baptism and Passion is equally emphasized: "I came to cast fire upon the earth; and would that it were already kindled! I have a baptism to be baptized with; and how I am constrained until it is accomplished!" (12:49-50).

The baptism of Jesus thus introduces us into the mystery of his death and resurrection. It is in the latter mystery that his baptism will be fully real, and it is then that he will pour out the Spirit. Peter's discourse on Pentecost shows us how fully the apostles understood all this, once the Spirit had descended on them:

> Jesus of Nazareth [was] a man attested to you by God with mighty works and wonders and signs which God did through him in your midst, as you yourselves know . . . you crucified and killed [him] by the hands of lawless men. But God raised him up. . . . Being therefore exalted at the right hand of God, and having received from the Father the promise of the Holy Spirit, he has poured out this which you see and hear. . . . Let all the house of Israel therefore know as-

> suredly that God has made him both Lord and Christ,
> this Jesus whom you crucified (Acts 2:22-36).

According to Peter, then, it was after the mystery of his
death and resurrection had been accomplished that Christ,
now exalted to the Father's right hand, poured out the Holy
Spirit he himself had received.

Such is the teaching of the New Testament about the
baptism of Jesus: that the baptism, which is a manifestation
of Jesus as Lord and Messiah, is also a manifestation of him
as Lord and Savior by reason of his Cross and resurrection.

Patristic commentaries

The Fathers rival each other in commenting on these two
aspects of the baptism of Jesus. We shall limit ourselves
here to the second aspect, since it is the one emphasized in
the Roman liturgy for the feast of the Savior's baptism. The
Church has chosen for the Office of Readings a homily of
St. Gregory of Nazianzus:

> I cannot restrain my joy; my heart is deeply moved
> and filled with delight. Forgetting my weakness, I
> long to undertake the mission of the great John the
> Baptist; though I am not the Precursor, I have indeed
> come from the desert!
>
> Christ receives the sacrament of enlightenment, or
> rather he enlightens us with his brilliance. He is bap-
> tized; let us go down into the water with him so that
> we may also come up with him. John is baptizing, and
> Jesus comes to him. Christ certainly sanctifies the
> man who now baptizes him, but his purpose is chiefly
> to bury the old Adam in the waters and, above all, to
> sanctify the waters of the Jordan by his baptism in
> them so that just as he was spirit and flesh, those who
> would later be baptized might be sanctified by the
> power of the Spirit and by water.
>
> John refuses; Jesus insists. "It is you that should be
> baptizing me!" says John. The torch addresses the
> Sun, the voice speaks to the Word.

Jesus comes out of the water, drawing the world with him, as it were, and raising it up when it had hitherto been sunk in the abyss. He sees the heavens, not being rent, but opening of their own accord. The first Adam had of old closed heaven to himself and us, just as he had seen the earthly paradise being closed to him, with a fiery sword barring access.

The Holy Spirit bears witness. Here all is in perfect harmony, for the testimony comes from heaven, just as he to whom the Spirit bears witness has come from heaven.[246]

In a homily on the baptism of Christ, St. John Chrysostom asks why Jesus had himself baptized. The first reason, he says, is that all might learn from Jesus' baptism that the baptism administered by John was meant for repentance and as a way of leading men to believe in the One who would come after John (see Acts 19:4).

The other reason is the one he himself [Jesus] gave. What is it? When John had said, "I should be baptized by you — and do you come to me?" he replied: "Let be. For it befits us in this way to fulfill all justice" (Matthew 3:14-15). . . . But what does "fulfilling all justice" mean? Justice is to be understood as the carrying out of all God's commandments. . . . Now, since all men were obliged to fulfill this justice and since no one in fact fulfilled it perfectly, Christ came to accomplish it. . . . When he came and found us debtors, he paid the debt, fulfilled the obligation, and liberated those who could not pay the debt and thus liberate themselves.[247]

The Fathers do not fail to note that the baptism of Jesus, which is a sign of our salvation, also reveals the Trinity to us. A homily attributed to St. Maximus of Turin, and certainly very old, expresses both of these aspects:

"Behold the Lamb of God, behold him who takes away the sins of the world." John is here saying: Cease now to ask for my baptism, which leads to repentance; here is a Baptist who takes sins away! Seek no longer to be baptized by me, your fellow servant, now that the Lord of us all is here. . . .

How marvelous the mystery in which our Lord Jesus, by mere bodily contact or the mere passage of his glory, sanctifies and gives life and light to his creature at every moment! For by being baptized he sanctifies the water; by being buried he sanctifies the earth; by rising he raises the dead; he glorifies everything in heaven by ascending to heaven and sitting at the right hand of God the Father.[248]

The Jordan, our Jordan

We must explain a little more fully how Jesus' baptism in the Jordan concerns us. It is undoubtedly the type of our own baptism; it is undoubtedly the proclamation of Christ's role as the Messiah who gives his life in order to reintegrate the broken world. But is not all that still rather remote from us?

We must go back briefly to a basic aspect of Jesus' baptism in the Jordan, referring the reader, as we do so, to the pages that have preceded. We saw that John the Baptist speaks of Christ as the "Lamb of God," and we tried to grasp the theological meaning of this expression. It tells us clearly that the role which now officially belongs to Jesus is to give his life for the redemption of the world.

There is a further point. When the Father speaks and presents his Son to us, each of his words are important, and each takes on its full meaning, with all its implications, only in the context of the statement as a whole. Thus we cannot correctly understand who and what the "Son" is unless we add that he is "my beloved." Moreover, for a complete understanding of the Father's words, we must read them together with those that the Father speaks at the transfiguration, when he adds, "Listen to him" (see Matthew 17:1-8; Luke 9:28-36).

We are confronted here with the "only-begotten" Son,

and our thoughts immediately go back to Isaac, the only son of Abraham. Such a connection already tells us a great deal about the way the Father conceives the role of his only Son. As we pointed out earlier, the word "Son" here has several resonances. Tradition sees it as meaning "servant" or "slave" as well as "child."

Elsewhere in John's Gospel we find a theme very dear to him: doing the Father's will. That is the mark of the true Son, as many texts assure us (John 4:32-38; 7:17; 14:31). The last words of Jesus on the Cross, "It is accomplished" (John 19:30 JB), serve as a perfect description of the Son: he is the one who has accomplished his Father's will. That is why the Father loves the Son, and that is why we must listen to him, that is, follow him along the road that he has shown to be the only true way to the Father.

If we broaden our vision and move a little further along this line, we find ourselves confronted with the history of salvation, with God's plan for reconstruction, and with our participation in his work. In what does that work consist?

The work of the Spirit is to rebuild and restore the world that was created as a unified whole for the glory of the Father but was then shattered by sin. The attempts at reconstruction in the Old Testament did not succeed. Then, when the time is ripe, the action of the Spirit turns history upside down, for he provides the eternal Word of God with a human nature. The Fathers connect the whole sacramental life with the activity of the same Spirit. According to them, we are to see in the Spirit's action on the water of baptism our own new creation and our entry into the life of God. The same Spirit who effected the coming of the eternal Word in the flesh also effects our birth in God.

In the life of Christ, the action of the Holy Spirit specifies the role of Christ, at his baptism in the Jordan and later at his transfiguration. We can say that at his baptism in the Jordan, Christ was officially appointed Prophet, Messiah, King, and Priest. May we not also think of our own confirmation, which is the sacrament of Christian "perfection" (i.e., completion), as corresponding to the Spirit's action at the Jordan, which is closely connected with his action at Pentecost and in which, like Christ, we are appointed to our role as prophets, messiahs, kings, and priests? After all, the anointing conferred upon us immediately after our baptism designated us as members of a priestly people.

When did Christ carry out the mission to which he was appointed? He did it when he brought to a successful end his paschal mystery, that is, his death, resurrection, ascension, and sending of the Spirit. At this moment he completed the work for which he had come among us and to which he was officially appointed. By preaching the word and giving his life in such a glorious way, Christ succeeded in restoring the world (in principle) to unity so that his Father might therein be glorified. When do we accomplish our own mission? We do it every time we celebrate the Eucharist, which renders present and active among us the paschal mystery of Christ. When we eat the bread and drink the cup, we proclaim the Lord's death until he comes again.

The baptism of Jesus in the Jordan is therefore indeed relevant to us. For in Jesus our own role is clearly specified, and in addition we learn what our own attitude should be as children of God who have been born again of water and the Spirit. We understand the close connection between the three sacraments of Christian initiation: baptism, the sacrament of birth; confirmation, the sacrament in which we are appointed to our proper function; and the Eucharist, in which we share in the work of rebuilding the world as we proclaim the paschal mystery and the end of time.

There can be no real confusion between the different priesthoods. In point of fact, there is but one priesthood, that of Christ. But there are two essentially different ways of sharing in it, both of them fully real: the ordained or ministerial priesthood, which, through the intervention of the Spirit, makes the paschal mystery efficaciously present; and the baptismal priesthood, which, once the mystery of the world's restoration has thus been rendered present, actively collaborates with Christ, who brings his work to completion with our help. There is thus an essential difference between the two priesthoods, and yet they complement each other.

There is no point in discussing in greater detail how the Jordan of Christ's baptism is also our Jordan and how our whole attitude to it depends on that of Christ.

19. CANA

Christmas, the visit of the Magi, and the baptism of Jesus have proved to be, not isolated episodes in the life of Christ, but links in the chain that is the paschal mystery. We have seen how in each of these liturgical celebrations the Church looks to the one center of the Christian year: the death and resurrection of Christ, with his return at the end of time. We find, now, the same preoccupation as we turn to the third facet of Epiphany, the marriage feast at Cana.

In celebrating these various events, the liturgy for Epiphany follows the sequence in the Fourth Gospel: first comes the manifestation of Christ at the Jordan and the witness of the Precursor; then a new manifestation to the disciples at the marriage feast of Cana (John 2:1-11).

In these opening chapters of the Fourth Gospel we get the impression that we are being presented with a catechesis. In the Prologue, John writes: "And the Word became flesh and dwelt among us, full of grace and truth; we have beheld his glory, glory as of the only Son from the Father" (1:14). This statement is immediately followed by the Precursor's witness to Christ: "He who comes after me ranks before me, for he was before me" (1:15). The Baptist will repeat his testimony after the baptism of Jesus, which is the latter's anointing as Messiah and represents the first fruits of our redemption. Finally the Evangelist tells us: "On the third day there was a marriage at Cana. . . . This, the first of his signs, Jesus did . . . and manifested his glory; and his disciples believed in him" (2:1-11).

The baptism of Jesus and the wedding feast at Cana are both of them manifestations of Jesus' glory. Moreover, they are not two totally separate manifestations, each isolated from the other, but they complete each other and overlap.

> On the third day there was a marriage at Cana in Galilee, and the other of Jesus was there; Jesus also was invited to the marriage, with his disciples. When the wine failed, the mother of Jesus said to him, "They have no wine." And Jesus said to her, "O woman, what have you to do with me? My hour has not yet come." His mother said to the servants, "Do whatever he tells you." Now six stone jars were standing there, for the Jewish rites of purification, each holding twenty or thirty gallons. Jesus said to them, "Fill the jars with water." And they filled them to the brim. He said to them, "Now draw some out, and take it to the steward of the feast." So they took it. When the steward of the feast tasted the water now become wine, and did not know where it came from (though the servants who had drawn the water knew), the steward of the feast called the bridegroom and said to him, "Every man serves the good wine first; and when men have drunk freely, then the poor wine; but you have kept the good wine until now." This, the first of his signs, Jesus did at Cana in Galilee, and manifested his glory; and his disciples believed in him (John 2:1-11).

If we read this second chapter of St. John carefully, we will be struck by the ambiguity of certain terms, and we may even feel a certain uneasiness as we attempt to interpret them. I am not referring only to the famous verse 4, where the exegetes flounder in their effort to rescue the respect that every Christian feels is due to the Mother of God. No, there are a number of points where the exegesis is difficult, if one wishes to be objective.

From the opening words it seems clear that the Evangelist wishes his account to carry a fairly precise over-all meaning. "On the third day" a marriage took place at Cana. This manner of dating the event is not accidental; it not only situates the event in an immediate temporal context but also shows St. John's desire to turn our thoughts toward the definitive "sign" of Christ's glory, namely, his resurrection. In other words, the wedding at Cana is not simply a sign of Christ's present glory, but a sign also of that future glory that is his "on the third day" after his death. It has been rightly noted that this phrase "on the third day" could not but remind the early Christians of the resurrection.[249] For St. John, then, the first sign, the changing of water into wine, prepares for, and is linked with, the supreme sign, the resurrection on the third day. Thus, from the very first words of the account, we glimpse the paschal significance that John intends the account of the wedding at Cana to have.

The central point in the whole account, namely, the changing of water into wine, brings us even closer to the paschal theme. In fact, the whole episode is so rich in signs that proclaim and prefigure the mystery of the Passion, the resurrection, our redemption, and the parousia that we must take them one by one, despite the fact that each is insepar-able from the others and complements them.

The "hour" of Christ

Christ's surprising reply to his Mother: (literally) "Woman, what to me and to thee?" has often preoccupied the exegetes more than the next words: "My hour has not yet come." And yet, if we are to understand Jesus' strange answer to his Mother, it is on these next words that we must focus our attention. The statement "My hour has not yet come" shows us that God's plan is set and that Jesus must conquer evil and be supremely glorified after a death that destroys sin.

"My hour has not yet come" is one of the expressions that

turn this whole account into a proclamation of the paschal mystery. It is a statement St. John puts on the lips of Jesus at several points in his Gospel. When Jesus, at Jerusalem, emphasizes his own divine origin, his enemies try to arrest him, but "no one laid hands on him, because his hour had not yet come" (7:30). Then, when he bears witness to himself while teaching in the Temple, "no one arrested him, because his hour had not yet come" (8:20). When he tells his disciples that his death and glorification are at hand, he does so by saying that his "hour" has at last come: "The hour has come for the Son of man to be glorified" (12:23). And when he is troubled by this thought, he prays: "Now is my soul troubled. And what shall I say? 'Father, save me from this hour'? No, for this purpose I have come to this hour. Father, glorify thy name" (12:27-28).

When the time comes for the Last Supper, John introduces it by saying: "Now before the feast of the Passover, when Jesus knew that his hour had come to depart out of this world to the Father . . ." (13:1). And Jesus himself, in his high-priestly prayer, addresses his Father: "Father, the hour has come; glorify thy Son that the Son may glorify thee" (17:1). The "hour" of Christ is the hour of his death, but also the hour of his passing to the Father (13:1), from whom he will receive the glory that crowns his victory.

We must not overlook the phrase John uses in 13:1, where he says that Jesus is to "pass" from this world to the Father. Exodus 12:11 had used the word "Passover" in the sense of "passage of the Red Sea."

Once again, then, in chapter 2 of John, the phrase "hour of Jesus" turns our thoughts to the paschal mystery of Christ's death, resurrection, and glorification.

"O woman, what have you to do with me?"

How are we to understand these words: "O woman, what have you to do with me? My hour has not yet come." There seems to be a lack of logic in the sequence of events. Jesus says his hour has not yet come, and he gently reproaches his Mother for not having grasped this clearly, and yet he accedes to his Mother's implicit request by changing water into wine! Some exegetes see in his action a proof of his condescension and of the effectiveness of his Mother's prayer: because she asks him, he pushes his hour forward. This solution may satisfy devotion, but it seems inadequate. After all, the "hour" of Jesus had been fixed from eternity by the divine plan of redemption; it is difficult to understand how the plan could be modified.

How, then, are we to understand Jesus' statement that the moment for his glorification has not yet come, when he proceeds to perform a miracle that is precisely a sign of that glory? The Mother of Jesus realized that despite his answer, he is going to do the miracle, for she tells the servants: "Do whatever he tells you." Her instructions contradict her Son's negative answer to her. Jesus has answered: My hour has not yet come for performing a sign that will reveal my glory and anticipate my definitive glorification. Yet his Mother here and now expects a sign that will be revelatory of that glory. Signs, as we know, were meant to prove that a prophet's mission was authentic. Moreover, at the end of the account, the evangelist specifically says: "[He] manifested his glory."

Some exegetes have sought to solve this difficult problem by supposing that Jesus was really asking a question: "Has my hour not come?"[250] The interpretation offered by some of the Fathers leans in this direction, but it finds no support in the rest of the Gospel, since whenever Jesus wishes to say that his hour has come, he always does so by using the indicative, not the interrogative, form: "The hour has come" (17:1; etc.).

In fact, however, no solution of the text is possible at the level at which the problem is too often placed. The account of the feast at Cana is not an anecdote whose every detail is to be examined with a magnifying glass and whose logic is to be carefully analyzed. The whole Gospel of John has a thesis, and it is a catechesis. Its unifying concept is the progressive manifestation of the glory of Jesus; its intent is not to present a sequence of stories, each of them obeying a human logic that is faithful to material facts. The facts serve simply as points of departure; in addition to providing historical anchorage, they have a special religious meaning that will emerge more and more clearly through the course of Jesus' life and in the narratives chosen by John.

Christ gently reprimands his Mother, and there is no reason for trying to soften the rebuke, any more than we should be shocked by the address "Woman," once we understand how it was used at that time. Is Jesus inconsistent with himself when he refuses to respond to his Mother's request, yet then performs the miracle? It does not seem that he is — provided we abandon our concern for the isolated episode and enter into the spirit that permeates the Gospel of John.

What Jesus is refusing is to manifest himself in his definitive (Easter) glory. In that sense, his hour has not yet come; it will come only in his death, resurrection, and ascension. But while refusing this complete manifestation of his glory, he does give an anticipatory sign of it, by reason of which the evangelist can say: "[He] manifested his glory." The miracle at Cana is, then, an anticipatory glorification, a first stage in the glorification of Jesus and one which, being a sign, is closely linked to the definitive glorification of Christ and his full self-revelation to the world at the end of time.

The sign of Christ's victory through death and resurrection in the Eucharist, which is prefigured in, and signified by, the changing of water in wine. At the same time, the Eucharist proclaims the triumphant death of the Lord until he comes again, and it is a figure of the messianic banquet.

Overlapping signs

Evidently we are dealing with signs that point to, and are connected with, one another. The wedding feast of Cana stands at the beginning of the linked series. In the mind of Jesus, to change water into wine is to prefigure the Last Supper. But the Supper is in turn the sign of the death and victory of Christ and, at the same time, of the eternal wedding feast that will begin when the Lord comes again. The Eucharistic celebration hastens the Lord's return by prefiguring the banquet that will begin on that day.

Now, against the background of these linked prefigurations that are so typical of St. John, we will be able to understand better the intervention of the Virgin at Cana. Jesus addresses her as "Woman," just as he will later on from the Cross (19:26) at the moment when Mary is appointed the new Eve, Mother of all the living (cf. Gen. 3:15-20). At that moment she will represent the Church and all of us. When we return to the Mary who intercedes with Jesus to obtain an anticipatory sign, are we indulging in exaggeration if we see in her the Church that celebrates the Eucharist and thereby hastens the return of Christ and the full revelation of his glory? Mary hastens this manifestation by asking for a sign, just as the Church hastens it by proclaiming the death and glorification of the Lord.

Such are the profound theological implications of the wedding at Cana. The wedding, like the resurrection, is celebrated "on the third day." Water is changed into wine, and sinful mankind passes, by way of baptism, from the law of Moses to the law of the Spirit. At the same time, the water changed into wine foretells the cup, that is, the hour of Jesus, namely his Passion. It prefigures the Supper that will be repeated and will make present in space and time the death and resurrection of Jesus. The wedding feast, like the Supper, also prefigures and leads to the eschatological banquet of the triumphant Christ, the wedding feast of the Lamb, which will be the wedding feast of God and men reunited in a restored world.

The key to the symbols

A narrative so rich in implications could not fail to attract the attention of the Fathers, and they study and comment on the wedding feast in all its aspects.

We shall cite, to begin with, a relatively rare yet very

meaning-filled kind of reflection on the wedding; it comes from Tertullian's treatise on baptism. Instead of dwelling on the miracle of the water changed into wine, Tertullian is interested more in the presence of the water and in the baptismal symbolism it has for him:

> What grace water has, before God and his Christ, for bringing out the meaning of baptism! Christ is never unaccompanied by water. He himself is baptized in water, and when he is invited to a marriage, he uses water in making his first show of power. . . . His witness to baptism continues right up to his Passion.[251]

In Tertullian's view, then, Cana is a prefiguration of baptism. Such an interpretation deserves notice, especially when we remember that the Roman liturgy celebrates on January 6 not only the self-manifestation of Jesus to the Magi and the world, but also his baptism and the wedding feast at Cana. We should remember, too, that the blessing of baptismal water in the Roman Rite (until the recent revision of the baptismal rite), as in the liturgies of Milan and Syria, connected the baptism of Jesus with the wedding feast at Cana.

The Fathers generally concentrate, however, on the more basic meanings symbolized in the Johannine narrative. Cyril of Alexandria, for example, picks up the words "on the third day," and comments: "The wedding is celebrated on the third day, that is, in the last age of this present world, for the number three signifies to us the beginning, middle, and end." He then quotes Hosea 6:2-3, a prophecy of the resurrection, and explains in a forceful way how Cana is a sign of Christ's triumphant resurrection and of our own transformation into Christ: "He also cured those afflicted with corruption and death, and did it on the third day, that is, not in the first nor in the middle, but in the last age, when, having become man, he healed human nature, raising it totally from the dead in himself."[252]

The Eucharistic and nuptial aspect of Cana is the one most fully developed by the Fathers. In their view, the wedding at Cana prefigures the marriage of Christ and the Church. The nations are invited to the wedding feast, since wine has now been substituted for the water of Jewish purifications. St. Cyprian, for example, writes:

> The Jews lacked spiritual grace, and therefore wine as well, though the house of Israel was meant to be the vineyard of the Lord of hosts (Is. 5:7). Then, to teach clearly that the nations were succeeding to the position the Jews had lost and that later on we too would succeed to it by faith, Christ changed water into wine. He showed thereby that after the Jews had defected, the Gentiles would flock in even greater numbers to the marriage of Christ and the Church.[253]

St. Cyril of Jerusalem, in one of his Catecheses, likewise interprets the wedding feast at Cana as a type of the Eucharist and of the marriage of Christ and his Church:

> At Cana of Galilee, he [Jesus] changed water into wine. Is he not to be believed, then, when he changes wine into Blood? When invited to an earthly marriage, he did this marvelous deed. Shall we not profess our faith even more readily when to the companions of the Bridgegroom he makes a present of the enjoyment of his Body and Blood?[254]

STRUCTURES AND THEMES OF THE EPIPHANY SEASON

20. EPIPHANY: Homage to the Lord

Contemplating the glory of the Lord

The central theme of the Gospel reading, in the context provided by the other two readings, is the manifestation of the Lord's glory to all peoples. The passage (Matthew 2:1-12) twice makes explicit the purpose of the Magi in coming from their home in the East: to prostrate themselves before the Lord.

The danger in the account of the Epiphany, with its element of the marvelous, is that we may be led astray into the exegesis of facts and signs. The number and names of the Magi, the star, the gifts, and many connected problems have, of course, a certain importance, and they cannot be simply ignored; but in choosing this passage for the liturgy, the Church presupposes the research of the scholars and has her eye on an aspect of the passage that is far more meaningful and important.

The principal interest of the account, in its liturgical context, is the manifestation of Christ the Lord to the whole world and the world's adoration of the infant King. Even here, however, the important thing is not the past but the present and the future that will emerge from the present. In other words, when the account is read in the liturgy, it is proclaimed as an actualization of the past event here and now, a dynamic actualization that is meant to lead the nations to the worship of the Lord and the acknowledgment of his glory.

The liturgy, then, has an eschatological vision of this worship of the glory of the God who is revealing himself; it is within that framework that the Church proclaims this Gospel. She sees the present people of God and indeed the entire world journeying toward the moment when God will definitively reveal his glory and men will adore that glory in a perfect way. That, after all, is the objective of the paschal mystery: to reunite and rebuild the world for the worship of the Lord of glory. The proclamation of this Gospel can be for us a striking example of the true function of the liturgical celebration of the word as an act in which the Lord himself actualizes a past event so as to lead us toward something definitive and everlasting.

As a matter of fact, in this same liturgy Isaiah has already offered us an eschatological vision, when he describes the nations walking toward the light and the kings advancing toward the light of the coming dawn. At the same time, this passage from Isaiah gives us a sense of God's presence in the Jerusalem where all men will ultimately be made one race again. Jerusalem is the mother of the scattered sons and daughters we see being gathered again. All the nations, even the pagan ones, come to Jerusalem; all of them seek to reach Jerusalem and the Lord in his glory.

The theme of the final reunion is, of course, found often in the Old Testament, for example, in Isaiah 2:1-4 and 66:18-21, and in Zechariah 14:16. In the city the prophets speak of, we Christians too find our heavenly Jerusalem; in today's Mass St. Paul speaks of that city and tells us she is our mother (Gal. 4:26). Thus, even in this opening phase of the paschal mystery, the Church already has an apocalyptic vision of the new heavens and the new earth, and "the holy city, new Jerusalem, coming down out of heaven from God, prepared as a bride adorned for her husband" (Apoc. 21:2). The glory of God is the city's light, and the Lamb is its lamp. "By its light shall the nations walk; and the kings of the earth shall bring their glory into it" (Apoc. 21:24).

Psalm 72, the responsorial psalm for the Epiphany Mass,

Readings for the Eucharist in the Epiphany Cycle

	Prophet	Apostle	Gospel
Epiphany	Is. 60:1-6	Eph. 3:2-3, 5-6	Matthew 2:1-12
Baptism of the Lord	Is. 42:1-4, 6-7	Acts 10:34-38	A. Matthew 3:13-17 B. Mark 1:7-11 C. Luke 3:15-16, 21-22
January 7		1 John 5:14-21	John 2:1-12

Readings for the Liturgy of the Hours

Epiphany	Is. 60:1-22
Baptism of Christ	Is. 42:1-9; 49:1-9
January 7	Is. 61:1-11

sings of this future reality as having already begun in a present that is the actualization of the past:

Lord, every nation on earth will adore you.

> May the kings of Tarshish and of the isles
>   render him tribute,
> may the kings of Sheba and Seba bring gifts!
> May all kings fall down before him,
>   all nations serve him!

The mystery revealed to all

In the second reading of the Mass we are offered the knowledge of the mystery of Christ. St. Paul tells us that the favor God has given him consists in the revelation to him of this mystery (Eph. 3:2-3), and he in turn reveals it to us on this feast of the Epiphany. Through him, the Lord makes the mystery of Christ known to us.

The journey into the mystery requires faith. The star is a sign to the Magi, who put aside all further questioning and set out for the place where they will prostrate themselves and do homage. But the same sign produces quite different effects, according to what we are told in the Gospel. To the Magi, the star is a revelation, and they promptly set off to glorify God. But the sign leads Herod deeper into blindness; its light does not illumine the dark places that his passions have created, and he sees it as a threat to his kingdom, whereas the Magi, being men of faith, see it as a guide that will lead them to the goal that every human being wants. The Magi bring the Lord their homage in the form of the traditional gifts.

The attitudes of the Magi are meant to be ours as well: to see the star, not to flee from its light, to believe in the sign God has given, to set out with the purpose of prostrating and adoring and offering ourselves under the sign of the Eucharistic gifts that are intended to represent our self-giving for the glory of the Lord.

The Epiphany is thus not a triumphalist celebration. No,

Epiphany is a feast of humility, for when the Church sees the bright light of the star, she is forced to ask herself whether she is constantly journeying to adore the Lord, whether that is her central and prodominant concern, and whether every Christian sees it as his essential purpose to surrender everything, in a spirit of faith, so that he may set out to adore and offer himself to the Lord. This kind of examination of conscience can be very realistic. Each one of us must search his own heart; the point at issue is the very meaning of Christian life.

The nations shall advance toward Jerusalem

The Gospel, then, as proclaimed in the liturgy, presents us with an eschatological vision, just as the first reading does (Is. 60:1-6). The new Sion of which Isaiah speaks is the lasting city, and so intent is the liturgy upon this eschatological vision that it adds the word "Jerusalem" to the text (In Isaiah 60:1). The addition of the word "Jerusalem" to the opening exhortation, "Arise, shine," gives a direction to our reading of the passage and thus indirectly to our reading of the Gospel as well.

St. Paul received the gracious light given to him, and communicated it to us; that was his essential mission. But it is also the mission of every baptized person. By being baptized in Christ Jesus, we receive the knowledge of his mysteries. Moreover, every sacrament is an epiphany, a star, a sign of the one mystery. The light of the revelation of Christ's mysteries that has been given to us must be passed on, so that the pagans share in the same inheritance as the Jews. All men are called to share the same promise of a definitive regathering of mankind in the heavenly Jerusalem, where they shall all pay homage to the glory of the Lord.

We already pay this homage when we celebrate the Eucharist. As the Communion antiphon says, "We have seen his star in the east, and have come with gifts to adore the Lord." The prayers of the Mass make the same connection between present and future: "Father, you revealed your Son to the nations by the guidance of a star. Lead us to your glory in heaven by the light of faith" (opening prayer), and "Father, guide us with your light. Help us to recognize Christ in this Eucharist and welcome him with love" (postcommunion prayer).

Christ, the Light of the nations

The preface for the Epiphany speaks of the enlightenment that has been brought to the peoples of the world. This preface is of Roman inspiration and is in harmony with the rest of the liturgy in emphasizing the same aspect of the Epiphany: its manifestation of Christ and revelation of his mystery to all the nations. What is special to the preface is its stress on the manner in which Christ manifests himself: through our human nature.

Here, of course, we have something that is supremely important for the Church and for all who seek Christ. It is the basis for the whole sacramental life of the Church, since Christ himself is already the sacrament of our meeting with God, and this epiphanic light continues to shine in and through the Church. In addition, in revealing himself by making our mortal flesh his own, Christ also re-created us. That is why we celebrate Epiphany, not as a simple memorial, but as a "sacrament," that is, the actualization of a mystery which we are thereby enabled to enter into profoundly here and now and which is inseparable from the paschal mystery of the reconstruction of the world.

The preface says: "Today you revealed in Christ your eternal plan of salvation and showed him as the light of all peoples. Now that his glory has shone among us you have renewed humanity in his immortal image." Since we are here emphasizing the paschal aspect of the Epiphany, it is worthwhile noting the original Latin text of the second sentence: *cum in substantia nostrae mortalitatis apparuit, nova nos immortalitatis eius gloria reparasti.* An accurate translation would bring out the opposition between our old

mortality and the immortality bestowed upon us through
redemption: "When he manifested himself in our mortal
nature, you [Father] re-created us by the new glory of his
immortal nature." A new glory, and not just a new light,
was manifested at the Epiphany.

The entrance antiphon sings: "The Lord and ruler is
coming; kingship is his, and government and power." *That*
is the glory manifested. It is from his vision of glory that the
light comes, when the nations see "his glory, glory as of the
only Son from the Father" (John 1:14).

21. THE BAPTISM OF THE LORD

The three evangelists

The entrance antiphon for the feast of the Lord's baptism
pinpoints the central theme of the celebration: "When the
Lord had been baptized, the heavens opened, and the
Spirit came down like a dove to rest on him. Then the voice
of the Father thundered: This is my beloved Son, with him I
am well pleased."

Only St. Luke, in the Gospel for Cycle C (Luke 3:15-16,
21-22), has the words: "You are my Son; today I have begotten you."[255] In Mark and Luke, the Father addresses the
Son directly; in Matthew he speaks of the Son in the third
person: "This is my beloved Son." Mark and Matthew,
moreover, have the Father use words reminiscent of Isaiah
42:1, "Behold my servant, whom I uphold, my chosen, in
whom my soul delights; I have put my Spirit upon him, he
will bring forth justice to the nations," while Luke, according to the better manuscript tradition, has the Father use
Psalm 2:7, "You are my son; today I have begotten you."

As we noted earlier, the Father speaks the same words
as at the baptism (as reported by Matthew and Mark). Thus,
while the facts reported are authentic, the text of the ac-

count of the baptism has been revised and shows, like many
other passages of the Gospel, the reactions of the early
Church. Luke's text uses, on the Father's lips, a verse from
a psalm that indicates the messiahship of Jesus. The other
two evangelists prefer to follow the text in Isaiah, but in so
doing, they also situate Jesus in a messianic context; in addition, they point out his role as Messiah: the role of "servant."

We also noted earlier that the expression "only [or:
only-begotten] Son" contains a reference to Genesis and
the account of the sacrifice of Isaac that was required of his
father, Abraham. The words "only son" occur three times in
the account: "Take your son, your only son Isaac, whom
you love . . ." (Gen. 22:2); ". . . you have not withheld your
son, your only son, from me" (22:12); ". . . have not withheld
your son, your only son" (22:16).

The words "only" and "whom you love" are enough to
tell us what a terrible sacrifice God was demanding. The
same holds for the baptism of Jesus. It is no exaggeration,
therefore, to speak of the baptism as being his investiture as
Messiah. That, surely, is what the evangelists are emphasizing. They use the same Old Testament text at the transfiguration; this latter event, coming as it did at a point nearer in
time to the Passover sacrifice Christ was to offer by offering
himself, made all the clearer the specific character of Jesus'
messiahship: He is the Servant who does the Father's will.

Every aspect of the Gospel account of the baptism is undoubtedly of interest, but we must observe, once again,
how the liturgy uses the passage with a particular end in
view; it does not scorn the other elements in the account,
but it does highlight one of them, not all.

The Servant

For the first reading the liturgy has Isaiah 42:1-4, 6-7, the
very passage that is closely related to the words put on the
Father's lips at the baptism in the accounts of Matthew and
Mark. Isaiah has: "Behold my servant, whom I uphold, my

chosen in whom my soul delights" (42:1), while Mark has: "Thou art my beloved Son; with thee I am well pleased." Isaiah goes on to say: "I have put my Spirit upon him," while the evangelist tells us that the Spirit descends on Jesus like a dove.

A Christian reading of Isaiah 42 turns our thoughts to God's action in the history of salvation, that is, to the love of the Father, who, through Christ and in the Spirit, renews the world.

The role that the Servant receives at the Jordan is spelled out for us in Isaiah 42. His first and foremost task is to re-unite the people to God: "I have given you as a covenant to the people" (42:6). But at the same time he is Messiah and Servant for all mankind: "I have given you as . . . a light to the nations." His task is to enlighten and set free: "to open the eyes that are blind, to bring out the prisoners from the dungeon, from the prison those who sit in darkness" (42:6-7).

The responsorial psalm (Ps. 29) sings of the Lord's "voice," the voice we shall shortly be listening to in the Gospel: "The God of glory thunders . . . and in his temple all cry, 'Glory!'"

Anointed by the Spirit

With this heading we come to the point that St. Luke (in Acts 10:34-38) regards as the most important thing about Jesus' baptism in the Jordan: through his baptism Jesus was anointed by the Spirit and filled with the Spirit's power. In the discourse of which this passage is a part, St. Peter does not speak of the event as though it were cut off from the course of history. On the contrary, it is a real historical event, with a real historical context: "You know . . . the word which was proclaimed throughout all Judea, beginning from Galilee after the baptism which John preached: how God anointed Jesus" (Acts 10:37). Similarly, Luke tells us in his Gospel that Jesus went about preaching in Galilee and Judea (Luke 23:5). Thus the anointing of Christ is situated in a definite historical context: his mission is beginning, and that of John is drawing to its end.

Jesus is anointed with the Spirit and his power. This description from Acts (10:38) reminds us of Isaiah's words in chapter 61:1, "The Spirit of the Lord God is upon me, because the Lord has anointed me to bring good tidings to the afflicted; he has sent me to bind up the brokenhearted."

God has chosen Jesus as recipient not only of the Spirit but of power as well. This "power" should be understood not as something distinct from the anointing of the Spirit but rather as part of the gift of the Spirit. St. Luke (in Peter's discourse) further specifies the effects of this anointing: "He went about doing good and healing all that were oppressed by the devil" (Acts 10:38).

The anointing makes of Jesus a prophet who brings the glad tidings of salvation, and Luke further observes that Jesus goes about doing good and healing those in Satan's power. These various effects, as we noted several times in our study of Advent, are a sign that the kingdom is present. Once again, then, the coming of the Spirit in the form of a dove is a sign of messianic investiture.

We can understand now why the Eastern liturgy celebrates the baptism in the Jordan on Epiphany. The baptism is a basic sign of our salvation in Jesus and tells the entire world that he is the Servant who has come to do the Father's will.

22. EPIPHANY IN THE LITURGIES
OF THE PAST

1. Epiphany in the Early Roman Liturgy

The table given below of the readings for Epiphany in the early Roman liturgy shows that a firm tradition had been established by the time of the surviving lectionaries. There are very few variations. The Missal of 1570 introduces one by substituting Galatians 4:1-7 for Titus 3:4-7 as the first reading for Mass on the Vigil of Epiphany.

The tradition is less unified for the feast of the Lord's baptism. John 1:29-34 appears by itself in two of the old lectionaries, but the Evangeliary of Würzburg offers a choice.

As for prayers, the Gelasian Sacramentary has an interesting preface for Epiphany that gives us an insight into this sacramentary's conception of the season:

> It is truly right and proper . . . that we should praise you as the God who are wonderful in all the works wherein you have revealed the mysteries of your kingdom. For a star pointing to the virginal birth preceded this feast and told the astonished Magi that the Lord of Heaven had been born on earth. Thus the God who was to be revealed to the world was announced by heavenly signs and, being born in time, was made known also by the help of temporal signs.[256]

2. The Celebration of Epiphany at Milan

The Milanese liturgy shows no originality in its choice of readings for the Mass of Epiphany. In fact, the readings proposed in, for example, the Bergamo Sacramentary are to be found in the other liturgies.

Vigil of Epiphany	Epiphany	Sunday after Epiphany
Titus 3:3-7 or 2:11–3:2	Titus 2:11 –3:2	Eph. 4:23-28
Matthew 3:3-17	Matthew 2:1-2	Luke 2:42-52

The Bergamo Sacramentary does, however, have some prayers that are original. Here, for example, is the preface for the Vigil of Epiphany, with its mention of the *tria*

	1	2	3	4	5	6
Vigil of Epiphany	Titus 3:4-7	Titus 3:4-7			Titus 3:4-7	Galatians 4:1-7
Epiphany	Is. 60:1-6	Is. 60:1-6	Matthew 2:19-23 Matthew 2:1-12	Is. 60:1-6	Matthew 2:19-23 Is. 60:1-6 Matthew 2:1-12	Matthew 2:19-23 Is. 60:1-6 Matthew 2:1-12
Baptism of Jesus			John 1:29-34	Mark 1:1, 4-11 John 1:29-34 Matthew 3:1-17	Is. 25:1 or 12:3-5 John 1:29-34	Is. 60:1-6 John 1:29-34
Sunday after Epiphany	Rom. 12:1-5	Rom. 12:1-5	Luke 2:42-52		Rom. 12:1-5 Luke 2:42-52	Rom. 12:1-5 Luke 2:42-52

1 = The Würzburg Epistolary. See p. 168ff, above.
2 = The Comes or Epistolary of Alcuin.
3 = The Würzburg Evangeliary, reconstructed earlier form. See G. Morin, "Liturgie et basiliques de Rome au milieu du VIIe s. d'après les listes d'évangiles de Wurzbourg," *Revue bénédictine* 28 (1911), pp. 296-330.
4 = The Würzburg Evangeliary, later stage.
5 = The Murbach Lectionary. See p. 168ff, above.
6 = Missal of Pius V (1570).

miracula, or "three mysteries," so dear to the Eastern Church:

> . . . for by his birth from heaven [Christ our Lord] introduced into the world the marvelous signs of his majesty: he showed the Magi the star they were to venerate; after a time the same Jesus Christ changed water into wine, and by his baptism sanctified the waters of the Jordan.[257]

The preface for Epiphany concentrates on the baptism:

> . . . eternal God who revealed yourself from heaven in the sound of thunder over the river Jordan in order to make known the Savior of the world and show yourself the Father of eternal light. You opened the heavens, blessed the air, purified the water-springs, and pointed out your only Son by sending the Holy Spirit in the form of a dove. The fonts today received your blessing and removed the curse that lay on us, offering to believers purification from all their sins and giving them birth into eternal life as adoptive children of God.[258]

3. The Celebration of Epiphany in Merovingian Gaul and in Spain

We limit our choice here to a few books that give the most characteristic readings. The table below shows the abundance of texts provided for the Merovingian liturgy in the Luxeuil Lectionary, the Wolfenbüttel Palimpsest, and the Bobbio Missal. We shall not cite any of the prayer texts, since those of the Bobbio Missal are not of any special interest.

The readings listed could be of help in constructing a liturgy of the word by way of preparation for the feast or as a meditation on the mystery celebrated in the feast of Epiphany.

For Spain, we note only the readings found in almost all the Spanish lectionaries, viz., Num. 24:3-9, 15-18; Titus 2:11-3:7; Matthew 2:1-15.

4. The Celebration of Epiphany in the East

The Eastern liturgy for Epiphany concentrates mainly on the baptism of Jesus; its formularies and texts are quite rich.

"Devotion" to the Jordan was so important that baptism was often so named, while even in our day baptismal fonts are still called "Jordan" in the East. Bede the Venerable (675–735) saw with his own eyes the wooden cross erected on the spot where John was supposed to have done his baptizing; the cross was as tall as a man and was submerged when the waves were high. A bridge crossed the Jordan at this point, connecting on the other side with a monastery dedicated to St. John the Baptist. St. Jerome tells us that catechumens preferred to be baptized in the Jordan and sometimes imprudently delayed their baptism until they could have their wish. St. Ambrose reacts against such a custom, telling his hearers that Christ is everywhere and that wherever Christ is, there the Jordan is as well.[259]

The Byzantine rite is, for most Western Christians, the most accessible of the Eastern rites. We shall therefore go into it in some detail.

On January 5, preparation begins for the feast of the holy Theophany. In the Office of Prime a troparion expresses the theology of Christ's baptism as elaborated by the Fathers:

> The Jordan once ran backward toward its source at the touch of Eliseus' mantle after Elias had been taken up, and the waters parted. Under his feet the river became a solid pathway and a realistic figure of baptism that enables us to cross the shifting waters of life. Christ manifested himself in the Jordan in order to sanctify the waters.[260]

The first part of this troparion is very reminiscent of a passage in Origen's commentary on the Fourth Gospel:

READINGS FOR THE EPIPHANY CYCLE IN MEROVINGIAN GAUL

	L	W	S	S¹	B
Epiphany	Is. 60:1-16 Titus 2:11-3:7 Matthew 3:13-17 Luke 3:23 John 2:1-11	Is. 59:21-60 Titus 2:11-3:7 Matthew 3:13-17 John 2:1-11 Matthew 15:29-31 John 6:1-2 John 6:5-14	Is. 60:1-6	Eph. 5:20-33	Titus 2:11-13 Matthew 3:13-17 Luke 3:23 John 2:1-11
Sunday after Epiphany	Is. 6:1-10 1 Cor. 10:26-31 Luke 4:16-22				

L = Lectionary of Luxeuil. See p. 177, above.
W = Wolfenbüttel Palimpsest, ca. 500. Edited in A. Dold, *Das älteste Liturgiebuch der lateinischen Kirche* (Texte und Arbeiten 26–28; Beuron, 1936). See Vogel, *op. cit.*, p. 290.
S = Lectionary of Sélestat. See p. 177, above.
S¹ = Fragment of a lectionary from Sélestat. See p. 177, above.
B = The Bobbio Missal. See p. 177, above.

We must observe again that Elias, when he was about
to be carried to heaven by a hurricane, having taken
his sheepskin and spread it out, struck the water
with it, which opened on either side, and they went
through one after the other; I mean himself and
Eliseus. So he was made fit to be taken up to heaven,
after having been baptized in the Jordan.[261]

The waters of Jordan are a figure of a "vehicle" that takes
men to heaven. St. Gregory of Nazianzus uses the image:
"Baptism is . . . the destruction of sin, the vehicle to carry
us to God,"[262] and St. Cyril of Jerusalem uses the same expression.[263]

An *idiomelos* [hymn with its own melody] based on a
poem attributed to St. Sophronius (ca. 560–638), patriarch of
Jerusalem, sings of Jordan's waters being sanctified for the
forgiveness of our sins:

On this day the element of water is consecrated; Jordan stops flowing and holds back its waters as it sees
the Savior purifying himself in them. . . . O Christ, our
King, as a man you went down into the river, hastening because of our sins to receive from the Precursor
the baptism meant for slaves.[264]

In this hymn the paschal theme is announced. The baptism of Jesus prefigures our redemption and continues the
incarnation in which the Savior took "the form of a servant"
(Phil. 2:7), for in his baptism he received a rite meant for
slaves.

The choice of readings is illuminating for a grasp of the
Eastern theology of the feast. The first reading is from
Isaiah 35:1-9, which contains these verses:

Behold, your God will come with vengeance, with the
recompense of God. He will come and save you. Then
the eyes of the blind shall be opened, and the ears of
the deaf unstopped; then shall the lame man leap like
a hart, and the tongue of the dumb sing for joy.
For waters shall break forth in the wilderness, and

streams in the desert; the burning sand shall become a pool, and the thirsty ground springs of water. . . . And a highway shall be there, and it shall be called the Holy Way; the unclean shall not pass over it, and fools shall not err therein. No lion shall be there, nor shall any ravenous beast come up on it; they shall not be found there, but the redeemed shall walk there (Is. 35:4-7a, 8-9).

This passage is especially appropriate. It announces salvation in terms that Jesus himself will use in answering the question of John the Baptist's disciples whom John had sent to Jesus from prison: "Go and tell John what you hear and see: the blind receive their sight and the lame walk, lepers are cleansed and the deaf hear . . ." (Matthew 11:4-5). The passage also develops the theme of the highway that we met in the troparion quoted earlier.

With regard to this highway Isaiah mentions a point not taken over in the New Testament. It is that on this highway, which the Jordan becomes, there are lions and beasts of prey, but henceforth they are excluded so that the redeemed may walk there as free men. What the liturgy is focusing on at this point is the theme of ransom from the devil; the ransoming is effected by water, after the latter has itself been freed from the domination of evil powers.

There are numerous other references to the crossing of the Jordan as being a victory over infernal powers. When Isaiah describes the end of time and the new creation it brings, he sees Yahweh crushing the dragon of the sea: "In that day the Lord with his hard and great and strong sword will punish Leviathan the fleeing serpent, Leviathan the twisting serpent, and he will slay the dragon that is in the sea" (Is. 27:1). Closer to the reading in the liturgy is another passage from Isaiah: "Was it not thou that didst cut Rahab in pieces, that didst pierce the dragon? Was it not thou that didst dry up the sea, the waters of the great deep; that didst make the depths of the sea a way for the redeemed to pass over?" (Is. 51:9-10).

Thus, in the first reading, the baptism of Jesus is already seen as a struggle with, and victory over, Satan. Once again, the paschal mystery begins with the baptism of Jesus.

The Eastern liturgies make frequent use of Psalm 74:13-14 during the celebration of Epiphany: "Thou didst divide the sea by thy might; thou didst break the heads of the dragons on the waters. Thou didst crush the heads of Leviathan." The baptism of the Lord is a mystery of our salvation.

The second reading is from the Acts of the Apostles (13:25-33). Here St. Paul quotes John the Baptist, who speaks of the one coming after him, whose sandals he is unworthy to loosen. Paul then tells the Jews that the message of salvation was addressed to them, but they, fulfilling the prophecies, put Jesus to death. God raised Jesus up, however, and now the good news can be preached that "what God promised to the fathers, this he has fulfilled to us their children by raising Jesus" (Acts 13:32-33).

The Gospel is Matthew 3:1-6, where we see John the Baptist preaching repentance and the crowds confessing their sins and receiving baptism in the Jordan.

The reading of the Gospel is followed by a *kontakion* (a liturgical song), which says: "The Lord went down today into the waters of the Jordan and said to John: 'Do not be afraid to baptize me, for I have come to save Adam, the first father.'" A kontakion is a troparion that sums up the theme of a feast. We can see, in this instance, how the kontakion emphasizes the paschal theme that has been sounded in the readings and earlier troparia.

Thus, beginning with the Vigil of Epiphany, the liturgy directs our attention to the Jordan, in which the mystery of our redemption is already under way. It would take too long to study each and every formulary connected with the vigil, but we may at least note some passages from the Office.

In an idiomelos at Terce we find the same emphasis on the paschal mystery and on Christ's victory over the demon:

> You came in the flesh to the Jordan to be baptized as a
> man, O life-giving Savior, in order that you might en-
> lighten us who were caught in error. . . . At the mo-
> ment when you were freeing us from all deception
> and all the dragon's snares, you received a testimonial
> from the Father, and the divine Spirit descended on
> you in the form of a dove.[265]

At the baptism of Jesus, the Trinity revealed itself:

> To us, on this day, did the Trinity, our God, reveal
> itself as undivided: the Father in a loud voice bore
> clear witness to his Son; the Spirit in the form of a
> dove descended from heaven; the Son bowed his sin-
> less head to the Precursor and received baptism. He
> freed the human race from slavery.[266]

At Sext, the theme of the struggle with Satan reappears in
an idiomelos: "I have hastened to destroy the enemy hidden in the waters, the prince of darkness, so that I might
free the world from his toils and give it eternal life."[267] The
poem thus puts an expression of the paschal mystery on
Christ's own lips: his struggle with the evil powers, followed by his victory and ours.

At None, an idiomelos gives voice to the theology of baptism: "He makes us children of God; in the realm of darkness he enlightens man through the water of his divine baptism."[268]

The feastday itself, January 6, is marked by a very rich
liturgy. In Vespers, celebrated on the eve, a beautiful
idiomelic sticheron briefly states the theme of the celebration of Theophany: "By bowing your head before the Precursor you crushed the heads of the demons; you stood
amid the waters and enlightened the universe so that it
might glorify you, O Savior, enlightener of our souls."[269]

These Vespers have fifteen readings; among them are
Genesis 1:1-13, which tells of land and waters being
separated; Exodus 14, the water springing from the rock;
Exodus 15, the springs of fresh water in the desert; Luke

3:1-18, John the Baptist preaching repentance and announcing another baptism.

After the readings comes the blessing of water, a lengthy ceremony containing an opening song, four readings, a diaconal litany, and a long prayer followed by the lowering of a crucifix into the water. Then the crucifix is kissed and a mouthful of water taken.

In some churches of the Latin rite, there used to be a blessing of water on Epiphany, in memory of the baptism in the Jordan. Pope Paul V authorized this custom wherever it already existed, and the Roman Ritual contains a formula for the blessing of water on the Vigil of Epiphany, although Pope Benedict XIV suppressed the formula in his revision of the Ritual; in any event, the custom had died out.

The feast of the Jordan

At least one traveler has brought back an account of this ceremony:

> At St. Petersburg, on Epiphany, the feast of the Jordan is celebrated with great solemnity on the Neva, in front of the Czar's palace. A richly decorated chapel, open on all sides, is built, with a hole in the center of the flooring and down through the ice. At ten in the morning, the metropolitan of St. Petersburg celebrates in this temporary chapel a solemn Mass, at which all the great dignitaries of the Church and the troops of the Imperial Guard are present. After the divine service, the Emperor arrives with his entire court. Then the metropolitan blesses the Neva by lowering a cross in the open hole, while cannon are fired and the troops, kneeling and bareheaded, present arms. Everyone then tries to touch his lips with the water that has just been blessed and to get some of it for himself by making holes in the ice. In some provinces, the peasants make a hole in the ice in order to plunge into the water themselves; elsewhere, people are content to gather the water in containers.[270]

The themes developed in this festival of the waters are those of the Spirit, the water, the forgiveness of sins, and salvation.

Early on, a troparion inspired by Isaiah sings of the Spirit's gifts: "The voice of the Lord resounds over the waters and says: 'Come, all of you, and receive from the Christ who has manifested himself the Spirit of wisdom, the Spirit of understanding, the Spirit of fear of the Lord.'"[271]

This is followed by two readings from Isaiah. The first (35:1-9) has already been read at Prime on January 5, and recalls the water springing up in the desert and the victory of the Messiah and the redeemed. The second (12:3-6) speaks of the wonderful things God has done for our salvation and invites us to draw water with joy from the fountain of salvation.

New Testament readings come next. The First Letter of St. Paul to the Corinthians reminds us that our fathers were all under the cloud, crossed the Red Sea, were baptized by Moses, and drank from the spiritual rock that followed them, that is, from Christ (10:1-4). Finally, the Gospel of St. Mark (1:9-11) tells us of Christ's baptism and the Father's witness to his Son.

While the deacon chants a liturgical prayer, the priest prays in a low voice:

> Thus did you clothe yourself in our poor weak nature. Though you are King of all creation, you submitted to the bonds of slavery and deigned to be baptized in the Jordan by the hand of one of your servants so that, being without sin, you might sanctify the waters and open to us, through water and the Spirit, the way of rebirth, and might restore us to our original freedom.[272]

Here we have the paschal theme of new life. The end of the prayer evidently recalls the words of Jesus in his conversation with Nicodemus: "Truly, truly, I say to you, unless one is born of water and the Spirit, he cannot enter the kingdom of God" (John 3:5).

The priest then prays aloud a long and beautiful collect that has been attributed to St. Sophronius, patriarch of Jerusalem. It is possible, however, that this prayer, so archaic in style, is even older than that. It served as a model for the prayer for blessing the water in the Armenian liturgy.[273]

This long prayer of thanksgiving spoken aloud is really a continuation and amplification of the prayer said just before it in a low voice. It begins with an expression of gratitude: "Accept from us a thanksgiving worthy of your greatness for the wonderful deeds and magnificent works you have done since the beginning of the world and especially in these last times as you effect your plan of sanctification."[274] There follows a listing of these divine wonders, which the priest proclaims aloud and speaks of as accomplished "today":

> . . . Today the grace of the Holy Spirit descends upon the waters in the form of a dove.
> . . . Today the waters of the Jordan are changed into a remedy by the presence of the Lord.
> . . . Today the sins of men are wiped away in the waters of the Jordan.
> . . . Today paradise is opened to mankind, and the Sun of Justice shines upon us.
> . . . Today the kingdom of heaven has become ours. . . .
> This is the feast of the Lord that we see today in the Jordan; we see him casting into the Jordan the death due us for our disobedience, the stinging goad of error, and the chains that bound Adam; we see him giving to the world the baptism that saves.[275]

This conclusion of the prayer leads over to a second thanksgiving in which the whole of creation is associated with man in praising God for the wonderful things he has done for the sake of our salvation.

This long and beautiful prayer of blessing is in the line of the "Jewish blessing" and the early anaphoras, or Eucharis-

tic Prayers, that we find in the third and fourth centuries.
The themes developed in the prayer are the ones we have
been seeing all along: Christ's baptism is the climax of
God's various comings to men since the sin of Adam; it is
the sign of our salvation and return to paradise.

Theophany

The same themes reappear in Matins for the feast of the
Theophany. The troparia of the first Ode are typical in this
respect:

> In the waters of the Jordan he creates Adam anew
> after he had undergone corruption; he crushes the
> heads of the dragons who have taken refuge there. So
> does the Lord, King of the ages, act, for he is clad in
> glory. . . . He who removes the filth from mankind by
> purifying himself in the Jordan on mankind's behalf
> has made himself like those who sit in darkness. So
> does the Lord act, for he is clad in glory.[276]

In this meditation on the paschal mystery, the last day
and the return of Christ are not forgotten:

> It is in the fire of the last day that Christ will baptize
> those who disobey him and do not believe that he is
> God. But it is in the Spirit and water that he renews
> through grace, and frees from their sins, all those who
> acknowledge his divinity.[277]

The celebration of the Liturgy, i.e., the Mass, has two
readings. One is from St. Paul: "For the grace of God has
appeared for the salvation of all men. . . . [It was] Jesus
Christ, who gave himself for us to redeem us from all iniquity and to purify for himself a people of his own. . . . He
saved us . . . by the washing of regeneration and renewal in
the Holy Spirit" (Titus 2:11-14; 3:4-7).[278]

The other reading, Matthew 3:13-17, makes the baptism
of Jesus the basis of our own purification: "'Let it be so
now; for thus it is fitting for us to fulfill all righteousness.'"

At the same time, it recalls the messianic anointing of Jesus: "'This is my beloved Son, with whom I am well pleased.'"

This profusion of texts does not cause the real focus of the celebration of the Theophany to be overlooked. The celebration is of the baptism of the Lord, but, in and through this, it is of the paschal mystery. The baptism is the anointing of the Messiah for his mission of cleansing the world of its sins and destroying the evil powers. Once the baptism of Jesus has taken place, we possess the waters of salvation and new birth, and we are on the road that leads us back to paradise. Finally, the baptism of Christ is the mystery of our definitive union with him.

Epilogue

A Journey into the Paschal Mystery

In this first volume of the series, we have been discovering the rich resources of Advent, Christmas, and Epiphany for our lives as we celebrate the liturgies of these seasons. As we end our survey, it will be worth our while to reflect briefly on the impressions we have derived from a study that was intended to make demands on us in our everyday lives.

We Catholics of today, unlike our predecessors of the first Christian generations, are in danger to some extent of having our attention and energies scattered. The early Christians celebrated only Sunday, including the special Sunday of Easter, and their attention was focused on the mystery of the death and resurrection of Christ. Breaking up the mystery of Jesus into several phases can indeed help in coming to grips with it, but only on one condition: that no phase is separated from the central paschal mystery. The Church has, of course, been aware of this condition, as we recognize by now. In her celebrations she frequently reminds us of the summit from which all grace flows and which is the source of all meaning for the life of the Church and for our individual lives. Advent, Christmas, and Epiphany are stages in a journey into the paschal mystery and from the latter derive their authentic effectiveness.

In our next volume we shall be studying Lent, from Ash Wednesday through to Holy Thursday morning and the reconciliation of sinners that used to be celebrated at Rome on that morning after a long period of conversion that was experienced not only by sinners and by catechumens preparing for baptism but by the whole Church as well. Once Lent begins, we are drawn more urgently toward the paschal mystery as presented to us in various liturgies we shall later be studying more closely.

At every moment, then, we are journeying toward the definitive reconstruction of the world in accordance with the eternal plan of God.

IMMACULATE CONCEPTION OF THE
BLESSED VIRGIN MARY
December 8

At the beginning of the eighth century we find in the East a feast celebrating St. Anne's conception of Mary. In the ninth century the feast appeared at Naples and, a century later, began to spread from there. It was still an optional feast, and the emphasis was on the special favor God gave to Anne of conceiving after so many years of barrenness; the celebration had no further dogmatic dimension. In about the eleventh century the feast became widespread in the west.

In the course of time, the celebration began to take on a greater solemnity and, above all, a new doctrinal meaning. Through a great deal of discussion in the theological schools, clarification was gradually achieved on the special privilege the Blessed Virgin had received of being preserved free from original sin. It was only in 1854, however, that Pope Pius IX proclaimed the dogma of the Immaculate Conception.

The Holy Spirit will come upon you (Luke 1:26-38)
See Fourth Week of Advent, pp. 152-161.

Enmity between you and the woman (Gen. 3:9-15, 20)
See the Tenth Sunday of Ordinary Time, Cycle B, in Volume 4, p. 195.

Chosen before the foundation of the world (Eph. 1:3-6, 11-12)
See January 1, p. 246.

The prayers and the preface bring out the essential content of the dogma: the fact that the Virgin was preserved from original sin by prevenient grace and thus prepared to be a worthy mother for God's Son. The preface also sees the Immaculate Virgin as prefiguring the Church, Christ's beautiful Bride that is without spot or wrinkle. We have recourse to Mary's intercession because she was chosen in a unique way from among all women and because she intervenes in behalf of God's people, for whom she is a figure of ideal holiness.

PRESENTATION OF THE LORD IN THE TEMPLE
February 2

In order to obey the Mosaic law, Mary took the child Jesus to the Temple forty days after his birth and presented herself for her legal purification. This required an offering; in her case it was the offering of the poor: a pair of turtle doves or of young pigeons. The elderly Simeon and Anna the prophetess received from God the great favor of meeting the child and recognizing in him the awaited Messiah.

In the East, the meeting of Jesus and Simeon was commemorated in a feast known as *Hypopantē* ("Meeting"). It is first attested, for the fourteenth of February, at Jerusalem toward the end of the fourth century. A procession was part of the celebration, and the day was spent in meditation on the words of Simeon, "A light for revelation to the Gentiles." It was probably around the middle of the fifth century that lamps were carried in the procession, with the intention of thus representing Christ as the Light that enlightens all mankind.

Under Pope Sergius I, a Syrian pope (687–701), the feast came to be celebrated at Rome, but on February 2, which was the fortieth day after the birth of Jesus. The celebration included a procession from the church of St. Hadrian to the basilica of St. Mary Major, and an Office containing elements of Eastern provenance. Only belatedly, beginning in the ninth century, did the feast spread from Rome throughout the West; for the most part it had something of a penitential character, especially at Rome.

The older liturgical books entitled the feast the Purification of the Blessed Virgin. Happily, this law-centered approach to the feast has been abandoned, and the feast now celebrates a new manifestation of Jesus as Messiah. In the new Missal the feast is known as the Presentation of the Lord.

"Mine eyes have seen thy salvation" (Luke 2:22-40)

The Canticle of Simeon, which has become one of the classic hymns of the Church and is recited at Compline in the Roman Office, proclaims the Messiah whom the old man recognizes in the child he holds in his arms. Anna the prophetess also recognizes in the child the one who is to liberate Jerusalem. The Presentation is thus a second feast of Epiphany. We, for our part, are being urged to recognize in the Church, in other human beings, and in events the salvation that is being offered to us. Above all, each sacrament is a manifestation of the Lord: we meet him in the sacrament, and he prepares us for the definitive meeting at the end.

The Lord comes into his temple (Mal. 3:1-4)

The reason why this passage is read today is not chiefly the mention of the temple but rather the fact that it concerns the coming and manifestation of the Lord. Malachias is describing a solemn epiphany and is also foretelling the role of John the Baptist: "I send my messenger to prepare the way before me." The Lord's coming is awesome: "Who can endure the day of his coming?" The images used to describe his power and action are strong ones, for his role is primarily to purify so that a sacrifice pleasing to the Lord may be offered.

The responsorial psalm (Ps. 24) was written for a glorious entry into Jerusalem, and it foretells the manifestation of the Savior: "Who is this King of glory? The Lord of hosts, he is the King of glory!"

A high priest who is like his brethren (Heb. 2:14-18)

God chose a unique way of saving the world: He sent his Son and bade him share the human condition; then, through the Son's death, he reduced to impotence the one who had the power to inflict death. The passage goes on, in a Pauline style and a Pauline theological vein, to explain God's plan as it was implemented in the *kenosis*, or self-emptying, of his Son. The result is that we have a High Priest who has been able to offer the perfect sacrifice and take away the sins of the world.

Today, this savior is presented in the Temple. The High Priest enters for the first time into the place of sacrifice, but his own sacrifice will be offered on the Cross and will be more efficacious than all the sacrifices hitherto offered.

SUNDAYS IN ORDINARY TIME
Sundays Two to Eight

SUNDAYS TWO TO EIGHT

IN ORDINARY TIME

CYCLE A
for years 1978, 1981, 1984, 1987, 1990

CYCLE B
for years 1979, 1982, 1985, 1988, 1991

CYCLE C
for years 1980, 1983, 1986, 1989, 1992

[An extended introduction to the Sundays of Ordinary Time is given in volume four of this series. For information on the Order of Mass, its constituent parts and purposes, including the rationale for the methodology pertinent to the following commentary on the Lectionary Readings, the reader is referred to this part of the present work.]

Table of readings

In the following table, the general theme of each celebration and the particular theme of each reading are indicated. If the second reading is connected with the general theme of the day, it will be commented on together with the first reading and the Gospel; such second readings are marked by an asterisk in the following list.

More often the second reading does not fit in with the theme proposed for the first and third readings. In such instances a heavy line separates the second reading from what precedes in the commentary below. This line of demarcation is to remind the reader to avoid looking for con-

nections between the semi-continuous reading of Paul's
Letters and the readings from the Old Testament and the
Gospel, since such connections are usually non-existent.
The commentary itself will be brief. We are dealing in the
second reading with a semi-continuous sequence in which
the liturgical context plays no part; no properly liturgical
commentary, therefore, is required. There are many exegetical commentaries on the Pauline Letters to which the
reader can easily refer. We shall limit ourselves to some
basic observations that may help the reader's personal
reflections and introduce him to the more extended commentaries.

CYCLE A

Sunday 2   GOD'S CHOICE
John 1:29-34 — The Son of God is here
Is. 49:3, 5-6 — Choice of the servant
*1 Cor. 1:1-3 — The apostle is called; so are we

Sunday 3   THE GOOD NEWS: A GREAT LIGHT HAS SHONE
Matthew 4:12-23 — Galilee of the Gentiles
Is. 9:1-4 — A great light has shone
1 Cor. 1:10-13, 17 — No divisions among us

Sunday 4   GOD CHOOSES THE POOR
Matthew 5:1-12a — Blessed are the poor in spirit
Zeph. 2:3; 3:12-13 — A people humble and lowly
*1 Cor. 1:26-31 — God has chosen the weak

Sunday 5   SALT OF THE EARTH AND LIGHT OF THE WORLD
Matthew 5:13-16 — Light of the world
Is. 58:7-10 — Your light shall rise in the darkness
*1 Cor. 2:1-5 — Proclaim a crucified Messiah

Sunday 6   A NEW LAW IN CONTINUITY WITH THE OLD
Matthew 5:17-37 — You have heard . . . but I say
Sir. 15:15-20 — Condemned to freedom
*1 Cor. 2:6-10 — Wisdom is revealed to us for our glorification

Sunday 5   OVERCOMING THE FORCES OF EVIL
Mark 1:29-39   He healed the sick
Job 7:1-4, 6-7   Suffering man
1 Cor. 9:16-19, 22-23   The duty of proclaiming the gospel

Sunday 6   WE ARE LEPERS
Mark 1:40-45   If you will, you can make me clean
Lev. 13:1-2, 45-46   The unclean man must dwell alone
1 Cor. 10:31–11:1   Christ our model

Sunday 7   THE FORGIVENESS OF SINS
Mark 2:1-12   The Son of man has authority to forgive sins
Is. 43:18-19, 21-22, 24b-25   God forgives sins
2 Cor. 1:18-22   Our "yes," to the glory of God

Sunday 8   THE MARRIAGE OF GOD TO HIS PEOPLE
Mark 2:18-22   The bridegroom with us
Osee 2:14b, 15b, 19-20   I will speak tenderly to my spouse
*2 Cor. 3:1b-6   Ministers of a new covenant

CYCLE C

Sunday 2	MARRIAGE	
	John 2:1-12	The marriage at Cana
	Is. 62:1-5	The marriage of Jerusalem
	1 Cor. 12:4-11	The same Spirit distributes all gifts

Sunday 3   THE WORD OF GOD PROCLAIMED TO ALL PEOPLES

	Luke 1:1-4; 4:14-21	He has anointed me to preach good news to the poor
	Neh. 8:2-4a, 5-6, 8-10	Listening to the word of God
	1 Cor. 12:12-30	The body and the members

Sunday 4   A PROPHET SPEAKS TO THE WORLD

	Luke 4:21-30	God speaks to the world
	Jer. 1:4-5, 17-19	A prophet to the nations
	1 Cor. 12:31–13:13	Charity the greatest of the three

Sunday 5   MESSENGERS OF GOD

	Luke 5:1-11	Henceforth you will be catching men
	Is. 6:1-2a, 3-8	Here am I! Send me
	*1 Cor. 15:1-11	The message of faith

Sunday 6   BLESSINGS AND CURSES
           Luke 6:17, 20-26   Blessed are you poor. Woe to you that are rich
           Jer. 17:5-8   Authentic riches and security
           1 Cor. 15:12, 16-20   If there is no resurrection, our faith is vain

Sunday 7   BE MERCIFUL
           Luke 6:27-38   Be merciful as God is to us
           1 Sam. 26:2, 7-9, 12-13, Spare your enemy
                22-23
           1 Cor. 15:45-49   We shall bear the image of the heavenly man

Sunday 8   THE WORD AND THE HEART
           Luke 6:39-45   The true disciple
           Sir. 27:4-7   The word and the heart
           1 Cor. 15:54-58   God gives us the victory through Christ

CYCLE A

pages 339-369
for years 1978, 1981, 1984, 1987, 1990

SECOND SUNDAY IN ORDINARY TIME

God's Choice

God's Son is here (John 1:29-34)

The continuous or semi-continuous reading of St. Matthew's Gospel does not begin until the third Sunday. During Ordinary Time passages from St. John's Gospel (which traditionally is read during Lent and the Easter season) are read on some Sundays. The second Sunday (all three cycles) is one of these.

The present reading from the Fourth Gospel is linked to the celebration of the Lord's baptism (first Sunday of Ordinary Time; Sunday after Epiphany), and continues the evangelist's meditation on John the Baptist. What is especially striking in John the Baptist's words is the designation of Christ and his role by the Spirit who descends from heaven and remains upon him. This is traditional language for describing God's choice of a prophet. "There shall come forth a shoot from the stump of Jesse, and a branch shall grow out of his roots. And the Spirit of the Lord shall rest upon him" (Is. 11:1-2). The rest of this chapter of Isaiah should be read here, for it shows the qualities and function of a person who is thus singled out by the Spirit.

Later on, Isaiah says: "Behold my servant, whom I uphold, my chosen, in whom my soul delights; I have put my Spirit upon him" (42:1). The Spirit here is the prophetic

Spirit of chapter 11. His outpouring is the great sign of the messianic age: "And it shall come to pass afterward, that I will pour out my spirit on all flesh. . . . And I will give portents in the heavens . . ." (Joel 2:28-30).

St. Luke describes for us the scene in which Jesus enters the synagogue at Nazareth and, when the moment comes for the reading from the prophets, takes the scroll and reads: "The Spirit of the Lord is upon me, because he has anointed me to preach the good news to the poor. He has sent me to proclaim release to the captives and recovering of sight to the blind, to set at liberty those who are oppressed, to proclaim the acceptable year of the Lord" (Luke 4:18-19; Is. 61:1-2). Jesus then comments on the passage by applying it to himself.

For John the Baptist, who would have been quite familiar with these various texts from the prophets, they must have taken on a vivid meaning, for he saw them fulfilled in a very concrete way at the baptism of Jesus. John was blessed by being able to identify Jesus as the person whom God had chosen and pointed out to his people: "He who sent me to baptize with water said to me, 'He on whom you see the Spirit descend and remain, this is he who baptizes with the Holy Spirit.' And I have seen and have borne witness that this is the Son of God" (John 1:33-34).

John fully understood Jesus and his mission. He bears witness to him by attributing to him all the qualities of God's Son. First, he asserts the eternity of the Son: "After me comes a man who ranks before me, for he was before me" (1:30). A true Son, however, is one who does his Father's will, and so John points to Jesus with the words: "Behold, the Lamb of God, who takes away the sin of the world!" (1:29).

The expressions "lamb" and "takes away the sin of the world" bring us back to Isaiah, but they also acquaint us straight off with the style and special concerns of St. John the Evangelist. The phrase "Lamb of God" immediately calls up the idea of sacrifice (cf. Exod. 13:13; 29:38; 34:25;

Lev. 3:7; Num. 28:9; Is. 7:9; Sir. 46:19; Is. 53:7; Jer. 11:19),
and especially the sacrifice of the Passover lamb (Exod.
12:3; 2 Chr. 35:7, 11). Both Isaiah and Jeremiah, though
with different references, speak of a lamb being sacrificed:
"Like a lamb that is led to the slaughter, and like a sheep
that before its shearers is dumb, so he opened not his
mouth" (Is. 53:7). "But I was like a gentle lamb led to the
slaughter. I did not know it was against me they devised
schemes" (Jer. 11:19).

When Isaiah speaks of the Servant of Yahweh as a lamb,
he anticipates John the Baptist's words, "Behold, the Lamb
of God." Jesus is the Son, but he is also the Lamb, the Servant who takes away the world's sins. In the prophets, the
word "lamb" emphasizes the innocence of the person who
is about to be sacrificed. "Taking away sins" is the Servant's function, for "the Lord has laid on him the iniquity of
us all" (Is. 53:6). "He has borne our griefs and carried our
sorrows [or: pains]" (Is. 53:4); "He bore the sin of many"
(53:12). Jesus is truly the Lamb, the Servant, the beloved
Son, because he does the Father's will. With the words
"Behold, the Lamb of God," John says in his own way what
the Father says of Jesus at the latter's baptism and transfiguration.

The Father, then, has chosen his only Son as Lamb and
Servant to take away the world's sins. The Spirit has remained upon him and chosen him for his task. The incarnation of the Word is for a service that brings him to death so
that the world may be redeemed and so that all who receive
him in his coming may become children of God.

Choice of the servant (Is. 49:3, 5-6)

The reading from Isaiah takes us back to one of the great
figures who typify Jesus and proclaim him in advance
across the centuries. There are four "Servant Songs" in the
Book of Isaiah (42:1-7; 49:1-9; 50:4-9; 52:13–53:12). There
is fairly general agreement among exegetes that these songs

were added later to the work of the original Isaiah and are in fact compositions of a later writer, whom they speak of as "Second Isaiah." The verses chosen for the present reading are those that speak of the choice of the servant (Is. 49:3, 5-6).

"He said to me, 'You are my servant, Israel, in whom I will be glorified" (v. 3). The choice of him by the Lord confers an important mission on the servant: that of gathering Israel and of being a light for the nations so that salvation may reach the ends of the earth (Is. 49:6).

Psalm 40, which serves as responsorial psalm after the first reading, has a refrain that emphasizes the special characteristic of the servant and the Lamb: "Here am I, Lord; I come to do your will." The servant offers himself as a victim, but what the Lord really wants is that the servant do his, the Lord's, will: "In the roll of the book it is written of me; I delight to do thy will, O my God" (Ps. 40:7b-8a).

The apostle is called; so are we (1 Cor. 1:1-3)

The second reading for this Sunday happens to fit in with the theme of the first reading and the Gospel: the theme of choice for a mission. In the opening words of his First Letter to the Corinthians, St. Paul speaks of himself as called by God's will to be an apostle of Jesus Christ. As John the Baptist was called to bear witness to Jesus, Paul has now been chosen to proclaim the good news of Christ. But the faithful, too, are the object of a divine choice; because of that call, they form a holy people and call on the name of the Lord Jesus Christ. In other words, they too have been chosen by the Lord and set apart to be witnesses to Christ.

If Paul has been chosen for the apostolate, the body of Christians has been chosen for holiness. The holiness is lived within the communion of the Church that calls upon the name of its Messiah and has for its principal function the offering of praise and adoration; these will in turn be the basis of the Church's witness and apostolate.

God's choice today

All that we have been reading and saying does not refer solely to the past. On the contrary, it applies very much to the here and now, and provides an occasion for us to try to understand better the teaching and spirituality of the liturgy generally. The liturgy is not interested in concepts but in concrete Christian life; it shows what it means to be chosen by God and what mission the choice involves. Nor is the liturgy interested in any abstract theology of God's choice; it intends rather to show us the God who chooses.

All this is relevant to us. We do not need theories about God's choice. We know for a fact that through our baptism we were chosen by God. Indeed, the name given in antiquity to those preparing for baptism was "the elect, the chosen." What they were elected to and chosen for was to share in God's life and to accept the consequences of that sharing. We must accept those consequences in our own lives.

THIRD SUNDAY

The Good News: A Great Light Has Shone

Galilee of the Gentiles (Matthew 4:12-23)

The semi-continuous reading of the Gospel of St. Matthew begins today in Cycle A. The choice of reading is very good, because it recalls the beginning of Jesus' preaching in Galilee, where there were many Gentiles. Matthew shows us Christ in his work of preaching the Good News, and sees it as a fulfillment of the Isaian prophecy found in the first reading for this day. One theme of Matthew's Gos-

pel is to show that Jesus is the true Messiah, whom the
pagans accept and the Jews reject.

John the Baptist had pointed him out. Now Jesus leaves
the region where John is working and comes to Galilee.
This is the first of his various shifts of locale, and it is important that the first such shift should be to Galilee, where
many pagans lived. John the Baptist was not the only one to
proclaim Jesus; Isaiah had done so before him.

Having been thus doubly proclaimed, Jesus begins his
ministry. His message is simple but staggering: "Repent,
for the kingdom of heaven is at hand" (Matthew 2:17). Jesus
goes about Gaililee always preaching the same message:
The kingdom is at hand; to back up his words, "he cured
the people of every disease and illness" (Matthew 2:23).
We have noted on several occasions throughout this series
of commentaries that such cures were the sign of the kingdom's presence.

Jesus shows the presence of the Messiah and the kingdom by another very special action: He begins to establish
his Church and to prepare for the building of it by gradually
shaping the columns that must support it. He looks around
among his fellowmen for those who will work with him in
helping the world achieve its freedom from Satan and sin;
those whom he chooses will be fishers of men. Simon, re-
named Peter, Andrew, James, and John are called.

In this passage Matthew twice stresses the fact that those
called immediately leave nets and boat and father to follow
Jesus. There can be no doubt that Matthew deliberately
emphasizes this "immediately." The light of Christ shines
out so strongly in this land of the Gentiles that nothing can
resist it. The first disciples do not sit down and discuss the
matter; they recognize Christ and immediately follow him.
It is then that Jesus begins to teach in the synagogues.

A great light has shone (Is. 9:1-4)

Matthew has chosen to hark back to Isaiah and see the
latter's prophecies fulfilled in the first events of Jesus' pub-

lic life. The passage from Isaiah relates to events connected with the invasion by the Assyrians of Northern Palestine — the land of Zebulun and the land of Naphtali — in 732. Many Galileans were deported. Isaiah sought to restore the people's confidence: "The people who walked in darkness have seen a great light" (9:2).

It is clear how this applies to the Messiah and the Good News. The people living in ignorance of God and enslaved by darkness now see the Messiah coming and his light shining upon them. On those dwelling in a land of deep darkness a light has shone; the yoke that weighed them down is broken. The words of the prophet sum up the whole mission of Christ, and St. Matthew quotes them to serve that purpose.

The light and the Good News are always being offered to us, for the work of evangelization goes on. But we are not simply to observe the work or to be the recipient of it — we are to share in it. The prophecy read today and the Gospel pericope are addressed to us in order to stir us to action. In fact, Christ stirs us to action at two levels. First, there is the inner spiritual movement incumbent upon us: the kingdom is at hand, proclaimed to us by the light we received at our baptism, and we must therefore unwearyingly carry on the work of our own conversion. But we must also leave all things and follow Christ in order to share with him the task of preaching the gospel.

The gospel is demanding, for we must take steps that are costly to our weak nature if we are to see the light and accept it. And yet the extension of the kingdom depends in part on us. The Church is already established, of course, and its supporting pillars are the apostles. But each of us is called to work for expansion of the Church and the spreading of the Good News. The sacrifices required of us in the pursuit of this goal may be hard ones. The apostles, the first men whom Christ called, responded without hesitation; not everyone else would do so, and the rich young man, though he had observed all the commandments, gave up when it came to following Jesus.

In the sometimes difficult following of Christ, the responsorial psalm, Psalm 27, can give us courage: "The Lord is
my light and my salvation; whom shall I fear?" (v. 1). There
is however a condition for acquiring this courage: we must
have our hearts set on a single goal, namely, to "dwell in
the house of the Lord" (v. 4). If we follow the guidance of
the Lord and look actively for his coming, we will receive
the courage and strength to follow in his steps: "I believe
that I shall see the goodness of the Lord in the land of the
living! (v. 13).

No divisions among us (1 Cor. 1:10-13, 17)

After only a very short time, divisions cropped up in the
life of the early Church. If, in this Letter to the Corinthians,
St. Paul adopts a serious, almost dramatic tone, it is because
divisions are, in his eyes, a basic contradiction to a properly
gospel outlook and a negation of the very being of the
Church. The men and women of this quite young community were filled with enthusiasm; unfortunately, the enthusiasm was directed to the special themes of each evangelist, to his person and his manner of teaching, rather than
to basic content and, more importantly, the person of
the Lord, who is Teacher of all Christians and in whom all
have been baptized.

The divisions in the Church of Corinth were due to their
proponents having failed to understand either Christ crucified or what it is that forms men and women into the people of God. The unanimity at which they should have
been aiming was a single faith and a common effort to
create unity because all had been reborn by the same sacrament of baptism and all had been saved by the same
Christ crucified.

How relevant such a passage is to us today! Despite our
contemporary concern with action, even excessive action,

people love to listen to speeches and are on the watch for new and original presentations of their faith. They are often more concerned with the manner of presentation than with the content, and their attachment to the "star" can even lead them to form autonomous cells within the Church. Is this a manifestation of the quest for God? It may well be regarded rather as a lack of genuine faith and of an understanding of what it means to belong to the Body of Christ, in which there should be, not uniformity on accidentals, but unity in faith for the good of the whole.

FOURTH SUNDAY

God Chooses the Poor

Blessed are the poor in spirit (Matthew 5:1-12a)

The gospel preaches a world turned inside out. This is not to say it claims poverty to be something good or that God's blessing cannot be manifested in the gifts of material things. The gospel does, however, foresee that it is difficult to keep our hearts free in the midst of earthly possessions. That is the point of the beatitudes, which we read today in St. Matthew's version of them (St. Luke's will be read on the sixth Sunday, Cycle C).

The beatitudes in St. Matthew form a paragraph of rhythmic prose. A comparison with the beatitudes of Luke shows that the two authors surely drew inspiration from a common source, but this is of little concern to us here. The power of the beatitudes over us becomes all the greater if we really believe that God is addressing his words to us here and now in the liturgical celebration.

Within the total context provided by the readings of this Sunday, the thematic beatitudes are poverty of spirit, meekness, mourning, hunger and thirst, and persecution — in short, everything that represents weakness, everything the world looks down its nose at and has trouble taking seriously. By contrast, if we think of the first beatitude: "Blessed are the poor"; the second: "Blessed are those who mourn"; the Fourth: "Blessed are those who hunger and thirst"; and the eighth: "Blessed are those who are persecuted," we have the essence of the beatitudes in relation to the coming kingdom. In his Sermon on the Mount, Jesus comes forward as preacher of the good news of the kingdom. Persecution, we may note, is mentioned both as a present and as a future reality, and is accompanied by a special exhortation to those who must experience it. The exhortation is in the form of a call to rejoice because the reward in heaven will be great.

The Gospel passage urges us to examine our life and especially our value judgments in the light of the new values with which Christ presents us and which are disconcerting to those who do not believe in the kingdom. Christianity will show the world people who suffer and yet rejoice, Christians who are persecuted and yet are filled with the joy of witnessing, families that lack the necessities of life and yet are marked, not by bitterness, but by youthfulness of spirit. Above all, Christianity will show the world people who may be materially rich but whose hearts are open, receptive, humble; people who are not puffed up by their wealth and who know that they have much to receive from others who are better than they in other than material ways.

We can never meditate seriously enough on this great charter of the Christian life or ever be done with the attempt to implement it fully. It can always be read with a still greater faith and a still deeper sense of God.

A people humble and lowly (Zeph. 2:3; 3:12-13)

If material poverty is not a good in itself, it does nonetheless help us toward the freedom that in turn enables us to search more effectively for God. This freedom is really what Zephaniah is talking about when he bids us seek righteousness, humility, and the will of God. These are the goals the humble and lowly set their hearts on. Such people will be protected against God's wrath on the last day, because it is to the last day and the Lord's coming that they have been looking forward to all along.

Against this background, we can see why the prophet speaks of Israel as a "shameless nation" (2:1). We may think of our own world, in which the rich and their children cannot dissipate their boredom and disgust with everything; a world that sets its heart on perishable material goods and yet is filled with an indefinable anxiety because there is nothing of the permanent and the absolute in their lives.

It is to be observed, however, that the prophet Zephaniah is not thinking simply of the material state of the humble and lowly. If God will preserve only those who are humble and lowly, it is because the latter will not sin or play false. In short, the ultimate concern is with a lowliness and a poverty that are above all spiritual, with what St. Matthew will call "poverty of spirit." The people who will survive will be no more than a remnant of Israel; this presupposes a major purge, indeed a catastrophe. The time will come when the only refuge is in the name of the Lord.

God has chosen the weak (1 Cor. 1:26-31)

The second reading on this day fits in very well with the theme of the other two readings. St. Paul fully grasped the inversion of values that the coming of Christ caused. From now on, God chooses what is weak in the world's eyes. No one can boast of himself before God.

It seems clear that Paul is here referring to a contemporary philosophical snobbery. He does not want Christians to be led astray by that kind of thinking, and so he calls their attention to some basic facts. He contrasts, for example, the wisdom of the world and the wisdom of God, and tells us that God alone is to be our wisdom and justice.

The church of Corinth had recruited its members from among the lowborn and despised; few were rich and influential, few were wise as men account wisdom. But God is not bound to the value judgments of men; he chooses precisely those for whom the world has little esteem, but it is he, after all, who knows how to judge properly! God chose "even things that are not, to bring to nothing things that are" (v. 28). He did this in order that "no human being might boast in the presence of God" (v. 29). The only pride a Christian can rightly cultivate is a pride in the Lord, from whom all that is worthwhile comes. Apart from Christ, nothing human is of value.

The readings for this Sunday really put everything in its proper place and are an invitation to the Christian to review his value judgments on persons and things. We ourselves have worth only in relation to God.

The responsory psalm, from Psalm 146, is full of meaning for us, and can be taken as a summary of the whole thought of the day. The response is from the Gospel: "Happy the poor in spirit; the kingdom of heaven is theirs." The verses chosen from the psalm are these:

> The Lord . . . executes justice for the oppressed;
>   he gives food to the hungry.
> The Lord sets the prisoners free;
>   the Lord opens the eyes of the blind.
> The Lord lifts up those who are bowed down;
>   the Lord loves the righteous.
> He upholds the widow and the fatherless;
>   but the way of the wicked he brings to ruin.

The lesson taught on this Sunday is truly fundamental for the Catholic of our day. God does not choose those who have sophisticated concepts of religion and the quest for God; he chooses, above all, the humble who have no theories about God and about how to follow him, but are open to the Lord and his demands. The lesson is undoubtedly a hard one for our contemporaries, who like to build conceptual systems and gnostic approaches to the search for

God. All that is irrelevant to God's choice; he has no interest in the little groups that spend hours developing methods of seeking God and deciding on the best way to follow him. God does not need that kind of workshop. He acts in ways that are usually quite unexpected, and chooses the weak things of the world.

FIFTH SUNDAY

Salt of the Earth and Light of the World

Light of the world (Matthew 5:13-16)

In the Gospel, this passage follows immediately upon the beatitudes. The Christian knows, in a general way, how he must conduct himself; he knows that he must follow Christ, and what this means. Now, employing rather strong images, Matthew wants to make his readers more fully aware of what they really are: the salt of the earth and the light of the world.

"Salt of the earth" is not a commonly used expression. It can be taken in a realistic sense as a salt that serves as fertilizer; of this St. Luke says that if it loses its strength, "it is fit neither for the land nor for the dunghill" (Luke 14:35). In the present passage, however, we have the impression that "earth" is rather a way of saying "world"; the meaning is would be that the disciple of Jesus is a power that should make the world bloom. Every Christian possesses within himself a power that should be active in the world. If he were to lose his "taste," he would also lose his meaning and would have to be "thrown out." These last words are strong ones, and we meet them elsewhere as indicating *eternal damnation*. St. Matthew uses the words on several occasions with reference to those who do not act as their vocation in Christ requires (7:19; 13:48, 50; 18:8, 9; 22:13). Jesus was probably using proverbial phraseology.

There is no point in puzzling here over the riddle of a salt that loses its taste. We are dealing with a proverb, and everyone knows quite well what the words mean as applied to human beings who should be living up to their responsibilities. The problem is one we all face. We have become the salt of the earth by reason of our baptism; we must continue to be salt for the world and develop the power given us and the dynamic, outgoing energy that in principle is at our disposal.

Christ still stands before us with the example of his life, and we are forced to ask ourselves to what extent each Christian in the Church is truly "salt" for the world. Do Christians simply "practice," or are they really "salt"? If they are no longer "salt," what significance do they still have? That is the problem, but only God can give the answer. We have no right to judge others, but we do have an obligation to examine ourselves and decide what we must do.

We are also "the light of the world." In thus designating his disciples, Christ enjoins on them the attitude that befits people in such a luminous state. The words in St. Matthew seem to imply a contrast and might be translated: "It is you who are the light of the world." The point would be that this function has now passed from the Jews, who formerly possessed it (Is. 42:6; 49:6; 60:3), to Christ's disciples and his new people.

Christians must proclaim the Messiah who has come and saved the world. It is by doing so that they will be a light in the darkness. Their situation as Christians imposes certain duties on them that they cannot simply shrug off: they must not let their salt loses its taste, nor put their light under a basket. At the same time, however, they must remember that while they may be legitimately proud of sharing in Christ's work and his Spirit-inspired activity in the world, they must not communicate their own light but that of Christ, who has come to enlighten every man.

The Christian's activity should lead all men to praise the Father for what he has done. The basis for praising God is the marvelous deeds he has done, and the Christian should be one of these deeds that leads men to wonder and praise of the Lord. When men thus glorify God, it is a sign of their conversion. Thus the Christian is really called to shed a light that will lead to the salvation of his fellowmen.

Your light shall rise in the darkness (Is. 58:7-10)

In this passage from the prophet, the shedding of light is connected with charity to others. If a man wants to be truly a light, he must shelter the homeless, clothe the naked, and not hide himself from his own flesh. If he does these things, his light will break forth like the dawn, and his own wounds will be quickly healed. If a man opens his heart to the hungry and satisfies the desire of the afflicted, his light will rise in the darkness, his gloom will become like noonday.

Thus, the light that the Christian is called to be cannot be translated into terms solely of faith and knowledge, but is intimately linked with love and concern for the neighbor. The verses of chapter 58 that precede those read today all move in the same direction. The point being made is that the prophet sent to Israel is an authentic prophet when he is open to the needs of others; similarly, we today are authentic Christians and authentic prophets when we too open our hearts to others. The aim is not merely to eliminate injustice; it is to build a just world. If we are this kind of Christian, the Lord is near at hand to us; we need only call and he will answer, "Here I am!" The "light," then, is in reality orthodox charity concretely shown to our neighbor.

Proclaim a crucified Messiah (1 Cor. 2:1-5)

The Corinthians seem to have been ever ready to divide into opposing groups according to the preacher they favored at the moment. St. Paul here reminds them that the effective preacher is not the one who is a master of language or a master of human wisdom. The preacher who is effective in God's eyes is the one who preaches Christ crucified and whose preaching manifests the power of the Spirit.

We may, without forcing things, link this second reading with the other two in terms of "light." We are meant to be the light of the world (the Gospel); we will in fact be a light to others only if we are inspired by charity and do the concrete works of charity (first reading). In addition, however, the light we are to bring is light concerning the central object of our faith, namely, Christ crucified. It is for this that the Spirit fills us with his power. To bring light to others, then, means to enable them to meet Christ, the crucified Messiah who is now the risen Lord of glory.

True faith is not grounded in the wisdom of men but in the power of God. For a man to receive the gift of faith, the "light," is for him to encounter the mystery of Christ or Christ himself in his paschal mystery. The true Catholic preacher — and this applies to every Catholic — is the one who enables others to encounter the Light, the Word-made-flesh who was crucified and then rose from the dead. It is the Spirit who really makes the mystery known to men and gives them the strength to embrace it.

SIXTH SUNDAY

A New Law in Continuity with the Old

You have heard . . . but I say (Matthew 5:17-37)

At first glance today's Gospel shows Jesus issuing a revolutionary challenge: "You have heard that it was said. . . .

But I say to you." And yet the impression soon proves ungrounded, for we are told at the very beginning of the passage: "Think not that I have come to abolish the law and the prophets; I have come not to abolish them but to fulfill them" (v. 17). In what does this fulfillment consist by which the law is not abolished but perfected to the fullest degree? An easy answer would be: the fulfillment consists in love. Doesn't St. Paul tell us so in his letter to the Romans, "Love is the fulfilling of the law"? (13:10).

If we stop here, we may remain rather vague — understanding without really understanding, and content with only a kind of superficial insight into this "fulfillment." The fulfillment is in fact the fulfillment of the law, but it is also the fulfillment of those who obey it, for the fulfillment of the law now consists in being able to become like God. As St. Matthew tells us later in this same chapter, "you must be perfect as your heavenly Father is perfect" (5:48). When did Jesus enable us to become as perfect as his heavenly Father? When did Jesus bring to fulfillment the purpose of the law and the prophets? *In and through his Passover mystery.* The law and the prophets were preliminary stages or pedagogical preparation unto the attainment of intimacy with God. In his Pasch Jesus achieved ontologically and to the fullest perfection the preliminary steps taken by the law and the prophets. Because of the Passion, death and resurrection of Jesus it has become possible, and necessary, for us to become perfect as our heavenly Father is perfect.

It is in this perspective that Christ does issue a revolutionary challenge: "You have heard that it was said. . . . But I say to you." He lists a whole series of areas with which the law dealt, but with regard to which the new covenant is much more demanding. Not only must a man not kill another; he must not even say an insulting word to him (Matthew 21:22). There is no point in bringing a ritual offering to the altar without first giving sincere signs of love and union with others (vv. 23-26). Not only must a man not commit adultery, but he is already guilty of adultery in his heart if he looks on a woman lustfully (vv. 27-30). It used to be that a man could dismiss his wife; henceforth marriage is indissoluble (vv. 31-32). Do not take oaths (vv. 33-36), but let your answers be simply "Yes" or "No" (v. 37).

This is not the place to study minutely each of Christ's statements, as, for example, the very important one about marriage being indissoluble. The focus of the liturgical proclamation is not on the details, for the point of reading this passage is to emphasize the fact that observance of the law has now entered upon the time of paschal fulfillment. Details become unimportant in view of the evident motive for the choice of the first reading.

Condemned to freedom (Sir. 15:15-20)

The phrase "condemned to freedom" aptly sums up man's condition from the moment of his creation.[279] Ben Sirach puts it in his own way: "It was he [God] who created man in the beginning, and he left him in the power of his own inclination" (v. 14; or, as the Jerusalem Bible expresses it more clearly: "and then left him free to make his own decisions"). This verse has unfortunately not been included in today's reading, but it lies behind the verses that follow, for the latter presuppose the full freedom of God's creature, man. In speaking of the commandments, it is important that we stress the fact that their fulfillment is within man's power and that he is, on the other hand, not forced to obedience (Sir. 15:15).

Man even has the privilege of choosing life or death; he needs only to stretch out his hand for whichever he wishes (vv. 16-17). These words must, however, be properly understood. It is true enough that even life and death are not forced on man, and that the choice men make is theirs. At the same time it is clear that those who obey God's commandments will receive life and blessing (Deut. 11:26-28); life is to be found by following the path of justice (Prov. 12:28).

Man is free indeed, but he must bear in mind that God possesses wisdom, that he knows all of a man's actions, and that his good will rests on those who fear him (Sir. 15:18-19). God offers man either life and blessing or death and wretchedness, but it is he who obeys the Lord's commandments who will live (Deut. 30:15-20). Wisdom, then, bids a man freely choose the ways of God and accept the wisdom of the Lord himself. This divine wisdom invites man to a life in which he observes the law and avoids sin. Ben Sirach puts the point negatively: "He has not commanded any one to be ungodly, and he has not given any one permission to sin" (Sir. 15:20).

The responsorial psalm for this first reading is taken from Psalm 119, which sings of the happiness of those who walk according to the word of God. You know, we can cultivate a certain simplism with regard to the Old Testament. We may think that the law of the Old Testament had nothing to do with love and that only Christ in the New Testament revealed the true way by teaching men to live in the spirit of love. Such an opposition is unfounded; we have failed to read the texts carefully enough. Both creation and God's gift of the law to his people were acts of love on his part, while the free man's observance of God's commandments was first and foremost an act of love on his part.

It is true enough, however, that Christ came to fulfill the purpose of the law, not to abolish it; moreover, the New Testament is clearly characterized by the supremacy it gives to love, even in the observance of the commandments, which man is obey freely but with love as well. This is not to say that man may not be weak and unfaithful or that he may not suffer interior conflicts. For all his freedom, man is also frail. St. Paul certainly makes no bones about this fact; he is not afraid to voice his own confusion at being unable to do what he wishes to do, while doing the opposite of what he wants (Rom. 7:14-20). The real point is that every Christian, like St. Paul before him, knows that his strength is from the Lord (Phil. 4:13).

Wisdom is revealed to us for our glorification (1 Cor. 2:6-10)

We would be exaggerating if we claimed that the second reading is fully integrated with the other two. But we can, without straining, find aspects that objectively link this reading to the other two and may therefore help enrich the theme of the law as being fulfilled perfectly in Christ's paschal mystery, and of its consequences for us.

The purpose of the law, reconciliation and union with God, was achieved objectively by Jesus as he accomplished God's way of redemption. But we are able freely to choose or reject God's way. If we do choose it, then no sooner have we bowed to God's will than we find wisdom. It is a wisdom revealed to us by the Spirit, who enables us to understand what God has prepared for those who love him; the Spirit reveals to us what no one has ever seen or heard, what no one has ever been able even to imagine (1 Cor. 2:6-10). As soon as the Christian sets out on the way of the gospel, his eyes are opened; the Spirit urges him on toward evangelical perfection and encourages him to be perfect as our heavenly Father is perfect (Matthew 5:48).

This perfection and wisdom cannot be grasped by the worldly mind, for they are on a different level than the things of this world. The "wisdom" that God gives relates in fact to the entire plan of salvation which God has prepared for us from the beginning of time. This wisdom comes to us through Christ, for by his paschal activity he is its revealer; the wisdom hidden in God through the ages is now revealed in Jesus.

Hidden wisdom is revealed to us by Jesus. This amounts to saying that as St. Paul uses the word, "mystery" does not mean something we cannot understand. On the contrary, the "mystery" is that which was formerly hidden in God but is now revealed to us. In the last analysis, the mystery is Christ himself, and in Christ we see the divine plan that he is carrying out. If we adhere to Christ and the saving plan he reveals, we become, by the power of the Spirit, perfect human beings, and we advance toward the glory whose first fruits we have possessed ever since we were baptized.

Yet this divine wisdom is foolishness to the wise men and the rulers of this world (1 Cor. 2:6). Only those who are mature in faith can draw near to the mystery and enter upon the path of wisdom; only they can become perfect by living according to this wisdom. They obey the law and, paradoxically, they become freer, for they are filled with the wisdom that the Holy Spirit of Jesus has revealed to them.

In the Office of Readings, the second reading is from St. Ephraem. In it he says: "The word of God is a tree of life that provides you with blessed fruit on every branch. It resembles the rock that was opened in the desert and produced a spiritual drink. As the Apostle says, 'All ate the same supernatural food and all drank the same supernatural drink.'"[280] The Book of Proverbs describes the quite different situation of those who refused to follow true wisdom through free obedience: "Because they hated knowledge and did not choose the fear of the Lord, would have none of my counsel, and despised all my reproof, therefore they shall eat the fruit of their way and be sated with their own devices" (Prov. 1:29-31).

SEVENTH SUNDAY

The Love of Others

Love your enemies (Matthew 5:38-48)

"You have heard that it was said. . . . But I say to you. . . ." Twice in today's passage we hear this solemn contrast voiced. In chapter 5 of Matthew's Gospel, it is repeated six times; today's passage contains the final two, both dealing with one's neighbor. And yet the contrast does not mean that Jesus has come to negate the law's purpose; rather, as he himself explicitly says, he has come to fulfill it.

The Code of the (old) covenant says: "If any harm follows [from a fight], then you shall give life for life, eye for eye, tooth for tooth, hand for hand, foot for foot, burn for burn, wound for wound, stripe for stripe" (Exod. 21:24-25). This is the "law of talion" (retaliation), but since there exists no evidence that it was ever actually implemented in the literal sense, we must understand it as the equivalent of the principle of just or legal compensation for injury done — a sanction imposed. What specifically the compensation would consist in, would be determined by a court of law. Jesus' law of love called for complete forgiveness, with no compensation for the injury inflicted.

Later on in this same Gospel of Matthew, Jesus will say that we must forgive seventy times seven times; in so saying, he deliberately juxtaposes his spirit against that of Lamech who said that if Cain was avenged sevenfold, he, Lamech, will be avenged seventy-sevenfold for any injury done him (4:24). In our present passage Christ also bids us turn the other cheek. If someone wants to sue us and take our coat, we should give him our cloak as well; if he forces us to go one mile with him, then go two miles; we should not refuse anyone who wishes to borrow from us.

Then Jesus issues a still more paradoxical order: Love your enemies! That is, we are not only to refrain from vengeance; we are to love the person who injures us! We must even pray for him! Perhaps St. Matthew was thinking of the difficulties the Church found herself in at the time when he was writing. In any case, the theme of persecution is repeated on three different occasions (5:10-11; 10:23; 23:33).

To act as Christ counsels us is to live as a child of the heavenly Father. Anyone who obeys this commandment becomes like God, who makes his sun rise on the just and the unjust alike. The thing that marks the Christian and distinguishes him from tax collector and Gentile is his attitude of forgiveness and love of neighbor.

Those who make this manner of life their own become perfect as the heavenly Father himself is perfect.

Love your neighbor (Lev. 19:1-2, 17-18)

"You shall be holy; for I the Lord your God am holy" (Lev. 19:1). The Gospel bids us be perfect as the heavenly Father is perfect. Yet Israel, too, was already holy, for it had been set apart (which is the basic meaning of "holy").

But Israel had also been always obliged to advance in the holiness bestowed upon her. Thus it is that the command of the Lord in the present text (vv. 17-18) contradicted existing custom: "You shall not hate your brother in your heart. . . . You shall not take vengeance." This does not mean, of course, that we are simply to accept everything others do. We must not hesitate to reprimand a fellowman, so that we may not share in his sin.

The text thus tries to strike a balance: on the one hand, no hesitation in reproaching; on the other, no hatred and no vengeance. We must hate the sin but love the sinner. In this passage from the Book of Leviticus, an attempt is probably being made to establish proper social relations between members of the same clan. Similar counsels given by Jesus are on a quite different level of application and prepare the way for the new law.

When all is said and done, we are to love our neighbor as we love ourselves. The point of this saying is not that we are to cultivate similar emotions, but that we are to acknowledge our neighbor's rights just as we want others to acknowledge ours, to respect others as we want others to respect us. The person who wishes to obey the Lord must be involved with his neighbor and must recognize the bonds that unite him to others.

The responsorial psalm tells us how the Lord acts toward us: "He does not deal with us according to our sins, nor requite us according to our iniquities" (Ps. 103:10). When the Christian pardons, he rises to the level of God himself. Vengeance is beneath a human being; it cannot be an ac-

ceptable attitude in a man of God. If you want to be perfect
as the Lord is perfect, you must love your neighbor. According to the Gospel, you must even love your enemy.

Love of neighbor will always be the distinguishing mark
of the Christian. A Christian is in danger of succumbing to a
more or less deliberately cultivated illusion: he can trust in
outward observances as his way to God, to the point of
forgetting his obligation to love his neighbor. Readings like
those of this Sunday should stir the hearer to a critical
evaluation of his Christian life today. Are there still Christians around who yield to the delusion that they can live a
Christian life without having a real love of others, even of
their enemies?

Boast not of men but of God (1 Cor. 3:16-23)

The seventh and eighth Sundays of Ordinary Time contain the final readings from the First Letter to the Corinthians. There can be no doubt that Paul found the community
at Corinth trying at times; it seems to have been constantly
in a state of high tension and always threatened by divisions. For all its attractiveness, the community seems to
have been rather superficial in its approach to things and to
have had its share of partisans who were more interested in
individual preachers and their ways of teaching than in
promoting unity and orthodox faith.

In their propensities the Corinthians seem to have been
driven by a false notion of what the preaching of the gospel
was all about. Paul is therefore careful to point out that he
is presenting Christ to them without relying on a particular
philosophy. His role is simply to bring men into contact
with Christ, to become all things to all men so that he may
help all to salvation. All who share the work of evangelization are working for the same goal, varied though the gifts
of each may be. All Christians toil in the field that belongs

to God; all share in the erection of a building that belongs to God, not to them.

In this semifinal reading from First Corinthians in Cycle A, Paul speaks of building the temple of God. The Christian community is precisely a temple of God. The community is not just any group; Paul has compared it to a body and to a building, and now he sees it as a holy temple, God's temple. What we have here is not really an image but the reality that expresses what the community really is. Christ, risen from the dead, is a temple that far transcends all temples built with hands, and Christians form the Body of that risen Christ. Woe to those who profane this temple! That, however, is what men do when they prefer the wisdom of this world, the reasonings that are simply wind.

St. Paul returns in this passage to his main concern: Christians must not find their pride in famous men. He then repeats also the theme of liberty, which has found expression on other Sundays. The Christian already lives and works in a temple that will last forever; he must rise above what is secondary, for he belongs to Christ, and Christ belongs to God. His words are an invitation to us all to discern in the community a dynamic presence that is greater than all else there and that requires us to rise in faith above worldly wisdom so that we may live as free men and women in Christ and in God our Father.

EIGHTH SUNDAY

Seek First the Kingdom

The duty of improvidence (Matthew 6:24-34)

A book written back in the thirties bore the intriguing title "The Duty of Improvidence."[281] The title captures the theme of today's passage from the Gospel. The Gospel is not telling the Christian to be neglectful of, or indifferent to, success in business or the security of his family. It is making a quite different point and inculcating a quite different attitude.

This different attitude may, however, involve such confidence in God that in certain situations we may abandon our habitual human prudence. Pope St. Gregory the Great, in his *Dialogues*, tells the story of a cellarer in St. Benedict's monastery who refused to give a poor man the only bit of oil left for the community's needs. St. Benedict was filled with a holy anger at the refusal, took the flask of oil, and threw it out the window. Then, however, all the receptacles for oil in the monastery were found to be filled to overflowing!

Whether or not the story is true, its aim is to teach a certain kind of improvidence. It is emphasizing, like the gospel itself, the one thing necessary, namely, to give absolute priority to the service of God, whether directly in himself or indirectly through the neighbor. The evangelical ideal of St. Francis of Assisi, which is shared by many groups today, even outside the religious Orders, is the pursuit of detachment so as to be totally at the service of God and his kingdom.

Rarely does a passage of the gospel address itself so clearly and, we might almost say, "brutally" to the contemporary world and the contemporary Christian. Do not serve two masters, for you will only end in a compromise that will not fool God! God's jealousy is a favorite theme in the Old Testament. At the time of the Exodus, it is applied to the Lord, who speaks of himself to Moses as "a jealous God" (Exod. 20:5). The same point is made in the Decalogue: "You shall worship no other God, for the Lord, whose name is Jealous, is a jealous God" (34:14). The Book of Deuteronomy applies the same adjective three times to God (Deut. 4:24; 5:9; 6:15). The proverb that Jesus cites in today's Gospel — no one can serve two masters — is related to the same theme of God's jealousy, especially when it comes to worshiping other gods. Deuteronomy, for example, shows the people rousing God's jealousy by adoring alien gods (32:16).

In the Gospel, the opposition is put in down-to-earth terms, with money (mammon) being treated as a god that is opposed to the true God. In the last analysis, however, the opposition is between what is definitive and eternal and what is weak, transient, of passing value, and perishable. The Christian is warned that there is an utter incompatibility between anxious worry about the morrow and the quest for the kingdom. It is on this kingdom that Jesus insists in the second part of today's passage.

Once again he speaks of the detachment that must be the mark of the Christian. His words remind us of the beatitudes, and especially of the happiness promised to the poor. A man has to be truly free if he is to enter the kingdom; that is why it is easier for a camel to pass through the eye of a needle than for a rich man to enter the kingdom (Matthew 19:23). The Scripture returns frequently to the subject of wealth and the rich — and justly so, for wealth is a real problem in this world, whether past or present.

The Bible stresses the uselessness of wealth as far as man's attainment of his ultimate end is concerned. The expressions it uses with regard to the rich are quite strong: "He swallows down riches and vomits them up again" (Job 20:15); "Man cannot abide in his pomp, he is like the beasts that perish" (Ps. 49:12); "The ransom of a man's life is his wealth" (Prov. 13:8); "Neither their silver nor their gold shall be able to deliver them on the day of the wrath of the Lord" (Zeph. 1:18).

But in contrast to this wealth that is useless for salvation, or even harmful, since it prevents man from hearing God's word (Mark 4:18-19; Luke 8:14), there is a genuine wealth: "The Lord is his inheritance" (Deut. 10:9); "You will have treasure in heaven" (Mark 10:21); the role of the apostle is to tell the pagans of "the unsearchable riches of Christ" (Eph. 3:8).

The kind of detachment needed cannot be reached without a deep faith in a provident God and a clear understanding of our own destiny. When St. Paul tells the Philippians, "The Lord is at hand. Have no anxiety about anything" (Phil. 4:5-6), he is making his appeal to a lively faith in Christ and in the coming kingdom. We must set aside all anxiety about temporal things so that we may believe in providence and spend our energies seeking the kingdom.

The second reading in the Office of Readings for this eighth Sunday is from St. Gregory the Great's commentary on the Book of Job:

> Anyone who yearns for the everlasting fatherland undoubtedly lives a simple and upright life — simple in works, upright in faith; simple in the good he accomplishes on earth, upright by reason of the supreme realities he knows in his heart. Some people are not simple in the good they do, because they do not seek their reward within themselves but look for the favor of others. As a wise man has well said, "Woe to the sinner who walks the earth on two paths." A sinner walks the earth on two paths when what he shows in his conduct belongs to God, but what he seeks in his heart belongs to this world.[282]

God does not forget us (Is. 49:14-15)

Isaiah here uses a powerful image to bring out God's continual concern for us: "Can a woman forget her sucking child, that she should have no compassion on the son of her womb? Even these may forget, yet I will not forget you." We do not have room here even to list all the passages in which Scripture speaks of God as a Father. The New Testament will emphasize this theme even more than the Old by developing the idea of our adoption.

Psalm 62, from which the responsorial psalm is drawn, sings of our self-surrender to the Lord, who is our only refuge: "Trust in him at all times, O people; pour out your heart before him; God is a refuge for us" (Ps. 62:8).

As we celebrate the Eucharist, we cannot but think of to-day's Gospel, in which the Lord tells us not to worry about material food. He will feed us, as he did at the multiplication of the loaves, but the food he gives is his own body and blood. We know that whoever eats his flesh and drinks his blood abides in God and God in him (John 6:56).

The preceding reflections may well appear to be nothing but pious babbling to many Christians of our day. And they would be right if we failed to make, not a compromise, but a realistic synthesis of the demands of the gospel and the demands of everyday life. What, then, can and should "the duty of improvidence" mean to a Christian of our day?

The improvidence of which the gospel speaks certainly does not mean a lack of concern for the advancement of the world and for the welfare of society. Quite the contrary, for it is precisely in this context that Jesus' words take on their real meaning. When God, beginning in the Book of Genesis, made men his collaborators in the work of creation ("Increase and multiply . . ." — Gen. 1:28), he evidently intended that they should be very much concerned with the world. The Christian, therefore, cannot excuse himself from an active concern for progress, be it of the technical order or, above all, of the social order. A person would have utterly failed to understand today's Gospel if he were to be unconcerned about technical and social advancement on the pretext that Jesus bids us seek the kingdom and be unconcerned about the passing things of time.

The Christian is serving God, not mammon, when he cooperates with efforts to secure progress and when he dedicates his human potentialities to the service of all — that is, to the service of his own family first of all, but as part of the larger world, not reserving his talents and efforts exclusively to the advantage of his immediate family but being open to the needs of all mankind. When the Christian who is working for technical, social, and political progress does not seek personal honor and wealth or the exaltation and increased prestige of his group, but looks above all for the kind of human advancement God wants, then he is perfectly in accord with the divine will. He is not a divided man.

Such a Christian outlook is admittedly difficult; it requires constant self-examination. A choice of this kind, which is required of every Christian, supposes true humility of soul and an unremitting readiness to abandon ways that may seem normal to other men but are in fact unconscious deviations from the Christian view of human activity. Here we see the importance of a true Christian community to which each individual can submit his problems and receive a Christian evaluation of them that is not inspired by passion or politics but is reached in the light of the kingdom, the ultimate point of reference in Christianity.

God will disclose the purposes of the heart (1 Cor. 4:1-5)

Once again Paul must issue a warning to the community at Corinth, which is so prone to divisions. He has already reproached them for being overly attached to the manner displayed by one or other preacher, that is, for not looking beyond the man and the manner to the message. They are also too attached to a philosophy and tend to be proud of their attachment.

St. Paul now tells his readers what an apostle should be: a servant of Christ and a steward of the mysteries of God. These titles say everything, and there is no point in looking for some further characteristic that will mark out the apostle. The only judgment we have a right to pass on him concerns his fidelity to his mission. Everything else is secondary, and he is not to be judged thereby.

Paul feels himself responsible before God for the way he acts. He does not, however, wholly trust his own conscience in this matter but looks to the judgment of God. He asks the Corinthians to do the same: to reserve their judgment and wait for the Lord to reveal what is in men, for he alone knows the secrets of the human heart. He alone will manifest men's hidden intentions, and it is certainly he who will give each man the praise he deserves.

The lesson is clear and is taught without any effort to be diplomatic. It is also an important lesson, one that still holds for us today. It is a serious matter to pass judgment on the Church, especially if we focus our attention on what is really peripheral. God alone knows men's real intentions, and we must leave justice to him.

CYCLE B

pages 370-403

for years 1979, 1982, 1985, 1988, 1991

SECOND SUNDAY IN ORDINARY TIME

The Call of God

Come and see (John 1:35-42)

I think it important to emphasize the fact that Christ chooses his future disciples in the milieu in which they live and in the social and professional situation proper to them. Those called to follow Jesus are human beings like other peoples, living in a certain context and devoting themselves to their trade or profession. This, however, does not prevent them from attending to the essential thing: the meaning of their own lives and the meaning of their people as a whole.

The men in question have attached themselves to John the Baptist as other Jews might to one or other rabbi. But now Jesus passes by, and a radical change is underway in the lives of the two disciples who happen to be accompanying John at the moment. John is entirely without egotism in his doctrine and spirituality; he has been forming disciples, not for his own benefit or according to his own desires, but for the sake of Jesus and the renewal of the world. Consequently, he points Jesus out to his disciples, and he does so in terms that leave no doubt in the minds of hearers who were well acquainted with the Scriptures: "Behold, the Lamb of God!" (John 1:36). In other words, here is the man Isaiah spoke of (ch. 53).

We must not forget that John the Evangelist reflects the thinking of the early Church. For the Christians of that time, John the Baptist was the supreme witness to the fulfillment of the Old Testament promises. He was the link between the Old Testament period and the new age inaugurated by Christ, and he brought his own disciples to Jesus because that new age was now beginning. The first two disciples did not miss the meaning of John's words and of Jesus' person. Andrew says to his brother Simon: "We have found the Messiah" (v. 41), and brings his brother to meet Jesus; a new disciple himself, he immediately goes and gets another to join him! Jesus then looks at Simon and says: "So you are Simon the son of John? You shall be called Cephas" (v. 42).

It would take too long, and not be very profitable, to analyze in detail all the words of the passage. It is important, however, to emphasize, as we have done on other occasions, the care with which St. John uses words.

Take, for example, the question Jesus puts when he sees the two disciples following him: "What do you seek?" (v. 38). John puts the same question on Jesus' lips on two other occasions. One is the moment in the Garden of Olives when the soldiers come to arrest Jesus, and he asks them: "Whom do you seek?" (18:4). The other is when Mary Magdalene at the tomb of Christ hears a man who looks like the gardener ask her: "Whom do you seek?" (20:15). These questions are in fact a manifestation of Jesus' knowledge of what is in men's hearts. He knows the answer before it is given, but he chooses to have men make it explicit.

Or take the question of the future disciples: "Where are you staying?" (1:38). They are not simply asking for the address of the man whose teaching they intend to follow. For St. John, the word "stay, dwell, abide" (Greek *menein*) has a more profound meaning, as we can see from several passages of his Gospel: "He who eats my flesh and drinks my blood abides in me, and I in him" (6:56); "Neither can you [bear fruit], unless you abide in me" (15:4); "He who abides in me, and I in him . . ." (15:5; cf. vv. 7,9). We should recall especially the Prologue: "The Word became flesh and dwelt among us" (1:14).

All this is an invitation to us to go beyond the simple material meaning of the words and discover the doctrinal themes at work. When Jesus bids the would-be disciples to "come and see" (1:39), we must remember that "seeing" for St. John is the starting point of faith and a new attitude. "Many believed in his name when they saw the signs which he did" (2:23); "What sign do you do, that we may see, and believe you?" (6:30); "This is the will of my Father, that every one who sees the Son and believes in him should have eternal life" (6:40); "Many of the Jews, therefore, who . . . had seen what he did, believed in him" (11:45); "If you had known me, you would have known my Father also; henceforth you know him and have seen him" (14:7); "Then the other disciple, who reached the tomb first, also went in, and he saw and believed" (20:8).

We too are meant to cultivate these attitudes: seeking, coming, seeing, believing. We have been called by Christ; we must become the children of God.

Hear the call and obey (1 Sam. 3:3b-10, 19)

The Old Testament gives a moving example of God's call in the story of the boy Samuel. There are many such calls reported throughout the Old Testament, calls to enter into the service of the people as a whole. These calls are always imperious, yet they leave the human being free to answer or not answer; that is why the Lord can complain, "when I called, you did not answer, when I spoke, you did not listen" (Is. 65:12).

Before he answers, however, a man must be sure it is indeed the Lord calling; this is part of the story of Samuel. Even though he live in the sanctuary itself, a man is not certain that it is God he hears, and so he is mistrustful; or he cannot believe that God really wants to enter into intimate dialogue with someone like himself. God's call often means suffering for the person chosen. The Servant (Is.

41:8; 43:10) shows the world what it means to hear God's call and to answer it without reserve.

The responsory psalm, Psalm 40 (same as in Cycle A), shows the kind of response God wants: "Then I said, 'Lo, I come . . . I delight to do thy will, O my God." "I waited patiently for the Lord; he inclined to me and heard my cry. . . . He put a new song in my mouth, a song of praise to our God."

Our bodies are the members of Christ (1 Cor. 6:13c-15a, 17-20)

This is an important passage. It shows us that Paul is unaware of any "taboo" in regard to the body; he sees only the body's dignity, and it is this that serves him as a basis for prescribing the conduct that Christians should observe. "Dignity," however, is here not primarily a moralist's term; for Paul, it springs from an ontology. Concretely, the dignity of the body is due to the fact that every Christian is incorporated into Christ, so that his very body is a member of Christ himself.

Paul is certainly not obsessed by fear of impurity, but impurity does seem to him to be especially opposed to membership in Christ and to the fact that we have become temples of the Holy Spirit. Nor, despite Paul's words about every sin but fornication being outside the body, do I think he concentrates too much on sins of impurity. (Did Paul have no knowledge of drug use? Was drunkenness rare in his day?) The point is rather that Paul is vividly aware of man's destiny; he knows that we do not belong to ourselves, that our bodies are for the Lord, and that our true life is in eternity. For these reasons, we must preserve the integrity of our bodies. We do not belong to ourselves, because our calling has made us temples of the Spirit, and our baptism has incorporated us into Christ.

Paul is deeply impressed by the unity that exists between the Christian and Christ, and by the unity that should exist among Christians themselves. To bring out this unity, he does not hesitate to use the example of a prostitute and her client (vv. 15-16): If a man joined with a prostitute becomes one flesh with her, much more does he become one with Christ, where the unity is spiritual. Through union with Christ, man is divinized and becomes a temple of the Spirit. We have been bought at a great price and must therefore glorify God in our bodies.

We might well ask whether an education based on this text, properly explained, would not be more successful than hours of "sex education" and depth psychology. Paul here presents us with a true analysis of what we are; we ought to reflect deeply on it.

THIRD SUNDAY

Be Converted and Believe

Repent and believe in the gospel (Mark 1:14-20)

In St. Mark, the Good News, or gospel, is the person of Jesus himself, to whom men must cleave through faith. When a human being comes face to face with the gospel that is Jesus himself, two things are required of him: he must repent and he must follow Christ in an act of faith.

Repentance and conversion are two words for the same reality. The most important thing in repentance is conversion of the heart. The prophets of the Old Testament had been chiefly concerned with this interior conversion. Hosea, for example, acknowledges a conversion as fruitful only when it is a profound, love-inspired conversion of the heart (6:1-6). Isaiah, for his part, emphasizes the uselessness of outward worship, or cultus, if it does not express an interior conversion (1:11-15). Sins that are as scarlet can become white as snow, but only if men walk in God's ways (1:16-20).

Following Isaiah, all the other prophets are unwearying in their stress on interior conversion. Jeremiah has perhaps the most striking formulas for bringing out the need of such conversion; a man must, for example, plow fallow ground and circumcise his heart (4:1-4). Ezekiel has more to say than the other prophets about the cultic regulations connected with repentance, but he is no less emphatic than they about conversion being a condition for true life (Ezek. 18:31). The Israelites are stubborn and a "rebellious house" (2:4-7), but the Lord will put his Spirit upon them so that they will repent of their ways (36:26-31).

Jesus too, when he calls for repentance, emphasizes the interior conditions of a true conversion. In fact, the evangelists offer us very rich perspectives on repentance as preached by Jesus. A man must obey the commandments and seek the kingdom of God and his righteousness (Matthew 6:33); he must make an energetic effort to change his ways. Above all, however, the act of conversion comprises humility and a confident turning to God amid the consciousness of man's own weakness (Luke 8:13). The Lord always retains the initiative in a conversion, as is made clear by the attitude of the father as he awaits the return of his erring son: the father sees him coming and welcomes him with great forgiveness (Luke 15:11-32). So, too, the real shepherd goes in search of his lost sheep (Luke 15:4).

Conversion is followed by adherence to Christ through faith. Conversion and faith are closely related attitudes. Thus, in the Acts of the Apostles we see conversion being followed by baptism (2:38). Conversion is required for baptism, but this is in part because a true conversion already involves an adherence to Christ (3:19), although the fullness of such adherence comes in baptism itself as a gift of the Spirit.

In today's Gospel, St. Mark gives a brief picture of the

apostle who is called by Christ, but he also gives a picture of persons who are called. First, the apostles. A first point that must be emphasized is that in their call Jesus takes and retains the initiative; it is he who approaches these men and calls them.

In the Old Testament, when God calls he does so in order to send someone to carry out a mission. God's choice is entirely his and cannot be justified by merely human considerations. Examples abound; all follow the same pattern: the person chosen is not chosen for his own sake but for the sake of a mission. This is true of Abraham (Gen. 12:1); it is true of Moses (Exod. 3:1-12); it is true of prophets like Amos (Amos 7:15), Isaiah (Is. 6:9), Jeremiah (Jer. 1:7), and Ezekiel (Ezek. 3:1-11).

Mark also calls attention to the attitude of those who answer Christ's call: they agree unhesitatingly to change their whole way of life. They set out on a new road by an act that is a brutal, almost unthinkable rupture with their past.

"Follow Jesus" is an expression frequently found in the New Testament; it occurs over thirty times, being used chiefly by St. Matthew. If we look at the words as they apply strictly to those who were being called to be Jesus' disciples, we may note the following passages: "'Follow me, and I will make you fishers of men.' Immediately they left their nets and followed him" (Matthew 4:19-20; cf. Mark 1:18; Luke 5:11); "Immediately they left their boat and their father, and followed him" (Matthew 4:22); "Follow me, and leave the dead to bury their own dead" (Matthew 8:22); "Follow me," says Jesus to Matthew (Matthew 9:9; cf. Mark 2:14; Luke 5:27-28); "He who does not take his cross and follow me is not worthy of me" (Matthew 10:38; cf. Mark 8:34; Luke 14:27; John 12:26; the same expressions occur again later on: Matthew 16:24; cf. Luke 9:23); "If you would be perfect, go, sell . . . and come, follow me" (Matthew 19:21; cf. Mark 10:21; Luke 10:28; 12:33; 18:22).

Those whom Jesus thus calls he intends to make "fishers

of men." In other words, their vocation will be to go and call others in turn.

The gospel also applies to the ordinary person who is called. We should bear in mind that St. Mark is writing his Gospel at a time when the Church is already established, although it is admittedly still in its beginnings and the evangelist is undoubtedly thinking primarily of those with the special calling to be apostles with Christ. Yet he is also thinking of his fellow Christians. That is to say, the calling of the apostles has become applicable to every man who wishes to enter the Church and live Christ's life therein. A man must leave his pagan or Jewish milieu if he is to enter the Church. More specifically, the Jew must leave the Jewish community and cast his lot with those who had been pagans.

Underlying the proclamation of this account in today's liturgy there is a realistic view of a close continuity between the call of the disciples and life of the Church today. Each of us has received and is constantly receiving a call to repent and follow Christ.

Turn from your evil ways (Jonah 3:1-5, 10)

Nineveh repented, and the instrument of its conversion was Jonah, a Jew sent by God to the pagans of that great city. But the prophet went despite himself; he was afraid of the pagan city and initially ran off in the opposite direction. But the Lord had his way, and almost incredible adventures led Jonah against his will to the place where he was supposed to preach conversion. Jonah succeeded where the prophets before him had failed. Indeed, the conversion of Nineveh was almost instantaneous: "And the people of Nineveh believed God"; their conversion was manifested by signs of mourning and especially by the fact that they "turned from their evil ways." As a result, God did not inflict the punishment he had threatened.

This passage, when taken together with the Gospel, teaches two lessons. the lesson of obedience to a mission and the lesson of conversion. The two lessons add up to a program that every disciple of Jesus must make his own in a spirit of trust in the Lord and his strength.

The responsorial psalm is taken from Psalm 25 and asks God to make his ways known to us and to lead us in the truth. To this petition for guidance from God is added praise for the God who saves us: "Good and upright is the Lord; therefore he instructs sinners in the way" (v. 8).

Live as free men (1 Cor. 7:29-31)

The second reading for today is an exception in that it happens to fit in with the other two readings. It teaches that we who are called to leave all and follow Christ must lead lives of complete freedom from all things. The basic reason for following Christ in this unconditional way is that time is limited. That is why we must leave everything: boat, nets, parents; why those who are married must live as though they were not married; why those who mourn must act as though they had no cause to mourn; why those who rejoice must live as though they had no cause to rejoice; why those who buy must act as if they owned nothing; why those who deal with the world must act as though they had no dealings with it. The Christian has no time to dally along the way as he goes about his mission; he must be ever intent on following Christ, because the world as we know it is passing away.

We must not think that St. Paul is showing contempt for marriage, which elsewhere he speaks of as a great mystery (Eph. 5:23-33; 1 Cor. 7:2-5). He is not saying the Christian has no right to feelings or that he is to be indifferent to suffering and joy. He is not arguing against private property nor teaching contempt of the world. Such interpretations would mistake the thrust of his teaching.

The point St. Paul is making is that, given the presence of the kingdom and the short time a man has to live, the Christian must make a pragmatic value judgment and live in complete detachment. We must love the values inherent in this world, we must love creation, we must work for the advancement of the world, but we must do so with detachment, standing back from all these things. This is the characteristic attitude of the saints, whose lives are sometimes distorted in the telling because we attribute to them a contempt for the world, when in fact they are simply judging the temporal and transient in the light of Christ who is eternal.

FOURTH SUNDAY

The Teaching of God

Teach in the name of the eternal God (Mark 1:21-28)

We should not let our attention be too much taken up with the evil spirit that Jesus casts out in today's Gospel. In the light of the first reading, greater interest is to be accorded to Jesus' teaching. This is not to deny, of course, that the kind of exorcism Jesus practices is connected with his teaching and gives it extraordinary authority. The evangelist notes the connection but also brings out the fact that it is secondary to the teaching proper. For, in fact, the crowd is not struck chiefly by the exorcism and violent dispelling of the demon; the words of the crowd as recorded by Mark concern rather the teaching: "Here is a teaching that is new and with authority behind it: he gives orders even to unclean spirits and they obey him" (v. 27 JB).

Both word and action highlight the authority — that is the point St. Mark wants to make. Jesus is manifesting himself as Messiah, and his teaching differs from that of others not only by its content but by the fact that it is linked to an effective power from on high. His teaching thus manifests his person and the fact that he has been sent from God.

St. Mark notes, at the beginning of the pericope, that
Jesus' teaching impressed his hearers because he spoke
with authority and not like the scribes. The account of the
exorcism conveys something to us of the same impression.
Jesus is not satisfied with words, nor does he give his hearers a catechesis that he could have learned in a rabbinic
school, where the concern was to explain the law. On the
contrary, his teaching is new in the sense that it seems to
come directly from God and is confirmed by acts of power,
such as the exorcism. In another context John writes: "The
words that I have spoken to you are spirit and life" (6:63);
these words provide one of the Alleluia verses for the Sundays of Ordinary Time.

Jesus has accustomed us to powerful words that find further expression in action; this pattern of word-and-action
has carried over from the Gospel into the sacraments of the
Church. In the latter case, the combination is one that Pope
St. Leo the Great often speaks of in his sermons as "sacred
sign and example" (*sacramentum et exemplum*), that is, an
efficacious sign and at the same time an example that conveys a lesson or a teaching to us. The words provide a succinct description of the whole life of Jesus as well as of the
Church's sacraments.

The authority of Jesus is acknowledged by the evil spirit,
who cries out: "I know who you are, the Holy One of God"
(v. 24). Thus it is that both the teaching and the actions of
Christ show him to be the Messiah, and his reputation
spreads throughout Galilee.

Word and sacrament — this phrase sums up, now and
until the end of time, the Church's activity to which she is
commissioned by Christ and the Father. The two together
represent the new teaching that astonished the crowd, according to Mark's account, and led men to faith throughout
Galilee. The two also represent the teaching of the Church,
whereby, under the guidance of the Spirit of Christ, she
carries on the teaching of him who was sent by the Father.
We are too accustomed to this kind of teaching and are less
sensitive than the crowds in Galilee were to this entirely

new manner of communicating God's word; it is teaching that has little in common with ordinary teaching, which is notional and conceptual in character.

The Church must indeed endeavor to prove the validity of her teaching and must engage in scholarly study of the truth and the message she is commissioned to transmit. She may not however be satisfied with mere study; her teaching must be primarily an action, a transmission from God of a power that renews the earth. That is what a sacrament is, and that is what the word of the Church has always been meant to be.

I will put my words in his mouth (Deut. 18:15-20)

Moses offers himself as the model by which the Israelites will be able to identify the prophet who is to come and whom God will raise up for us. Moses reminds the people that at Horeb they had bidden him ask the Lord to appoint someone to serve as intermediary between them and the Lord, and that the Lord had promised a prophet. Moses himself had served as the first intermediary, the first in the line of prophets, who are men chosen from among their brethren. God, not the people, does the choosing of each and every prophet, and his way of choosing often proves disconcerting. He guides his people and chooses those who are to be sent in his name.

What is to be the role of the chosen prophet? "I will put my words in his mouth, and he shall speak . . . all that I command him" (Deut. 18:18). This means that God looks upon the prophet as another self. Men must therefore heed his words; not to listen to him is to refuse God, and God will demand an accounting of this refusal. The prophet must speak exactly what is entrusted to him; otherwise he will betray his mission.

Who is the future prophet who is like Moses? We know that in Jesus' time such a prophet was expected, for John the Baptist sends his disciples to ask Jesus whether he, Jesus, is the awaited prophet (John 1:21). It becomes clear,

when Jesus asks his disciples who men think he is, that
people were expecting a new Elias or a new Jeremias (Matthew 16:14; for Elias, see also Matthew 11:14); in short, a
prophet was indeed expected to come soon.

Jesus, for his part, acts like a prophet, that is, a man who
speaks in behalf of God: "But I tell you. . . ." St. Luke reports Jesus as saying: "Whoever receives me receives him
who sent me" (9:48; cf. Matthew 18:3; Mark 9:37; John
13:20). In the Fourth Gospel, Jesus frequently refers to the
One who sent him: "He whom God has sent utters the
words of God" (3:34); Jesus has come to do the will of him
who sent him (4:34); in all things he seeks the will of him
who sent him (5:30); his teaching is not his own, but his
who sent him (7:16). Evidently, then, he is presenting himself as the long-expected mediator. If he speaks as he does,
it is in order that men may believe that the Father has sent
him (11:42). Eternal life consists in believing in the one
who has been sent (17:3), for in the last analysis he who
sends and he who is sent are one.

Jesus clearly thinks of himself as doing what is expected
of the great prophet whom God had promised to raise up
from among his brethren. Consequently, the reading from
Deuteronomy does much to bring home the full significance
of the Gospel pericope from St. Mark.

Today the Church carries on the prophetic function of
Christ. The Lord puts his words in her mouth, and she
teaches in the name of the Lord. The whole revelation has
been given, and the task of the Church in her teaching is to
make it known by explaining it and, under the guidance of
the Spirit, drawing further conclusions from what Christ
and the Father have revealed to us in the Scriptures. For us
Catholics, the Church is the only one who can interpret the
Scriptures with absolute authority; it is in and through her
that the Scriptures manifest to us their authentic meaning.

To say this is in no way to play down the charisms that
existed in the past and that, according to the Church herself, still exist today.[283] But the prophetic role connected
with the charisms is today, as in St. Paul's time, subordinate

to revelation and to the Church. The Church is guided in her development and adaptation by the Spirit of Christ, but she is also helped by the charisms. The latter have only too often been viewed with distrust; today we are more open to them, although the concrete manifestations of them must still be examined to determine whether they are truly from God.

The responsorial psalm is from Psalm 95. The response is from verses 7-8, "O that today you would hearken to his voice! Harden not your hearts."

The unmarried woman and the concerns of the Lord (1 Cor. 7:32-35)

As read here apart from their context, St. Paul's statements regarding the dedication of one's life to the Lord may appear one-sided and insufficiently mindful of the sacrament of marriage, concerning which he himself elsewhere writes, "This is a great mystery" (Eph. 5:32). However, it is easy enough to put today's pericope back into its context and to read it as it should be read.

St. Paul is addressing the community of Corinth, with which previous readings have already familiarized us. We know how rich this community was in persons and gifts; we also know that it had its troubles, inasmuch as its responses were not always those that its gifts should have elicited. In a new Christian community of this kind, the sexual problem was bound to make itself felt. St. Paul does not, however, spend a lot of time discussing serious situations in which his only response can be to condemn, situations involving incest and fornication (5:1-5; 6:12-19).

Whenever a Church that is enthusiastic about its faith and its Christian life finds licentiousness being practiced by some of its members, there is always the likelihood of a reaction to the other extreme. So it was at Corinth. Paul has received a letter telling him that a group within the community has chosen the unqualified position that there must be abstention from marriage: "It is well for a man not to touch a woman" (7:1). In response, St. Paul makes some needed distinctions and takes up the various possible states: married people, widowed individuals, celibates, etc.

St. Paul makes it clear that his own preference is for what we today would call the "consecrated life." Does this preference betray a certain scorn for marriage or a negative vision of a state of life that he seems to consider only as a means of retaining one's moral balance: "It is better to marry than to be aflame with passion" (7:9)? Quite the contrary. We receive the impression that Paul regards the way God set down in the Book of Genesis as being the natural and normal way of life for mankind; he even emphasizes the practice of intercourse for husbands and wives (7:5).

It does seem to me, however, that if we limit ourselves to the Letter to the Corinthians, we will not easily grasp the very positive view Paul has of marriage. To this end, we must also read the Letter to the Ephesians (5:21-33), where we find Paul expressing his admiration for the sacrament of marriage. He sees marriage as symbolized in the union of Christ with his Church and gives the spouses a primordial role in the building and extension of the kingdom.

In today's reading, Paul's emphasis is more on the eschatological dimension of Christian life. He would like to see Christians truly free, not for selfish fulfillment, but for the sake of a more direct and constant union with God and for the service of others. This kind of freedom from all things gives the person who dedicates himself to God the ability to go wherever the Lord calls him.

The First Letter to the Corinthians, when taken together with the Letter to the Ephesians, gives us the basic Christian teaching on marriage and virginity. Virginity is seen as a gift in which a person renounces the way God has providentially set down for mankind in general. It is a response to a divine choice and a step forward into what is humanly unknown, but a step taken in the conviction that the Lord is ever present and will guide his disciple.

The problem, in a sense, is only with the starting point: Does this person really have the charism of virginity? There are signs that argue against it. Paul, for his part, knows of no commandment from the Lord in this matter, and he has no desire to trap anyone. Humility, prayer, love, and devotion to neighbor will bring the light needed to discover God's choice.

FIFTH SUNDAY

Overcoming the Forces of Evil

He healed the sick (Mark 1:29-39)

Today's Gospel acquaints us with two facts. The first is that the Good News is gradually spreading and that healings symbolize the radical newness that the Good News represents, for it is the good news of spiritual healing, resurrection, and new life. The other fact is that the crowds do not look beyond the material sign to its real meaning. (This is, unfortunately, always the case, and yet, while the Church should not be preaching to empty bellies [St. Augustine's phrase], her primary aim must be spiritual healing, not raising the standard of living.) This situation, and the conflict it embodies, runs through the whole of Jesus' public life.

In this passage of Mark's Gospel we find Jesus healing the sick and, in particular, driving out demons. What is the significance of the healing of Peter's mother-in-law? Mark uses a word that may provide a clue when we compare this passage with the Letter of St. James, where the same word occurs. We are told that Jesus "lifted her up" ("helped her up": NAB and JB) and the fever left her. The Greek word represented by "lift up" is *egeiro*. Now St. James, in speaking of the sacrament of the sick, uses the same word: "The prayer of faith will save the sick man, and the Lord will *raise* him *up*" (James 5:15). The Greek verb *egeiro*, in its active form, has a number of meanings: wake, rouse; raise, help to rise; relieve; restore to life. In our view, we should not try to limit the word to a single meaning but should utilize the various meanings. The mother-in-law of Simon Peter gets up and begins to serve the guests. This is very much like what we find in the sacrament of the sick, where the person is healed so that he can take his place once again in the Christian assembly.

Jesus heals; his coming is a sign of life, and life in turn is a sign that the kingdom is present. The Good News is the news of life, and we must not make that life either exclusively spiritual or exclusively physical. That is the kind of mistake the crowds make when they see only the material side of Christ's gifts to them. When that happens, the Lord leaves them; he withdraws from them.

In this passage of Mark, Jesus moves on to another place, and we sense a certain disillusionment about his going. The crowd seeks him out only because it wants physical healings, but Jesus must concentrate rather on preaching the Good News: "That is why I came" (v. 38). In the parallel passage Luke has "I was sent for this purpose" (4:43), thus specifying "came" as "was sent," that is, by the Father. Mark seems satisfied simply to emphasize the fact that Jesus' primary purpose is to preach the Good News, not to perform physical cures.

The "messianic secret" plays a part in the passage, as elsewhere. This is a favorite theme of St. Mark. The demons, of course, recognize Jesus for who he is (v. 34), as the possessed man in the synagogue had (1:24). Jesus does not wish, however, to be acknowledged solely because of physical healings; these are but signs that should lead to faith, and faith must go further. Therefore he imposes silence.

Men must discover only gradually who he is, and they must not be motivated chiefly by their own material interests. The healings he performs are meant to prod men into asking who Jesus really is. If they once recognize him to be the Messiah, they must then go a step further and accept him as the Messiah who must die and rise from the dead for the salvation of the world, and whom they themselves must follow in death and resurrection.

Suffering man (Job 7:1-4, 6-7)

This passage from the Book of Job raises in a brutally direct way the problem of human existence and suffering. People often have a one-sided impression of the Book of Job, as though it preached a passive submission to the will of God. As this passage shows us, however, the book is about a normal man with violent reactions to suffering. He is a man who rebels angrily against the injustice of his lot and complains bitterly about his human state. He has known months of emptiness, and his nights are times of misery. And ahead lies death, after a life that passes as swiftly as a weaver's shuttle moves. But though he cannot solve the problem raised by his physical and spiritual suffering, Job has not despaired. He knows that he can encounter God and that God is mindful of him.

Job doubtless had no conception of an afterlife, and he ends this chapter with the statement: "Now I shall lie in the earth; thou wilt seek me, but I shall not be" (viz., living on earth; 7:21). And yet he knows that God is mindful of him. God is mindful indeed. Eventually he sends his Son to proclaim the good news of life and to bring men, not necessarily a cure of present ills, but a life that will last for ever.

The real solution to the problem of suffering is not to be found in a philosophy of simple resignation but in the absolute certainty that any and all suffering is part of building a new world with Christ, who himself died but then rose from the dead. Sin, as a consequence, has been forgiven, and there is the prospect of a new life whose full energies are hidden from us as yet and whose joys we can only try to imagine.

The duty of proclaiming the gospel (1 Cor. 9:16-19, 22-23)

Paul depicts himself as all the prophets had before him: as a man who cannot renounce preaching the word. He cannot renounce it, not only because God has chosen him but also because of what his mission means to other people. To preach the gospel is to be the servant of all, so as to win over to Christ as many as possible. It is to be all things to all men for the sake of saving some. That is the purpose of preaching; in the last analysis it is meant to bring men into contact with God and his salvation.

Preaching is thus not primarily a matter of teaching doctrine or teaching any thing at all; it is a matter of touching a person in such a way that he enters into close contact with the Lord who speaks the word through his apostle. In order to carry out his mission, Paul is determined to be utterly free and at the service of all. He renounces his right to a salary, he eagerly lives with others and shares their way of life. He is not the kind of teacher who remains apart from and above those he instructs. He teaches a way of life, and this kind of teaching is communicated only through example, through becoming all things to all men.

SIXTH SUNDAY

We Are Lepers

If you will, you can make me clean (Mark 1:40-45)

Today's Gospel could well be the subject of a lengthy commentary, since it raises a number of problems. But to go into such problems in connection with the Sixth Sunday of Ordinary Time would be to lose sight of the real meaning the passage has within the liturgical celebration. For this reason, we shall make a few brief remarks, by way of a digression, in order to satisfy those who are intrigued by certain statements. These remarks, however, are not the main concern; we shall quickly leave them behind and concentrate on the essential point of today's message.

The same story is found in the other Synoptic Gospels (Matthew 8:2-4; Luke 5:12-16). The moment in Jesus' life at which the event takes place is different in the different Gospels, since each evangelist uses the story when it fits in best with his catechetical presentation of the life of Jesus.

The passage confronts us once again with the "messianic secret," as Jesus forbids the leper to make his cure known. The cure of the leprous is one of the signs of the Messiah (Matthew 11:5), but Jesus wants to avoid having the Jews mistake the meaning of his coming. He has no desire to establish an earthly kingdom, as the Jews expect the Messiah to do. On the contrary, if men want to understand the real meaning of his mission, they will find it in his Passion and death. Jesus was evidently quite justified in imposing silence on the leper, for once the leper spoke of the cure, Jesus could not openly enter a town without crowds running to him for miracles.

Christ does send the former leper to the priests and urges him to follow the prescriptions set down by Moses for his legal purification. Thus, while he does not want the thoughtless crowd to know of the cure, he does not seem to have wanted to keep it a secret from the priests. The priests were presumably more enlightened, and when the leper went to them to testify to his cure, he would make it known to them that the Messiah had come.

This passage of the Gospel touches all of us closely. Spiritual leprosy is a reality in every age; that is why the Fathers make frequent use in their preaching on the various Gospel pericopes that speak of leprosy.

The unclean man must dwell alone (Lev. 13:1-2, 45-46)

The Old Testament, as we know, considers leprosy not only as the most terrible of afflictions but also as a legal impurity.

We should not let the Book of Leviticus put us off entirely. Admittedly, its subject matter is not what we would expect in an inspired book, but we would be wrong if we saw there only the juridical details. If we look beyond the latter, we will find interesting teachings on sin and the mercy of God and on the means of atoning for sin, especially through sacrifices. Moreover, the concepts of the book are not purely culture-bound and reflective solely of a now dead civilization. If we look more deeply into the thought of the book, we will find the same teaching that God had given to Moses along with the law.

It was taken for granted in the Old Testament that sickness was connected with sin; in fact, so deep-rooted was this assumption that Jesus would later find it necessary to insist that a direct link was not always present. Furthermore, the Old Testament regarded leprosy as the very type, or fullest visible form, of divine chastisement. We should observe here that the assumption of a connection between sickness and sin was not peculiar to the people of the Old Testament; many other cultures have taken the same view of sickness. Be that as it may, the person who wished to be acknowledged as cured had to present himself to a priest and confess his sin. The Book of Job, we may remember, likewise gives a 'moral" vision of leprosy; that is, leprosy is regarded as sent by the Lord (Job 19:20-21) and as cured by the Lord (Job 5:18). Leprosy rendered impure the person afflicted with it. It is quite understandable that the seriousness of the illness and its contagious character should have led men to cast out anyone afflicted with it and to regard him as impure in the eyes of the law. Such is the situation in the background of today's Gospel passage.

We shall not insist further on this background, despite the cultural interest it may have for us, because today's liturgy does not dwell on the point. The message today is not that we should be divided into the pure and the impure. The point is rather to show us that sin is what separates and that the power of God can heal us.

Both leprosy and sin separate us from others. Too often today, sin is considered as an entirely personal matter; its necessarily social character is overlooked. For in fact every sin is necessarily social in its bearing; even if the sin is hidden, it influences the world and the Church. That is why tradition has insisted on the confession of sin to the Church, for which that sin created a spiritual "crisis." The value of excommunication was that it emphasized this social aspect of sin, the separation that sin caused. But whether or not a man's sin is known, the sinner is in fact someone "separated." The ancient monastic Rules, too, provided for "excommunications"; these were inspired by the fear that a guilty monk might morally contaminate the community, and they were also a punishment intended to make the guilty person reflect on his sin.[284]

At the same time, the sinner and his sin should never be thought of apart from the mercy of God and the divine power to heal. In today's passage from St. Mark, Jesus sends the healed leper to the priest. Jesus does not say whether he thinks of the leper as a sinner whom God has punished; his chief reason for sending the man is that the priest and his associates may be forced to acknowledge the presence of the messianic age. Henceforth leprosy can be cured, because the Lord who pardons and heals is now present.

St. Matthew emphasizes the faith of the sick. Jesus uses his authority and power in order to bring out into the open the priests' stubborn refusal to accept any testimony that may tell in favor of Jesus.

St. Luke, who has his eye on pagan readers, wants to emphasize the power of Christ, who heals men by freeing them from sin. St. Mark, as we have seen, is more interested in stressing the presence of the messianic age and on bringing out the true nature of the kingdom. The messiahship of Jesus has nothing to do with the coming of a restored earthly kingdom.

The lesson being taught on this Sunday is not a useless one, for the Church is still made up of sinners who are looking for healing. The first reading and the Gospel pericope should guide us in our quest for salvation by making us more fully aware of the social aspect of our sins as well as of our responsibility in today's world. Other people accept the fact that a Christian is a sinner, but the Christian himself cannot simply accept it; in fact, only if he does not accept it can he be a Christian despite his sin.

The Christian is a person with a deep faith in the Lord's power to heal him. He is aware of his responsibility and is able to evaluate properly the things of this world. He knows that if he asks God's mercy he will be pardoned, but that his earthly life will not thereby become a paradise. For when the Lord pardons, he does not promise a life of happiness in the earthly sense; to think that he does is to misunderstand the messianic message of Jesus. When Christ forgives sin, he does however heal us interiorly and gives us access to the life that constantly enlivens his Church.

Christ our model (1 Cor. 10:31–11:1)

St. Paul has already emphasized to the Corinthians the disinterestedness of his work. He has pointed out that in order to be all things to all men, a man must be free. The freedom in question is not simply a freedom from material concerns or even from attachment to human beings. It is also — and this is the point Paul is making in today's short pericope — a more continuous and radical liberation in which all our actions are dedicated to the glory of God. Whether we eat or drink or do anything else, we must do it for God's glory.

Paul is thus not afraid to speak of the need to be free. He emphasizes it several times in the First Letter to the Corinthians. "Am I not free?" (9:1; cf. 9:1-12). "All things are lawful" (10:23) for one who is fully dedicated to God's glory. But though there may be no interior obstacle to using this freedom, charity may at times bid the apostle not to use it, precisely so that he may continue to be all things to all men. Paul is very much aware of the limitations that charity sometimes imposes on an individual, and he insists on them in today's passage: "Give no offence to Jews or to Greeks or to the church of God" (10:32).

In all this, the Corinthians can take Paul as their model. The real model, however, is Christ, whom Paul seeks to follow in everything. Of what is Christ a model? Of self-sacrifice to the will and the glory of the Father, for the sake of saving everyone. If we are to imitate Paul in his quest of freedom (as limited by the bidding of charity), we must look beyond Paul and follow Christ, who did not hesitate to lay down his life for the salvation of all.

SEVENTH SUNDAY

The Forgiveness of Sins

The Son of man has authority to forgive sins (Mark 2:1-12)

Despite the startling character of the miracle and the unusual circumstances in which Jesus worked it, the narrative

is concerned primarily with the forgiveness of sins. That is
the main point, and the evangelist doubtless described the
scene in order to highlight this central issue: sin is forgiven.
The witnesses are utterly amazed; they glorify God and
claim that they have never seen anything like it. That is the
first step toward the assent of faith, for what the sign is
showing is the power of Jesus and the mystery of his person.

The scribes realize what is going on, and they tell themselves that only God can forgive sins. In fact, Jesus claims
and exercises two powers, one of which (healing) is the sign
of the other (forgiveness of sins). The second is essential,
since Jesus has come to save men. What good would his
coming do, then, if he did not forgive sins?

Jesus is the Lamb who takes away the sins of the world.
Thus, this story, like others of the same kind, is an attempt
to bring to light the true person of Jesus. The scribes are
aware of the danger Jesus represents to them; they can only
take Jesus's words, "Your sins are forgiven," as a blas-
phemy, for they realize that, in a sense not yet fully clear to
them, Jesus is claiming equality with God.

At the time when St. Mark was writing, the power to forgive sins was being exercised in the Church. Perhaps the
evangelist was highlighting the power of Jesus in order to
help his readers understand the power he had left to his
Church.

God forgives sins (Is. 43:18-19, 21-22, 24b-25)

In this passage, forgiveness is presented as a form of renewal: We are to forget the past. God says that Israel has
treated him as a servant and weighed him down with the
sins of his people. Yet he forgives and will no longer remember their sins!

The New Testament throws light on what God says here
through Isaiah, for according to the New Testament, forgiveness is an act by which God creates anew. In its full
form, then, forgiveness is an eschatological reality: "Be-

hold, I make all things new" (Apoc. 21:5). The whole purpose of the coming of Jesus and of his paschal mystery was to renew the world. St. Paul, for his part, writes: "Therefore, if any one is in Christ, he is a new creation; the old has passed away, behold, the new has come" (2 Cor. 5:17).

The Christian is thus uniquely privileged in that he does not have a past! God's forgiveness means that God no longer remembers our sins. Despite our ingratitude, despite the fact that we have treated him like a servant, he wants to forget and, in keeping with his covenant plan, to forgive and make us new beings. This determination of God to forgive is perhaps his most incomprehensible aspect. St. Paul was deeply impressed by this mystery: "God has consigned all men to disobedience, that he may have mercy upon all. . . . How unsearchable are his judgments and how inscrutable his ways!" (Rom. 11:32-36).

The responsorial psalm sings of the God who helps men on their sickbed and brings them healing: "Thou hast upheld me because of my integrity, and set me in thy presence for ever" (Ps. 41:12).

Our "yes" to the glory of God (2 Cor. 1:18-22)

The community at Corinth was not fully convinced by Paul's first Letter, and the Saint was offended by certain attitudes of the Corinthians concerning which we have no direct information. He did not return to Corinth but sent Titus in his stead. Through the latter he learned that peace seemed to have been restored in the community and that tempers had been chastened. Therefore he writes to them again. In our present passage he writes in the first person plural, showing that he, Silvanus, and Timothy are agreed.

The Corinthians may have offended Paul by saying that he did not preach a clear and sincere message, but that on

the contrary he spoke and acted with duplicity. Such at
least is the background the letter suggests. If so, Paul does
not attempt to justify himself, nor does he make repeated
claims to have spoken and acted in a straightforward way.
For his own teaching and actions, he refers simply to the
teaching of Christ. Christ was not Yes and No, for he was
the very incarnation of truth and taught us that we should
speak a clear Yes or a clear No, without ambiguity (Matthew 5:37).

In this passage, then, Paul is claiming to be a genuine
apostle. The authenticity of his mission has God himself as
its guarantor, since it is God who chose and consecrated the
apostles and put his seal upon them. The seal is a sign that
something is authentic. Consequently, the anointing by the
Spirit and the gift of the Spirit are the two sources from
which the Apostle's evangelizing activity draws its value.
That is what the community at Corinth must ever keep in
mind.

EIGHTH SUNDAY

The Marriage of God to His People

The Bridegroom with us (Mark 2:18-22)

The Gospel for this Sunday provides a good example of
the liturgical reading of a biblical text. The passage invites
the exegete to go into the importance of fasting and the way
Jesus thinks of it. In today's liturgy, however, the first reading provides the context within which the Gospel is to be
read and tells us that in reading Mark, we are to concentrate
chiefly on the presence of the Bridegroom and on the behavior this presence suggests. In other words, Jesus' answer
to his questioners is not to be taken as a facile defense of

his disciples, who do not fast, but rather it bids us think in symbolic terms, which we must now try to specify.

A narrowly exegetical approach might lead us, as it has led others, to challenge the authenticity of the passage as perhaps having been inserted in Mark's text as a justification for the practice of fasting in the early Christian community. Such an interpretation (which in any case is completely hypothetical and lacks any real basis in the text) bears no relation to the liturgical proclamation of the passage.

The passage speaks to us of the presence of the Bridegroom and of his disciples' attitude while he is present and after he has gone. The element of fasting appears as secondary in relation to the prediction of Jesus' departure, a departure Jesus himself seems to foresee as marked by violence.

The overarching context for the whole account is the presence of the kingdom. The various cures that Jesus works (cc. 2 and 3) are signs of the kingdom, as Jesus elsewhere tells the disciples of John the Baptist (Matthew 11:5). They are "signs of the times" (Matthew 16:3). The kingdom, however, means the presence of the Bridegroom, that is, of the definitive covenant, which is described as a marriage. The "marriage" in this instance is not simply a juridical entity but a personal relationship: God is united to his people as his people are to him, and when his people is unfaithful, God is jealous.

The prophet Hosea was the first to compare the covenant to a marriage. Jeremias will then use the same image (2:2, 20), as will Ezekiel (16:1-43, 59-63). Isaiah, too, will make poetic use of it (54:4-8; 61:10; 62:4).

The covenant is made eternal by Christ, whose coming is the most important step toward making the marriage fully real (Matthew 9:15; Mark 2:18-22; Luke 5:33-39). St. John thinks of John the Baptist as "the friend of the bridegroom" (3:29). We know how often Jesus describes the kingdom as a wedding feast that a king prepares for his son (see, e.g., Matthew 22:2).

Since the covenant is here and the kingdom has begun, there can be no question of fasting. Let those fast who do not realize that the Bridegroom is present and that a marriage is to be celebrated. But, we may ask, how is it that John the Baptist and his disciples fast? Is not John being illogical, since he also proclaims the kingdom? No, he is not illogical, for he fasts precisely as a preparation for the coming of the kingdom. Jesus is really anticipating the full reality of the kingdom; his attitude here and his approval of what his disciples are doing are a further sign that the kingdom has begun.

Jesus then moves on to a new point: "The days will come, when the bridegroom is taken away from them" (Mark 2:20). The words are an evident allusion to his own violent death. (The Bible elsewhere uses the expressions "take away" or "cut off" to indicate a tragic death: Is. 53:8; Jer. 11:19; Matthew 24:40; Luke 23:18; John 19:15.)

The important thing here, however, is not how the Bridegroom will cease to be present, but the very fact of his future absence. His absence will be a sign to the disciples that the time for fasting has come. We must, moreover, not take "fasting" in a narrowly literal way, but must interpret it more broadly to include the sufferings of the disciples and the persecution they will undergo. In addition, the fast in question is not necessarily associated with mourning, since the Bridegroom who departs from the disciples rises and ascends to heavenly glory. Thus the fast will be accompanied by expectation of the Bridegroom's return and will therefore be of a festive kind.

It is against this background that the Church established her custom of the nocturnal vigil spent in fasting and prayer, with the vigil and the fating ending in the celebration of the Eucharist. The great examples were the vigils of Easter and Christmas.

The pericope from Mark ends with two short parables: the parable of the old garment that cannot be repaired by sewing new cloth onto it, and the parable of the old wineskin that cannot be used for new wine. The two parables are closely related to each other and to what precedes. The point being made is that the kingdom that is now present is a new creation; it introduces men into a new world in which they must rid themselves of an outmoded outlook and acquire new attitudes.

Such a change is no easy matter. It is difficult to keep and renew customs which are really unadaptable but to which, nonetheless, people cling more than they do to charity. It has always been so, and so it is today. We know how St. Paul was forced to be constantly shaking up his contemporaries who were too attached to customs that were without a point. Recall, for example, the dispute about circumcision (Gal. 5). Jesus began a new era in history, and we live in a new dispensation.

Clothing often serves as a symbol in Scripture, especially in the Old Testament. Shining garments, white as snow, appear in Daniel's vision (7:9) and again in Jesus' transfiguration (Matthew 17:2; Mark 9:2-3, Luke 9:29); the angel at the tomb, when Mary and Salome come to anoint Jesus' body, is likewise wearing shining white garments (Matthew 28:3; Mark 16:5; Luke 24:4; John 20:12). The image of a worn-out garment as representing a decaying civilization is used in Isaiah: "The earth will wear out like a garment" (51:6). Psalm 102 develops the same poetic image more fully: "Of old thou didst lay the foundation of the earth, and the heavens are the work of thy hands. They will perish, but thou dost endure; they will all wear out like a garment. Thou changest them like raiment, and they pass away" (vv. 25-26).

Thus those who listened to Jesus were familiar with the image. So too, in a country where viticulture was important, everyone had a background of experience for appreciating the little parable of the old wine and the new wineskins. They could grasp the point that the institutions proper to the old law would not serve for the renewal of the world through the new covenant.

Jesus is not urging his contemporaries to abandon ascetical practices; on the contrary, he himself (Matthew 6:16-18) and the early Church (Acts 13:2; 14:23; 2 Cor. 6:5; 11:27) recommend them. Moreover, he claimed to fulfill the old law, not to abolish it (Matthew 5:17). What he is urging, then, is a new attitude of freedom and openness that goes beyond the letter of the law.

This new outlook joins ascetical practice to the joy of the Eucharistic banquet, which is a sign of the kingdom. Jesus is proclaiming a new life in which the Catholic, who has put on Christ, accepts trials and testings, and tries to maintain his balance with the help of ascetical practices; in which he is not attached to the letter but to the spirit, and constantly tests his own adaptation to the new dispensation that Jesus has established through his paschal mystery.

In this we have an extremely valuable lesson for life in the Church today. The most important thing, we are being told, is faith in the presence of Jesus and his new covenant. This faith is constantly finding expression in the Church: in the gathered assembly, in the prayer group, and especially in the celebration of the Eucharist. At such moments the members become aware ever anew of the presence of Christ the Bridegroom with his new and eternal covenant. This presence, which we grasp through faith, is absolutely basic to the Church and to the life of each individual; from it come joy and freedom. Yet to attain such a constant faith and to be able to enter into the covenant and meet the bridegroom, we need asceticism; ascetical practices enable us to concentrate more fully on essentials.

I will speak tenderly to my spouse (Hosea 2:14b, 15b, 19-20)

Faith in the presence of the Bridegroom with his new covenant, while requiring a new outlook, also makes dialogue with God possible. Hosea had already made this point. When he presents Yahweh as husband of Israel, he makes us privy to an overwhelming religious experience in which Israel received the revelation of God who loves. Hosea gives us access to this experience by way of his own experience.

The people of Israel could look back to all that their God had done for them in rescuing them and establishing them as a nation; for Israel, God was truly a covenant God. And yet the Israelites remained a weak people who allowed themselves to be seduced by the less demanding gods of Canaan, whose worship flattered the instinctive urge to drunkenness and sexual expression.

Meanwhile, the prophet had had his own special experience. At the Lord's command, he had taken a prostitute as wife, but the woman, named Gomer, abandoned him (Hosea 1:2). In the passage we read today, Hosea links the two experiences, his own and that of his people, when he tells us of God's words to his unfaithful spouse: "Therefore, behold, I will allure her, and bring her into the wilderness, and speak tenderly to her."

For us today, the dialogue is that of God with his Church and with each of us. In this dialogue God constantly renews us; we become a new garment, new wine: "There she shall answer as in the days of her youth, as at the time when she came out of the land of Egypt."

The Christian, despite his infidelity, does not have a past weighing upon him. Moreover, the mystery of his liberation by divine love is ever alive, ever renewed: "I will betroth you to me for ever." Three times the Lord repeats his "I will betroth you to me," and each time it is accompanied by new gifts. "I will betroth you to me for ever": the Lord asserts his intention of being faithful to his covenant; he is always with us and always will be with us, ever searching us out. "I will betroth you to me in righteousness and justice, in steadfast love, and in mercy": these are the gifts specific to the covenant, which establishes social justice and love in human society. "I will betroth you to me in faithfulness; and you shall know the Lord": there will be an intimate union between God and us; we shall be able to draw close to him as we acknowledge his constant gifts and as we experience his fidelity and our own.

These statements of God in Hosea describe the life of the Church and of each Christian: the primacy of God's love for us and our love for him (our love being inseparable from love for other men as well). Other things — various observances, rituals, customs — are not to be neglected, for they help in a measure to foster love and fidelity; the sacraments, in fact, even give the grace to love and to be faithful. But the chief thing in the life of the Church and the individual should be the profound sense of God's loving presence.

Ministers of a new covenant (2 Cor. 3:1b-6)

St. Paul speaks to the Corinthians with assurance and firmness. The assurance is not grounded in his own abilities but comes from God, who has made him minister of a new covenant. The Apostle does not depend on his personal qualifications but on God. All the apostles are "ministers" of a new covenant, that is, they are "servants" of this new covenant.

In two other places Paul emphasizes the humble and demanding role of servant that is his. "What then is Apollos? What is Paul? Servants through whom you believed, as the Lord assigned to each" (1 Cor. 3:5). Here Paul has been obliged to intervene when the community was divided by clannish allegiances. Later on he is forced to write to the Corinthians once again: "What we preach is not ourselves, but Jesus Christ as Lord, with ourselves as your servants for Jesus' sake" (2 Cor. 4:5).

The apostle's role is to implement the covenant between God and men, the marriage of God with his people. Thus the idea of the covenant links this second reading with the first reading and the Gospel. It is in Jesus Christ that the covenant of which the apostles are servants is fully realized. The Spirit of the new covenant gives men a new heart and leads them in a love that goes beyond the letter of the law, and it is this Spirit of Christ that the apostolic ministry serves (2 Cor. 3:8). "The law of the Spirit of life in Christ Jesus has set me free from the law of sin and death" (Rom. 8:2).

The Corinthians, then, are Paul's "letter of recommendation," for they are now new creatures united to the Lord in a new covenant. In fact, the whole community at Corinth is Paul's letter of recommendation, since he became their father in Jesus Christ through the gospel (1 Cor. 4:15).

CYCLE C

pages 404-432
for years 1980, 1983, 1986, 1989, 1992

SECOND SUNDAY IN ORDINARY TIME

Marriage

The marriage at Cana (John 2:1-12)

The wedding at Cana has already played a part in the
Liturgy of the Hours for the feast of the Epiphany, but the
approach to the event is different in the present Mass. The
main point, of course, is always the same: Jesus' self-
manifestation through his first miracle, which is a "type" of
the Eucharist.

In this Mass, however, the first reading, as we shall see,
provides a context that requires us to take a somewhat
broader view of the Cana event. The first reading, too, is
concerned with a marriage (Is. 62:1-5). This does not mean
that we are to think of Jesus' action at Cana as being simply
a blessing of human marriage. Cana, like the multiplication
of the loaves, represents a proclamation of the messianic
banquet, which is often compared to a wedding feast. The
messianic banquet presupposes a new world, a new wine, a
new love, and the new people of God made one in the joy
of the kingdom.

We may leave aside the scene itself, though the description of it possesses high literary quality and presents certain
difficulties, such as Christ's attitude to his mother: "O
woman, what have you to do with me?" (John 2:4). The important thing for us here is the sign motif: Jesus "man-

ifested his glory" (2:11). The thought is a continuation of
the Prologue: "The Word became flesh and dwelt among us
. . . we have beheld his glory" (1:14).

The messianic banquet, as we indicated, is often represented as a marriage feast. This is true of the Synoptic Gospels. The Apocalypse speaks of "the marriage of the Lamb"
(19:7). We should note, in this context, that the wedding at
Cana took place "on the third day" (John 2:1), that is, on the
same day on which Christ later manifested his glory
through his resurrection. This wedding feast, therefore, is
the wedding feast of the triumphant Christ who came
among us and showed the glory that he acquired by shedding his blood and that is still present among us in the
Eucharist. He will give us a share in that glory at the wedding feast that is the eschatological banquet at the end of
time, when he shall bring all together in love.

The marriage of Jerusalem (Is. 62:1-5)

The theme of this very beautiful poem is the new creation: Jerusalem will be renewed. The notion of glory runs
through it: "All the kings [shall see] your glory" (v. 2; "You
shall be a crown of beauty in the hand of the Lord" (v. 3).
For the poem is proclaiming the messianic age, the time
when the successful covenant will be celebrated by a marriage. The poet quite naturally uses marriage symbolism:
the Lord who has rebuilt Jerusalem will marry her. We
think immediately of the Apocalypse: "And I saw the holy
city, the new Jerusalem, coming down out of heaven from
God, prepared as a bride adorned for her husband" (Apoc.
21:2).

Later in this same passage from the Apocalypse we read
that "the former things have passed away" (21:4). It is the
time now for wine, not for water; for covenant, not for division; it is the time, not for the forsaken spouse, but for her
who is "My delight," the city whom her Spouse, the divine
Architect, will rebuild.

Do we find this Mass rather "mystical" and rather far removed from our situation and concerns? I personally do not think the impression is justified; I would say rather that the readings penetrate to the very heart of our problems. For in the last analysis, what we look for, especially today, is a renewal, a new wine, a new world, a renewed love, a transformation of our age. We look for it, and we have a right to look for it; unfortunately, we often go about our looking in the wrong way and end up confusing what should be kept distinct.

The newness we should be looking for is first and foremost our own interior renewal, the new man who comes into being through baptism and the Spirit. We were once water, now we are wine, and are judged worthy of the wedding feast. The bride can now be reunited to her Spouse; she is no longer forsaken, but is the beneficiary of the eternal covenant in the blood of the Lamb whose marriage we celebrate. We are being invited, then, to meditate on this renewal of our selves, of our institutions, and of everything around us, but we must bear in mind that the renewal will come in its fullness only at the wedding feast on the last day.

The same Spirit distributes all gifts (1 Cor. 12:4-11)

No one can prevent political positions, sociological choices, and the laws of anthropology from having their repercussions and exerting their influence even in the Church. St. Paul was probably faced with a kind of "democratic spirit" that did not grasp the deeper meaning of ministries in the Church.

The distribution of these ministries does not point primarily to a hierarchy of officials who may argue about their relative dignity, nor is the distribution primarily a juridical matter. Ministries, on the contrary, are gifts given to certain persons for the service of the whole community.

The bestowal of a ministry is not primarily a legal investiture and a handing over of authoritarian powers. Rather, each minister, depending on his rank and office, is to be a mediator and distributor of gifts to others. In the Church, all offices are ministries or services.

St. Paul here lists some functions that correspond to particular gifts. He then insists that these gifts have been distributed according to God's will, that they all come from the same Holy Spirit, and that they are all given in order to form the one people of God.

The conciliar documents on the Church, the bishops, the priests, and the laity pay a good deal of attention to the different ministries and roles. There is need of avoiding not only clericalism but a false democratic approach as well. For example, in the liturgical celebration a great effort must be made to bring out the unity of all who make up the assembly, but this end is not to be achieved by giving everyone a uniform and identical role. It is not to be achieved by leaving the congregation uncertain about who the celebrant is or by preventing him from assuming his role in accordance with the teaching of St. Paul in today's passage from the First Letter to the Corinthians.

The celebrant's function, which must be brought out liturgically by insignia and by the place he occupies, is not primarily hierarchic indicating superiority; it is ontological. That is, the entire ascending activity of the assembly and the entire descending activity of God necessarily pass through the celebrant. Christ is the primary celebrant of the liturgy, and the priest represents him. Not to understand this and to obscure what should be a visible ministry because of the democratic feeling in this or that place is not progress but confusion. We must accept that the Spirit distributes his gifts to each individual as he chooses, but always for the service of all.

THIRD SUNDAY

The Word of God Proclaimed to All Peoples

He has anointed me to preach the good news to the poor (Luke 1:1-4; 4:14-21)

On this third Sunday in Cycle C we begin the reading of St. Luke's Gospel, and by a happy choice the Prologue has been included. A happy choice, because the Prologue tells us how the evangelist conceived his mission of writing a Gospel.

His main concern is clear: the events he is to narrate represent to some extent a break with the past, but they are first and foremost a fulfillment, since in them what the prophets foretold has been accomplished. Luke is not the first to have written down the message received from Jesus. He is well aware of this, and yet he thinks it necessary that he in his turn should put it in writing for the sake of his local community.

We know to some extent the problem that his Church was facing. Luke was writing around 70, and the Acts of the Apostles, which is also his work, enables us to put our finger on his basic concern. Chapter 11 of the Acts of the Apostles shows us the struggle going on between Peter and the Jewish Christians who were finding it difficult to accept the admission of Gentiles to baptism and the Church. By the time Luke was writing, specific positions had been taken, such as those of the Council of Jerusalem (Acts 15), but this did not mean that the problem had been completely resolved.

People continued to ask about the importance of the Jewish law for the Christian. Jewish Christians continued to attend the temple, while also celebrating the breaking of bread. But what of the pagans who were entering the Church? Furthermore, if the Church were not to see in Judaism the work of the Lord who had now himself come upon the scene of the world in order to save mankind, would she not be introducing a break pure and simple into the plan of God? Must she not safeguard at any price the unity of the divine plan that was continuing in the New Testament and the Church? The continuous reading of St. Luke's Gospel will show that the evangelist's concerns were still keenly felt. The problem he faced in his apostolate was not yet wholly resolved.

Nonetheless, at the beginning of his Gospel, Luke asserts the continuity of the Old and New Testaments. He also asserts a transition, although he does not go so far as to call it a complete break with the past.

The passage chosen for today jumps now from the Prologue to the latter part of chapter 4, and to Christ as predicted by the prophet Isaiah. Before we continue with the text, however, it will be helpful to recall briefly what we know about the synagogal liturgy. (In point of fact, we project the synagogal liturgy of the time of Jesus chiefly through the liturgy of our own time and through partial reconstructions.) The liturgy was quite simple in form: first came the word of God, and then the prayer of the congregation. It is the same scheme that we find in chapter 67 of St. Justin's *First Apology*: reading of the prophets and the apostolic writings, followed by the prayers of the people.

The later evolution of the synagogal liturgy parallels that of the Roman liturgy: now the service begins with preparatory prayers; after these come the readings. We should note that in the synagogue the law was read first and then the prophets. It is to this sequence that Jesus frequently alludes when he speaks of "the law and the prophets."

In our passage today, Jesus attends the synagogue; when the time for the reading from the prophets comes, he is offered the book. He reads the assigned passage and then, as was customary, comments on it; this was the original pattern of the synagogal liturgy.

The decisive moment, of course, comes when Jesus proclaims that the passage he has read is now fulfilled: "Today this scripture has been fulfilled in your hearing" (4.21). He knows that it is of him that the prophet was speaking, and therefore he declares that he himself is the long-awaited Messiah. He has been anointed and sent to preach good news to the poor. The prophecy of Isaiah goes on to list the signs by which the Messiah's coming can be recognized; they are the signs of which John the Baptist is told as he lies in prison. Here, in a solemn manner, during the liturgy of the word in the synagogue, Jesus asserts that the prophecy is fulfilled in himself.

Luke, then, while placing his main emphasis on the coming of the Messiah and the inauguration of a new age, also links this event to the past — in other words, he writes both as historian and as theologian. He has his sources — the entire Christian tradition — and makes perhaps a fuller use of them than the other evangelists do. But he does not write simply as a historian. After all, Theophilus, for whom he writes, already knows a good deal; but it is not enough for him simply to know, he must also make the full commitment of faith. It is to help Theophilus achieve that goal that St. Luke writes his Gospel. It is consistent with this that the evangelist is not writing for Theophilus alone or even for Christians alone; he knows that many, including pagans, will read his Gospel, and that is what he wants.

The prophecy of Isaiah is actualized every time it is read in the Christian assembly of our own day, and everyone who hears it hears it as actualized for himself, according to the role he plays in the Church. Each bishop, priest, and deacon hears his own missionary vocation in the Church set before him; so does each Christian, for the prophetic vocation of every Christian must not be forgotten, since it is part of his commitment to the faith and the Gospel.

Listening to the word of God (Neh. 8:2-4a, 5-6, 8-10)

The first reading is taken, not from Isaiah whom Jesus reads in the Gospel, but from the Book of Nehemiah, in which we hear of God's word being proclaimed. The choice of this reading is an indication to us that in today's liturgy the emphasis is on the actualization of the word and on the work of proclaiming it, rather than on the designation of the person who is to speak it. In the passage from the Book of Nehemiah, it is the Torah, or "law" (really, "instruction"), that is being read and that will always be the main focus of the synagogal liturgy. Read the whole ritual as described in Nehemiah and you will see the origin of the Jewish synagogal liturgy as well as of our own liturgy of the word.

According to the passage, the people stand to hear the word of God; after it has been read, it is translated so that all may understand, and then a commentary on it is provided. The passage notes that the people weep as they listen to the words of the law, for these words are so many signs of God's love for his people. The whole day was given over to the Lord who spoke to his people, and it was a day of joy.

The responsorial psalm, from Psalm 19, emphasizes the power of God's word: "The law of the Lord is perfect, reviving the soul." Further on, praise turns into petition: "Let the words of my mouth and the meditation of my heart be acceptable in thy sight, O Lord, my rock and my redeemer."

Today's liturgy is an invitation to us, early on in Ordinary Time, to meditate on the importance of the proclamation of God's word. This proclamation is like a constantly renewed confirmation of our calling and an active reminder of what we are and must become. We are to listen to the word in faith and pass it on to others.

The body and the members (1 Cor. 12:12-30)

Paul is seeking to restore some order and, above all, a sense of unity in the church of Corinth, which seems to have been a very lively but also a somewhat troubled place. He seeks to achieve his purpose with the help of the image of a human body. Once he has presented his paradigm, the practical applications become obvious, and his readers will know what they must do if they wish to be true to themselves as Christians.

With the passage of time, however, Paul's paradigm has lost the power it had when he first used it. We must even say that in our day it can serve as only a partial image of the Church. At a very early time, by the third century in fact, Church law began to develop, and "body" soon came to have juridical connotations. We are familiar today with professional groups that are "bodies," with a single head, the same laws for all, and the same purpose guiding all. The Church is likewise an institution with a single head, a code of law, and a goal. It is, however, more than an institution.

In order to get beyond the factors that would lessen the power of St. Paul's image, we must have recourse to St. John's Gospel, chapter 17, where Christ, in his prayer to the Father, asks that "they may be one [thing] even as we are one [thing]" (v. 22). The word "united" still implies entities that are separate each from the other, whereas we Christians are not simply "united" (in that sense) but have become, through baptism, a single entity. This is no way destroys the personhood of each member: the Father and the Son are distinct Persons and yet they are also "one [thing]," a single Being.

The rich gifts bestowed on the community at Corinth should therefore not fragment the community or make its members jealous of one another. St. Paul lists the various gifts and ministries, and gives the latter first place among the charisms. He sees no opposition between charism and hierarchy as far as ministries are concerned, since ministries are also charisms. It can even be said that he regards ministries as the most important charisms.

When there is an abundance of varied gifts, Christians, instead of thanking God for the variety of riches, may act so as to tear their communities apart. Pluralism in accidentals, if it is to work, always presupposes a very orthodox faith binding Christians together under, and in, a single Lord.

FOURTH SUNDAY

A Prophet Speaks to the World

God speaks to the world (Luke 4:21-30)

The passage chosen for today's Gospel is hard on the Jews, and we can understand why it made the hearers angry. It is a condemnation of the Chosen People for not receiving Jesus as a prophet. Because his countrymen do not accept him, all that he does is done for the sake of non-Jews. Like Elias, he does not respond only to the needs of an Israel that rejects him, but he turns to the pagans as well. Jesus has been sent to save, but the salvation is intended for the entire world and not just for the Jews. In fact, it is really not just his rejection by the Jews that determines him to go to the pagans; his very mission is to proclaim salvation to all flesh (cf. Acts 2:17).

The drama being played out here is basic to the entire future history of the Church. In reporting the scene in the synagogue at Nazareth, Luke really has in mind the Church's mission. Without giving up on the Jews, the Church had to free herself from her Jewish connections and put aside all nationalistic views so that she might preach the Good News to the entire known world. The Church had to speak to all men. This was the challenge Paul faced: The Church must not limit herself to the Jewish people, who in any case refused to listen; the prophet's mission is to the world.

The Church has always understood the true nature of her mission, but she has not always found it easy to address the word of God to all nations. In doing it, she has sometimes imposed upon various nations the lifestyle and thinking of an alien culture, with the result that the true point of the Christian mission was to some extent lost from view. When the Church has moved onto new terrain, her problem has always been to distinguish the essentials of the Gospel it-

self from the cultural forms with which she is already familiar. The Church faced this challenge at the very beginning,
and she is still facing it today.

We become aware of the problem even as we study the
life of Christ. Our study groups and prayer groups are always in danger of confusing the essential with the accidental, and of therefore closing themselves off to others.
Though the professed aim is to widen the boundaries of the
Church, people actually cut themselves off from the Church
at large, even in celebrations that should be most open
to the universal Church, namely, celebrations of the Eucharist. People want to celebrate the Eucharist in a small
group, but they forget that the legitimacy of the small group
depends on a firm determination not to create an exclusive
group of the "pure," but a living assembly to which every
comer is welcome.

Today, this particular Gospel pericope has an importance
that cannot be overemphasized. We must be open to all; we
must not let the universal message be limited to some
small group or other but must preach the Good News
everywhere; we must proclaim it to the world at large by
trying to distinguish clearly between its essentials and the
cultural form that a particular nation or civilization has developed. Salvation is for all — that is what the Savior is
insisting on in this passage. If we close our minds and
hearts to this truth, salvation may be given only to others,
for we may keep the grace of the Lord from entering us.

A prophet to the nations (Jer. 1:4-5, 17-19)

The life of the prophet Jeremias (see. Jer. 36–45) contains
a wealth of teaching for us. We see him unable to speak and
yet forced to do so by God in the face of the hostility his
message arouses on all sides. He overcomes his fear and
continues to preach as the Lord commands him: "Thus says
the Lord." He has been chosen by God, who takes the initiative without regard to human qualifications and makes of

the prophet "a fortified city, an iron pillar, and bronze walls, against the whole land" (1:18).

Jeremias prefigures Christ, and his life enables us better to understand the life of Jesus, who is the supreme Prophet. Jesus is chosen from among his brethren; the latter do not accept him, but his determination is unswerving: to proclaim the eternal Father's plan of salvation that has been prepared since the creation of the world. Until the very end of his life, Jesus will be the Prophet who preaches what the Father has bidden him communicate to men; that is what he has been sent to do.

The attitude of Jesus must find an echo in the attitude of all his followers. According to the teaching of St. Thomas Aquinas, which has been repeated by Vatican Council II in its *Dogmatic Constitution on the Church*, baptism brings us a share in the priesthood of Christ. This means that the baptized shares in the Godward role of Christ: that of offering sacrifice to the Father, and in his manward role: that of bearing witness among men through word and attitude.

Each Catholic should examine himself with regard to his prophetic role. How does he conceive of it? How does he carry it out? Too often he may think of himself as a prophet, even though he is in disagreement with the norms of holy living as proposed by the Church. The baptized Catholic is not given a share in Christ's priesthood so that he can set himself up against the Church! He is given it so that he may help her to fulfill her task, even while he may respectfully tell her his own views. The criterion of the true prophet will always be his basic accord with the Church, even though this may entail suffering and the acceptance of what he personally finds difficult to accept.

The prophet's function is to stimulate persons and institutions to reflection and needed change. Often, however, persons and institutions are excessively attached to what they like to think of as "tradition," but what is in fact at times a fad or a comfortable way of doing things. It is quite to be expected, therefore, that the prophet will not be well re-

ceived. This is the test that proves the prophet's authenticity. If he rebels, if his enthusiasm dissipates, if he becomes
bitter, if he turns harshly critical, above all if he does not
bow to what those in authority require of him or if he even
forms a group apart from the community and attacks the
community in a loveless way, then we cannot trust him in
his prophetic claims.

Good sense, good judgment, timeliness (which is not the
same as opportunism), and respect for others are some of
the criteria by which we can know the true prophet. The
Church certainly needs such prophets. When St. Catherine
of Siena remonstrated harshly with the Pope, she was act-
ing as a prophet. She said what she was bound to say; but
though she used hard words, made concrete criticisms, and
kept nothing back, she did so with the deep love of one
whose aim is to heal, not to wound.

The texts for this liturgy should make us reflect on the
role of the prophet today. Our approach should not be negative but should be marked by the moderation that is the
sign of authenticity.

Charity the greatest of the three (1 Cor. 12:31–13:13)

The community of Corinth must have been a difficult one
to lead. It was rich in gifts but also rather turbulent and
outspoken in its reactions. In chapter 12, Paul has been
speaking of the various gifts, ministries, and activities in the
Church. Unfortunately the gifts, which are meant to
strengthen the unity of the Church, have at times been the
reason for disagreements. Paul has therefore emphasized
the fact that a gift is given not primarily for the benefit of
the person who receives it but for the benefit of the entire
community. He has listed these gifts that are meant for the
service of all and has ended with the gift of tongues. This
last, sensational though it is, is not the greatest of the gifts;

moreover, there is a way superior to the whole range of the charisms. With this he turns to the theology of charity.

Hitherto, Paul has not spoken of any radical difference between the three virtues of faith, hope, and charity, which are bound up each with the others. Nor does he now deny their interaction. He does, however, see in charity the basic dynamism behind all Christian activity, and the virtue that must accompany every other gift. If the Corinthians do not live in accordance with charity, of what use are the other gifts which they have received and of which they are so desirous and proud?

The charity that Paul is speaking of is not just any "charity"; it is a higher gift given by the Spirit of God. Paul takes the opportunity to write almost a lyric poem on the power and splendor of charity. It is the indispensable foundation for everything else (13:1-3); it is the source of fruitful energy (13:4-8a); it will last forever (13:8b-13), whereas the other two basic virtues will necessarily cease to exist when our definitive encounter with the Lord takes place.

Such is the teaching that is ever vital to the Church's life and that we in turn must call to mind and keep vivid before us. We may be tempted to yield to our yen for the extraordinary and to substitute some new way for the way of charity, a new way that will be more showy — and require less sacrifice. But charity will always provide the basic criterion for separating the wheat from the chaff.

FIFTH SUNDAY

Messengers of God

Henceforth you will be catching men (Luke 5:1-11)

It is easy to sense the deep joy that filled St. Luke's soul when he began to write this chapter. He is describing the time when Jesus is beginning his ministry to the crowds, now that he has gathered his band of disciples. Preparations are already being made for the future Church.

Jesus comes forward here as the Master who teaches the crowds. Luke describes the scene, for the moment is an important one: Simon Peter is about to be given his mission, and Jesus will manifest the meaning of the Church and its activity in language that Luke deliberately makes rather solemn. The crowd presses around Jesus, and he gets into a boat that puts out a little from the shore, not so that he may separate himself from the crowd but simply so that he may teach them better. The boat he picks is Peter's. Does Luke see something symbolic in this? Well, at least he does call attention to the fact.

The miraculous catch of fish follows. This is not simply a reward to Peter for his blind obedience (if the night fishing was so unprofitable, the daytime fishing would be even more so!) It is quite clear, on the contrary, that the catch is leading up to something further. The very fact that so many details of the miracle are given proves that Luke sees it as extraordinarily important. So marvelous is the wonder that Peter and his fellows become quite fearful. Peter falls down and worships God for this manifestation of power. He does so with the humility so typical of him; we may also think, however, that Luke, writing as he was after Peter's later denial, was himself deeply moved, so that he naturally puts on Peter's lips the words, "I am a sinful man, O Lord."

Then the climax: Jesus reveals to Peter his future activity, and the various disciples, on reaching land, leave everything and follow him. "'Henceforth you will be catching men.' And when they had brought their boats to the land, they left everything and followed him." Here we already have a picture of the Church and its mission, which will reach its full and mature form after Pentecost. The Lord is already preparing his disciples for their important role of preaching the Good News, healing and saving men, and bringing men into the bark of Peter.

Here am I! Send me (Is. 6:1-2a, 3-8)

Isaiah was affected by his vision very much like Peter by the miraculous catch. Every contact with God is to some extent terrifying. Isaiah saw the Lord and was therefore sure that he was lost, just as Peter is made deeply aware of his sinfulness. Isaiah is even more deeply affected, because he has seen the King who is Lord of the universe. After the theophany, which despite its aura of majesty is comparable to the event of which St. Luke tells us, the prophet receives his mission and asks to be sent. So too, after revealing his power, Jesus sends Peter to be a fisher of men. The lips of the prophet are purified by a burning coal; Peter repents of his sins.

In its own way, the Old Testament was already preparing for the Church and its mission. At every point it was God who chose men, and God who sent them on their missions. Any extension of his rule was always his doing rather than men's. Psalm 138, the responsorial psalm, implicitly makes this point when it says: "Thy steadfast love, O Lord, endures for ever. Do not forsake the work of thy hands." The Spirit of the Lord continues to choose men and carries on the work of building up the Church.

In silence of heart and humble acceptance of their spiritual and human condition, men today still encounter the majestic Lord who purifies their lips with a coal; they leave everything to follow Jesus and become fishers of men. This miracle occurs often; we do not see it or even think of it, yet it is a source of life for the Church. Because of it, no persecution has ever been able to kill the impulse that Christ gave to his apostles long ago at the miraculous catch of fish. Christ's words, "You will be catching men," continue to echo in our world today, and nothing can diminish their power.

The message of faith (1 Cor. 15:1-11)

Being a fisher of men does not mean priding oneself on one's own intellectual resources or one's own psychological or pedagogical methods. The mission of a fisher of men is first and foremost to proclaim the Good News as Christ gave it to us and to help men observe it without altering it. The message is absolutely basic: Christ died, was buried, rose on the third day, and appeared, first to Peter, then to the Twelve, and then to a large number of other people. In other words, the message is the mystery of Christ.

It is possible that in this passage Paul's intention is to emphasize the essentials of the message. As we know, the Corinthians were proud of their knowledge and their philsophy. Doubtless they do not go so far as to deny the resurrection, although the current philosophies were not favorable to such a doctrine; the least that can be said, however, is that the Corinthians tended to give priority to human wisdom.

Faced with this attitude, St. Paul reminds his readers of a very simple profession of faith; perhaps it was even the formula in use in that community: "Christ died for our sins in accordance with the scriptures . . . he was buried . . . he was raised on the third day in accordance with the scriptures." These are historical facts: Christ's death, his entombment, his resurrection. But the facts were also redemptive events: Christ died for our sins, and his resurrection is the pledge of ours. There you have the Christian message. Paul is able to refer to witnesses of the resurrection and of the apparitions of Christ. Christ even appeared to Paul himself, who is an apostle by the grace of God and a preacher of the message of faith.

SIXTH SUNDAY

Blessings and Curses

Blessed are you poor. Woe to you that are rich (Luke 6:17, 20-26)

The discourse on the beatitudes is usually thought of as part of the Sermon on the Mount (Matthew 5–7; see fourth Sunday, Cycle A). Luke, however, introduces the discourse as being delivered on a "level place" where many listeners were assembled. If we compare the beatitudes in the Gospels of Matthew and Mark, we will find many points in common but also some differences. The exegetes usually conclude to the existence of a common source, unknown to us, on which both accounts drew. We may note the rhythmic style of Luke's four beatitudes and the fact that there are four corresponding curses.

It makes a deep impression to hear Jesus himself addressing the congregation and each of us with the words: "Blessed are you. . . ." They are indeed addressed to us, for we honestly seek to follow him. We are weak indeed, yet the four curses seem addressed, not to us, but to those who do not seek him.

"Blessed are you poor." Those who are deeply concerned with social problems feel their urge to do good aroused when they hear the Lord thus honoring the disinherited. Nor are they mistaken. We have perhaps too quickly turned the poverty of which Jesus speaks into something "spiritual." Recent scholarly study of the Scriptures has shown that Jesus is indeed speaking of material poverty, just as in the corresponding curse he is speaking of material wealth. It is to those who are materially poor that the promise of joy in the future kingdom is given, for, in Luke's view, material poverty leads to a surer detachment. The quest for material poverty in the Desert Fathers and the religious Orders has no other purpose; the goal is not asceticism or poverty for its own sake but the detachment from material things that makes it easier for men to attach themselves to authentic values.

It will be worthwhile to see what Luke's thoughts on poverty are elsewhere in his Gospel. A reading of these other passages shows us that what Luke is concerned with is a genuine liberation that enables us to follow Christ without compromise. Thus, later in this same sixth chapter we read: "Give to everyone who begs from you; and of him who takes away your goods do not ask them again" (v. 30) and "lend, expecting nothing in return" (v. 35).

Later on, in chapter 11, detachment is presented as a means of acquiring a purer vision of all reality: "Give for alms those things which are within; and behold, everything is clean for you" (11:41). In chapter 14 Jesus says: "You will be blessed, because they [the poor, etc., to whom you have given] cannot repay you. You will be repaid at the resurrection of the just" (v. 14). Zacchaeus, a man attached to earthly goods, proves the reality of his conversion when he says: "Behold, Lord, the half of my goods I give to the poor; and if I have defrauded any one of anything, I restore it fourfold" (19:8). And Jesus tells the rich ruler: "One thing you still lack. Sell all that you have and distribute to the poor; and you will have treasure in heaven; and come, follow me" (18:22).

The parables that Luke puts in the lips of Christ certainly have to do with material poverty; this is true of the parable about Lazarus the beggar (16:19-31) and of the incident in which Jesus sees the poor widow making her gift in the temple (21:2). When he urges action that involves the "poor," he means those who are materially poor: "When you give a feast, invite the poor" (14:13); "Go out quickly to the streets and lanes of the city, and bring in the poor" (14:21). It is to the really poor that the Good News is preached (4:18), in accordance with the prophecy of Isaiah (61:1-2).

And yet, material poverty is not enough; a man must have the heart of one truly poor, as St. Matthew tells us (5:3). When Jesus speaks of humble service, he tells us: "When you have done all that is commanded you, say, 'We are unworthy servants; we have only done what was our duty" (17:10). Yet, even such interior poverty is not a value in itself; it is not to be sought for its own sake but as a means of detachment in the following of Christ.

St. Luke has a real fear of riches. He speaks of wealth as "unrighteous mammon" (16:9) and shows us Jesus telling the money-loving Pharisees: "What is exalted among men is an abomination in the sight of God" (16:14). We will recall the abundance of detail Luke uses in the parable of the rich man and the beggar Lazarus, and how he describes the reversed lots of the two after death, with the rich man being tormented and Lazarus sitting at the banquet table in the kingdom (16:23-28). In the *Magnificat*, Mary sings: "He has filled the hungry with good things, and the rich he has sent empty away" (1:53), and Jesus later tells the rich: "You have received your consolation" (6:24). And finally there is the great saying: "Where your treasure is, there will your heart be also" (12:34).

In addition, Jesus gives a series of instructions that evidently caught St. Luke's interest: "Take nothing for your journey" (9:3); "Carry no purse, no bag, no sandals" (10:4); "Sell your possessions, and give alms" (12:33). The disciples tell Jesus: "Lo, we have left our homes and followed you" (18:28). Later on, when describing the life of the early community in the Acts of the Apostles, St. Luke twice mentions that "they had everything in common" (2:44; 4:32).

Such poverty must even become indifference to the opinion and respect of men. The disciple must not love the best places in the assembly (11:43) but should take the lowest place (14:10); he must be glad to be scorned for the sake of the Son of Man.

Poverty, then, is an ascetical means to life in the kingdom.

Authentic riches and security (Jer. 17:5-8)

The first reading presents us with a very simple yet utterly decisive antithesis. The literary procedure is different than in Luke, inasmuch as Jeremias speaks first of those who are cursed because they put their trust in weak men; he then turns to the man who is blessed and finds joy because he puts his trust in the Lord. Note how serene the man is who attains true detachment; he has nothing to fear.

Many of the psalms praise trust in the Lord as the way to joy and peace. The psalm chosen as the responsorial psalm today gives poetic expression to this idea: "Blessed is the man who walks not in the counsel of the wicked . . . but his delight is in the law of the Lord. . . . He is like a tree planted by streams of water, that yields its fruit in its season, and its leaf does not wither" (Ps. 1:1-3).

If there is no resurrection, our faith is in vain (1 Cor. 15:12, 16-20)

Faith in Christ as "the first of those who rise from the dead" is the principle on which the whole logic of Christian life is based. If Christ be not risen, faith is useless; we are still in our sins, and those who died before us in Christ have perished. If, moreover, it be a genuine truth that the dead do not rise, then Christ cannot be risen!

The reader may be tempted to reproach the author of these volumes for not adverting to modern theologies of the resurrection and to the way some contemporary theologians deal with the mystery, when he comes to discuss the paschal mystery. Some readers may reproach him on the same counts for this short commentary on the First Letter to the Corinthians. But the liturgy is not interested in hypotheses on the resurrection, be they old or new. Its aim is simply to bring the Scriptures alive; it has nothing in common with the study of the manner of the resurrection or the conditions required for it. The liturgy, like faith itself, is content with the fact. If our hope in

Christ related only to our present life, we would be indeed the most pitiable of mankind.

SEVENTH SUNDAY

Be Merciful

Be merciful as God is to us (Luke 6:27-38)

We should recall here the passage from St. Matthew that is read in Cycle A for this Sunday, since in the present passage Luke deals with the same subject and draws inspiration from the same verse of Leviticus: "You shall be holy; for I the Lord your God am holy" (19:2). Luke has changed the slant somewhat, however, for he writes: "Be merciful, even as your Father is merciful" (6:36).

The end of this passage, "The measure you give will be the measure you get back" (v. 38), reminds us of the petition in the Our Father: "Forgive us our debts, as we also have forgiven our debtors" (Matthew 6:12). The Fathers, in commenting on the Lord's Prayer, emphasize the idea that we are the ones who determine the limits of God's mercy, which in itself is infinite. Those limits are the ones we ourselves place on the forgiveness we give to our fellowmen.

It is in this matter of forgiveness that we see the true originality of the gospel and of the Christian lifestyle. While the world goes its way around him, the Christian lives a special kind of life; he is not understood and is regarded as a fool by those who judge according to a purely human criterion. What a difficult ideal to attain! And yet no one can say he is truly a Christian unless he pursues that ideal.

Spare your enemy (1 Sam. 26:2, 7-9, 12-13, 22-23)

The Old Testament reading provides us with a remarkable example of generosity and respect for an enemy's life and for his person, which is consecrated by God. The story is an attractive one and becomes even more so when we put it into its context. The Lord has already regretted anointing Saul (1 Sam. 15:11, 35), and the Spirit of the Lord has already laid hold of David (1 Sam. 16:13). David is being pursued by Saul's soldiers. Now Abishai sees, as anyone would, that Saul is in their power; this is providential, and David must take advantage of it.

David's reaction is quite different, for it is inspired by the Lord. He instinctively respects God's action in originally choosing Saul, and he needs far clearer signs before he can bring himself to kill someone who, though his enemy, was once anointed by God. Therefore he refuses to lift his hand against the anointed king and leaves it to the Lord to see justice done: "The Lord rewards every man for his righteousness and his faithfulness" (v. 23). David will not take the law into his own hands. Thus, whereas Abishai sees the Lord delivering Saul into David's hands, David interprets the event quite differently; he prefers to respect God's plan and to look to God for justice.

This is a splendid story; even today it strikes us as one that does honor to mankind. The Christian of today should have the same respect for God's plan as it affects every created person.

The merciful David has been seen as a prefiguration of Christ. He, David, was a man anointed, and he foretold the great Anointed One who was to come and who would forgive his enemies from the Cross.

We shall bear the image of the heavenly man (1 Cor. 15:45-49)

St. Paul has told the Corinthians how important he thinks the resurrection is, but he has made no effort to analyze how the resurrection took place. He does, however, now attempt to clarify the essential meaning of the resurrection, which is so central to our faith.

His explanation begins with a parallel between the two Adams: the first, a human being who received the gift of life; the last (Christ), a spiritual being who gives life. The first Adam came from the earth, the last from heaven. But now, through the saving intervention of Christ, human beings, who are of the earth, belong to heaven. We are now in the image of the earthly Adam, but someday we shall be also in the image of the heavenly Adam.

This is a splendidly simple explanation of the doctrine of our resurrection. It tells us that we have a twofold being: we are made from the earth in the image of the earthly Adam, but we have become spiritual in Christ and are now modeled after the image of the heavenly man. The body of Christ was raised up in glory; we shall rise glorious like him.

EIGHTH SUNDAY

The Word and the Heart

The true disciple (Luke 6:39-45)

In this passage, once again, there is a many-sided teaching, and the aspect we are meant to attend to when the passage is read in the liturgy is determined by the first reading. In this light, the primary emphasis in the Gospel is on the word that comes from a man's mouth and shows what he is. The true disciple of Christ is to be recognized by what he says as well as by what he is. For in the first reading, the word a man speaks is said to be a norm for judging his person.

What Jesus has to say about the "abundance of the heart"

is not to be taken as simple moralism; rather, it tells us something about the "ontology," or very being, of the disciple. If the disciple has indeed put on Christ and if he has indeed been anointed at baptism with the Spirit, then what he says will make this manifest. The tree is to be judged by its fruits. The whole person of the baptized individual is affected by baptism; the change wrought by baptism and the fact of belonging to Christ involve the person in his entirety.

This does not mean that the Christian is to be closed in upon himself. It does mean that there are ideas and principles he cannot accept, and that his exclusiveness in this respect is not imposed from outside but springs from his very being as a Christian. The baptized person must live within the limits set by the Body of Christ to which he belongs. The Christian lives in the world, but he is not therefore free to move in any of the directions the "world" happens to favor. There are even political commitments he will not accept, not because of a discipline imposed on him from without, but because a balanced prudence that is a reflection of God's wisdom bids him not compromise the Body of Christ to which he belongs.

In many matters the Christian is not dependent on the Church advising him or acknowledging that his attitude is correct. The Christian can only speak as a Christian. At the same time, however, we must recognize that it is not always a simple matter for the individual to judge whether what he wants to say is always in keeping with orthodox thinking. When this difficulty arises, he must have the humility to ask advice, not because a law binds him to do so, but because he respects his own religious commitment. He knows that men will judge him and the Church by what he says; they will judge the tree by its fruits.

It is perhaps artificial to link what we have been saying with the beginning of the Gospel pericope, which states that one blind man cannot lead another. A guide is a person who accepts a responsibility. Not everyone is in a position to accept such a responsibility; Luke may well have in mind certain dangerous prophets who lacked the ability to lead others. That is why he goes on to remind us of the need of submitting to a teacher. He himself is surely thinking of Jesus, but we should certainly think of the Church and its teaching authority; to her we must submit even if this means at times putting up with delays or a lack of understanding or openness. If the disciple puts forth doctrines that are not those of the Church and are dangerous, he speaks indeed out of the abundance of his heart, but it is a proud man speaking, not one who has become a member of Christ's Body through baptism.

Some may regard the judgment we have just expressed as regressive and will not accept it. There can be no question, of course, of canonizing every suppression and every condemnation. Yet there are plenty of illustrious examples of submission to the Church that show us the possibilities inherent in true discipleship. Those who have humbly conformed to what was commanded them have often reached a level of holiness and even of human renown that confounds the rebellious, most of whom end up empty and bitter.

Nor is the disciple free to issue severe criticisms and judgments of his neighbor. Here again the mouth speaks out of the heart's abundance. It is pride that leads to harsh criticism and judgment of others, not the spirit of merciful forgiveness that we find in God and Jesus, and should find in every disciple.

The word "hypocrite" that Jesus here applies to a certain type of person is itself harsh, even offensive. We must bear in mind, however, that it does not mean quite what it does in modern parlance. For us, hypocrisy means hiding one's real thought and character behind a deliberately adopted but false front. The Hebrew word that lies behind the Greek of the Gospel means rather a person who is far from God because he is unwilling to discern the truth. Jesus uses the word elsewhere with this same meaning. For example, when the multitudes prove unwilling to discern the signs of the times, Jesus treats them as "hypocrites," that is, people who are blind and incapable of objective judgment and who therefore depart from God's ways (Luke 12:56).

The statements of Jesus that are grouped here (in Luke 6:39-45) were probably made at different times. For St. Luke, they must have been connected in ways we cannot always readily see. In any case, the teaching of this Sunday's Gospel is more important today than ever before: The true disciple will be known by his outlook.

The word and the heart (Sir. 27:4-7)

This short passage from Ben Sira, which is subtle in its analysis though harsh in its language, determines the point of view for reading the Gospel of the day: "Do not praise a man before you hear him reason, for this is the test of men" (v. 7). In three images the writer gives us criteria for testing a man. The sieve and the refuse: a man's utterances show us what is mean in him. The kiln that tests the potter's vessels: a man's words test him. The tree and its fruits: a man's words make his thoughts known. This last parallel we have already seen in the Gospel pericope: the disciple is known by his words.

The disciple of Christ must live in accordance with his profession as a baptized person who has put on Christ. Everything he says and does involves his discipleship, and therefore Christ and the Church as well. For though we live in the world, we are part of a new creation. This does not at all mean that we can be unconcerned about the world and withdraw into a cocoon so that we may be sure of living in perfect accordance with what we are. On the contrary! If we are really aware of what we are, we will feel constrained to enter more and more fully into the service of the world. This service, however, requires precisely that the disciple be what he should be and that his utterances never be inspired by political calculation but be those of a person who has become God's messenger.

God gives us the victory through Christ (1 Cor. 15:54-58)

This passage is a very encouraging one for the Christian as he attempts to live his life of faith. This whole chapter concerns the resurrection, and we have already heard Paul's reflections on the subject (sixth and seventh Sundays, Cycle C). Here he goes into a little more detail.

"When the perishable puts on the imperishable, and the mortal puts on immortality. . . ." Paul likes the image of "putting on"; here, as in his other writings, it refers not to a mere external form but implies a real change in the person. Thus when he says that "as many of you as were baptized into Christ have put on Christ" (Gal. 3:27), he means that we have been reborn and utterly transformed. So here, in putting on immortality, we will again be transformed. The garment of immortality is something heavenly (1 Cor. 15:40, 47-49; 2 Cor. 5:2). Our lowly bodies, he tells us elsewhere, will become like the glorious body of Christ (Phil. 3:20-21).

Given this belief, the Christian should think of death in an entirely different way than does the person who does not believe and has not been baptized. The words of Scripture, says Paul, will come true for him. Where does Paul get these words? In fact, they do not occur as such in the Bible but are based by Paul on two different passages. The first statement, "Death is swallowed up in victory," derives from, or is based on, the Book of Isaiah (25:8), where the prophet writes: "He [the Lord] will swallow up death for ever." It makes no difference whether or not Isaiah was thinking of a real resurrection; it is with the resurrection in mind that Paul uses them here. The second quotation derives from the Book of Hosea (13:14), "O Death, where are your plagues? O Sheol, where is your destruction?" The oracle is a threat to destroy Israel utterly. Paul turns it into a promise of resurrection and of the integral survival of the Christian. If we read the passage with faith, Paul gives us an overwhelming sense of confidence and security in the face of death.

The thing that makes death fearful for every human being is sin. In itself, death might possibly be a simple transition to a glorious state; it is the sting of sin that makes death hateful to us, while the law reinforces the power of sin, because it tells us what is wrong but does not give us the power to avoid doing wrong (Rom. 7:7). Instead of freeing man from evil, the law only makes him sin more. Christ alone can deliver us from the tutelage of the law (Rom. 7:1-6) and rescue the conscience of man, which is prisoner to evil (Rom. 7:14-25). Because of Christ's redemptive action, the law is no longer external to us; the Spirit transforms us and writes the law in our hearts by pouring out God's love therein (Rom. 5:5). How grateful we should be, then, to God who gives us the victory through Jesus Christ!

The Christian, then, while remaining a realist, should also be a fearless optimist, for he has already conquered death in and through the risen Christ. No place, then, for real sadness; nor should any event be able to take away our assurance of winning through to the end. Death after a "life in Christ" can only be a Passover to Easter beatitude.

NOTES

[1] *CL*, no. 10 (Flannery, p. 6).

[2] See *Foi et vie*, no. 63 (1964), p. 49.

[3] *Loc. cit.*, pp. 57–58.

[4] *Ibid.*, and *Rivista Liturgica* 56(1969), p. 576.

[5] G. Thils, "Désacralisation et sécularité," in *Au service de la Parole: Mélanges A.-M. Charue* (Gembloux, 1969), p. 395.

[6] See H.-J. Kraus, "Gottesdienst im Alten und im Neuen Bund," *Evangelische Theologie* 23 (1965), pp. 171–206.

[7] For further discussion of these viewpoints, see Y. Congar, "Situation du 'sacré' en régime chrétien," in *Liturgie après Vatican II*, ed. J.-P. Jossua and Y. Congar (Unam sanctam 66; Paris, 1967), pp. 385–403; L. Maldonado, *Vers une liturgie sécularisée* (Paris, 1971); A. Nocent, *Le temps de la liturgie est-il passé?* (Paris, 1968).

[8] St. Justin Martyr, *Dialogus cum Tryphone* 12, 3 (*PG* 6:499).

[9] Origen, *Contra Celsum* VIII, 23, trans. Henry Chadwick (Cambridge, 1953), p. 468

[10] Abraham Heschel, in an article on time quoted by R. Aron in "La liturgie juive et le temps," *La Maison-Dieu*, no. 65 (1961), p. 13.

[11] R. Aron, *art. cit.*, p. 19.

[12] See L. Maldonado, *op. cit.*, p. 170.

[13] St. Leo the Great, *Sermo* 29, 2 (*CCL* 138:148).

[14] *Sermo* 36, 1 (CCL 138:195).

[15] *Sermo* 37, 1 (*CCL* 138:200).

[16] *Sermo* 26, 1 (*CCL* 138:125).

[17] *Sermo* 52 (*CCL* 138A:307).

[18] *Sermo* 63, 6 (*CCL* 138A:386).

[19] See, for example, Th. Filthaut, *Die Kontroverse über die Mysterienlehre* (Warendorf, 1947); French translation, *La théologie des mystères: Exposé de la controverse*, by J.-C. Didier and A. Liefooghe (Paris, 1954). L. Bouyer, *Liturgical Piety* (Notre Dame, 1955), pp. 86–98, provides a good synthesis and a clear, constructive critique.

[20] *CL*, nos. 5–7 (Flannery, pp. 3–5).

[21] See Tertullian, *De resurrectione mortuorum* 8, 3 (*CCL* 2:931): *Caro salutis est cardo* ("The flesh is the hinge of salvation").

[22] *CL*, no. 7 (Flannery, pp. 4–5).

[23] *CL*, nos. 7 and 33 (Flannery, pp. 4–5 and 11–12).

[24] Paul VI, encyclical *Mysterium fidei*, no. 29 (*AAS* 57 [1965], p. 764; *TPS* 10 [1964–65], p. 319).

[25] S. Marsili, *Anamnesis* 1: *La liturgia, momento nella storia di salvezza* (Turin, 1974); see p. 92. This is the first volume of a projected three- or four-volume series by the professors of the Pontifical Liturgical Institute at San Anselmo, Rome.

[26] This inscription was found at Autun in 1839 and can be assigned to the end of the second century. The text may be seen in, for example, the article "Abercius," in the *Dictionnaire d'archéologie chrétienne et de liturgie* 1:83.

[27] The *rudimenta gloriae* is a very old expression still preserved in our present baptismal ritual; cf. 2 Cor. 4:18; Rom. 8:24.

[28] Is. 1:21-27; 2:1-5. *LH*, Monday of first week of Advent.

[29] Is. 29:13-24. *LH*, third Sunday.

[30] Is. 16:1-5; 17:4-8. *LH*, Thursday of first week.

[31] Matthew 3:1-12. Mass, second Sunday (A).

[32] Is. 48:17-19. Mass, Friday of second week.

[33] Phil. 1:4-6, 8-11. Mass, second Sunday (C).

[34] Heb. 10:5-10. Mass, fourth Sunday (C).

[35] Mark 13:33-37. Mass, first Sunday (B).

[36] Matthew 3:1-12; second Sunday (A). Mark 1:1-8; second Sunday (A). Luke 3:1-6; second Sunday (C).

[37] Is. 40:1-5, 9-11; second Sunday (B). Bar. 5:1-9; second Sunday (C).

[38] Matthew 21:28-32. Mass, Tuesday of third week.

[39] Is. 39:19-21, 23-26. Mass, Saturday of first week.

[40] Matthew 9:35–10:1, 5a, 6-8. Mass, Saturday of first week.

[41] Is. 35:1-10. Mass, Monday of second week.

[42] St. Cyril of Jerusalem, *Catecheses* 15, 1 (*PG* 33:870; W. K. Reischl and J. Rupp [eds.], *Cyrilli Hierosolymorum archiepiscopi opera* [Hildesheim, 1967]).

[43] *CL*, no. 10 (Flannery, p. 6).

[44] S. Pinckaers, "L'espérance de l'Ancien Testament est-elle la même que la nôtre?" *Nouvelle revue théologique* 77 (1955), pp. 785–99; A. Hulsbosch, "L'attente du salut d'après l'Ancien Testament," *Irénikon* 27 (1954), pp. 1–20; J. Van Der Ploeg, "L'espérance dans l'Ancien Testament," *Revue biblique* 61 (1954), pp. 481–507.

[45] See C. Tresmontant, *A Study of Hebrew Thought*, trans. M. F. Gannon (New York, 1960).

[46] See A. Gelin, "The Expectation of God in the Old Testament," in A. Gelin *et al.*, *Son and Saviour: The Divinity of Jesus Christ in the Scriptures*, trans. A. Wheaton (Baltimore, 1960), p. 22. [This volume is a translation of *Lumière et vie*, no. 9 (1953).]

[47] J. Daniélou, *The Lord of History: Reflections on the Inner Meaning of History*, trans. N. Abercrombie (Chicago, 1958), p. 341.

[48] See L. Bouyer *op. cit.*, ch. 15.

49 Invitatory for December 17–23. Responsory at Lauds on December 24.

50 St. Irenaeus of Lyons, *Adversus haereses* IV, 14, 3 (*PG* 7:1011; *SC* 100:546).

51 Rom. 13:11-14. Mass, first Sunday (A).

52 See the Second Letter to the Thessalonians.

53 Teilhard de Chardin, "Modern Unbelief: Its Underlying Cause and Remedy," in his *Science and Christ*, trans. R. Hague (New York, 1968), p. 115.

54 H. de Lubac, *Catholicism: A Study of Dogma in Relation to the Corporate Destiny of Mankind*, trans. L. C. Sheppard (New York, 1950).

55 *Homiliae in Ezechielem* 9, 1 (*PG* 13:732).

56 See I.-H. Dalmais, *Introduction to the Liturgy*, trans. R. Capel (Baltimore, 1961), p. 58.

57 See L. Bouyer, *op. cit..*, pp. 257–71.

58 Yves de Montcheuil, "Vie chrétienne et action temporelle," *Construire*, no. 12, p. 103.

59 St. Augustine, *Epistola* 55 (*PL* 33:2–5; *CCL* 34:170).

60 *Sermo* 29, 1 (*CCL* 138:148).

61 Th. Spassky, "La Pâque de Noël," *Irénikon* 30 (1957), pp. 289–306.

62 Gregory of Tours, *Historia Francorum* X, 31 (*PL* 71:566; *Monumenta Germaniae Historica: Scriptores rerum merouingicarum* 1/1 [2nd ed.]:444–45).

63 See J. Hild, "L'Avent," *La Maison-Dieu*, no. 59 (1959), pp. 10–24.

64 See J. Audet, *La Didachè: Instructions des apôtres* (Paris, 1958).

65 *De bono patientiae* 13 (*CSEL* 3:406). *LH*, Saturday, first week.

66 *Constitution on the Church*, no. 48 (Flannery, pp. 407–8). *LH*, Tuesday, second week.

67 *Enarrationes in Psalmos*, Ps. 109:1-3 (*PL* 37:1446–47; *CCL* 40:1601–3).

68 On "Blessed are the poor," see J. Dupont, *Les Béatitudes*, 3 vols. (Paris, 1969–73).

69 Or: Joy for the saved of Israel: Is. 4:2-6.

70 Or: The Lord is in your midst: Zeph. 3:14-18a.

71 [Translated from the author's French. The translation in the Sacramentary reads: "Increase our strength of will for doing good that Christ may find an eager welcome at his coming. . . ." Latin: "Da, quaesumus, omnipotens Deus, hanc tuis fidelibus voluntatem, ut, Christo tuo venienti iustis operibus occurrentes. . . ."]

72 [Translated from the author's French. The Sacramentary: "Grant that we may be ready to receive Christ when he comes in

glory and to share in the banquet of heaven." Latin: "ut, veniente Christo Filio tuo, digni inveniamur aeternae vitae convivio, et cibum caelestem, ipso ministrante, percipere mereamur."]

73 [Translated from the author's French. The Sacramentary: "that we may rejoice at the coming of your Son." Latin: "ut, de Filii tui venientis praesentia consolati. . . ."]

74 [Translated from the author's French. The Sacramentary: "Free us from sin and bring us to life. Support us by your power." Latin: "Magna nobis virtute succurre, ut, quod nostra peccata praepediunt, gratia tuae propitiationis acceleret."]

75 [Translated from the author's French. The Sacramentary: "Remove the things that hinder us from receiving Christ with joy, so that we may share his wisdom and become one with him when he comes in glory." Latin: "In tui occursum Filii festinantes nulla opera terreni actus impediant, sed sapientiae caelestis eruditio nos faciat eius esse consortes."]

76 A. Lods, *Histoire de la littérature hébraïque et juive depuis les origines jusqu'à la ruine de l'état juif* (135 *après J.-C.*) (Paris, 1950), p. 239; quoted in J. Steinmann, *Le prophète Isaïe: Sa vie, son oeuvre et son temps* (Lectio divina 5; Paris, 1955), p. 31.

77 St. Irenaeus, *Adversus haereses* IV, 20, 5 (*PG* 7:1035; *SC* 100:638–40).

78 *Dogmatic Constitution on Divine Revelation*, no. 4 (Flannery, pp. 751–52). The words "as a man among men" are from the *Epistle to Diognetus* 7, 4.

79 St. Augustine, *Enarrationes in Psalmos*, Ps. 37, 14 (*PL* 36:404; *CCL* 38:382).

80 Origen, *Homiliae in Lucam* 4, 6 (*PG* 13:1811; *SC* 87:134).

81 B. Botte, *La Tradition Apostolique de saint Hippolyte: Essai de reconstitution* (Liturgiewissenschaftliche Quellen und Forschungen 39; Münster, 1963), p. 14.

82 L. Bouyer, *The Seat of Wisdom: An Essay on the Place of the Virgin Mary in Christian Theology*, trans. A. V. Littledale (New York, 1960), pp. 128–29.

83 St. Leo the Great, *Epistulae* 31, 2–3 (*PL* 54:792).

84 St. Irenaeus, *Adversus haereses* III, 20, 3 (*PG* 7:944; *SC* 34:342–44).

85 See J. Guillet, *Themes of the Bible*, trans. A. J. LaMothe, Jr. (Notre Dame, 1960), pp. 25ff.

86 *Ibid.*, p. 55.

87 See *The Jerusalem Bible*, note on Exod. 3:14.

88 R. Poelman's *De la plénitude de Dieu* (Tournai, 1959), which is a selection of texts from St. Irenaeus, has a section entitled *La divine extension des mains*. Among other texts is the following: "By the divine outstretching of his hands Christ gathered the two peoples into the one God" (*Adversus haereses* V, 17, 4, on p. 70).

⁸⁹ Botte, *op. cit.*, p. 15.

⁹⁰ Edition of the lectionary: G. Morin, "Le plus ancien lectionnaire de l'Eglise romaine," *Revue bénédictine* 27 (1910), pp. 41–74. For its history, see C. Vogel, *Introduction aux sources de l'histoire du culte chrétien au Moyen Age* (Biblioteca degli "Studi Medievali" 1; Spoleto, n. d. [1965]), pp. 309–10, 313–14, 322–23.

⁹¹ G. Morin, "Liturgie et basiliques de Rome au milieu du VIIᵉ s. d'après les listes d'évangiles de Wurzbourg," *Revue bénédictine* 28 (1911), pp. 296–330.

⁹² Edition: A. Wilmart, "Le Comes de Murbach," *Revue bénédictine* 30 (1913), pp. 26–59.

⁹³ L. C. Mohlberg (ed.), *Sacramentarium Veronense* (Rerum ecclesiasticarum documenta, Series maior: Fontes 1; Rome, 1966), pp. 166–70.

⁹⁴ "Nativitatem panis aeterni" (Mohlberg, *op. cit.*, p. 168, ll. 20–21).

⁹⁵ L. C. Mohlberg (ed.), *Liber sacramentorum Romanae Aeclesiae ordinis circuli (Sacramentarium Gelasianum)* (Rerum ecclesiasticarum documenta, Series maior: Fontes 4; Rome, 1968).

⁹⁶ A. Chavasse, *Le sacramentarie gélasien* (Paris, 1958), 442; *idem*, "L'Avent romain du VIᵉ au VIIᵉ siècle," *Ephemerides Liturgicae* 57 (1953), p. 297.

⁹⁷ Gel. 1120: "Excita, domine, potenciam tuam et veni, et quod aecclesiae tuae usque in finem saeculi promisisti, clementer operare."

⁹⁸ Gel. 1124: "Repleti cibo spiritali alimoniae supplices te depraecamur, omnipotens deus, ut huius participacione mysterii docea nos terraena dispicere et amare caelestia, adque omni nexu mortifere cupiditatis exutos regno perpetuae libertatis consortes efficias."

⁹⁹ Gel. 1123: "Propiciare supplicacionibus nostris et aecclesiae tuae misericordiam tuam quam confitentur ostende, manifestans plebi tuae unigeniti tui mirabile sacramentum, ut in uniuersitate nacionum perficiatur quod per uerbi tui evangelium promisisti, et habeat plenitudo adopcionis quod pertulit testificacio ueritatis."

¹⁰⁰ A. Paredi (ed.), *Sacramentarium Bergomense* (Monumenta Bergomensia 6; Bergamo, 1962), pp. 28–37; M. Ceriani (ed.), *Missale Ambrosianum Vetus* (Monumenta Sacra et Profana 8; Milan, 1912). See Vogel, *op. cit.*, pp. 301–302.

¹⁰¹ *Sacramentarium Bergomense*, p. 51: "Deus qui in unigenito tuo novam creaturam nos tibi esse fecisti, respice propitius in opere misericordiae tuae et in adventu Filii tui ab omnibus nos maculis vetustatis emunda."

¹⁰² *Sacramentarium Bergomense*, p. 54: "cuius incarnatione salus facta est mundi et passione redemptio procurata est hominis procreati. Ipse nos, quaesumus, ad aeternum perducat praemium, qui

redemit de tenebris infernorum. Iustificet que in adventu secundo, qui nos redemit in primo."

[103] *Sacramentarium Bergomense*, p. 60: "De cuius ventre fructus effloruit, qui panis angelici munere replevit. Quod Eva voravit in crimine, Maria restituit in salute. Distat opus serpentis et Virginis. Inde fusa sunt venea discriminis, hinc egressa mysteria salvatoris. Inde partus occubuit, hinc conditor resurrexit. A quo humana natura non iam captiva sed libera restituitur; quod Adam perdidit in parente, Christo recepit auctore."

[104] P. Salmon (ed.), *Le Lectionnaire de Luxeuil* (Collectanea Biblica 7 and 9; Rome, 1944 and 1953). See Vogel, *op. cit.*, p. 291.

[105] P. Cagin (ed.), *Le sacramentaire gélasien d'Angoulême* (Angoulême, 1918).

[106] *Op. cit.*, no. 1516: "Conscientias nostras, quaesumus, omnipotens deus, cotidie visitando purifica, ut veniente Filio tuo domino nostro paratam sibi in nobis inveniat mansionem."

[107] *Op. cit.*., no. 1519: "Animae nostrae, quaesumus, deus, hoc potiantur desiderio, ut a tuo spiritu inflamentur ut sicut lampades divino munere saciati ante conspectum venientis Christi filii tui, velut clara lumina fulgeamus."

[108] *The Bobbio Missal*, no. 363, p. 108.

[109] See Vogel, *op. cit.*, pp. 302–303.

[110] J. Pérez de Urbel and A. González y Ruiz-Zorrilla (eds.), *Liber commicus: Edición crítica* (Monumenta Hispaniae Sacra, Series liturgica 2–3; Madrid, 1950–55).

[111] See Vogel, *op. cit.*, p. 304.

[112] *Ibid.*

[113] M. Férotin (ed.), *Liber mozarabicus sacramentorum* (Monumenta ecclesiae liturgica 6; Paris, 1912).

[114] *Op. cit.*, p. 12: "O Verbum Patris quod caro factum es, tu habitares in nobis, praesta nobis, ut qui te venisse iam credimus, et venturum adhuc speramus, ab omni peccatorum eruamur contagione."

[115] *Op. cit.*, pp. 15–16: "Confortentur, quaeso, Domine Jesu Christe, in adventu tuo corda fidelium, tuoque in nomine genua roborentur debilium. Tua visitatione vulnera curentur egrorum, tuove tactu oculi inluminentur cecorum: tuo regimine vestigia firmentur claudorum, tuaque miseratione vincula absolvantur peccaminum. Quosque prospicis adventum suscipere, hos facito in secundum iudicii tui adventum ad te exsultantibus animis pervenire, atque in amenitate paradisi iucundaturos induce."

[116] B. Botte (ed.), *La Tradition Apostolique de saint Hippolyte: Essai de reconstitution* (Liturgiewissenschaftliche Quellen und Forschungen 39; (Münster, 1963), p. 14.

[117] B. Botte, *Les origines de Noël et de l'Epiphanie* (Louvain, 1932), p. 105.

[118] L. Duchesne, *Christian Worship: Its Origin and Evolution*, trans. M. L. McClure (London, 1903), pp. 257–65.

[119] C. Mohrmann, "Epiphania," *Revue des sciences philosophiques et théologiques* 37 (1953), p. 664. Article reprinted in C. Mohrmann, *Etudes sur le latin des chrétiens* 1 (Rome, 1961), pp. 245–75.

[120] *Art. cit.*, p. 644.

[121] Botte, *Les origines de Noël*, p. 33.

[122] L. Duchesne, in *Bulletin critique* 2 (1890), p. 41.

[123] *Sermo* 187, 1 (*PL* 38:1001).

[124] *Epist.* 54, 1 (*PL* 33:200).

[125] See *Constitution on the Sacred Liturgy* (*Sacrosanctum Concilium*), no. 7 (in A. Flannery, ed., *Vatican Council II: The Conciliar and Postconciliar Documents* [Collegeville, 1975], pp. 4–5).

[126] *Epist.* 55, 1, 1 (*PL* 33:205).

[127] *Ibid.*

[128] See J. Gaillard, "Noël: *memoria* ou mystère?" *La Maison-Dieu*, no. 59 (1959), p. 43.

[129] A. Baumstark, *Comparative Liturgy*, rev. B. Botte and trans. F. L. Cross (London, 1958), p. 156.

[130] *Sermo* 190, 1 (*PL* 38:1007).

[131] *Sermo* 29, 1 (*CCL* 138:147).

[132] *Sermo* 28, 1 (*CCL* 138:139).

[133] *Loc. cit.*

[134] *Sermo* 25, 1 (*CCL* 138:117).

[135] See Gaillard, *art. cit.*, pp. 50–51.

[136] H. Jenny, *The Paschal Mystery in the Christian Year*, trans. A. Stehling and J. Lundberg (Notre Dame, 1962), p. 32.

[137] *In vigilia Nativitatis Domini sermones* 3, 1–2. 6 (*PL* 183:94–99).

[138] J. Condamin, *Le livre d'Isaïe* (Paris, 1905), p. 58.

[139] On all this, see A. Gelin, *The Key Concepts of the Old Testament*, trans. G. Lamb (New York, 1955); A. Robert, "Considérations sur le messianisme du Ps. 2," *Recherches de science religieuse* 39 (1951), p. 95.

[140] Translated in J. Connelly, *Hymns of the Roman Liturgy* (Westminster, Md., 1957), p. 56.

[141] The first, third, and fourth of these are translated in *The Hours of the Divine Office in English and Latin* (Collegeville, Minn., 1963–64), 1:1166, 1249, 1253.

[142] For example, Gen. 24:27; Exod. 18:10-11.

[143] *Didache* 9, 2. Text in A. Hänggi and I. Pahl (eds.), *Prex Eucharistica: Textus e variis liturgiis antiquioribus selecti* (Spicilegium Friburgense 12; Fribourg, 1968), p. 66.

[144] St. Clement of Rome, *Letter to the Corinthians* 59, 2. Text in

K. Bihlmeyer, *Die Apostolischen Väter* 1 (Tübingen, 1924). The Letter dates from the second half of the first century.

[145] *Martyrdom of Polycarp* 14, trans. in H. Musurillo (ed.), *The Acts of the Christian Martyrs* (Oxford, 1972), p. 13.

[146] Anaphora of Serapion of Thmuis (Egypt) 1, 3. Text in Hänngi-Pahl, *op. cit.*, p. 128.

[147] See L. Brou, "Saint Grégoire de Naziance et l'antienne *Mirabile mysterium* des laudes de la Circoncision," *Ephemerides liturgicae* 58 (1944), pp. 14ff.

[148] H. Denzinger and A. Schönmetzer (eds.), *Enchiridion Symbolorum* (32nd ed.; Freiburg, 1963). Translated in J. M. Carmody and T. E. Clarke, *Christ and His Missions: Christology and Soteriology* (Sources of Christian Theology 3; Westminster, Md., 1966), p. 120. [Two words left in Greek in this translation have here been translated into English. — Tr.]

[149] *Catecheses* 4, 9 (*PG* 33:466–67).

[150] *Sermo* 27, 1 (*CCL* 138:133).

[151] Translated in Connelly, *op. cit.*, p. 54.

[152] L. Cerfaux, "Le Fils né de la femme," *Bible et vie chrétienne*, no. 4 (1953–54), p. 60.

[153] *Adversus haereses* III, 19, 1 (*PG* 7:939).

[154] A paschal homily of St. Cyril of Alexandria, in the *Homiliaire patristique* (Paris, 1949), p. 121.

[155] St. Cyril of Alexandria, *Quod unus sit Christus* (*PG* 78:1268).

[156] See Th. Spassky, "La Pâque de Noël," *Irénikon* 30 (1957), pp. 289–306.

[157] Connelly, *op. cit.*, p. 54.

[158] St. Leo, *Sermo* 21, 1 (*CCL* 138:85).

[159] Connelly, *op. cit.*, p. 56.

[160] *Sermo* 29, 1 (*CCL* 138:146–47).

[161] *Sermo* 21, 3 (*CCL* 138:88).

[162] The history of the text has been studied by B. Capelle, "La postcommunion de la seconde messe de Noël," *Questions liturgiques et paroissiales* 22 (1937), pp. 298–308. For the text, see p. 308.

[163] *Sermo* 25, 5 (*CCL* 138:122).

[164] *Expositio Evangelii secundum Lucam* II, 50 (*SC* 45:95).

[165] *Ibid.* II, 60 (*SC* 45:99).

[166] *Sermo* 21, (*CCL* 138:88).

[167] *Homiliae in Evangelia* 8, 1 (*PL* 76:1103).

[168] F. Mercenier and F. Paris, *La prière des Eglises du rite byzantin* (2 vols.; Amay, 1937–39), 2:119.

[169] *Sermo* 62, 1 (*CCL* 23:261).

[170] See B. Botte, *Les origines de Noël*, p. 105. The text of the treatise *De solstitiis et aequinoctibus* is printed on pp. 93–105; see ll. 434–39.

171 See above, pp. 3ff., 9, 90.

172 *Homilia in Transfigurationem Domini* 18 (*PG* 76:573).

173 *Oratio in diem natalem Christi* (*PG* 46:1129).

174 "Le principe fondamental de la théologie morale," *Recherches de science religieuse* 42 (1954), p. 490.

175 *Ad Ephesios* 19, 1–3 (*SC* 10 [3rd ed.]:89).

176 *Sermo* 22, 5 (*CCL* 138:98).

177 *Adversus haereses* III, 22, 4 (*PG* 7:958–59).

178 See p. 173.

179 *Hymn to the Blessed Virgin Mary* 1, 2, in T. J. Lamy (ed.), *Sancti Ephraem Syri hymni et sermones* (4 vols; Malines, 1882–1902), 2:522.

180 See Exod. 3:16; 4:31; 13:13; Ruth 1:6; Judith 4:15; 8:33; Ps. 79:16; Sir. 46:16; Is. 29:6; Jer. 29:10; Amos 3:2.

181 *Sermo* 21, 1 (*CCL* 138:85).

182 *Sermo* 21, 3 (*CCL* 138:88).

183 Christmas Preface I.

184 Prayer over the gifts, January 1.

185 See C. Vogel, *Introduction aux sources de l'histoire du culte chrétien au Moyen Age* (Biblioteca degli "Studi Medievali" 1; Spoleto, n.d. [1965]), pp. 317–18.

186 *Ibid.*, p. 310.

187 *Ibid.*, p. 316.

188 L. C. Mohlberg (ed.), *Sacramentarium Veronense* (Rerum ecclesiasticarum documenta, Series maior: Fontes 1; Rome, 1956), Section XL, nos. 1239–72 (pp. 157–63). (Referred to henceforth as Ver. with number of text.)

189 See Ver. 1239.

190 Ver. 1242.

191 Ver. 1243: "Largire, quaesumus, domine, famulis tuis fidei et securitatis aumentum; ut qui de natiuitate domini nostri filii tui gloriantur, et aduersa mundi te gubernante non sentiant, et quae temporaliter celebrare desiderant, sine fine percipiant: per."

192 Ver. 1258: "Deus, qui restaurationem condicionis humanae mirabilius operaris, quam substantiam condedisti: tribue, quaesumus, ut simul perficatur in nobis et quod creavit uerbi tui divina generatio, et quod eius hominis facti gloriosa natiuitas reformauit: per."

193 L. C. Mohlberg (ed.), *Liber sacramentorum romanae aeclesiae ordinis anni circuli (Sacramentarium Gelasianum)* (Rerum ecclesiasticarum documenta, Series maior: Fontes 4, Rome, 1960), no. 5. (Henceforth, Gel. with number of text.)

194 Ver. 1241: "Uere dignum: quoniam quidquid christianae professionis deuotione celebratur, de hac sumit sollemnitate principium et in huius muneris mysterio continetur."

[195] A. Paredi (ed.), *Sacramentarium Bergomense* (Monumenta Bergomensia 6; Bergamo, 1962).

[196] The prayer is called the *Post pridie* and comes after the consecration. Text in M. Férotin (ed.), *Liber mozarabicus sacramentorum* (Monumenta ecclesiae liturgica 6; Paris, 1912), p. 116: "Haec, Domine, dona tua et praecepta servantes, in altare tuum panis ac vini holocausta proponimus: rogantes profusissimam tuae misericordiae pietatem, ut eodem Spiritu, quo te in carne Virginitas incorrupta concepit, has hostias Trinitas indivisa sanctificet; ut cum a nobis fuerint non minori trepidatione quam veneratione perceptae, quidquid contra animam male vivit intereat, et quidquid interierit nullatenus revivìscat."

[197] *Ibid.*, p. 195: "Qui ante tempus natus et te Deo Patre, tecum pariter et cum Spiritu Sancto condidit tempora, dignatus nasci et ipse sub tempore ex utero virginis Mariae. Qui tamen, cum sit sempiternus, statutos annorum decrevit decursus, per quos evolutus duceretur hic mundus. . . . Terram quoque fructibus reple; animas corporaque facito morbis delictisque carere; scandala remove; contere hostem. . . ."

[198] See note 189 and corresponding text.

[199] Ver. 1260.

[200] Ver. 1250.

[201] Ver. 1241.

[202] Gel. 59, and J. Deshusses (ed.), *Le sacramentaire grégorien* (Spicilegium Friburgense 16; Fribourg, 1971), no. 89: "Quia cum unigenitus tuus in substantiae nostrae mortalitatis apparuit, in nouam nos immortalitatis suae lucem reparauit."

[203] Gel. 57: "Corda nostra, quaesumus, domine, uenturae festiuitatis splendor inlustret, quo mundi huius tenebras carere ualeamus, et perueniamus ad patriam claritatis aeterne."

[204] Gel. 60: "Inlumina, quaesumus, domine, populum tuum et splendore gratiae tuae cor eius semper accende, ut saluatoris mundi stella famulante manifestata natiuitas mentibus eorum et reueletur semper et crescat."

[205] Gel. 65.

[206] Gel. 66.

[207] On this subject, see Botte, *Les origines de Noël*; J. Leclercq, "Aux origines du cycle de Noël," *Ephemerides liturgicae* 60 (1946), p. 25; Mohrmann, *art. cit.*, p. 658.

[208] Mohrmann, *loc. cit.*, thinks, however, that the early feast of the Epiphany in the East could not have been concerned solely with the birth of Christ; if it had been, how are we to explain the fact that once the feast of Christmas was introduced in the East, Epiphany should then have focused on the baptism of Christ? The answer is that even in the early stage the object of interest in the

feast of the Epiphany was, as the word itself indicates, the manifestation of the divinity.

[209] According to one view, the feast of Epiphany was introduced into Spain and came thence to Rome (Botte, *op. cit.*, p. 57). According to another view, it was introduced into Africa and passed thence simultaneously to Rome and Spain (Leclercq, *art. cit.*, p. 25).

[210] See P. Benoit, *L'Evangile selon saint Matthieu* (La Bible de Jérusalem [in fascicles]; Paris, 1950), p. 31.

[211] See *Jerusalem Bible* (Garden City, N.Y., 1966), *New Testament*, p. 12.

[212] See L. Cerfaux, *La voix vivante de l'Evangile au début de l'Eglise* (Tournai, 1946), pp. 48–49.

[213] *Ibid.*, p. 54.

[214] It provides the first reading in the Office of Readings in the new Liturgy of the Hours; it supplied the second and third of the nine readings in the older Breviary.

[215] *Sermo* 31, 1 (*CCL* 138:161).

[216] *Sermo* 31, 3 (*CCL* 138:163).

[217] *Sermo* 32, 1 (*CCL* 138:165).

[218] *Sermo* 32, 3 (*CCL* 138:171).

[219] *Homiliae in evangelia* 10, 2 (*PL* 76:1111).

[220] A. Feuillet, "La conversion et le salut des nations chez le prophète Isaïe," *Bible et vie chrétienne*, no. 22 (1958), p. 5.

[221] See J. Steinmann, *Le prophète Isaïe: Sa vie, son oeuvre et son temps* (Lectio divina 5; 2nd ed., Paris, 1955), p. 129.

[222] See Feuillet, *art cit.*, p. 13.

[223] *Sermo* 32, 4 (*CCL* 138:176).

[224] *Sermo* 33, 5 (*CCL* 138:176).

[225] *Sermo* 35, 1–2 (*CCL* 138:193).

[226] *Sermo* 36, 1 (*CCL* 138:195).

[227] Connelly, *op. cit.*, p. 66.

[228] See note 14.

[229] See the entrance antiphon for Epiphany.

[230] Literal translation of the Latin antiphon for the *Magnificat* at First Vespers for Epiphany: "Hoc signum magni Regis est."

[231] The old but still valuable work of J. Corblet, *Histoire dogmatique, liturgique et archéologique du sacrement de Baptême* (Paris, 1881), gives a list of the representations of Jesus' baptism by John (2:524–50).

[232] *Commentaria in Evangelium Joannis* VI, 28 (*PG* 14:281).

[233] *Homiliae in S. Lucam* 33, 5 (*SC* 87:399).

[234] *Commentaria in Evangelium Joannis* VI, 27 (*PG* 14:281).

[235] See J. Daniélou, *Origen*, trans. W. Mitchell (New York,

1955), pp. 57–58; *idem, The Bible and the Liturgy* (Notre Dame, 1956), pp. 99–113.

[236] *Oratio adversus eos qui baptismum differunt* (PG 46:420–21), trans. in Daniélou, *The Bible and the Liturgy*, pp. 102–103.

[237] F. M. Abel, "Exploration de la vallée du Jourdain," *Revue biblique* 10 (1913), p. 240.

[238] On all this, see J. Bonsirven, *Le judaïsme palestinien au temps de Jésus-Christ: Sa théologie* (Paris, 1935), vol. 1.

[239] See G. Vermès, *Discovery in the Judean Desert* (New York, 1956), who gives a translation of the *Rule* edited by M. Burrows in 1951. On the baptism of the Essenes, see L. Cerfaux, "Le Baptême des Esséniens," *Recherches de science religieuse* 19 (1929), pp. 248–65.

[240] Is. 1:25; Zech. 13:9; etc.

[241] Is. 10:16-19; 30:27-33; 31:9; etc.; Jer. 21:14; etc.

[242] The last section (cc. 55–66) of the Book of Isaiah is not regarded as having been written by Isaiah himself.

[243] There is a good study of the theme of God's fatherhood in L. Bouyer, *The Meaning of Sacred Scripture*, trans. M. P. Ryan (Notre Dame, 1958), ch. 21: "Our Adoption by the Father and the Gift of the Spirit."

[244] Bouyer, *op. cit.*, p. 219.

[245] A summary of the various interpretations, with bibliography, may be found in M.-E. Boismard, *Du baptême à Cana* (Lectio divina 18; Paris, 1956), pp. 43–47. See also P. Joüon, "L'Agneau de Dieu," *Nouvelle revue théologique* 67 (1940), pp. 318–21.

[246] *Oratio* 39: *In Sancta Lumina* (PG 36:349ff.)

[247] *Homilia de Baptismo Christi et de Epiphania* 3–4 (PG 39:368–69).

[248] *Homilia* 34: *De baptismo Christi homilia* 6 (PL 57:297–98).

[249] See Boismard, *op. cit.*, p. 136; C. H. Dodd, *The Interpretation of the Fourth Gospel* (Cambridge, 1953), p. 300; L. Bouyer, *The Fourth Gospel*, trans. P. Byrne (Westminster, Md., 1964), p. 70.

[250] H. Seemann, "Aufgehellte Bibelstellen," *Benediktinische Monatschrift* 28 (1952), nos. 5–6. Boismard, *op. cit.*, p. 156, adopts this solution. But L. Bouyer, *The Paschal Mystery*, trans. Sr. Mary Benoit (Chicago, 1950), pp. 37–41, and C. Charlier, "Les noces de Cana," *Bible et vie chrétienne*, no. 4 (1953–54), p. 81, seem to come closer to the true solution of the problem.

[251] Tertullian, *De baptismo* 9, 3–4 (CCL 1:284).

[252] *Commentaria in Evangelium Joannis* II (PG 73:228).

[253] *Epist.* 63, 12 (PL 4:394–95).

[254] *Catecheses Mystagogicae* 4, 2 (PG 33:1098–99; SC 126:136).

[255] [Apparently the French lectionary the author is using has the

variant reading that he mentions at the end of this paragraph. — Tr.]

[256] Gel. 65: "Uere dignum: te laudare mirabilem deum in omnibus operibus tuis, quibus regni tui mysteria reuelasti. Hancque enim festiuitatem index puerpera uirginalis stella praecessit, quae natum in terra caeli dominum magis stupentibus nuntiaret, ut manifestandus mundo deus et caelesti denuntiaretur inditio, et temporaliter procreatus signorum temporalium ministerio panderetur. Et ideo."

[257] *Sacramentarium Bergomense*, p. 189: ". . . quia puerperio caelesti intulit mundo suae miracula maiestatis, ut adorandum magis ostenderet stellam, et transacto temporis intervallo aquam mutaret in vinum et suo quoque baptismate sanctificaret fluenta Iordanis idem Iesus Christus. . . ."

[258] *Sacramentarium Bergomense*, p. 199: ". . . qui te nobis super Iordanis alveo de caelis in voce tonitrui praebuisti, ut salvatorem caeli demonstrares, et te patrem lumis aeterni ostenderes. Caelos aperuisti, aerem benedixisti, fontem purificasti, et tuum unicum filium per speciem columbae Sancto Spiritu declarasti. Susceperunt hodie fontes benedictionem tuam et abstulerunt maledictionem nostram. Its ut credentibus purificationem omnium delictoru exhibeant, et Deo filios generando adoptive faciant in vitam aeternam. . . ."

[259] See Corblet, *op. cit.*, 1:104–107.

[260] Mercenier and Paris, *op. cit.*, p. 151.

[261] *Commentaria in Evangelium Joannis* VI, 46, quoted in Daniélou, *The Bible and the Liturgy*, pp. 107–108.

[262] *Oratio* 36 (*PG* 36:361), quoted in Daniélou, *op cit.*, p. 55.

[263] Daniélou, *ibid.*

[264] Mercenier and Paris, *op. cit.*, p. 151.

[265] *Ibid.*, p. 155.

[266] *Ibid.*

[267] *Ibid.*, p. 159.

[268] *Ibid.*, p. 163.

[269] *Ibid.*, p. 166.

[270] Blanchard, *Un hiver à Saint-Petersbourg*, in *Le tour du monde*, 3:206; quoted in Corblet, *op. cit.*, 1:111.

[271] Mercenier and Paris, *op. cit.*, p. 170.

[272] *Ibid.*, p. 172.

[273] A translation of the Armenian prayer may be found in J. Lemarié, *La manifestation du Seigneur: La liturgie de Noël et l'Epiphanie* (Lex orandi 23; Paris, 1957), Appendix II, p. 525.

[274] Mercenier and Paris, *op. cit.*, p. 172.

[275] *Ibid.*, pp. 172–76.

[276] *Ibid.*, p. 185.

[277] *Ibid.*, p. 189.

[278] The first part of the passage (2:11-14) is the Epistle for the Christmas Midnight Mass in the Roman rite.

[279] Jean Paul Sartre saw this and brought it out in his book *Existentialism and Humanism*, trans. P. Mairet (London, 1948).

[280] St. Ephraem, *Commentarium in Diatessaron* 1, 18–19 (*SC* 121:52–53).

[281] Isabelle Rivière, *Sur le devoir d'imprévoyance: Petit traité d'économie pratique* (reprinted: Paris, 1946).

[282] St. Gregory the Great, *Moralia in Job* I, 36 (*PL* 75:543–44).

[283] See Vatican Council II, *Dogmatic Constitution on the Church*, nos. 4 and 7.

[284] St. Benedict, *Regula*, cc. 23, 24, 26, 27, 28, 30, 44.

ABBREVIATIONS

AAS	*Acta Apostolicae Sedis*
CCL	*Corpus Christianorum, Series Latina.* Turnhout, 1953–.
CL	*Constitution on the Sacred Liturgy*
CSEL	*Corpus Scriptorum Ecclesiasticorum Latinorum.* Vienna, 1866–
Flannery	*Vatican Council II: The Conciliar and Post Conciliar Documents*, Austin Flannery, O.P., General Editor. Collegeville, Minn., 1975
LH	*Liturgy of the Hours*
PG	*Patrologia Graeca*, ed. J. P. Migne. Paris, 1857–66
PL	*Patrologia Latina*, ed. J. P. Migne. Paris, 1844–64
SC	*Sources Chrétiennes.* Paris, 1942–
TPS	*The Pope Speaks.* Washington, 1954–
TDNT	*Theological Dictionary of the New Testament.* Grand Rapids, 1964–74